FARMHOUSE COOKING

FARMHOUSE COOKING

Mary Blackie

CRESCENT BOOKS
New York • Avenel, New Jersey

Photograph and Illustration Credits

All photographs were taken by Joseph Filshie, except as stated below:
Bay Picture Library: pages x, 110
Andre Martin: page 114 (stylist: Lisa Hilton)
Oliver Strewe: page 349
Rodney Weidland: pages ii, 13 (stylist: Robin Duffecy), 17 (stylist: Robin Duffecy), 45 (stylist: Sheridan Rogers), 63 (stylist: Robin Duffecy), 103 (stylist: Sheridan Rogers), 127 (stylist: Sheridan Rogers), 150 (stylist: Robin Duffecy), 153 (stylist: Sheridan Rogers), 214 (stylist: Sheridan Rogers), 292 (stylist: Robin Duffecy), 293 (stylist: Sheridan Rogers), 312 (stylist: Sheridan Rogers)

All illustrations were taken from the previous edition of *Farmhouse Cooking* (published as the *Great Country Cookbook*), illustrated by Linda Arnold, Brendan Pittaway and Christine Brown

Some herbs and plants are dangerous and the author and
publisher accept no responsibility for any mishaps arising
from the use of herbs and plants mentioned herein

This 1994 edition published in the USA by Crescent Books, distributed by
Outlet Book Company, Inc., a Random House Company,
40 Engelhard Avenue, Avenel, New Jersey 07001.

Random House
New York • Toronto • London • Sydney • Auckland

by arrangement with HarperCollins*Publishers* (Australia) Pty Limited

First published in Australia in 1985 by
Angus & Robertson Publishers as
The Great Australian Country Cookbook
Second edition published 1988

This edition published in Australia in 1994 by
Angus&Robertson, an imprint of
HarperCollins*Publishers* Pty Limited
25 Ryde Road, Pymble NSW 2073, Australia

No Library of Congress Cataloging Publication Data
available at the time of printing

ISBN 0 517 10195 5

Photography by Joseph Filshie
Styling by Georgina Dolling, Georgina Dolling Productions
Food prepared for photography by Southerly Dolling
Typeset in Australia by Midlands Typesetters, Maryborough
Printed in China
9 8 7 6 5 4 3 2 1
97 96 95 94

To my family

Contents

Acknowledgments • viii
Preface • ix

PART I
Recipes

Important Notes • 1

PART II
Preserving

Introduction • 311

PART III
Herbs & Spices

Introduction • 351

Acknowledgments

I wish to acknowledge the following source of material, reproduced by permission of the publishers:
- Court Bouillon—adapted from a recipe of the same name in *The Cookery Year*, © Reader's Digest Association Ltd, 1973.

My sincere thanks go to Mrs Valerie McNicol who spent many hours typing the first draft of this book from difficult handwritten scripts. Her excellent typing never failed me.

Thanks also to Ray Richards whose professional advice has been invaluable.

I wish to offer sincere thanks and gratitude to the parents who taught me to understand and love the country and who first inspired in me an interest in gardening and cooking.

Above all, my thanks go to my husband Malcolm who, besides eating his way through the contents of this book, gave constant advice, support and encouragement!

I thank you all.

Mary Blackie

Preface

My initial intention in writing a cookbook twelve years ago was as a sequel to my husband's book *Successful Smallfarming*, written following our smallholding ventures in New Zealand and Western Samoa. In that book, he described how to produce your own food. My book was to be what to do with it after harvesting.

However, my interest in cookery as a science and an art led me to write more than I'd intended. The more I cooked and learned, the more I wanted to learn. The more research I did, the more I cooked and learned again . . . and so it went on. The result was *The Great Country Cookbook*, the predecessor to this volume.

My interest has always been in simple country fare, perhaps influenced by happy memories of a childhood spent in rural Gloucestershire—we played in and explored England's 'green and pleasant land' and brought home its 'spoils' of flowers, fruits and nuts.

Traditional cookery is living history, linking our own lives to those of our forebears, throughout the ages past.

There is much to learn and cook beyond what I offer here. I am still cooking and learning. I hope you will too!

PART I
Recipes

Important Notes

The recipes given in this book are based around the general methods described for each section. I have made a number of assumptions in the writing of these recipes which are important to note.

- All cup measurements given in this book are for both US and metric cups. The small difference in size between these measures has been absorbed, and will not affect the recipes. Imperial measurements are given after cup measurements. Where millilitres and fluid ounces only are given, the fluid ounce measurement is for both imperial *and* US measures. Tablespoon and teaspoon measurements are treated as universal. As with cups, the difference in tablespoon measures between countries has been absorbed, and will not affect the recipes. Some units of measurement and their metric equivalents are as follows:

Spoon and Cup Measurements

(All countries use the same teaspoon measures)

	AUSTRALIA	NEW ZEALAND	UNITED KINGDOM	UNITED STATES
1 tablespoon	20 ml	15 ml	15 ml (½ fl oz)	15 ml (½ fl oz)
1 cup (fluid)	250 ml	250 ml	300 ml (10 fl oz)	240 ml (8 fl oz)

Small differences in metric units have also been absorbed (eg 125 g and 130 g are both converted to 4½ oz) and will not affect the recipe. Just use your discretion where necessary.

- Oven temperatures are given in both Celsius and Fahrenheit. For a guide to equivalent gas marks, please use table over page. However, to find the correct gas mark setting for your own oven, please refer to the manufacturer's instruction manual. The following conversion chart for gas ovens should be used as a guide only. Gas mark calibrations vary from old to new models and from manufacturer to manufacturer. The following guide to selecting temperature settings has been prepared by British Gas.

Oven Temperatures and Gas Marks

CELSIUS	FAHRENHEIT	GAS MARK	HEAT
110°C	225°F	¼ (S)	very cool
120°C	250°F	½ (S)	very cool
140°C	275°F	1	cool
150°C	300°F	2	cool
160°C	325°F	3	moderate
180°C	350°F	4	moderate
190°C	375°F	5	fairly hot
200°C	400°F	6	fairly hot
220°C	425°F	7	hot
230°C	450°F	8	very hot
240°C	475°F	9	very hot
260°C	500°F	10	very very hot

Note: The gas mark S is a special setting available on some ovens used for cooking slowly, eg meringues.

- It is assumed that all vegetables used are already basically prepared. For example, where the recipe reads 'thinly slice onion and cut carrot into thin rounds', I assume that the onion has already been skinned and had root and leaf area cut away, and that the carrot has been washed, 'topped and tailed', and scraped or peeled if necessary. Please refer to 'Vegetables, salads and dried beans' (*see* p. 4) and under the individual listing if at all in doubt.
- I have used herbs in most recipes in amounts I think would be generally accepted. If you are not fully acquainted with the flavour of herbs, be quite conservative with the amounts used until your palate is used to their aromatic flavours. I suggest halving the quantities given in the recipes. Also, and of utmost importance, I always use *fresh* herbs and quantities given refer to this. If you are using dried herbs, reduce quantities by one-half.
- Some recipes specify the amount of seasoning, eg '¼ teaspoon paprika' or 'pinch of cayenne'. Where no quantity is given, as in 'black pepper' or 'paprika', cooks should use their discretion, and flavour according to taste. All herbs and spices used are described in Part III.
- For US readers, some recipes in this book use golden syrup (light treacle). This really is the best ingredient, especially in recipes such as Brandy Sauce and Carrot Cake. However, if golden syrup is unavailable, corn syrup can be substituted.

- As a general rule, I try to use wholemeal (whole-wheat) flour in the belief that it is superior nutritionally to refined flour. Wholemeal flour varies greatly between brands, depending on the:
  - gluten content
  - proportion of wheat germ and wheat bran
  - milling process used, eg stone-ground flour I've 'battled' with in cooking.

  Where some wholemeal flours are excellent for cake baking and sauce thickening, others will not be. Discerning cooks will soon discover which of their local brands are best. Some recipes require that bran be sieved out prior to use. Chocolate sauce is much lighter and better tasting if bran is removed from wholemeal flour. Other recipes, eg fish batter, must of necessity use refined white flour.
- Quantities in this book assume dark soy sauce (Soy Superior) is used. Light soy sauce (Superior Soy) may also be used. However, quantities should be adjusted according to taste. Dark soy sauce is darker, thicker and stronger than light soy sauce because it has been matured for longer. Light soy sauce is light in colour but quite salty. It is especially good for stir-frying. Low or no salt soy sauce is also available.
- Where tomato purée is given as an ingredient, it refers to sieved (strained) tomato, *not* tomato paste or concentrate. You can make your own according to the recipe given on p. 221, or use commercially prepared tomato purée. This also applies to other recipes throughout the book which are used as ingredients (eg curry powder and tomato sauce (ketchup)). You may wish to start from scratch and use your own produce or to use readily available store-bought ingredients. The choice is yours.
- Finally, a general note about kitchen equipment. I believe stainless steel or enamel to be the best materials for saucepans. Cast-ironware is excellent for stewing and casseroling dishes and frying pans (skillets), but not suitable for cooking vegetables or fruit. A chemical reaction often occurs where the fruit or vegetable will change colour and taste a little of iron. Take great care with cast-ironware. Follow the manufacturer's instructions carefully and keep pans oiled a little to prevent surface rust and subsequent tainting of food's flavour.

  I must make note here of my oven temperature. Though I believe the temperature dial on my stove (cooker) to be correct, I find it a rather hot oven. That is, in cooking, foods tend to get a little overdone or even burned on the bottom, especially with biscuits (cookies and crackers) and cakes. However, I believe enthusiastic cooks like me will know their oven and will be able to make adjustments to oven temperature if necessary. To overcome the problem of a hot oven, one can place a heavy baking tray (sheet) on the bottom shelf (or on the top shelf if a fierce top element is your problem). A tip given to me by a Viennese friend, and one of particular use when baking cakes and biscuits, is this: place a baking or roasting tray containing water to a depth of 1–1½ cm (approx. ½ in) at the bottom of the oven. Not only does it prevent burning or scorching underneath (the water acts as an insulating layer), but the water acts as a humidifier and so prevents the food drying out. This is particularly useful when baking large cakes such as Christmas or simnel cake which require a long, slow, even cooking. My friend hastened to add, however, that the water-filled tray should never be used when baking bread or in other yeast cookery.

vegetables,

salads &
dried beans

The term 'vegetable' is rather a loose one I think. It describes any part of a plant that is eaten as a savoury dish. Cauliflower and broccoli are the flowers of their respective plants, tomatoes and eggplants (aubergines) are fruits, a potato is an underground swollen stem, a carrot is a swollen root, spinach the leaf, celery the leaf stalk and peas and beans the seed.

Vegetable cooking can be creative, interesting and stimulating to the palate. It is therefore disappointing that the vegetable is often provided almost as an afterthought to meat, over which great care and attention is always taken. It was with this in mind that I wrote this chapter. I hope that it will open new avenues of vegetable cookery for a few, if not many, people.

I suggest that you always buy fresh vegetables. Frozen vegetable packs in the supermarket are not only costly, but also contain overcooked, tasteless vegetables. I occasionally freeze a few packs of summer vegetables from my garden as a winter treat, but as a general rule prefer to eat seasonal vegetables only—what a joy it becomes to savour a mouthful of the first green peas of the season after the long winter months. Similarly, the taste of leeks well cooked but still firm, in a tangy cheese sauce, means long winter evenings around a log fire, chores complete and the animals safe in their houses tucked away from cold winds and rain.

Look around carefully for vegetable shops or supermarkets that provide a wide variety of vegetables and buy as many different kinds as you can find. Limiting ourselves to carrots, cabbage and potatoes is no way to open up creative avenues of vegetable cooking. Also, potatoes need not be included in every meal. In the past, potatoes were important because they were a cheap source of bulk and energy, and vitamin C. Today, our diet is much improved. It does not lack energy, and potatoes are not always cheap.

I think it was during our life in New Zealand in a rural district that my attitude towards vegetables was changed. We had just bought a piece of land to rear sheep, milking goats, hens and ducks. Naturally our system involved quite a sizeable vegetable garden, and whilst the vegetables matured fairly quickly, our meat supply did not. Being short of money, it seemed ridiculous to go out and buy meat, so I decided to make the best use possible out of the vegetables we had produced. I experimented with different methods of preparation and sauces, and discovered to my delight a whole new area of vegetable tastes. This inspired me to expand my garden to include the less usual vegetables. Cooking these when they matured interested me further and we became so engrossed in our vegetable meals we forgot the absence of meat. If you have a glut of cabbage, the rule is don't just boil it—steam it or stir-fry it, stuff it, sauerkraut it, steam and add a tangy tomato sauce, cook it in a cheese sauce, boil and add chopped cooked bacon and grated cheese, curry it or simply eat it raw—do anything to make it different. You would be surprised how versatile the humble cabbage can be with just a little imagination.

Below I list the vegetables that I use. Avocados and tomatoes are included in this list, even though they are strictly fruits. Mushrooms are also included here.

asparagus	beetroot (beets)
avocados	broccoli
beans, broad (fava)	Brussels sprouts
beans, green (French, runner or string)	cabbage, green (round head)
beans, purple	cabbage, white (drum head)
beans, yellow (wax)	capsicum (sweet peppers)

carrots	onions
cauliflower	parsnips
celery	peas, green
chokos (chayotes, mirlitons)	potatoes
corn (maize)	pumpkin (winter squash)
cucumber	radishes
eggplant (aubergines)	silverbeet
Jerusalem artichokes	spinach
kohlrabi	spring onions (green onions, scallions)
leeks	sweet potatoes, kumara and yams
lettuce	tomatoes
marrow (summer or yellow squash)	turnips
mushrooms	zucchini (courgettes)
okra (lady's fingers, gumbo)	

Here I must add that besides the above, which are accepted culinary vegetables, there is a vast array of vegetables all around you as 'weeds' which are waiting to be eaten. Have you ever tried dandelion leaves with lemon butter sauce, nasturtium leaves and flowers in a salad, or fat-hen, chickweed or nettles lightly steamed? Richard Mabey's well-known book *Food for Free* is a good addition to our kitchen library. Remember that most of these plants must be picked young, tend to be bitter and are acquired tastes. Do try your garden 'weeds'. If nothing else, you will find them an interesting topic of conversation. A male friend of ours (with a very conservative taste in food) came to stay for several months just at the time I was experimenting with this new source of food. One evening, fired with more enthusiasm than usual, I prepared a 'healthy' meal of dandelion leaves in lemon butter sauce and couch grass (twitch grass) soup. (I had learned that during wars, when flour was in short supply, English villagers used the white, starchy underground stem of couch grass, finely ground, as a substitute.) I had assumed that the stems would soften and become like noodles with cooking. However, the dandelion leaves I had chosen were old and very bitter, and the soup more reminiscent of string stock. After braving it for five minutes, my husband and our friend took one look at each other, nodded in agreement and rushed away to the safety of the local fish and chip shop! Unfortunately for them, their conservatism did not dull my enthusiasm!

If care is taken to select as wide a range as possible, one benefits not only from variation in flavours, but in the vitamins, minerals and trace elements that each provides.

Preparation

Preparation of vegetables prior to eating raw or cooking is of great importance. I see far too many people torturing their vegetables. Try not to peel a vegetable: except in the case of really tough fibrous skins, eg kohlrabi and beetroot (beets), there is little need to peel. Most of the vitamin C content lies directly under the skin and even the thinnest paring will remove some of this vitamin and open the cells to allow greater vitamin loss during cooking. The skins are also a tasty part of the vegetable. If picked *very* young, peas and broad (fava) beans can be eaten in their pods. As the pod gets older it becomes fibrous, is not pleasant to eat and must be discarded. Choose the very young pods when the pea or bean has hardly developed. Cabbage, Brussels sprouts, onions and leeks will need their outer leaves removed.

Wash the vegetable in fresh cold water and drain. If the vegetable is to be peeled, cut or chopped, this should be done immediately before eating or cooking. Many people prepare their vegetables early and leave them sitting in cold salted water. This is wrong. Many of the nutrients are water-soluble and are lost even before cooking starts. Similarly, a salad should be crisp in texture, and preparing it even an hour in advance of eating can render it limp. The ideal is to pick from the garden, prepare and eat in as fast a succession as possible for full nutritive value. Obviously, for those cooks without a vegetable garden this is not possible. When buying, always choose firm vegetables, bright in colour, and store in a cool, dry, dark place.

Eating raw vegetables is best for obtaining full nutritive value. Vegetables contain fibre called cellulose which is essential to our digestive system. Cooking breaks down this fibre. Many of our digestive problems today—eg constipation—arise from a lack of fibre in the diet. More serious problems such as cancer of the colon and cholesterol build-up in the arteries are thought by some doctors to be in some part due to the lack of fibre in today's overcooked, overprocessed foods. Eating raw vegetables maintains the fibre content and ensures no loss of nutrient value. Where cooking is necessary—eg leeks and Brussels sprouts—or desired, the cooking time should be reduced to a minimum.

The method of cooking affects the flavour of a vegetable. Compare the taste of carrots when they are raw, boiled, stir-fried, roasted or baked. You will find that they all taste different. If you mix carrot with another vegetable and cook them together, you will again find a slightly different taste. With a little experimentation, you will find vegetable cookery and vegetable tastes take on new and exciting dimensions.

Finally, a note about salt. Most vegetables have a delicate sweetish taste which is completely destroyed rather than enhanced, in my opinion, by the addition of salt during cooking. I omit salt entirely, but allow access at the table for salt-lovers.

Methods of Cooking
Boiling

This is the most usual method of preparation and is, on the whole, done badly. I try not to boil vegetables because much of the nutrient value is lost to the water. This water is ideal for making gravy, stocks and soups, but there is a limit to the amount of soups we enjoy, and I always feel guilty discarding all the goodness. Besides, boiling seems to me to be the most destructive of taste and texture of all the different methods of cooking.

If you are going to boil vegetables, there are a few points worth remembering. Only peel where absolutely necessary. Cut into pieces of the required size, and pop into boiling water. There should be just enough water to cover the vegetables. Make sure the pan has a tightly fitting lid. This maintains the high temperature of the water and reduces the cooking time. Time the cooking carefully. I do not wish to give boiling times for each of the vegetables, as I find the degree of hardness enjoyed varies according to individual tastes. I prefer to eat cooked vegetables when they are softened just enough not to be termed raw. They are firm, bright in colour and still crisp to eat. Others may prefer a softer texture and so a longer cooking time will be required. Experiment and you will find your own preferences. Remember though that the longer the cooking time, the greater the loss of texture, colour and nutritive value.

Leaf vegetables, eg spinach, cabbage, chickweed and stinging nettle, should be dealt with in a slightly different manner. The bottom of the pan is covered shallowly with water and, when boiling, the chopped leaves are added. No lid is required on the pan. As the water boils rapidly, it evaporates as steam. Cooking is done more by steam than boiling water and takes only a few minutes, eg about 2 minutes for spinach and nettles, 5 minutes for cabbage which is finely sliced. By the time cooking is complete, no water should be left in the pan. It will probably take you some time to learn the correct amount of water required, which will vary of course depending on the quantity of leaf vegetable you intend to cook. Once mastered you will find leaf vegetables cooked in this way do not end up in a soggy green heap! Leaf vegetables are delicate in structure and need to be softened only slightly.

Seasoning The boiling water may be seasoned with herbs, eg mint, marjoram or basil. Alternatively, the cooked and drained vegetables may be seasoned with black pepper, paprika, cayenne or finely chopped herbs. You may also toss the cooked, drained vegetables in garlic or lemon butter.

Steaming

The idea behind steaming is to cook the vegetable without allowing it to come in contact with the boiling water. In this way, the colour and taste are maintained and nutrients are not lost to the boiling water. In order to cook the vegetables quickly, and so avoid softening them too much and destroying a lot of vitamin C, a properly designed steamer is required. This consists of two saucepans. The bottom one will contain the boiling water, and the second pan sits on top of the first. The second pan has holes in the base (bottom) through which steam passes. The vegetables sit in this second pan and cook in the steam. A tightly fitting lid should be used to maintain a high temperature. As with boiling, each vegetable has it own cooking time, but you can, if you wish, steam more than one vegetable at a time by successive additions. Adjust cooking times to personal taste.

Seasoning Sprinkle before or after cooking with paprika, black pepper, cayenne and/or chopped fresh herbs. Vegetables may be tossed in garlic or lemon butter after cooking.

Pressure Cooking

Pressure cookers are efficient pieces of equipment and are excellent for tenderising tough meat or reducing the cooking time (and also fuel use) of meats, soups and stews. Because they are so efficient, I feel they are far too damaging to the delicate tissues of vegetables. Also, if more than one vegetable is to be cooked, it is important to add them in succession according to their cooking times. For example, a delicate leaf vegetable such as cabbage is bound to the same cooking time as potatoes. You end up with either soggy cabbage and well-cooked potato or well-cooked cabbage and raw potato.

Baking

Baking is oven-cooking and can be performed with dry or moist heat. It is not suitable for the delicate leaf vegetables such as spinach or lettuce. Cabbage leaves, which are slightly tougher, may be baked for a short time prior to stuffing in order to soften them and avoid splitting.

Dry-baking involves placing vegetables in an uncovered dish or directly on the oven bars. Vegetables to be moist-baked are placed in a covered dish. Either the bottom of the dish is shallowly covered with water or a sauce is poured over the vegetable. The oven temperature should be around 180°–200°C or 350°–400°F, and cooking time adjusted to suit personal taste. For example, a medium-sized potato would take 1 hour dry-baked at 180°C or 350°F. A piece of pumpkin (winter squash) (about a 3 cm (1 in) cube) would take 15–20 minutes at 200°C or 400°F. A dish of unsliced leeks in cheese sauce would take 1 hour at 180°C or 350°F.

Seasoning Moist-baked vegetables can be seasoned with the usual chopped herbs, black pepper, paprika and cayenne.

Roasting

Only tougher vegetables are suitable for roasting, eg kohlrabi, potato, pumpkin (winter squash), carrot and onion. Green peas and (French or runner, string) beans, together with leaf vegetables, are not cooked this way. The traditional method of roasting is to place vegetables around a joint of meat where they are cooked in fats and meat juices, absorbing flavour from the meat. Small potatoes, carrots and onions may be roasted whole, while larger ones are cut into cubes of about 5–8 cm (2–3 in). Vegetable oil or animal fat is poured to shallowly cover the bottom of the dish and vegetables are added. They are turned several times to ensure an even coating of oil. The dish is placed in the oven (covered or uncovered) at 150°–200°C or 300°–400°F. It is necessary to turn vegetables occasionally to ensure even cooking.

Seasoning Season the oil prior to cooking or sprinkle the seasoning over the vegetables once served in the dish.

Stir-frying

This is the method used in Chinese cooking. Essentially, the vegetable is very finely sliced and cooked quickly at a high temperature in a small quantity of vegetable oil. The oil is really only to prevent sticking, as the heat of the metal softens the vegetable's fibres. Traditionally a wok is used by the Chinese. The metal is thin and attains a high and even temperature. I find a good-quality, heavy-bottomed frying pan (skillet) or even a saucepan may be substituted, although a wok really is the best. The bottom of the pan or wok is thoroughly covered with oil and placed on the heat source. When the oil is beginning to smoke, the vegetable is thrown in and stirred continuously. I find the addition of a small quantity of water helps to maintain moisture in the vegetable.

This method is suitable for a wide range of vegetables. Potatoes, carrots and the tougher vegetables must be sliced very thinly and they take approximately 5 minutes to cook. Cabbage, onion and other leaf vegetables are finely chopped and need 1–2 minutes. Again, cooking time varies according to personal taste.

Seasoning Garlic, black pepper, paprika and cayenne should be added to the oil before adding the vegetables. Herbs can be used to season. If the herbs are dried, they should be added to the oil with the other seasoning. If fresh, they should be lightly chopped and added at the same time as the vegetables.

The Vegetables

The following list runs through each vegetable outlining the most suitable methods of cooking, according to my personal tastes. For example, boiling green capsicum (sweet peppers) is not suitable in my opinion, but if you enjoy your capsicum this way, then go ahead with this method. Similarly, if you find raw, grated beetroot (beets) completely inedible, omit this vegetable from your salads. The key factor is experimenting to suit your personal tastes.

Asparagus

Use only the green end of the shoots.
- Eat raw.
- Steam.
- Boil.
- Slice thinly and stir-fry.
- Moist-bake in a sauce.

Avocados

A native of tropical climates, but frequently imported into temperate countries, it is a popular vegetable. Generally it is eaten raw, plain or made into a cold savoury dish. New Zealanders often eat avocado sprinkled with raw or brown (demerara, soft light brown) sugar. It can also be made into a cold sweet mousse.

Beans, Broad (Fava)

Remove from pod.
- If very young, eat raw.
- Boil.
- Steam.
- Stir-fry.
- Bake in a sauce.

Beans, Green (French or Runner, String), Purple and Yellow (Wax)

Remove tips and tails. Wash. Slice diagonally, transversely or lengthwise, or leave whole.
- Boil.
- Steam.
- Eat raw.
- Stir-fry.
- Bake in a sauce.

Beetroot (Beets)

Trim leaves to within 2 cm (¾ in) of beetroot (beet) and wash well.
- Bake whole (wrap first in aluminium foil for best results) for 1 hour.
- Boil whole and peel before eating (approx. 1 hour for medium-sized).

Note: Beetroot leaves may also be eaten—lightly steamed with garlic butter.

Broccoli

Wash.
- Steam.
- Boil.
- Bake in a sauce.
- Break or cut into small pieces and stir-fry.
- Eat raw.

Brussels Sprouts

Remove yellow and tougher outside leaves. Wash. Make a cross-cut in the stalk end for a more even cooking.
- Boil.
- Steam.
- Bake in a sauce.

Cabbage, Green (Round Head)

Treat as for white (drum head) cabbage, but this is not such a good vegetable for raw eating or baking.

Cabbage, White (Drum Head)

Remove yellowed or bruised outer leaves.
- Chop finely and
  - eat raw
  - stir-fry
  - boil
  - steam
  - bake in a sauce
- Halve, remove innermost leaves, stuff and bake.

Capsicum (Sweet Peppers)

Wash, discard 'heart' with seeds and stalk.

- Eat raw.
- Slice thinly and stir-fry.
- Slice and bake in a sauce.
- Stuff and bake for 25–30 minutes.

Carrots

Wash. Top and tail. Peel if necessary.

- Eat raw.
- Slice lengthwise, diagonally or transversely (½–1 cm (¼–½ in) thick) and boil.
- Slice as above and steam.
- Slice very thinly and stir-fry.
- Roast small carrots whole and larger ones cut into chunks (2–3 cm (¾–1 in) thick).
- Moist-bake in 2–3 cm (¾–1 in) chunks.
- Moist-bake in a sauce in 2–3 cm (¾–1 in) chunks for 35 minutes.

Cauliflower

Wash and trim away thick stalk area. Include younger, more delicate leaves in cooking if desired. If cooking whole, make a deep incision up through the stalk area for a more even cooking.

- Break into florets and
  - eat raw
  - stir-fry.
- Break into florets or leave whole and
  - boil
  - steam
  - bake in a sauce.

Celery

Wash and trim away root areas. Leafy tops may be used if desired.

- Eat raw.
- Cut into lengths and
  - boil
  - steam.
- Moist-bake in a sauce.
- Moist-bake.
- Slice thinly and stir-fry.

Chokos (Chayotes, Mirlitons)

The choko (chayote, mirliton) is a very bland-tasting vegetable and needs herbs or spices, or a tasty sauce, to make it interesting. The larger the choko, the more insipid the taste. I think stir-frying is the best method of cooking. Cooking in hot oil seals in the little flavour there is. In times of need, I have substituted choko for bamboo shoots or water chestnuts in a Chinese-style stir-fry dish. It does not of course impart their characteristic flavour, but in its

own way it enchances the flavour of the food. In tropical Western Samoa where apples are a luxury, I was taught to use chokos instead—cut peeled choko into thin slices or even grate it, and boil in a little water until very soft. Sweeten to taste, then use in pies and crumbles in place of cooked apple.

Peel away all traces of thick, tough, fibrous skin and remove inner seeds. You may prefer to do this under running water to wash away the sap which otherwise dries on the skin and can be unpleasant.

- Cut into 3–4 cm (1–1½ in) cubes and
  - boil
  - steam.
- Slice thinly and
  - stir-fry
  - bake in a sauce.

Corn (Maize)

Remove outer leaves and silks.

- Leave kernels on the cob or remove and
  - boil
  - steam
  - eat raw.
- Remove kernels from cob and
  - stir-fry
  - bake in a sauce.

Cucumber

Wash. Some varieties may need to be peeled as their skins are bitter and tough.

- Slice thinly or into chunks and eat raw.
- Slice thinly and stir-fry.

Eggplant (Aubergines)

Wash and remove stalk. When used sliced, you may prefer to lightly salt slices and allow to 'rest' for 10–20 minutes. They are then washed and dried before cooking. This salting will remove any slight bitterness plus excess water. Eggplant has a high water content so you will find that during frying it can soak up quite a lot of oil, with a tendency to become soggy rather than crisp. The salting is not necessary, however, and I usually don't bother.

- Slice thinly and stir-fry.
- Halve and boil.
- Dry-bake whole (slit skin first).
- Cut lengthwise, stuff and bake in aluminium foil or covered dish.
- Slice and moist-bake.

Jerusalem Artichokes

Flavour is rather nutty, so take care with blending of flavours when adding to other foods. Preparation and cooking as for potatoes.

Kohlrabi

Trim away leaves and root area. Peel, making sure to remove all fibrous area. This can be quite thick on older kohlrabi.

- Cut into 3–4 cm (1–1½ in) cubes and
  - boil
  - steam
  - moist-bake
  - roast.
- Slice thinly and
  - stir-fry
  - bake in a sauce.
- Eat raw.

Leeks

Remove tough outer leaves and root area—trim back darkest green leaf tip, but much of the paler, softer green areas can be used. Wash well as leeks can be very sandy/gritty.

- Slice transversely into rounds 1–2 cm (½–¾ in) thick and boil.
- Slice as above and steam.
- Moist-bake sliced or whole.
- Moist-bake sliced or whole in a sauce.
- Roast whole.

Lettuce

Discard tough outer leaves and wash well.

- Tear rather than cut into pieces and eat raw.

- Chop finely and
  - steam
  - stir-fry
  - add to a sauce.
- Halve, remove innermost leaves, stuff and eat raw.

Marrow
(Summer or Yellow Squash)

Remove skin, discard seeds (*see* later use of seeds on p. 43).
- Cut into ½–1 cm (¼–½ in) cubes and
  - boil
  - steam
  - roast
  - moist-bake
  - bake in a sauce.
- Cut lengthwise, scoop out seeds, stuff and bake.

Mushrooms

Wash well. Peel only if old and badly blemished.
- Eat raw.
- Leave whole and
  - boil
  - steam
  - roast
  - bake in a sauce.
- Leave whole or slice and
  - stir-fry
  - add to a sauce.

Okra
(Lady's Fingers, Gumbo)

Use young okra only. Older pods will be tough, stringy and not so palatable. Cut away stalks and tip.

- Eat raw, thinly sliced.
- Slice thinly and
  - boil
  - stir-fry
  - bake in a sauce.

Onions

Remove brown outer leaves and cut away top and root area.
- Slice thinly and eat raw.
- Boil (whole if small, otherwise halved or quartered).
- Steam as above.
- Bake in a sauce (whole if small, otherwise halved or quartered).
- Roast (whole, halved or quartered).
- Remove centres, stuff and moist-bake for 30 minutes.
- Slice thinly and stir-fry.
- Slice thinly, boil in milk until soft and and use with milky juices to make a sauce.

Parsnips

Old parsnips have a central core of tough, fibrous tissue which must be discarded. The outside flesh is cut into cubes or chunks, and then cooked. Old parsnips have a very pungent flavour and should be treated cautiously when blending flavours. Young parsnips may be cooked whole or cut into slices or chunks.

- Cut into 2–3 cm (¾–1 in) pieces and
  - boil
  - steam
  - roast (leave young parsnips whole).
- Slice thinly and bake in a sauce.
- Slice very thinly into slivers and deep-fry into 'chips'.
- Slice cooked parsnip into regular chip-sized pieces and deep-fry until brown.

Peas, Green

Remove from pod. However, if peas are very young, they may be eaten whole. This is particularly the case with snow peas (mangetouts) and sugar snap peas which have edible pods (*see* 'Preparation', p. 7).
- Boil.
- Steam.
- Stir-fry.
- Eat raw.
- Moist-bake in a sauce.

Potatoes

Wash well. Peel only if the skin is very old, tough and heavily blemished. Cut away green areas or discard entirely if there is a lot of green.
- Cut into 3–4 cm (1–1½ in) cubes or, if small, leave whole.

- Boil.
- Steam.
- Roast.
- Leave unpeeled and dry-bake.
- Slice thinly and stir-fry.
- Chips—slice thinly or in 'fingers' and deep-fry.
- Slice thickly and bake in milk or a sauce.
- Cut into 3–4 cm (1–1½ in) cubes or, if small, leave whole. Serve mashed with butter.
- Duchesse potato—mash 500 g (1 lb) of boiled potato with 25 g (1 oz) of butter and 1 egg. Pipe into swirls with a piping (pastry) bag onto a baking tray (sheet). Bake for 10 minutes at 180°C or 350°F.

Pumpkin (Winter Squash)

Wash. Some pumpkin (winter squash) skins, though very tough in appearance, do soften considerably when cooked; others do not. Experiment with varieties and leave the skin on where possible.
- Cut into 3–4 cm (1–1½ in) cubes and
  - boil
  - steam
  - roast
  - moist-bake.
- Grate and eat raw.
- Slice thinly and
  - stir-fry
  - bake in a sauce.

- Bake whole, scoop out seeds and use soft flesh as a purée or as a basis for soup.

Note: Varieties available most frequently in the UK favour use in savoury rather than sweet dishes. Experiment to find most suitable for each recipe.

Radishes

Wash and trim off leaves and root.
- Eat raw.
- Slice thinly and stir-fry.

Silverbeet (Swiss Chard)

Discard old, tough leaves. The white stalk may be used, but discard thick, tougher areas at base. Wash well.
- Choose young leaves, discarding thick white stalk and midrib. Shred or tear into pieces and add to a salad.
- Shred and
  - boil
  - steam
  - stir-fry
  - 'quick boil'—make a layer no more than 10 cm (4 in) deep in a wide pan. Cover with water and heat. Boil rapidly with pan uncovered until only 1 tablespoon of liquid remains. Remove from heat. Serve as is, or add a little butter, stir and boil further until only a tablespoon or two of liquid remains.

- Dip each leaf in boiling water for 1 minute to soften, spread with a filling, roll and moist-bake for 45–50 minutes.

Spinach

Spinach oleracea is the true spinach, of which there are many varieties. Silver beet, Swiss chard, New Zealand spinach and spinach beet can be used in its place, and are in fact often referred to as 'spinach'.

Wash well and remove blemished and insect-damaged leaves. You may prefer to remove all or part of the tougher stem, depending on the variety.
- Chop finely and
  - add sparingly to a salad
  - boil rapidly in a minimum of water
  - add to a stir-fry dish
  - add sparingly to a mixture of meats and/or vegetables which is to be baked slowly, eg stuffing inside cabbage, pumpkin (winter squash), poultry or pie.

Spring Onions (Green Onions, Scallions)

Remove roots, thin, papery outer leaves and very dark, tougher leaf tips.
- Eat raw.
- Chop and stir-fry.
- Chop and add to a sauce.

Sweet Potatoes, Kumara and Yams

Delicious, nutritious and filling. Preparation and cooking as for potatoes. However, as yams generally have tough, 'barky' skin, peel where necessary.

Tomatoes

Wash.

- Eat raw.
- Halve and dry-bake.
- Halve, scoop out centres, stuff and eat raw or dry-bake.
- Halve and grill (broil), can be topped with grated cheese.
- Halve or quarter. Heat in a pan, stir and press tomatoes into a pulp.
- To skin (peel)—dip in boiling water for about 1 minute until skin splits. Cool and peel.

Turnips

Trim away leaf and root area. Peel. Young small turnips may be left whole; otherwise slice or quarter according to recipe. Old turnips have a stronger flavour and tougher tissue and are best used in stews, soups or in vegetable stocks. Young turnips are more versatile, but even with these, cautious regard must be given to their somewhat bitter flavour. Turnips are often served as a

vegetable side dish with a tasty sauce or are well seasoned. They can be mashed with plenty of butter and again well seasoned.

- Grate finely and add to a salad (*young* turnips only).
- Quarter or slice 2–3 cm (¾–1 in) thick and
  - steam
  - boil.
- Quarter or, if small, leave whole and
  - roast
  - dry-bake wrapped tightly in aluminium foil.

- Slice very thinly and moist-bake in a tasty sauce.

Zucchini (Courgettes)

Wash and trim away stalk.

- Eat raw.
- Halve, leave whole or cut into 5 cm (2 in) lengths and boil.
- Slice thickly and steam.
- Slice thinly and stir-fry.
- Halve lengthwise and moist-bake.
- Moist-bake in a sauce (whole or in thick or thin slices).

Garden 'Weeds' and Flowers

Most garden weeds are edible though not necessarily palatable, and you must experiment to find those you like. Take care with selection. Those growing along dusty roadsides, in fields which may have been sprayed with agricultural chemicals or in places easily accessible to visiting canine friends are probably best left alone. Choose fresh, bright-green, healthy-looking plants and pick only the youngest, tenderest parts. Weeds become stringy and bitter very early in life! Again I suggest you refer to Richard Mabey's book *Food for Free*, but I will list the ones we found most acceptable. I also suggest that you refer to a fairly comprehensive herb book as most of those mentioned will be described in more detail. On no account eat, or drink the tea of, any leaf, flower, seed or berry until you are absolutely sure of its identity. Although most plants are edible, there is no sense in taking chances—if in doubt, your local botanic gardens or university department of botany will, I am sure, offer assistance.

chickweed	plantain
comfrey	salad burnet (garden burnet)
dandelion	sorrel
fat-hen	sow thistle (hare's lettuce, milkweed, puha)
marigold (calendula)	stinging nettle
nasturtium	watercress
nipplewort	

Methods of Cooking

- Eat raw.
- Chop finely and lightly boil with just enough water to cover the bottom of the pan—more of a light steaming than boiling.
- Chop and stir-fry (1 minute).
- Chop and add to a sauce, cook for a further 2 minutes.

Chickweed Family: Caryophyllaceae, *Stellaria media* (annual)
Delightful lightly steamed/boiled, and tossed in garlic butter. Alternatively, add to a soup or eat raw in salads. It is said to be rich in copper and iron.

Comfrey Family: Boraginaceae, *Symphytum officinale* (perennial)
It is best eaten cooked owing to its rather rough, hairy leaves. Comfrey contains vitamin B_{12}, which is especially important to strict vegetarians, but it only contains small amounts so it cannot be solely relied upon as a source of this essential vitamin.

Dandelion Family: Compositae, *Taraxacum officinale* (perennial)
Only the very young leaves are palatable as bitterness develops quite early. Dandelion is a good salad herb, or can be chopped finely and used in a meat or hot vegetable dish. It contains

potassium, calcium, manganese, sodium, sulphur and silicic acid. The root cleaned and roasted may be ground into a 'coffee' rather like chicory. The roots can also be eaten like parsnips or grated into salads. The flowers make an excellent wine.

Fat-Hen Family: Chenopodiaceae, *Chenopodium album* (annual)
Check identification thoroughly as several weeds go under the name 'fat-hen', a close relative being *Chenopodium bonus-henricus*—Good-King-Henry. Use young leaves only; the older ones are stringy. Young stem tips may also be eaten. Equally good cooked or in a salad. Certain American Indian tribes used seeds ground into flour to make a kind of bread. Fat-hen can be used as a substitute for spinach and is rich in vitamins A and C. It is also popular for its spinach-like leaves loaded with iron.

Marigold (Calendula) Family: Compositae, *Calendula officinalis* (annual)
A pretty flower commonly found in home gardens and parks. It has a thickish leaf with a yellow or orange flower, or rather a group of florets as with all Compositae. Young leaves and outer florets are excellent in salads. The outer florets may be added to cakes and biscuits (cookies). A 'tea' of the petals may be used to colour butter. The Romans used *Calendula* flowers in place of saffron when the latter was in short supply.

Nasturtium Family: Tropaeolaceae, *Tropaeolum majus* (or *minus*) (annual)
A very common garden flower. Once grown, it seeds itself every year. The leaves have a hot mustard-like flavour and are excellent in salads. The flowers are also used and are delicious in sandwiches. The seeds picked when green and pickled may be used as a substitute for capers. They were also used as a substitute for pepper in Britain during World War II. The whole plant is said to be rich in vitamin C and minerals.

Nipplewort Family: Compositae, *Lapsana communis* (annual)
Found in Europe, parts of Asia and America, it is a rather bitter herb. One or two small leaves finely chopped in a mixed salad is sufficient. It also may be used in a hot vegetable dish or hot meat dish.

Plantain Family: Plantaginaceae, *Plantago minor* (perennial)
This plant tends to lie flat on the ground. The leaves are rather thick, heavily ribbed and are dark green in colour. They contain much mucilage. It is only palatable if a very small quantity of leaves is used, chopped very finely and disguised in a hot vegetable or meat dish. During a drought year in New Zealand, an organically orientated sheep farmer found this plant invaluable. It did not die with the lack of rain and was a 'lifesaver' for his sheep.

Salad Burnet (Garden Burnet) Family: Rosaceae, *Sanguisorba minor* (*Poterium sanguisorba*) (perennial)
A very pretty herb found wild in the UK together with a close relative, burnet minor—*Pimpinella sanguisorba*. It is often found on chalk land and cliff sides—I remember seeing it in large quantities on the cliffs of Portishead above the Bristol Channel in England. It has a strong flavour rather like cucumber skin and can be used finely chopped in salads, eg cucumber salad, or it may be added to meat and vegetable dishes. Salad burnet is one of the few herbs available all year round and it will even sprout enough for picking through snow. It makes an attractive garnish.

Sorrel Wood Sorrel *(Oxalis acetosella)*

Garden (Broad Leaf) Sorrel *(Rumex acetosa)*

Sheep Sorrel *(Rumex acetosella)*

French (Buckler Leaf) Sorrel *(Rumex scutatus)* (perennial)

All recipes in this book using sorrel refer to French sorrel.

All of the above sorrels can be eaten, but wood sorrel should only be consumed in very small quantities. All are rich in vitamin C and have been well known for years as cures for and preventives against scurvy. All are rich in oxalic acid (which can be toxic in large doses) and should not be used too frequently. The sorrels have a slightly acid, rather lemon-like flavour and may be used in salads, soups, stews, sauces or as cooked greens—eg in place of spinach. French sorrel (though often confusingly called garden sorrel) is traditionally used by the French for soup. Garden sorrel and wood sorrel were much used in Britain in the past as a basis for green sauce to accompany meat and fish. Sheep sorrel was also very popular in Britain during Henry VIII's reign. Lightly boiled and puréed sorrel may be used to accompany the more greasy meats—pork, goose or lamb—in place of the usual sauces like apple and mint sauce.

Note: Because of its acidity, do not cook sorrel in a copper or aluminium pan.

Sow Thistle Family: Compositae, *Sonchus oleraceus* (perennial)

Sow thistle is also known as hare's lettuce or milkweed. Its Maori name is puha. The leaves are rather prickly and the prickly parts may be cut away when used in salads. Said to be rich in minerals and iron, especially vitamin C, it makes a fine addition to soups and stocks. It can also be used in meat or vegetable dishes. It was once thought that sows sought out this weed to increase their milk flow, hence the name.

Stinging Nettle Family: Urticaceae, *Urtica dioica* (perennial)

The presence of nettle is said to indicate a soil rich in nitrogen. Owing to its sting, cut the plant with scissors over a bowl or a basket, and cut only the new, young shoots. Makes an excellent soup or can be lightly steamed, tossed in garlic butter and topped with poached eggs.

Watercress Family: Cruciferae, *Nasturtium officinale* (perennial)

A well-known herb that grows wild as well as cultivated in running water, it has a hot, peppery taste and is best used in salads or soups. It is delicious in sandwiches. Said to be rich in minerals and iron. Watercress was an important green vegetable to us during our two years in Western Samoa. I had a form of watercress in my garden in Harare, Zimbabwe, called land cress. It is very similar in appearance and taste, and grows well in a moderate, damp soil alongside the oregano and marjoram.

Salads

I have to admit to being a 'nibbler' in the kitchen. As I prepare, I nibble and taste. In this way I have discovered that many vegetables we consider only as a cooked dish have an interesting texture and flavour in the raw state. Have you ever tried raw pumpkin (winter squash) or cauliflower or tried raw grated swede (Swedish turnip, rutabaga) in a salad? I would suggest that you try each vegetable raw before you cook it and see if you like it. Remember though that if in the past you have consumed vegetables as I described earlier, mostly peeled and boiled, you must keep an open mind and train your palate to these new tastes and textures.

A salad to most people means lettuce, tomato, cucumber, beetroot (beets) and perhaps spring onions (scallions). The term 'salad' really indicates a mixture of cold raw vegetables, but I use the term to mean any mixture of raw or cooked vegetables that is eaten cold as a savoury dish. Once you have decided which vegetables you enjoy raw, use a mixture of them in as many different combinations as you can. In recent years, interest in salads has increased and many takeaway (carry-out) restaurants and delicatessens offer salads as a matter of course.

Preparation

Returning to salad preparation—wash all vegetables well and leave skins intact where possible. Chop or slice vegetables to a medium fineness and mix together. If too finely sliced, I find vegetables lose their individuality in mixed salad. Also good tooth and gum exercise is lost! Cooked vegetables—eg potatoes, beans, corn (maize) kernels—may be used either as a base or in addition to other raw vegetables. Include as many garden 'weeds' as possible. To the basic mixture of raw and/or cooked vegetables, add any one or several of the following:
- raw fruit, eg apples, oranges
- dried fruit, eg dates, sultanas (golden raisins), prunes
- cold cooked rice
- cold cooked pasta, eg macaroni
- cold cooked meat, eg bacon, chicken, pork, beef, lamb cubes, salami, liverwurst (liver sausage)
- nuts or seeds, eg sunflower seeds, roast pumpkin (winter squash) seeds (pepitas), peanuts (groundnuts), cold cooked beans
- eggs, chopped hard-boiled, or cold scrambled eggs
- cheese, cubed or grated.

Secondary Salads

This is the term I use to describe a salad of which the base is not vegetables. For example, a rice salad may be predominantly cold cooked rice perhaps with chopped tomato, sultanas (golden raisins) and chopped lettuce added. It is served as a cold savoury accompaniment to a main meat or vegetable dish, forming the carbohydrate source in the meal. A 'true' salad (ie predominantly raw vegetables) may also be served.

Another example would be cold cooked macaroni with chopped hard-boiled egg and raw or cooked corn (maize) kernels added. Remember that a salad can consist of any mixture of cold foods that you enjoy. Experiment with different combinations and you will find salad eating far more exciting. I find many people still consider it to be 'rabbit food', ie uninteresting and non-filling—it need not be so.

Seasoning Remember that aromatic plants also make tasty additions to any salad. Try a little finely chopped marjoram, oregano or chives and see how they 'lift' the overall taste of the salad. Season also with crushed or finely chopped garlic, black pepper, paprika or cayenne.

Dressings To your salad you may add a mayonnaise or salad dressing, or simply a spoonful of a good quality oil, eg sunflower, safflower (Mexican saffron) or olive. Very often I find that the juices from the raw vegetables seep out after cutting and are enough to moisten the salad. A little orange, lemon or apple juice may be used instead of a dressing.

Recipes for salad dressings and mayonnaise are given on pp. 227–9.

Dried Beans

My concern here is for all types of dried beans or peas, eg red kidney, pinto, black eye, soya (soy), lima (butter), haricot (navy or pea), lentils and split peas. Awareness of their high protein content and versatility in cookery has emerged in the last 20 years, alongside the concern for the high energy input required for meat production. Meat as a source of protein is coming to be regarded as a luxury, while vegetable protein is more cheaply and easily produced. Beans have a high protein content and are also rich in minerals and vitamins.

If beans are soaked in cold water before cooking they will take much less time to cook, saving on fuel. With smaller dried beans, this soaking is less important and with lentils it can be omitted entirely. For beans of lima (butter)/haricot (navy or pea)/black eye/soya (soy)/red kidney size, soak for at least 12 hours in plenty of cold water. In a tropical climate (or even a temperate zone heatwave), it is best to place the pan of soaking beans in the refrigerator to eliminate possible fermentation, which can affect flavour. Dried beans double their original volume after soaking and cooking. There are three basic methods of cooking beans:
- boiling
- baking
- pressure cooking.

Boiling

1. Drain water from soaked beans and re-cover with fresh water.
2. Bring to boil, reduce heat and simmer. Stir once or twice when first boiling as one or two beans may stick to the bottom of the pan. It is important to boil beans vigorously for 10 minutes before simmering, in a partially covered saucepan.
3. Simmer beans until cooked (making sure they are always well covered in water). Time will depend on size of beans and degree to which they were softened during soaking. Beans are cooked when they are soft but not mushy. Most people will remember the ubiquitous canned baked beans on toast of childhood days—aim for that kind of softness, perhaps a little less. For beans soaked in water for 12 hours before cooking, the following should act as a guide:

black eye	—	50 minutes
haricot (navy or pea)	—	50 minutes
jugo	—	50 minutes
lima (butter)	—	60 minutes
pinto	—	60 minutes
red kidney	—	60 minutes

soya (soy)	—	50 minutes
split peas	—	15 minutes (soaked)*
sugar	—	50 minutes

Note: * It is not necessary to soak split peas. If soaked, they should be simmered for 15 minutes. If unsoaked, simmer for 30 minutes.

4. Drain beans. If beans are to be used for a salad, rinse again in fresh cold water.

Boiling Lentils

1. Place lentils in saucepan and cover with three to four times their own volume of water.
2. Bring to boil. Reduce heat and simmer until lentils are soft. It does not matter if they are a little mushy. In fact, for a recipe such as lentil patties, it is desirable for them to be 'mashable' (15–20 minutes is about right).
3. Drain (do not rinse in fresh water).

Baking

Presoaked beans are placed in an ovenproof dish, covered in water and baked in a cool to moderate oven (150°–180°C/300°–350°F) for 2–2½ hours. I have never used this method, but believe it achieves good results. It certainly saves on fuel if you already have the oven on for cooking.

Pressure Cooking

The main advantages of this method are twofold:

• Presoaking is not necessary.
• Cooking time can be significantly reduced, which saves fuel. Time is reduced by about two-thirds with the pressure setting at 7 kg (15 lb).

If you use this method, approx. 20–25 minutes cooking time will be sufficient. Any underdone beans may be finished off on the top of the stove (cooker). Note which varieties need extra cooking and adjust future pressure cooking times accordingly.

Note: 1. This method is *not* suitable for lentils.
2. If you add 1 tablespoon of vegetable oil to the water in the pressure cooker, it will reduce frothing.

Sprouting Beans

Sprouted or germinated beans and seeds are superior in food value to unsprouted ones. It is for this reason that health enthusiasts around the world sprout alfalfa, soya (soy) and other beans seen on sale in health-food stores. The East Asians of course are also aware of their value and one therefore finds in Asian cookery quantities of bean sprouts. The beans mostly used in Chinese cookery are mung (moong dal) beans. They can be easily sprouted at home, taking only a few days to grow to the required size.

Strictly speaking, any bean that is edible should be suitable as a sprouted bean. In our family, we find a few we really enjoy. Alfalfa seeds in salad are a favourite, as are mung (moong dal) beans in Chinese cookery. As with all cookery, experiment and find what suits you and your family best. The following methods may be used for all types of beans.

Method 1

1. Soak beans for 24 hours in warm fresh water. Two to three tablespoons of beans should be sufficient for one batch.
2. Drain, wash several times in warm to hot water. Drain again and place in a large jar.
3. Cover open neck of jar with muslin (double cheesecloth). Secure in place with a tight rubber (elastic) band or string, or the screw band of a preserving jar.
4. Invert jar and allow for drainage. I sit the inverted jar in a sieve sitting in a bowl—it sounds a bit cumbersome but does work. Anything which allows water to drain away and beans to breathe is suitable. Place jar in a dark, warm place or cover with a thick cloth.
5. Leave jar for 4–5 days, but rinse beans several times (about three times daily) in warm to hot water. Drain away excess water and return to position described in the previous point. The number of days required to germinate is 2–5. The crop can be harvested 2–5 days later when sprout is three times the length of the bean.

Method 2

1. Soak beans for 24 hours in warm fresh water.
2. Line a large wide bowl with wet muslin (cheesecloth)—preferably muslin which has been soaked in warm water.

3. Drain beans. Rinse with several changes of warm to hot water.
4. Drain finally. Place beans in the muslin-lined bowl.
5. Cover bowl with a plate to exclude light and maintain a damp atmosphere. Set bowl in a warm place.
6. Leave for 4 to 5 days, but remove beans three times daily and rinse in several changes of warm water. Drain, rinse muslin in warm water. Replace muslin and beans in dish. Cover.

The seed coats and sprouted beans may be separated by floating them in water or by washing them through a wide-meshed sieve (the seed coats pass through and are discarded).

Cooking
- Serve raw in a salad.
- Lightly boil.
- Stir-fry.

(*See* Tai Tapu Beef on p. 105 and Lamb with Bean Sprouts on p. 130.)

Hot Vegetables

BEAN AND CORN PIE

Serves 5–6

PASTRY
75 g (1/3 cup, 3 oz) margarine
150 g (1¼ cups, 5½ oz) wholemeal (whole-wheat) flour
2 tablespoons water

FILLING
450 ml (1¾ cups, 15 fl oz) milk
1 tablespoon margarine
2 tablespoons wholemeal (whole-wheat) flour
100 g (¾ cup, 3½ oz) green (French or runner, string) beans
100 g (½ cup, 3½ oz) corn (maize) kernels
25 g (1 oz) bacon rashers (slices), chopped (optional)
1 teaspoon oil
½ teaspoon summer savory, finely chopped (optional)

PASTRY
Rub margarine into flour with fingertips. Sprinkle in water. Mix into a soft dough. Roll out thinly. Use to line a greased 18 × 3 cm (7 × 1¾ in) pie dish (plate).

FILLING
Pour milk into a saucepan and bring to boil. Stir well to prevent boiling over. Reduce heat and simmer until reduced in volume to 270 ml (1 cup, 9 fl oz). In a separate pan, heat margarine until sizzling. Stir in flour. Remove from heat. Carefully blend in milk, avoiding lumps. Reheat gently until sauce thickens. Set aside. Thinly slice green beans. Steam or boil with corn until tender. Set aside. Cut bacon (if used) into small pieces. Fry gently in oil until well cooked. Stir beans, corn, bacon and savory into sauce. Pour into pastry case (shell). Bake at 180°C or 350°F for 35–40 minutes.

Opposite: Bean and Corn Pie — perfect for a simple lunch, even more so when produce fresh from the garden can be used.

GRILLED CHEESY VEGETABLES

Serves 2–4

75 g (½ cup, 2½ oz) green (French or runner, string) beans
50 g (2 oz) bacon rashers (slices), chopped
1 teaspoon oil
50 g (½ cup, 1½ oz) sorrel or lettuce, chopped
1 tablespoon chives, finely chopped
100 g (3½ oz) tomatoes
125 ml (½ cup, 4½ fl oz) Basic Wholemeal (Whole-Wheat) Sauce (see sauces, p. 218)
50 g (½ cup, 2 oz) cheddar cheese, grated

Cut green beans into pieces 2–3 cm (¾–1¼ in) long. Boil or steam until tender. Drain and place in a shallow ovenproof dish.

Cut bacon into tiny pieces (approx. 1–1½ cm (½ in) square). Fry gently in oil until cooked. Add sorrel and chives. Cook gently for 2 minutes, stirring well. Remove from heat. Layer bacon mixture over beans. Cut tomatoes into small pieces. Layer over bacon.

Prepare wholemeal sauce. Stir grated cheese into sauce. Spoon this sauce over tomato layer in dish. Place under a medium grill (broiler) for several minutes until sauce is bubbling and beginning to brown.

SAGE BEANS

Serves 4

200 g (1½ cups, 7 oz) green (French or runner, string) beans
1 onion
1 teaspoon sage, finely chopped
½ tablespoon oil
50 g (¾ cup, 2 oz) wholemeal (whole-wheat) breadcrumbs, fresh
black pepper
2 tomatoes

Slice beans. Boil or steam until just tender. Meanwhile, thinly slice onion. Gently fry onion and sage in oil. When onion is soft, add breadcrumbs. Season with black pepper. Cook gently for 1 minute. Chop tomatoes into small pieces. Add to breadcrumbs and onion mixture. Cook gently for a further minute. Remove from heat.

When beans are cooked, drain and place in a warmed, shallow ovenproof dish. Layer breadcrumb mixture over beans. Place under a hot grill (broiler) for 2–3 minutes.
Alternative Sprinkle with a tablespoon of grated Parmesan or cheddar cheese before placing under hot grill.

SESAME BEANS

Serves 4

1 large tomato
2 teaspoons oil
1½ tablespoons sesame seed
150 g (1 cup, 5½ oz) green (French or runner, string) beans

Skin tomato, chop into small pieces and set aside. Heat oil and sesame seed in a small pan. Cook over a fairly high heat until seeds are browned. Add tomato and cook, stirring continuously, for 1 minute. Remove from heat, but keep hot.

Slice beans. Boil or steam until soft. Drain. Add hot tomato mixture to beans. Stir well. Spoon into a warmed shallow dish. Serve immediately.

BUCKWHEAT BRUNCH

Serves 2

100 g (⅔ cup, 3½ oz) buckwheat,
whole but hulled

1 onion

50 g (⅓ cup, 2 oz) green (French or
runner, string) beans

2½ tablespoons oil

2 teaspoons (sweet) marjoram,
finely chopped

25 g (¼ cup, 1 oz) borage, shredded

salt and black pepper

Soak buckwheat in water for 30 minutes, drain and set aside.

Finely slice onion and thinly slice green beans. Place both in a heavy-based frying pan (skillet) with oil. Cook over a medium heat, stirring frequently, until beans are tender. Add buckwheat, marjoram, borage, a little salt and plenty of black pepper (dish should be peppery in flavour so season generously with this). Continue cooking over a medium heat, stirring constantly, for 2–3 minutes. Serve with fresh, crusty wholemeal (whole-wheat) bread.

Note: An unusual dish which I serve for breakfast, brunch, supper or as an hors d'oeuvre. Opinions on it vary—I love it but my husband hates it!

STIR-FRIED CABBAGE WITH EGGS

Serves 3–4

1 clove garlic

pinch of paprika

1 tablespoon oil

75 g (⅔ cup, 2½ oz) white (drum
head) cabbage, shredded

25 g (1 oz) carrot

1 medium green capsicum
(sweet pepper)

4 eggs, lightly beaten

2 teaspoons soy sauce

Finely chop garlic. Place in a heavy-based frying pan (skillet) with paprika and oil. Thinly slice cabbage, carrot and capsicum. Stir-fry in oil until tender.

Break eggs into a separate bowl and beat a little. When vegetables are tender, pour egg into pan (over vegetables). Cook over a medium heat allowing egg to set (rather like making an omelette). When just set, cut egg into chunks and pour in soy sauce. Stir gently for half a minute. Remove from heat. Serve immediately.

CABBAGE WITH CHEESE

Serves 3–4

200 g (2 cups, 7 oz) white (drum
head) or green (round head) cabbage,
shredded

40 g (⅓ cup, 1½ oz) mature (sharp)
cheddar cheese, grated

1 tablespoon sesame seed, toasted

pinch of cayenne

Thinly slice cabbage. Steam or lightly boil until just tender. Mix together remaining ingredients. Drain the cooked cabbage. Add cheese mixture. Mix thoroughly. Serve immediately.

Alternative Add 1 rasher (slice) of cooked lean bacon chopped into small pieces at same time as cheese mixture.

STUFFED CABBAGE

Serves 4
1 small white (drum head) or green
(round head) cabbage (about
375 g/14 oz)
1 small onion
1½ teaspoons oregano, finely chopped
½ tablespoon oil
100 g (½ cup, 3½ oz) cottage cheese,
sieved (strained)
75 g (¾ cup, 2½ oz) peanuts (ground-
nuts) or sunflower seeds, ground
3 tablespoons water
3 tablespoons white wine
salt and black pepper

Cut cabbage into halves. Remove inner leaves from each half, leaving behind a shell or outer layer (1½–2 cm (½–1 in) thick). Take inner leaves and discard about one-third. Finely chop remaining two-thirds. Thinly slice onion. Place chopped cabbage, onion, oregano and oil in a frying pan (skillet). Fry gently until onion and cabbage are just tender. Remove from heat. Stir in cottage cheese and nuts (or seeds). Use this mixture to stuff each cabbage half. Tie two stuffed halves together using white cotton (string). Place in a deep ovenproof dish. Pour over water and wine. Season with a little salt and black pepper. Cover and bake at 180°C or 350°F for 50 minutes. (Baste two or three times during cooking.)

CABBAGE AND CORIANDER PIE

Serves 4–6
PASTRY
75 g (⅓ cup, 3 oz) margarine
150 g (1¼ cups, 5½ oz) wholemeal
(whole-wheat) flour
2 tablespoons water

FILLING
300 g (2½ cups, 10½ oz) white (drum
head) cabbage, shredded
1½ tablespoons oil
1 tablespoon coriander (Chinese
parsley) seed, coarsely ground
3 tablespoons milk
2 eggs
1½ teaspoons coriander (Chinese
parsley) seed, coarsely ground (extra)
100 g (1 cup, 3½ oz) mature (sharp)
cheddar cheese, grated
black pepper

PASTRY
Rub margarine into flour with fingertips. Sprinkle in water. Mix well to make a soft dough. Roll out pastry fairly thinly on a well-floured board. Use to line a greased 20 × 3 cm (8 × 1¼ in) pie dish (plate).

FILLING
Finely shred or slice cabbage. Set aside. Heat oil and 1 tablespoon of coriander in a large frying pan (skillet) or wok. When quite hot, add cabbage and stir-fry until tender. Layer inside the pastry-lined pie dish. Pour milk into a bowl, add eggs and extra coriander. Beat well. Add grated cheese to bowl. Season with a little black pepper, mix well and pour over cabbage. The cheese will collect on top, so spread it evenly over cabbage. Bake pie at 190°C or 375°F for 30 minutes.

Opposite: *This crisp and colourful dish of Baked Red Cabbage, topped with melted cheese, is a far cry from the usual limp serving of ordinary boiled cabbage.*

BAKED RED CABBAGE

Serves 3–4

1 medium onion
1 teaspoon dill seed
½ tablespoon oil
150 g (1¼ cups, 5½ oz) red cabbage,
shredded
1 large green capsicum (sweet pepper)
salt and black pepper
2 tablespoons white wine
50 g (½ cup, 2 oz) mature (sharp)
cheddar cheese, grated

Thinly slice onion. Place in a small frying pan (skillet) with dill and oil. Fry gently until onion is soft.

Thinly slice cabbage and capsicum. Add to cooked onion and mix well. Turn into a shallow ovenproof dish. Season with salt and black pepper. Spoon over white wine. Sprinkle with grated cheese. Cover and bake at 200°C or 400°F for 25 minutes.

CARROT TART

Serves 4

PASTRY

75 g (⅓ cup, 3 oz) margarine
150 g (1¼ cups, 5½ oz) wholemeal
(whole-wheat) flour
2 tablespoons water

FILLING

75 g (⅓ cup, 3 oz) butter
3 teaspoons mace sticks
(flakes or blades)
300 g (1⅔ cups, 10½ oz) carrot,
grated
salt and black pepper
3 tablespoons thickened
(double, whipping) cream

PASTRY

Rub margarine into flour with fingertips. Sprinkle in water. Mix into a soft dough. Roll out thinly. Use pastry to line a greased 18 × 3 cm (7 × 1¾ in) pie dish (plate).

FILLING

Heat butter in a small pan until sizzling. Add mace. Reduce heat and cook mace gently for 2 minutes. Strain butter into a larger pan. Add grated carrot to butter. Cook over a gentle heat, stirring frequently, until carrot is tender—do not allow to brown. Remove from heat. Season with a little salt and plenty of black pepper. Stir in cream. Spoon into prepared pie dish. Bake at 190°C or 375°F for 25–30 minutes.

Note: I use mace sticks in preference to powdered (ground) mace as I believe they achieve a more subtle flavour. The latter may be substituted if preferred. Use about ¼ teaspoon and add to butter at same time as carrot.

CHEESE, CARROT AND CARAWAY PASTIES

Makes 10

FILLING

200 g (7 oz) potatoes
150 g (¾ cup, 5½ oz) carrot, grated
1 teaspoon butter or margarine
200 g (1¾ cups, 7 oz) mature (sharp)
cheddar cheese, grated
1½–2 teaspoons caraway seed
¼ teaspoon paprika
salt and black pepper

PASTRY

200 g (7 oz) margarine
400 g (3 cups, 14 oz) wholemeal
(whole-wheat) flour
5 tablespoons water
a little beaten egg

FILLING

Peel potatoes, cut into pieces and boil or steam until tender. Drain well, place in bowl, mash a little and set aside. Place grated carrot in pan with butter and just enough water to cover. Boil with pan uncovered until tender. Drain off any remaining liquid. Add carrots to potatoes. Add cheese, caraway seed, paprika, salt and black pepper to potato and carrots. Using a fork, mix all ingredients until thoroughly blended. Set aside.

PASTRY

Rub margarine into flour with fingertips. Spoon in water. Using a fork, work mixture into a soft and even dough. Roll out on a floured board. Cut into ten circles of 14 cm (5½ in) diameter.

Divide filling into ten portions. Take one portion and place centrally on one of the circles. Moisten pastry edges with a little water. Bring sides up and over filling to meet at top. Press edges together firmly and place the pasty on a well-greased baking tray (sheet). Repeat with remaining pasties. Brush each with a little beaten egg. Bake at 200°C or 400°F for 20–25 minutes or until lightly browned.

ROSEMARY CARROTS

Serves 4
2 teaspoons butter
½ teaspoon rosemary, finely chopped
125 g (4½ oz) carrots
black pepper

Gently heat butter until melted, but do not allow to sizzle. Add rosemary. Continue heating gently for 2 minutes. Remove from heat. Set aside, but keep warm. Slice carrots into rounds ½ cm (¼ in) thick. Boil or steam until tender. Drain and retain 1 teaspoon of cooking liquid—blend with butter and rosemary. Add to drained carrots and mix well. Season with black pepper.

Note: There are many variations upon the same theme, eg:
1. green (French or runner, string) beans with winter savory butter
2. green peas with mint butter
3. green peas with chive butter.
I often prepare herb butter an hour or two in advance to allow the flavour to fully permeate butter.

CAULIFLOWER WITH MUSHROOM CREAM SAUCE

Serves 6–8
1 large cauliflower
1 quantity Mushroom Cream Sauce
(see sauces, p. 222)

Prepare cauliflower in usual way and cook whole. Just before cauliflower is cooked, prepare mushroom sauce. Drain cauliflower and place on a heated shallow dish. Pour over cream sauce. Serve immediately.

SPICY CAULIFLOWER CHEESE

Serves 5
1 medium cauliflower

SAUCE
250 ml (1 cup, 9 fl oz) Basic Whole-meal (Whole-Wheat) Sauce (see sauces, p. 218)
black pepper
pinch of paprika
½ teaspoon ground cumin
75 g (¾ cup, 2½ oz) cheddar cheese, grated

Prepare wholemeal sauce. Mix in black pepper, paprika, cumin and grated cheese. Stir until cheese has melted. Cover and set aside.

Cut cauliflower into florets. Boil or steam until tender. Drain and place in a warmed ovenproof dish. Cover. Set aside but keep warm. Reheat sauce until almost boiling, pour over cauliflower and serve.

Alternatives 1. Use *plain cheese sauce*, ie omit cumin.
2. Use *sorrel and cheese sauce*: substitute 2 tablespoons shredded sorrel for cumin.
3. Use *sage and cheese sauce*: substitute 1 teaspoon finely chopped sage for cumin.

Note: Cheese sauce goes well with most vegetables and seems a particularly popular way of serving vegetables for young children. Try a mixture of vegetables, eg corn (maize), green (French or runner, string) beans and carrot.

CAULIFLOWER WITH TURMERIC SAUCE

Serves 6
1 large cauliflower
250 ml (1 cup, 9 fl oz) Turmeric
Sauce (see sauces, p. 223)
2 lemon slices

Steam or boil cauliflower until tender. (This may be done whole or with florets separated.) Prepare Turmeric Sauce. Arrange cauliflower in a warmed shallow dish. Pour over Turmeric Sauce. Serve garnished with lemon slices.

STIR-FRIED CHOKO (CHAYOTE, MIRLITON) WITH HERBS

Serves 2–3
200 g (7 oz) chokos
(chayotes, mirlitons), peeled
1 small onion
2 cloves garlic
1 small handful mixed greens (mild
greens eg chickweed or fat-hen)
1 small green capsicum (sweet pepper)
2-3 tablespoons oil
1 tablespoon garlic (Chinese) chives,
chopped
1 tablespoon cream cheese (optional)
black pepper

Thinly slice choko, onion and garlic. Chop greens and thinly slice capsicum. Set aside. Stir-fry choko, onion and garlic in oil. When almost cooked, add capsicum, garlic chives and greens. Continue stir-frying until choko is tender. Remove from heat. Stir in cream cheese (if used). Spoon into a warmed serving dish and sprinkle with black pepper.

EGGPLANT (AUBERGINE) RUFFLE

Serves 2–3
50 g (¼ cup, 2 oz) rice
150 g (5½ oz) eggplant (aubergine)
1 onion
1 tablespoon oil
½ teaspoon French tarragon,
finely chopped
4 tablespoons water
1 clove garlic
1 green capsicum (sweet pepper)
5 tablespoons tomato purée
(see p. 221)
black pepper

Boil rice until cooked, drain and set aside. Slice eggplant into rounds ½–1 cm (¼–½ in) thick. Cut into strips ½–1 cm (¼–½ in) wide. (Do not skin eggplant.) Thinly slice onion. Place eggplant, onion, oil, tarragon, water and finely chopped garlic in a frying pan (skillet). Fry over a medium heat with pan covered, stirring occasionally, for 10 minutes. Thinly slice capsicum. Add to pan. Also add tomato purée. Stir well. Simmer gently for 3 minutes. Add rice. Continue to simmer, stirring continuously, until rice is thoroughly heated. Season with freshly ground black pepper. Serve.

SARDINE-STUFFED EGGPLANT (AUBERGINE)

Serves 2–4

1 large onion

1 clove garlic

1 tablespoon sardine oil

1 teaspoon dill seed

¼ teaspoon paprika

black pepper

1 large eggplant (aubergine)

(about 400 g/14 oz)

1 large tomato

2 teaspoons Dijon/French mustard

1 small can sardines in oil

Thinly slice onion and garlic. Place in a frying pan (skillet) with oil (in which sardines were canned), dill seed, paprika and black pepper. Fry gently until onion is soft. Halve eggplant lengthwise. Scoop out flesh leaving a fairly thin shell. Chop flesh into small pieces. Cut tomato into small pieces. Add tomato, chopped eggplant and mustard to cooked onion. Continue cooking over a medium heat for 4–5 minutes. Drain and discard any remaining oil from sardines. Mash well. Mix thoroughly into onion mixture. Use this mixture to stuff each eggplant shell. Place stuffed shells side by side in a shallow ovenproof dish. Cover and bake at 180°C or 350°F for 45 minutes.

Note: Allow half a shell per person for an hors d'oeuvre, or one if for a main course.

STUFFED EGGPLANT (AUBERGINE)

Serves 2–4

1 onion

1 tablespoon oil

2 teaspoons marjoram, finely chopped

1 clove garlic

½ teaspoon dill seed

1 large eggplant (aubergine)

(about 400 g/14 oz)

6 tablespoons tomato purée

(see p. 221)

200 g (7 oz) steak mince

(ground beef)

black pepper

1½ tablespoons natural

(plain) yoghurt

25 g (¼ cup, 1 oz) cheese

(eg cheddar), grated

Finely chop onion. Place in a large frying pan (skillet) with oil, marjoram, finely chopped garlic and dill seed. Fry gently until onion is soft. Halve eggplant lengthwise. Scoop out flesh, leaving a casing about ½ cm (¼ in) thick. Chop flesh into small pieces. Add chopped eggplant, tomato purée and mince to onion. Cook over a medium heat for 10 minutes, stirring frequently. Remove from heat, season with black pepper and stuff each eggplant half. Place side by side in an ovenproof dish. Cover and bake at 200°C or 400°F for 30 minutes.

Mix yoghurt and grated cheese. Spread over each stuffed half. Replace in oven for a further 3 minutes to allow cheese to melt.

GRILLED CHEESY CHOKOS (CHAYOTES, MIRLITONS) Follow recipe for Grilled Cheesy Vegetables (p. 26), substituting 75 g (2½ oz) peeled, sliced chokos (chayotes, mirlitons) in place of green (French or runner, string) beans.

CHOKOS (CHAYOTES, MIRLITONS) WITH ORIENTAL SAUCE Follow recipe for Oriental Sprouts (p. 46), substituting 500 g (1 lb) peeled, sliced chokos (chayotes, mirlitons) in place of sprouts.

EGGPLANT (AUBERGINE) BAKE

Serves 4–6

1 large onion
2 cloves garlic
2 tablespoons oil
1 large eggplant (aubergine)
(300 g/10½ oz)
80 ml (⅓ cup, 3 fl oz) water
50 g (⅔ cup, 2 oz) rolled oats
(regular oatmeal)
100 g (¼–½ cup, 3½ oz) greens
(eg lettuce, sorrel, borage), chopped
salt and black pepper
100 g (¾ cup, 3½ oz) green (French
or runner, string) beans
6 tomatoes, skinned (peeled)
2 teaspoons basil, finely chopped
2 green capsicum (sweet peppers)
100 g (1 cup, 3½ oz) mature (sharp)
cheese (eg cheddar), grated

Finely chop onion and 1 clove of garlic. Fry gently in oil. Thinly slice eggplant (do not peel). Cut into strips. When onion is tender, add eggplant and water. Cover pan and cook over a medium heat for 5 minutes. Stir occasionally. Remove lid from pan. Add rolled oats. Stir well. Allow to cook for 1 minute. Add chopped greens. Cook for a further minute. Remove from heat. Season with salt and black pepper. Layer mixture on the bottom of an ovenproof dish. Slice green beans very thinly (about ½ cm (¼ in) thick). Layer over eggplant.

Skin (peel) tomatoes and chop into small pieces. (Alternatively, put tomatoes through a blender (liquidiser) for 1 minute and sieve.) Place tomato and basil in a saucepan. Heat gently. Chop remaining garlic clove very finely. Add to tomato. Slice capsicum very thinly. Add to tomato. Allow to simmer for 2 minutes. Stir well. Season with black pepper. Pour over beans in dish. Cover and cook at 200°C or 400°F for 30 minutes. Remove from oven. Sprinkle cheese over top. Return to oven uncovered for several minutes until cheese has melted.

SAVOURY KUMARA FLAT CAKE

Serves 4

250 g (9 oz) kumara
(red sweet potato)
50 g (½ cup, 2 oz) cabbage,
finely chopped
50 g (½ cup, 2 oz) mature
(sharp) cheese, grated
1 egg
black pepper and paprika
3 tablespoons oil
4 tomato slices
4 sprigs parsley
4 lemon wedges

Peel kumara, cut into 2–3 cm (¾–1¼ in) cubes and boil or steam until tender. Drain and set aside. Meanwhile, very finely chop cabbage. Stir-fry until tender. Set aside. Mash kumara or press through a sieve. Stir in cabbage, cheese, egg, black pepper and paprika. Mix thoroughly. Heat oil in a heavy-based frying pan (skillet) (12–15 cm (5–6 in) diameter). When almost smoking, spoon in kumara. Gently spread mixture evenly across pan to make a flat cake. Cook for ½–1 minute at high heat to seal bottom of 'cake'. Turn heat to low. Allow to cook very slowly until well set—the bottom will be well browned and crispy. Be patient, as this takes some time. Leave 'cake' completely alone while cooking or it will fragment. Cut into four portions in pan, gently lift each onto a plate, and garnish with tomato slices and parsley. Serve with lemon wedges.

SPICED KUMARA AND SPINACH

Serves 5–6

400 g (14 oz) kumara
(red sweet potato)
200 g (5 cups, 7 oz) spinach,
finely chopped
4 tablespoons oil
1 teaspoon ground coriander
½ teaspoon ground ginger
½–1 teaspoon ground turmeric
1 teaspoon curry powder (see p. 114)
6 cardamom seeds, crushed (optional)
black pepper
2 tablespoons raisins
2 tablespoons nuts (eg roasted peanuts
(groundnuts)) or sunflower kernels
4 tablespoons thickened (double,
whipping) cream
2 tablespoons natural (plain) yoghurt

Cut kumara into cubes of 1–2 cm (½–1 in). Boil or steam until just tender. Drain and set aside. Meanwhile, discard spinach stalks and very finely chop green leaves. Gently heat oil and all spices in a wok or large heavy-based pan for 1–2 minutes. Add spinach. Stir-fry over a medium heat until spinach is tender. Add kumara and cook, stirring continuously, for 3–4 minutes. Add raisins, nuts and 3 tablespoons cream. Stir for ½ minute. Remove from heat. Spoon into a shallow, warmed serving dish. Quickly mix yoghurt with remaining cream. Dribble decoratively over kumara and spinach mixture. Serve as a side dish to a curry, or as an hors d'oeuvre to a curry meal.

Note: Silverbeet (Swiss chard) or similar can be substituted for spinach.

CHEESY LEEK AND BACON PIE

Serves 6

FILLING
300 g (10½ oz) leeks, sliced
50 g (2 oz) bacon rashers (slices) or
chunk bacon, sliced
1 teaspoon oil
250 ml (1 cup, 9 fl oz) Basic Wholemeal (Whole-Wheat) Sauce
(see sauces, p. 218)
80 g (¾ cup, 3 oz) cheese, grated
paprika and black pepper
2 small tomatoes

PASTRY
75 g (⅓ cup, 3 oz) margarine
150 g (1¼ cups, 5½ oz) wholemeal
(whole-wheat) flour
1 teaspoon thyme, finely chopped
2 tablespoons water

FILLING
Rinse leeks well after slicing. They can be very sandy/gritty. Steam or boil leeks until just tender. Drain and set aside. Lightly fry bacon in oil, drain well and set aside. Prepare sauce. While still hot, add cheese and stir until melted. Season with paprika and black pepper. Add leeks and bacon. Mix well. Set aside.

PASTRY
Rub margarine into flour with fingertips. Stir in thyme. Sprinkle in water. Mix well to make a soft dough. Roll out fairly thinly on a well-floured board. Use pastry to line a greased 20 × 3 cm (8 × 1¼ in) flan dish (quiche pan). Spoon leek and bacon mixture into pastry case (shell). Slice tomatoes and arrange on top of pie. Bake at 180°C or 350°F for 35–40 minutes.

LEEKS AND POTATOES

Serves 4
100 g (3½ oz) leeks, sliced
150 g (5½ oz) potatoes
3 teaspoons oil
½ teaspoon French tarragon,
finely chopped
pinch of paprika
salt and black pepper
1 teaspoon cider vinegar

TO PREPARE LEEKS

Slice leeks, including some of the green part, into rounds ½–1 cm (¼–½ in) thick. Rinse well. Leeks can be very gritty/sandy.

METHOD

Cut potatoes into small pieces (about 1½–2 cm (½–1 in) cubes). Place in a pan, cover with water and boil. When potato is half-cooked, add prepared leeks. Continue boiling until both potatoes and leeks are tender. Drain and set aside to keep warm.

Mix remaining ingredients in a bowl. Spoon over potatoes and leeks. Serve hot or cold.

LEEKS IN PEANUT (GROUNDNUT) SAUCE

Serves 4
500 g (l lb) leeks
250 ml (1 cup, 9 fl oz) Basic Whole-
meal (Whole-Wheat) Sauce
(see sauces, p. 218)
3 teaspoons peanut butter (see p. 346)

Prepare and boil leeks until just tender, making sure you rinse them well before cooking. Meanwhile, prepare wholemeal sauce. Gradually blend in peanut butter. Place leeks in a warmed serving dish and pour over peanut sauce.

Alternative Leeks also taste delicious with a cheese sauce (*see* p. 218). Bake in the oven at 180°C or 350°F for ½ to 1 hour, depending on size of leeks.

MUSHROOM QUICHE

Serves 6
FILLING
1 onion
1 tablespoon oil
150 g (5½ oz) mushrooms
black pepper
pinch of paprika
3 eggs, lightly beaten
100 ml (3½ fl oz) thickened
(double, whipping) cream

PASTRY
75 g (⅓ cup, 3 oz) margarine
150 g (1¼ cups, 5½ oz) wholemeal
(whole-wheat) flour
1 teaspoon thyme, finely chopped
2 tablespoons water

FILLING

Thinly slice onion. Fry gently in oil until tender and only lightly browned. Remove from heat and set aside. Thinly slice mushrooms and add to cooked onion. Season with a little black pepper and paprika. In a separate bowl, beat eggs a little. Stir in cream. Add onion and mushroom mixture. Mix well. Set aside.

PASTRY

Rub margarine into flour with fingertips. Stir in thyme. Sprinkle in water. Mix well to make a soft dough. Roll out fairly thinly on a well-floured board. Use pastry to line a greased 20 × 3 cm (8 × 1¼ in) flan dish (quiche pan). Pour in mushroom mixture. Bake at 180°C or 350°F for 30 minutes.

Opposite: Okra, spiced with curry powder, makes a refreshing change from the more usual vegetable dishes.

MUSHROOMS IN RED WINE

Serves 3–4

1 tablespoon butter

150 g (5½ oz) mushrooms, sliced

3 tablespoons red wine

salt and black pepper

Heat butter in a small frying pan (skillet) until sizzling. Add sliced mushrooms. Cook on a gentle heat for 1 minute, stirring all the time. Pour in red wine. Continue cooking gently for a further 2 minutes. Season and serve immediately.

SAVORY ROLLS

Serves 2

2 bread rolls

75 g (2½ oz) mushrooms

1½ teaspoons summer savory, finely chopped

2 tablespoons butter

50 g (½ cup, 2 oz) cheese, grated

black pepper

Halve bread rolls. Pull out inside bread, leaving a hollow shell approx. 1 cm (½ in) thick. Crumble inside bread and set aside.

Chop mushrooms into tiny pieces. Place in a pan with savory and butter. Fry mushrooms gently until tender, add crumbled bread and stir well. Remove from heat, but keep hot. Toast bread shells under a medium grill (broiler) until crisp and lightly browned. Fill each with one-quarter of mushroom mixture. Top with grated cheese. Place under a medium grill for 2–3 minutes to warm thoroughly and melt cheese. Sprinkle with freshly ground black pepper. Serve.

Note: Half to one teaspoon marjoram or basil can be substituted for summer savory.

INDIAN OKRA
(LADY'S FINGERS, GUMBO) 1

Serves 4

250 g (9 oz) okra

(lady's fingers, gumbo)

a little oil

½ tablespoon margarine or butter

½ teaspoon curry powder (see p. 114)

1 tablespoon wholemeal

(whole-wheat) flour

125 ml (½ cup, 4½ fl oz) milk

1 teaspoon sweet chutney

Slice okra into rounds ½ cm (¼ in) thick. Stir-fry in a little hot oil. Place in a warmed bowl. Set aside, but keep hot.

SAUCE
Heat margarine and stir in curry powder. When sizzling, add flour, stirring well. Remove from heat. Gradually add warmed milk, blending carefully to avoid lumps. Return to heat. Cook, stirring continuously, until sauce thickens. Remove from heat, add chutney, stir well and pour over cooked okra. Serve immediately.

INDIAN OKRA
(LADY'S FINGERS, GUMBO) 2

Serves 4
200 g (7 oz) okra
(lady's fingers, gumbo)
2 teaspoons oil
1 teaspoon curry powder (see p. 114)

Slice okra into rounds ½ cm (¼ in) thick. Set aside. Heat oil and curry powder in a heavy-based frying pan (skillet). When quite hot, add okra. Cook over a medium heat for 2–3 minutes until okra are tender.

STUFFED MARROW
(SUMMER OR YELLOW SQUASH)

Serves 4
1 medium marrow (summer or
yellow squash)
(800 g–1 kg/1¾–2¼ lb)
salt and black pepper
1 large onion
1½ tablespoons oil
3 cloves garlic
½ teaspoon each of rosemary, winter
savory (optional), sage, thyme,
oregano, paprika
50 g (¼ cup, 1½ oz) greens (eg borage,
lettuce, sorrel, comfrey, spinach),
chopped
400 g (14 oz) steak mince
(ground beef)
150 ml (⅔ cup, 5½ fl oz) tomato
purée (see p. 221)
125 ml (½ cup, 4½ fl oz) water

Peel marrow and trim ends. Halve, scoop out and discard seeds (leaving a 1–2 cm (½–1 in) thickness of marrow flesh). Season both halves, inside and out, with salt and black pepper. Thinly slice onion. Fry until browned and soft in 1 tablespoon of oil. Add 2 finely chopped garlic cloves, herbs, paprika, greens and a little salt and black pepper. Stir in meat. Cook over a medium heat for 2 minutes, stirring continuously. Add tomato purée, stir well and simmer for 10 minutes, stirring occasionally. Remove from heat and cool slightly. Stuff each half of the marrow with meat mixture. Fit the two marrow halves together again. Tie in three or four places with cotton thread/string. Place in an ovenproof dish with approximately the same dimensions as the marrow (I often cut the stuffed marrow into two pieces to fit my round casserole dish). Pour in water and remaining ½ tablespoon of oil. Add the third garlic clove, finely chopped. Cover and cook at 180°C or 350°F for 50–60 minutes. Baste occasionally during cooking.

PEAS WITH FRENCH SORREL

Serves 3
250 g (9 oz) green peas, unshelled
2 mint leaves
3 French sorrel leaves, shredded
2 tablespoons milk
1 egg yolk
salt and black pepper

Shell peas. Place in a pan with mint leaves. Cover with water and boil until peas are just tender. Drain and remove. Discard mint leaves. Replace peas in pan. Shred sorrel leaves. Add sorrel, milk and egg yolk to pan. Heat gently, stirring continuously, until mixture thickens. Season with salt and black pepper.

HERBED STUFFED ONIONS

Serves 4

4 medium onions

1 tablespoon borage, finely chopped

½–1 teaspoon sage or rosemary,
finely chopped

2 tablespoons wholemeal
(whole-wheat) breadcrumbs

black pepper and paprika

4 tablespoons white wine

1 tablespoon water

2 tablespoons oil

Remove tough, brown outer leaves of onion, and stalk and root area. Remove a central core of 1–1½ cm (½ in) diameter from each onion. Finely chop two of the cores and place in a bowl. Discard the other two cores. Add borage, sage (or rosemary) and breadcrumbs. Season with black pepper and paprika. Mix well and moisten with 2 tablespoons of white wine. Stuff each onion and place in an ovenproof dish. Pour over remaining 2 tablespoons of white wine, plus the water and oil. Cover and bake at 180°C or 350°F for 1 hour.

PARSNIP AND CARROT PURÉE

parsnips

carrots

butter

salt and black pepper

paprika

herbs (eg rosemary, winter savory,
sage), finely chopped

cheese, grated (optional)

Take equal quantities of parsnips and carrots, cut into pieces and boil or steam until very tender. Mash or press through a sieve. Flavour by stirring in plenty of butter. Season with salt, black pepper, paprika and finely chopped herbs. Grated cheese may be stirred in for added flavour.

PARSNIP NEST

Serves 5

300 g (10½ oz) parsnips

Creamy French Sorrel (see p. 46)

4 tablespoons cream cheese

salt and black pepper

paprika

¼ teaspoon ground caraway seed

Peel and, if necessary, core parsnips. Cut into pieces and boil or steam until very tender. Prepare sorrel according to recipe. Set aside but keep hot. Drain parsnips. Mash well or press through a sieve. Stir in cream cheese. Season with a little salt, black pepper, paprika and caraway seed. Make a ring or 'nest' of parsnip on a large plate. Spoon Creamy French Sorrel into nest. Serve.

Note: Spinach or silverbeet (Swiss chard) prepared in the same way can be substituted for sorrel.

Opposite: *Capsicum or sweet peppers are a rich source of vitamin C. In Potato-Stuffed Capsicum (Sweet Peppers), their vibrant primary colours make this simple meal a visual treat.*

POTATO-STUFFED CAPSICUM (SWEET PEPPERS)

Serves 4

300 g (10½ oz) potatoes

6 tablespoons tomato purée
(see p. 221)

50 g (½ cup, 2 oz) mature (sharp)
cheddar cheese, grated

1½ tablespoons chives, finely chopped

pinch of cayenne (optional)

pinch of paprika

black pepper

3 eggs, beaten

butter

4 medium capsicum (sweet peppers)

Peel potatoes, cut into pieces and boil or steam until soft. Drain and mash a little. Stir in tomato purée, cheddar cheese and finely chopped chives. Season with cayenne (if used), paprika and black pepper. Set aside.

Beat eggs. Pour into a well-buttered hot frying pan (skillet). Cook gently. Allow eggs to set, making a kind of flat omelette. Remove from heat, chop into small pieces and add to potato mixture. Slice off stalk area (tops) and remove and discard seeds from capsicum. Fill each with potato and egg mixture. Place stuffed capsicum side by side in a deep ovenproof dish. Cover and bake at 200°C or 400°F for 20 minutes.

VEGETARIAN STUFFED CAPSICUM (SWEET PEPPERS)

Serves 4

4 medium green capsicum
(sweet peppers)
50 g (2 oz) green (French or runner,
string) beans
50 g (2 oz) green peas, shelled
75 g (¾ cup, 2½ oz) mature (sharp)
cheddar cheese, grated
pinch of paprika
1 teaspoon sage, finely chopped
3 eggs

Wash capsicum, remove stalk area, remove and discard seeds. Place in a deep ovenproof dish. Slice beans into rounds approx. ½ cm (¼ in) thick. Place in a pan with peas. Add enough water to cover both. Bring to boil and cook until tender, drain and place in a bowl. Grate cheese into same bowl. Add paprika and sage. Stir well. Finally, break eggs into bowl. Mix ingredients together thoroughly. Spoon into capsicum. Cover dish. Bake at 190°C or 375°F for 30 minutes.

Baked Potatoes

These are basically dealt with in the general methods (*see* pp. 10–11), but here are a few variations:
- Make small incision in prepared potato, slip in a leaf or two of rosemary and bake as usual.
- Serve baked potatoes:
  - with natural (plain) yoghurt flavoured with dill—¼ teaspoon dill seed to 125 ml (½ cup, 4½ fl oz) yoghurt
  - with herb butter
  - with sour cream sprinkled with toasted sesame seed.

BAKED POTATO LAYERS

Serves 6–8

350 g (12½ oz) potatoes
200 g (7 oz) young marrow
(summer or yellow squash) or
zucchini (courgettes)
1 onion
1 rasher (slice) bacon
½ tablespoon oil
50 g (¼ cup, 1½ oz) greens (eg borage,
comfrey, lettuce, spinach), chopped
150 g (5½ oz) tomatoes, skinned
(peeled)
6 tablespoons tomato purée
(see p. 221)
3 teaspoons marjoram, finely chopped
black pepper

Peel potatoes if necessary. Cut into slices ½–1 cm (¼–½ in) thick. Place half at the bottom of an ovenproof dish. Set aside remainder.

Slice marrow or zucchini ½–1 cm (¼–½ in) thick. Layer half of them over potatoes in dish. Set aside remainder. Thinly slice onion and cut bacon into small pieces. Fry both in oil. Remove from heat. Stir in chopped greens. Place mixture over marrow layer in dish. Place second half of marrow or zucchini over bacon, onion and greens. Finish with a layer of remaining potato.

Chop tomatoes into small pieces and place in a saucepan. Add tomato purée and finely chopped marjoram. Season with black pepper, heat and simmer gently for 3–4 minutes. Pour over vegetable layers. Cover dish and bake at 180°C or 350°F for 50 minutes.

Note: A young marrow can weigh up to 400 g (14 oz). At this size, skin and seeds are soft and do not have to be removed.

OVEN-COOKED POTATOES

Serves 4–6

500 g (1 lb) potatoes
1 small onion
1 teaspoon sage, finely chopped
black pepper
150 ml (²/₃ cup, 5½ fl oz) milk

Scrub potatoes well. Peel if necessary. Slice into rounds approx. ½ cm (¼ in) thick. Peel onion and cut into thin rounds. Make several layers of potato in a shallow ovenproof dish. Sprinkle sage over potato. Season with pepper. Place sliced onion on top of potato. Pour over milk. Cover with a lid or aluminium foil. Bake in oven for 45 minutes at 180°C or 350°F.

SAVORY POTATO AND MARROW (SUMMER OR YELLOW SQUASH)

Serves 3–4

150 g (5½ oz) potatoes
150 g (5½ oz) marrow (summer or yellow squash)
black pepper
½ teaspoon summer savory
1 teaspoon sesame seed, toasted
3 tablespoons natural (plain) yoghurt

Peel potato if necessary. Cut into small pieces (approx. 1½–2 cm (½–1 in) cubes). Peel marrow if necessary. Cut into similar-sized pieces. Boil potato in water. When almost cooked, add marrow. Boil until both are tender (be sure not to overcook marrow, which leaves it soggy and tasteless). Drain vegetables. Place in a serving bowl. Season with black pepper.

Mix together summer savory, sesame seed and yoghurt. Spoon or pour over potatoes and marrow. Serve hot or cold.

Note: Whenever possible, prepare yoghurt sauce in advance to allow flavour of summer savory to be absorbed into yoghurt.

STUFFED PUMPKIN (WINTER SQUASH)

Serves 6–8

1 pumpkin (winter squash)
(about 1¼ kg/2¾ lb)
50 g (¹/₃ cup, 2 oz) brown rice
1 onion
1 tablespoon oil
½ teaspoon ground nutmeg
2 teaspoons ground coriander
½ teaspoon ground cinnamon
100 g (¾ cup, 3½ oz) green (French or runner, string) beans
100 g (½ cup, 3½ oz) sultanas (golden raisins) or raisins
salt and black pepper

Wash outside of pumpkin well. Cut a 'lid' or circular piece from top. This will expose seeds inside. Scoop out and discard all seeds.* This leaves pumpkin with a thick wall, but a large cavern in the middle. Boil rice until tender. Drain and set aside.

FILLING

Thinly slice onion. Place in a frying pan (skillet) with oil, nutmeg, coriander and cinnamon. Fry gently until onion is soft. Cut beans transversely into very thin rounds (½ cm/¼ in thick). Add rice, beans and sultanas to onion. Mix well. Season with salt and black pepper. Use to stuff pumpkin. Replace lid. Place on a baking tray (sheet). Bake at 180°C or 350°F for 1 hour.

Note: * Remove all flesh from pumpkin seeds and spread seeds one layer thick over a baking tray (sheet). Place in oven alongside stuffed pumpkin. Bake until seeds are well browned (about ½ hour). Remove and cool. Sprinkle with a little salt and eat. Good as a between-meal nibble for children.

SAVOURY PUMPKIN (WINTER SQUASH)

Serves 4

50 g (¼ cup, 2 oz) white rice or
50 g (⅓ cup, 2 oz) brown rice
250 g (9 oz) pumpkin (winter squash)
1 onion
½ teaspoon ground cumin
½ teaspoon paprika
1 teaspoon ground coriander
½ tablespoon oil
3 tablespoons French sorrel leaves,
finely chopped
salt and black pepper

Boil rice until cooked. Drain and set aside. Slice pumpkin into pieces ½–1 cm (¼–½ in) thick. Boil or steam until tender. Thinly slice onion. Place in a small frying pan (skillet) with cumin, paprika, coriander and oil. Fry gently until onion is soft. Add sorrel and rice. Heat very gently for 2–3 minutes until rice is warm and sorrel cooked. Season with salt and black pepper. Set aside.

Layer pumpkin in a shallow ovenproof dish. Layer rice mixture over top. Place under a hot grill (broiler) for several minutes, until pumpkin and rice are thoroughly heated.

Note: This dish is not strong in flavour despite use of spices. I prefer to use it as a side dish to accompany a more flavourful meat or vegetable dish.

PEPPERY RICE

Serves 4

150 g (¾ cup, 5½ oz) white rice
1 medium green capsicum
(sweet pepper)
1 teaspoon oil
pinch of paprika
2½ tablespoons tomato purée
(see p. 00)
salt and black pepper

Boil rice until cooked. Drain. Meanwhile, chop capsicum into tiny pieces. Stir-fry in oil until tender. Remove from heat. Add paprika and tomato purée. Stir into cooked rice. Season with salt and black pepper. Serve hot or cold.

Note: White rice is preferable to brown for this recipe.

SILVERBEET (SWISS CHARD), CHICKEN AND NOODLES

Serves 4

1 kg (2 lb) chicken pieces (portions)
Cream Sauce (see p. 220)
1 teaspoon tarragon, finely chopped
paprika and black pepper
100 g (3½ oz) flat noodles
150–200 g (4–5 cups, 5½–7 oz) sil-
verbeet (Swiss chard), shredded
2 teaspoons butter

Boil, steam or bake chicken pieces. When cool, remove and discard bone and skin. You should be left with around 400 g (14 oz) of meat. Cut into small- to medium-sized pieces. Set aside. Prepare Cream Sauce according to recipe. Season with tarragon, a little paprika and black pepper. Set aside but keep warm. Plunge noodles into boiling water. Cook until al dente. Shred silverbeet and 'quick boil (*see* p. 16). As soon as beet is tender and liquid has evaporated, stir in butter and chicken. Cook gently, stirring continuously, until reheated. Pour in Cream Sauce. Allow to reheat gently for 1–2 minutes. Add noodles, mix well and serve.

STUFFED SILVERBEET
(SWISS CHARD) LEAVES

Serves 4

4 large silverbeet (Swiss chard) leaves

1 small onion

250 g (9 oz) sausagemeat
(fresh sausage)

1 teaspoon winter savory,
finely chopped

2 cloves garlic, finely chopped

paprika and black pepper

Fresh Tomato Sauce (see p. 220)

pinch of cayenne or chilli powder
(optional)

Cut off and discard stalks from silverbeet. Plunge leaves one at a time for 1 minute each in boiling water to soften. Place on a plate to cool. Chop onion very finely. Place in a bowl. Add sausagemeat, savory, garlic, paprika and plenty of black pepper. Mix thoroughly. Divide into four equal portions. Shape one portion into a ball, place in centre of one silverbeet leaf and flatten gently so it covers the middle third of leaf. Fold leaf tip over top of meat and then leaf base over top of that. You should now have a flat 'envelope'. Repeat with remaining meat and leaves. Place envelopes in a shallow ovenproof dish, side by side or so that they overlap. Cover dish tightly with aluminium foil. Bake at 350°F or 180°C for 1 hour.

Prepare tomato sauce. Set aside but keep hot (cayenne or chilli powder, if used, is added with garlic). Remove dish from oven. Pour tomato sauce over top. Serve.

Note: 1. One 'envelope' per person is a small- to medium-sized helping. 2. It is best to use finely minced (ground) sausagemeat.

TURMERIC RICE *See* recipe for Fruity Chicken Curry (p. 142).

CREAMY FRENCH SORREL

Serves 4–5

250 g (9 oz) French sorrel, shredded

2 tablespoons thickened
(double, whipping) cream

salt and black pepper

Shred sorrel, discarding tough stalks. Place in a large saucepan. Add just enough water to cover bottom of pan. Heat and boil rapidly for 2 minutes, stirring a little to ensure even cooking. The sorrel will soften and turn dull green. Remove from heat and drain. Add cream, replace on heat and cook gently for 1 minute, stirring continuously. Season and serve immediately.

ORIENTAL SPROUTS

Serves 6

500 g (1 lb) Brussels sprouts

250 ml (1 cup, 9 fl oz) Basic Wholemeal (Whole-Wheat) Sauce
(see sauces, p. 218)

½ teaspoon mild curry powder
(see p. 114)

1 teaspoon mild sweet chutney
(banana or mango is best)

2 tablespoons cottage cheese, sieved
(strained)

Prepare sauce in usual way. Add curry powder, chutney and cottage cheese to sauce. Blend thoroughly. Cover pan and set aside.

Boil or steam Brussels sprouts until tender. Drain and place in a warmed serving dish. Cover and keep warm. Reheat sauce until almost boiling, pour over sprouts and serve.

TOMATO AND BASIL PIE

Serves 6

PASTRY

75 g (⅓ cup, 3 oz) margarine

150 g (1¼ cups, 5½ oz) wholemeal
(whole-wheat) flour

2 tablespoons water

FILLING

2 medium onions

3 tablespoons oil

600 g (1¼ lb) tomatoes, skinned
(peeled)

½–1 tablespoon basil, finely chopped

black pepper

PASTRY

Rub margarine into flour with fingertips. Sprinkle over water. Using a fork, work mixture into a soft dough. Roll out on a well-floured board. Use pastry to line a greased shallow pie dish (plate) 20 cm (8 in) in diameter.

FILLING

Thinly slice onions. Fry gently in oil until tender, but not browned. Chop tomatoes into small pieces. Add tomatoes and basil to onion. Season with plenty of black pepper. Bring to boil, reduce heat and boil gently or simmer (uncovered) for 15 minutes, stirring frequently. Spoon filling into pastry case (shell). Bake at 200°C or 400°F for 30 minutes.

TOMATO HORS D'OEUVRE

Serves 4

500 g (1 lb) tomatoes, skinned
(peeled)
1 green capsicum (sweet pepper)
1 medium onion
½ teaspoon dill seed
1 clove garlic
2 teaspoons marjoram, finely chopped
1 tablespoon oil
black pepper

Roughly chop tomatoes and set aside. Slice capsicum very thinly and set aside.

Thinly slice onion. Place in a heavy-based frying pan (skillet). Add dill seed, finely chopped garlic, marjoram and oil. Cook over a medium heat until onion is soft, stirring occasionally. Add tomatoes and capsicum. Season with black pepper. Cook over a medium heat for 5 minutes, stirring frequently. Serve with hot, crusty fresh bread.

Alternatives One of the following (about ¼ cup) may be added at the same time as tomato and capsicum:
- flaked cooked fish, eg sardines, cod
- cooked chopped meat or poultry, eg bacon, lamb, chicken
- cooked chopped vegetables, eg green (French or runner, string) beans, cauliflower.

Note: This can also be used as a simple and easily prepared lunch dish.

STUFFED TOMATOES 1

Serves 4

2 tablespoons white rice
1 rasher (slice) bacon
1 small onion
1 teaspoon oil
1 teaspoon basil, finely chopped
pinch of paprika
2 large firm tomatoes
(about 275 g/10 oz)
25 g (1 oz) mushrooms
salt and black pepper
Parmesan cheese, grated

Boil rice until tender, drain and set aside.

Cut bacon into small pieces. Finely chop onion. Place both in a pan and add oil, basil and paprika. Cook gently until onion is soft. Meanwhile, cut tomatoes in half. Scoop out middle from each half. Chop flesh into small pieces. Chop mushrooms into small pieces. Add chopped tomato, mushroom and rice to cooked onion. Cook gently for 1 minute. Season with salt and black pepper. Use to fill each tomato half. Place stuffed tomatoes in a shallow ovenproof dish under a medium grill (broiler) for 5–7 minutes. Cooking time will depend on how firm you prefer your tomato 'shells'. Sprinkle with a little Parmesan cheese. Serve.

Note: 1. It is best to use young mushrooms or button mushrooms to prevent discoloration in the mixture.
2. Alternative method: Bake uncovered at 180°C or 350°F for 12–14 minutes.
3. Vegetarians—omit bacon.

STUFFED TOMATOES 2

Serves 3 or 6
Dark Mince (Ground Beef) (see p. 99)
3 tomatoes (300 g/10½ oz)
parsley to garnish

Prepare Dark Mince according to recipe. Set aside.

Cut tomatoes in halves. Scoop out middle from each. Chop flesh into small pieces and stir into mince (ground beef). Fill each tomato half with mince. Place stuffed tomatoes in a shallow ovenproof dish. Place under a medium grill (broiler) for 5 minutes. Garnish each with a tiny piece of parsley before serving.

Note: 1. Stuffed tomatoes can be used as an hors d'oeuvre or a lunch dish. For the former, offer one half per person, and for the latter offer two halves per person.

2. Alternative method: Bake at 180°C or 350°F, uncovered, for 12–14 minutes.

VEGETARIAN MOUSSAKA

Serves 5–6
200 g (7 oz) potato
250 g (9 oz) eggplant (aubergine)
2 tablespoons oil
250 g (9 oz) zucchini (courgette)
75 g (⅔ cup, 2½ oz) French sorrel,
borage, comfrey or lettuce, chopped
1 large onion
2 cloves garlic
2 green capsicum (sweet peppers)
50 g (2 oz) mushrooms
2 teaspoons oregano, finely chopped
2 teaspoons marjoram, finely chopped
125 ml (½ cup, 4½ fl oz) tomato
purée (see p. 221)
black pepper and salt
250 ml (1 cup, 9 fl oz) Basic Whole-
meal (Whole-Wheat) Sauce
(see sauces, p. 218)
2 egg yolks, beaten

Cut potato into thick slices and boil. When cooked, drain and set aside. Slice eggplant into rounds ½ cm (¼ in) thick. Set aside one half of eggplant. Layer second half at bottom of an ovenproof dish. Sprinkle over ½ tablespoon oil. Slice zucchini into rounds ½ cm (¼ in) thick. Set aside one half of zucchini. Layer second half over eggplant in dish. Cover with chopped sorrel. Evenly space potato on top of sorrel. Cover with reserved zucchini slices.

Now prepare tomato sauce. Thinly slice onion and garlic. Fry both gently in 1 tablespoon oil until soft. Thinly slice capsicum and mushrooms. Add capsicum, mushrooms, oregano, marjoram and tomato purée to cooked onion. Stir well. Cook gently for 2 minutes. Season with black pepper. Spoon sauce over zucchini in dish. Make a final layer using reserved eggplant. Sprinkle with ½ tablespoon oil. Season with salt and black pepper. Cover dish. Bake at 180°C or 350°F for 40 minutes.

While cooking, prepare moussaka sauce. Prepare wholemeal sauce in usual way. As soon as sauce thickens, stir in 2 egg yolks. Cook very gently for 2 minutes. Remove from heat and set aside. When moussaka has cooked for full 40 minutes, remove from oven. Spread moussaka sauce over eggplant. Cover dish and return to oven to cook a further 15 minutes.

Opposite: A mouthwatering variation of the Greek dish of the same name, Vegetarian Moussaka includes the usual eggplant (aubergine) and cheese sauce, but without the meat.

TASTY TURNIP DISH

Serves 4

50 g (¼ cup, 2 oz) rice
250 g (9 oz) young turnips
1½ tablespoons butter
1 teaspoon winter savory,
finely chopped
½–1 cup cooked beans*
2 tablespoons nuts (eg roasted peanuts
(groundnuts)) or sunflower kernels
150 g (5½ oz) cooked sausage
Fresh Tomato Sauce (see p. 220)
50 g (½ cup, 2 oz) cheese, grated or
2 tablespoons Parmesan cheese

Boil rice until tender, drain and set aside. Peel turnips, cut into 1–2 cm (½–1 in) cubes and boil until tender. Drain. Gently heat butter in a large pan, add turnip and winter savory. Cook gently for several minutes. Remove from heat, add beans, rice and nuts. Mix thoroughly. Thinly slice sausage, add to pan and mix well. Spoon into a shallow baking dish and set aside. Prepare tomato sauce according to recipe. Pour over turnip mixture. Place under a medium grill (broiler) or in a hot oven until thoroughly heated and bubbling. Remove and sprinkle over cheese. Serve.

Note: * When cooked, 50 g (2 oz) dried beans, eg haricot (navy or pea), red kidney or sugar beans, will give the required amount.

TURNIP BED

Serves 4

500 g (1 lb) turnips
8 sausages*
Cream Sauce (see p. 220)
2 teaspoons parsley, finely chopped
2 sprigs parsley

Peel turnips, cut into thick (2 cm/1 in) slices and boil or steam until tender. Meanwhile, grill (broil) sausages until well cooked. Prepare Cream Sauce according to recipe, adding parsley with flour. Set aside but keep hot. When sausages are cooked, lay side by side in a warmed serving dish, drain turnips and pile over sausages. Pour over Cream Sauce. Garnish with parsley sprigs.

Note: * Sausages are a good choice to accompany turnips because of their dominant flavour. You can, however, substitute a meat such as boiled silverside or brisket, or boiled pressed tongue. About 650 g (1½ lb) is enough for four people.

VEGETABLE VARIETY

Serves 4

1 small eggplant (aubergine)
(100-150 g/3½-5½ oz)
2 tablespoons oil
2 tablespoons water
3 tablespoons red wine
1 zucchini (courgette) (50 g/2 oz)
200 g (7 oz) pumpkin (winter squash)
75 g (½ cup, 2½ oz) brown rice
50 g (2 oz) mushrooms
4 teaspoons marjoram, finely chopped
¼ teaspoon paprika
3 eggs, beaten
1 onion
2 cloves garlic
1 large green capsicum (sweet pepper)
1 teaspoon dill seed
4 tablespoons natural (plain) yoghurt
black pepper

Slice eggplant into rounds 1 cm (½ in) thick. Place in a heavy-based frying pan (skillet). Add 1 tablespoon oil, 2 tablespoons water and 1 tablespoon red wine. Cover pan. Cook over a medium heat until eggplant is soft, stirring occasionally. Remove eggplant from pan when cooked. Layer at bottom of an ovenproof dish. Slice zucchini thinly and place over eggplant. Peel pumpkin if necessary. Cut into slices 1 cm (½ in) thick. Boil until tender, drain and make a layer over zucchini.

Boil rice until cooked. Drain and place in a bowl. Thinly slice mushrooms. Place in pan in which eggplant was cooked. (It should not have been washed in the interim.) Add 2 tablespoons red wine to mushrooms. Cook gently until mushrooms are just tender. Add to rice. Also add 2 teaspoons marjoram, mix well and season with paprika. Layer rice over pumpkin.

Break eggs into a separate bowl, beat well and pour over rice layer. Thinly slice onion and garlic. Place in same (still unwashed) frying pan as was used for mushrooms. Pour in 1 tablespoon oil and fry gently for 2 minutes. Thinly slice capsicum and add to onion. Add 2 teaspoons marjoram and dill seed. Cook for 3 minutes, stirring well. Remove from heat and stir in yoghurt. Season with black pepper. Pour over eggs (which by this time will have soaked through rice layer a little). Cover dish. Bake at 190°C or 375°F for 30 minutes. Serve as a main dish at a vegetarian meal or as an hors d'oeuvre. Serve hot or cold.

Note: If cooked in a rectangular dish or tin (pan) and served cold, this vegetable dish can be cut into thick slices rather like a vegetable loaf.

OATMEAL-STUFFED
ZUCCHINI (COURGETTES)

Serves 4

4 medium zucchini (courgettes)

1 small onion

2 teaspoons marjoram, finely chopped

1 tablespoon oil

2 tablespoons water

4 tablespoons dry white wine

4 tablespoons coarse oatmeal or rolled oats (regular oatmeal)

Halve zucchini lengthwise. Scoop out flesh leaving behind a thin shell. Chop flesh into very tiny pieces. Set aside. Finely chop onion. Add to a small frying pan (skillet) with marjoram and oil. Fry gently until onion is soft. Add zucchini flesh. Continue to fry gently until tender, stirring frequently. Pour in water and white wine. Add oatmeal or rolled oats. Cook for 2–3 minutes, stirring continuously. Remove from heat. Use to stuff each zucchini shell. Place stuffed zucchini side by side in a shallow dish. Cover and cook at 180°C or 350°F for 30 minutes.

STEWED ZUCCHINI (COURGETTES)

Serves 4

1 small onion

2 tablespoons oil

1 clove garlic

400 g (14 oz) zucchini (courgettes)

125 ml (½ cup, 4½ fl oz) water

3 tablespoons dry white wine

black pepper

Finely slice onion. Fry gently in oil with finely chopped garlic until soft. Slice zucchini into fairly thin rounds (½ cm/¼ in thick). Add zucchini, water and wine to onion. Season with a little black pepper. Bring to boil. Simmer with pan uncovered until zucchini are tender. Turn onto a warmed serving dish. Serve.

APIA FRUIT
ZUCCHINI (COURGETTES)

Serves 4–6

6 zucchini (courgettes) (about 500 g/1 lb)

1 medium onion

1 tablespoon oil

½-1 teaspoon basil, finely chopped

¼ teaspoon paprika

black pepper

50 g (⅔ cup, 2 oz) rolled oats (regular oatmeal)

4 tablespoons water

200 g (7 oz) fruit (pawpaw (papaya), peach or apricot)

100 g (1 cup, 3½ oz) cheddar cheese, grated

Halve zucchini lengthwise. Scoop out flesh leaving a thin shell. Chop flesh into very tiny pieces and set aside. Thinly slice onion. Fry gently in oil until soft. Add basil and paprika. Season with black pepper. Add rolled oats, zucchini flesh and water. Stir ingredients well. Cook on a medium heat for a few minutes until zucchini are soft. Meanwhile, peel, pit or seed fruit and chop into very small pieces. Add to cooked zucchini. Also add three-quarters of grated cheese. Stir well. Cook very gently for 1 minute. Remove from heat.

Place zucchini shells side by side in a shallow ovenproof dish or on a baking tray (sheet). Fill each with fruity mixture. Sprinkle remaining grated cheese over top. Place under a medium grill (broiler) for 5 minutes until sizzling and a little browned. The zucchini shells should still be quite crisp.

ZUCCHINI (COURGETTE) QUICHE

Serves 5–6
PASTRY
75 g (⅓ cup, 3 oz) margarine
*150 g (1¼ cups, 5½ oz) wholemeal
(whole-wheat) flour*
2 tablespoons water

FILLING
250 g (9 oz) zucchini (courgettes)
3 large eggs, lightly beaten
60 ml (¼ cup, 2 fl oz) milk
½ teaspoon summer savory
paprika and black pepper

PASTRY
Rub margarine into flour with fingertips. Sprinkle in water.
Mix to form a soft dough. Roll out thinly. Use pastry to line
a greased 18 × 3 cm (7 × 1¾ in) pie dish (plate).

FILLING
Thinly slice zucchini and set aside. In a bowl, beat eggs a little.
Stir in milk. Season with savory, paprika and black pepper. Mix
thoroughly. Stir in zucchini and pour mixture into pastry case
(shell). Bake at 180°C or 350°F for 30 minutes.

ZUCCHINI (COURGETTE) PIE

Serves 6
PASTRY
75 g (⅓ cup, 3 oz) margarine
*150 g (1¼ cups, 5½ oz) wholemeal
(whole-wheat) flour*
1 teaspoon thyme, finely chopped
2 tablespoons water

FILLING
450 ml (1¾ cups, 15 fl oz) milk
1 tablespoon margarine
*2 tablespoons wholemeal
(whole-wheat) flour*
1 egg
300 g (10½ oz) zucchini (courgettes)

PASTRY
Rub margarine into flour with fingertips. Stir in thyme. Sprinkle
in water. Mix into a soft dough and roll out on a well-floured
board. Line a greased 20 × 3 cm (8 × 1¼ in) pie dish (plate)
with the pastry.

FILLING
Pour milk into a saucepan. Bring to boil. Stir well to prevent
boiling over. Reduce heat. Simmer milk until reduced to only
270 ml (1 cup, 9 fl oz). Remove from heat and set aside. In
a separate pan, heat margarine until sizzling. Stir in flour. Remove
from heat and gradually blend in milk, avoiding lumps. Reheat
gently until sauce thickens. Beat in egg and set aside. Thinly
slice zucchini. Arrange several layers deep in pastry case (shell).
Pour over sauce. Bake at 180°C or 350°F for 40 minutes.

Opposite: *Zucchini (Courgettes) with Rosemary Sauce is a delicious and filling meal for both vegetarians and non-vegetarians alike.*

ZUCCHINI (COURGETTES) WITH ROSEMARY SAUCE

Serves 4

200 g (7 oz) zucchini (courgettes)
125 ml (½ cup, 4½ fl oz) Basic
Wholemeal (Whole-Wheat) Sauce
(see sauces, p. 218)
¼ teaspoon rosemary, finely chopped
black pepper
2 tomatoes
50 g (2 oz) mushrooms
½ tablespoon oil
1 tablespoon Parmesan cheese, grated

Top and tail zucchini, halve lengthwise and make layers of them in an ovenproof dish. Prepare wholemeal sauce and stir in rosemary. Season with black pepper. Pour sauce over zucchini, cover dish and bake at 180°C or 350°F for 20 minutes. Meanwhile, slice tomatoes and set aside. Slice mushrooms and fry gently in oil. Set aside.

When zucchini are cooked, remove dish from oven. Layer mushrooms over zucchini then make a layer of sliced tomato. Sprinkle over Parmesan cheese. Place under a hot grill (broiler) for 2–3 minutes.

TARRAGON LUNCH

Serves 2
3 zucchini (courgettes)
(about 200 g/7 oz)
1 tablespoon oil
2 large tomatoes
1 small green capsicum (sweet pepper)
½ teaspoon French tarragon,
finely chopped
1 clove garlic
black pepper
2 eggs
50 g (½ cup, 2 oz) cheddar cheese,
grated

Slice zucchini into thin rounds. Gently fry in oil, stirring frequently. When tender, place zucchini in bottom of an oven-proof dish, leaving behind in the pan any oil and vegetable juices.

Chop tomatoes into small pieces and thinly slice capsicum. Add tomato, tarragon, capsicum and finely chopped garlic to pan containing juices remaining from zucchini. Simmer gently for 2–3 minutes. Season with black pepper. Spoon mixture over zucchini. Break 2 eggs onto tomato mixture. Sprinkle with grated cheese, cover dish and cook at 200°C or 400°F for 12–15 minutes. The white of the eggs should be set and the yolk partly set.

STUFFED ZUCCHINI (COURGETTES)

Serves 3–6
6 medium zucchini (courgettes)
(about 500 g/1 lb)
1 small onion
1 tablespoon sardine oil (reserved
from can of sardines)
¼ teaspoon French tarragon,
finely chopped
1 teaspoon salad burnet,
finely chopped
salt and black pepper
1 small can sardines in oil

Halve zucchini lengthwise. Scoop out flesh leaving a thin shell. Chop flesh into tiny pieces and set aside. Thinly slice onion. Place in a small frying pan (skillet) with oil, tarragon and salad burnet. Season with a little salt and black pepper. Cook gently until onion is soft. Add zucchini flesh. Continue cooking gently, stirring frequently, for 2 minutes. Drain any remaining oil from sardines, mash them a little and add to onion mixture. Cook for a further 2 minutes, remove from heat and use mixture to fill each zucchini half.

Place stuffed zucchini side by side in a shallow ovenproof dish. Place under a medium–hot grill (broiler) for 5 minutes. The zucchini should be piping hot, with shells quite crisp.

Salads

The recipes in this section are salads I have made and will serve as a guide to the sort of cold food combinations possible. I hope that the reader will use these recipes as a beginning from which further experimentation may follow.

Note: The dishes listed below may be served as either hot or cold dishes. The recipes are to be found in the previous section, 'Hot vegetables':
1. Leeks and Potatoes (p. 36)
2. Savory Potato and Marrow (p. 43)
3. Peppery Rice (p. 44)
4. Vegetable Variety (p. 50)

CHEESY AVOCADO

Serves 4–5
50 g (½ cup, 2 oz) cheddar cheese,
grated
1 egg
2 large avocados
salt and black pepper
2 teaspoons chives, finely chopped

Put cheese in a pan, break egg into pan and mix well. Cook over a medium heat until consistency of scrambled egg. Set aside to cool.

Halve avocados and remove stone (pit). Scoop flesh into a bowl and mash well. Add cooled cheesy egg and mix thoroughly. Season with salt and black pepper. Serve in small individual dishes with plain wholemeal (whole-wheat) crackers or fresh wholemeal bread. Garnish with chives.

Note: If avocado is not to be served immediately, adding a little lemon or lime juice to the mashed avocado mixture will help prevent discoloration.

AVOCADO BOATS

Serves 4
2 eggs, lightly beaten
2 teaspoons milk
pinch of cayenne
pinch of paprika
40 g (⅓ cup, 1½ oz) cheddar cheese,
grated
2 avocados
4 nasturtium flowers (optional)
black pepper

Break eggs into a small pan. Beat lightly. Add milk, cayenne and paprika. Cook gently, stirring continuously, until eggs are scrambled. Remove from heat. Stir in cheese. Set aside to cool.

Halve avocados and remove stone (pit). Scoop flesh into a bowl and mash well. Finely chop nasturtium flowers (if used). Add nasturtium flowers and egg mixture to mashed avocado. Mix thoroughly. Spoon into avocado shells. Sprinkle with a little freshly ground black pepper. Serve.

Note: If avocado is not to be served immediately, adding a little lemon or lime juice to the mashed avocado mixture will help prevent discoloration.

STUFFED AVOCADO

Serves 4
2 medium avocados
1 small clove garlic
75 g (¾ cup, 2½ oz) cheese
(eg Cheshire, Caerphilly,
mild cheddar), grated
4 small tomatoes
black pepper
4 teaspoons sesame seed, toasted

Halve avocados lengthwise. Remove stone (pit). Scoop flesh into a bowl and retain skins or shells. Mash flesh well. Finely chop garlic and cut tomatoes into tiny pieces. Add garlic, tomato and grated cheese to mashed avocado flesh. Mix thoroughly. Season with black pepper. Fill each avocado shell with mixture. Place in refrigerator for 5 minutes to chill slightly. Remove and sprinkle with toasted sesame seed. Serve immediately.

Note: 1. The garlic flavour comes through very strongly: reduce quantity used or omit altogether if preferred.
2. If avocado is not to be served immediately, adding a little lemon or lime juice to the mashed avocado mixture will help prevent discoloration.

AVOCADO SALAD

Serves 2–4

1 large avocado

½ cucumber (about 100 g/3½ oz)

1 medium green capsicum
(sweet pepper)

black pepper

1 tablespoon mayonnaise
(see sauces, p. 227)

Halve avocado, remove and discard stone (pit). Scoop out flesh. Cut into fairly large pieces and place in a bowl. Peel cucumber if necessary. Cut into small cubes (1–1½ cm (½ in)). Add to avocado. Slice capsicum as thinly as possible and cut into small lengths. Add to bowl. Season with black pepper and thoroughly mix in mayonnaise. Serve slightly chilled.

Note: 1. Serve as an hors d'oeuvre or as a side salad.
2. The avocado can be be sprinkled with lemon juice to prevent discoloration.

AVOCADO IN TARRAGON DRESSING

Serves 6

½ teaspoon French tarragon,
finely chopped

2 teaspoons cider vinegar

2 teaspoons oil

2 large avocados

black pepper

Mix together tarragon, vinegar and oil. Set aside for 30 minutes. Peel and stone (pit) avocados and cut flesh lengthwise into thick slices. Arrange on a plate or shallow dish. Chill slightly. Spoon over tarragon dressing. Serve seasoned with a little freshly ground black pepper.

Note: The avocado can be sprinkled with lemon juice to prevent discoloration.

SPICY AVOCADO

Serves 4–6

2 large avocados

1 clove garlic

1½ teaspoons ground cumin

1 tablespoon spring onion (scallions),
finely chopped

2 tablespoons chives, finely chopped

1 tablespoon cheddar cheese, grated

black pepper

1 tomato (to garnish)

Halve avocados and remove stone (pit). Scoop flesh into a bowl and mash well. Finely chop garlic. Add garlic and remaining ingredients to avocado. Mix well and chill slightly. Spoon into individual dishes or onto small plates. Garnish with tomato slices.

Note: 1. The cumin flavour is rather strong: reduce quantity if preferred.
2. If not to be served immediately, adding a little lemon or lime juice to the mashed avocado mixture will help prevent discoloration.

BEETROOT (BEETS) WITH LEMON SAUCE

Serves 6

12 small beetroot (beets),
cooked and cooled
125 ml (½ cup, 4½ fl oz) Basic
Wholemeal (Whole-Wheat) Sauce
(see sauces, p. 218)
2 teaspoons raw (demerara,
turbinado) sugar
1 lemon rind, finely grated
juice of 1 lemon

Peel cold cooked beetroot. Place in a shallow dish. Prepare sauce in usual way. While still warm, add sugar and stir until dissolved. Allow to cool. Add lemon rind and lemon juice, stir well and pour over beetroot. Serve immediately.

Note: When preparing wholemeal sauce, I often sieve the bran from the flour before use.

RED CABBAGE SALAD

Serves 4

100 g (1 cup, 3½ oz) red cabbage,
shredded
50 g (2 oz) salami
2 eggs, hard-boiled
1½ tablespoons Orange Dressing
(see dressings, p. 229)
50 g (½ cup, 2 oz) sunflower kernels
(seeds) or nuts, chopped

Thinly slice cabbage and place in a salad bowl. Cut salami into small chunks. Shell eggs and cut into small pieces. Add salami and eggs to salad. Add Orange Dressing and toss salad well. Chill slightly. Add sunflower kernels (or nuts) immediately before serving.

MIXED GREEN SALAD

Serves 4

75 g (⅔ cup, 2½ oz) white (drum
head) or green (round head) cabbage,
shredded
50 g (⅔ cup, 2 oz) lettuce, shredded
75 g (2½ oz) cucumber
50 g (2 oz) cooked sausage, cold
3 teaspoons Plain Salad Dressing
(see dressings, p. 228)

Finely shred cabbage and lettuce. Place in a salad bowl. Peel cucumber if necessary and slice thinly. Cut sausage into thin rounds. Add cucumber and sausage to bowl, sprinkle in salad dressing and toss salad well. Serve slightly chilled.

Alternative Substitute 1 small peeled and sliced avocado for the sausage.

CAULIFLOWER SALAD

Serves 4

200 g (7 oz) cauliflower
1 rasher (slice) bacon
a little oil
1 medium green capsicum
(sweet pepper)
1 large tomato
30 g (1 oz) green peas, shelled
1 teaspoon marjoram, finely chopped
salt and black pepper
2 teaspoons mayonnaise
(see sauces, p. 227)

Lightly boil or steam cauliflower. Cool and break into florets. Gently fry bacon in a little oil. Cool and cut into small pieces. Thinly slice capsicum and tomato. Lightly boil peas or leave raw, according to preference. Mix together in a bowl the cauliflower, bacon, tomato, capsicum, peas and marjoram. Season with a little salt and black pepper. Stir in mayonnaise. Mix thoroughly.

EASTER SALAD

Serves 4

200 g (7 oz) cauliflower
25 g (1/3 cup, 1 oz) lettuce, shredded
50 g (2 oz) feta cheese
1 orange
25 g (1/4 cup, 1 oz) sunflower kernels
(seeds)

Break cauliflower into florets. Lightly boil or steam, or leave raw, according to preference. Shred lettuce and cut cheese into small cubes (½–1 cm/¼–½ in). Peel orange and cut into thin slices. In a bowl, mix the cauliflower, lettuce, orange and cheese. Chill slightly. Add sunflower kernels immediately before serving.
Note: No salad dressing is required, the juice from the orange is sufficient.

STUFFED CELERY STICKS

Serves 4

75 g (1/3 cup, 2½ oz) cottage cheese,
sieved (strained)
1 teaspoon marjoram, finely chopped
2 nasturtium flowers, finely chopped
(optional)
1 teaspoon chives, finely chopped
pinch of paprika
black pepper
75 g (2½ oz) celery
2 teaspoons sesame seed, toasted

In a bowl, blend the cottage cheese, marjoram, nasturtium flowers (if used), chives, paprika and a little black pepper. Wash celery well. Trim away leaves and any discoloured parts. Cut celery into pieces 4–5 cm (1½–2 in) long. Fill hollow of each piece with cottage cheese mixture. Arrange on a small plate. Sprinkle with sesame seed. Serve as an appetiser or party snack.

Opposite: *Cucumber and Dill Salad is a cooling and simple salad for a summer barbecue or picnic.*

CUCUMBER AND DILL SALAD

Serves 4–6

½ teaspoon dill seed

4 tablespoons natural (plain) yoghurt

200 g (7 oz) cucumber

1 slice of lemon

Stir dill seed into yoghurt. Set aside for 1 hour. Peel cucumber if necessary. Slice thinly and arrange in a shallow dish or plate. Spoon yoghurt and dill over cucumber. Cut lemon slice in two halves and use to garnish.

Note: This is a good salad to serve with curry or fish.

FENNEL SALAD

Serves 4

1 bulb of Florence fennel (finocchio)

3 tablespoons French Dressing

(see *dressings*, p. 228)

1 sprig of fennel leaves

Trim away any discoloured or bruised outer leaves from fennel. Trim away root area. Slice thinly, wash well to remove any soil trapped between leaves. Drain well. Lay the fennel in a shallow dish (plate) and spoon over French Dressing. Garnish with fennel leaves.

EGG SALAD

Serves 4

4 eggs, hard-boiled
50 g (¼ cup, 2 oz) carrot, grated
50 g (½ cup, 2 oz) cheese, grated
8 borage flowers (optional)
4 camomile flowers (optional)
6 nasturtium flowers (optional)
black pepper
1 tablespoon oil
½ teaspoon lemon juice or cider vinegar

Shell eggs, cut into eighths and place in a bowl. Add carrot, cheese and borage flowers. Halve camomile flowers and finely chop nasturtium flowers. Add both to eggs. Season with black pepper. Add oil and lemon juice. Mix thoroughly.

AUTUMN SALAD

Serves 4

50 g (⅔ cup, 2 oz) lettuce, shredded
2 French sorrel leaves
1 apple
2 teapsoons Plain Salad Dressing
(see dressings, p. 228)

Shred lettuce and sorrel. Place in a bowl. Core apple, but do not peel. Cut into thin slices. Add to bowl. Spoon in salad dressing and toss salad well. Serve slightly chilled.

MIXED HERB SALAD

Serves 4

50 g (⅔ cup, 2 oz) lettuce, finely shredded
1½ teaspoons each of tansy and dandelion leaves, finely chopped
12 borage flowers
1 tablespoon sesame seed, toasted
2 teaspoons nasturtium leaves, finely chopped
1 large apple
4 nasturtium flowers
50 g (2 oz) green peas, shelled
3 teaspoons Plain Salad Dressing
(see dressings, p. 228)
1 banana

Finely shred lettuce and place in a salad bowl. Add tansy, dandelion, borage flowers, sesame seed and nasturtium leaves. Cut apple into small chunks. Finely chop 3 nasturtium flowers. Add apple and nasturtium flowers to salad. If peas are young and tender, add raw—otherwise lightly boil or steam, cool and add to salad. Sprinkle dressing over salad. Toss well. Chill slightly. Immediately before serving, add sliced banana, mix thoroughly and garnish with remaining nasturtium flower.

Note: Tansy can be toxic in large doses, so avoid frequent use or large amounts. However, used sparingly in salads it is not dangerous. Pregnant women should avoid eating tansy.

HERBS AND LETTUCE SALAD

Serves 3–4
½ small lettuce
1 French sorrel leaf
2 small tender borage leaves
2 teaspoons each of bergamot (bee
balm), lemon balm and salad
(garden) burnet, chopped
12 borage flowers
5 camomile flowers
4 marigold flowers
1 tablespoon French Dressing
(see dressings, p. 228)

Finely chop lettuce, sorrel and borage leaves. Place in a salad bowl. Add bergamot, lemon balm, salad burnet and 6 borage flowers. Cut camomile flowers in halves. Add to salad. Remove outer yellow or orange ray florets from marigold flowers. Add to salad. Discard central 'core' (disc-florets receptacle and stalk). Sprinkle in the French Dressing, toss salad well and serve at room temperature decorated with 6 remaining borage flowers.

SPICY LEEKS

Serves 4
300 g (10½ oz) leeks, prepared
black pepper

SPICY SAUCE
2 tablespoons soy sauce
1½ tablespoons oil
1 teaspoon cider vinegar
1 teaspoon Worcestershire sauce

TO PREPARE LEEKS
Pull off tough and damaged outer leaves. Cut away root area and tough green leaves. Slice remainder (white and light-green parts) into rounds ½–1 cm (¼–½ in) thick. Rinse well, as leeks can be very gritty/sandy.

Boil or steam prepared leeks, drain and set aside until cold. Season with black pepper.

SPICY SAUCE
In a cup or small bowl, thoroughly mix together spicy sauce ingredients. Pour over cold cooked leeks. Serve.

MACARONI SALAD

Serves 6
100 g (⅔ cup, 3½ oz) wholemeal
(whole-wheat) macaroni
125 g (¾ cup, 4½ oz) green (French
or runner, string) beans, cooked
2 teaspoons oil
1 tablespoon marjoram,
finely chopped
4 eggs, hard-boiled
salt and black pepper

Boil macaroni until al dente, drain and allow to cool. Place in a salad bowl. Cut beans into tiny pieces. Add beans, oil and marjoram to bowl. Hard-boil eggs and allow to cool. Shell and cut into eighths. Add to bowl. Mix salad well. Season with salt and black pepper.

VAL'S MUSHROOMS

Serves 4

1 tablespoon Dijon/French mustard

1 tablespoon olive oil or good-quality cooking oil

½ teaspoon French tarragon, finely chopped

2 teaspoons lemon juice

salt and black pepper

100 g (3½ oz) fresh young mushrooms

Spoon mustard into a bowl, add olive oil and blend well using a fork. Add tarragon and lemon juice. Mix thoroughly. Season with salt and black pepper.

Cut mushrooms into quarters, place in a bowl and pour sauce over them. Stir well until each piece of mushroom is coated in sauce.

Note: 1. This dish is rather spicy and small portions are preferable.
2. It makes a good hors d'oeuvre dish if served with hot crusty bread.

POTATO SALAD

Serves 4

500 g (1 lb) potato, cooked

100 g (¼ cup, 3½ oz) shelled peas, (cooked or raw)

3 tablespoons chives, finely chopped

2 rashers (slices) bacon

1 teaspoon oil

4 tablespoons Basic Wholemeal (Whole-Wheat) Sauce (see sauces, p. 218) or 3 tablespoons mayonnaise (see p. 227)

black pepper

Cut potato into small cubes. Place in a bowl. Add peas—cooked or raw, according to preference. Add chives. Cut bacon into small pieces. Fry in oil until well cooked. Drain. When cool, add to ingredients in bowl. Stir in sauce or mayonnaise. Mix well. Season with black pepper.

BROWN RICE SALAD

Serves 4–6

50 g (⅓ cup, 2 oz) brown rice

100 g (¾ cup, 3½ oz) green (French or runner, string) beans

50 g (½ cup, 2 oz) cheddar cheese, grated

1 teaspoon oil (optional)

1 tablespoon chives, finely chopped

50 g (⅓ cup, 2 oz) raisins or sultanas (golden raisins)

black pepper

Boil rice until cooked, drain and allow to cool. Slice beans into small rounds (½ cm/¼ in thick), boil until just tender, drain and allow to cool. Mix beans, rice, cheese, oil, chives and raisins in a salad bowl. Season with black pepper. Serve at room temperature.

Alternatives • Add sliced bananas to salad just before serving.
• Use 2 teaspoons of Orange Dressing (see sauces, p. 229) in place of oil.
• Leave beans raw if preferred.

PINEAPPLE SALAD

Serves 4–5

175 g (6 oz) fresh pineapple, peeled
75 g (2½ oz) feta cheese
25 g (¼ cup, 1 oz) watercress
75 g (2½ oz) lean (chunk) bacon
1 teaspoon oil

Cut pineapple into small cubes of approx. 1 cm (½ in). Place in a bowl. Cut feta cheese into same-sized cubes. Add to bowl. Wash watercress well. Cut away and discard any tough, bitter stalks. Chop into fairly large pieces and add to cheese and pineapple. Fry bacon in oil until crispy and drain away all oil—on paper towels (absorbent kitchen paper) if possible. When bacon is cool, add to salad. Mix ingredients thoroughly. Serve.

Note: No dressing is required on this salad.

PINEAPPLE AND PAWPAW (PAPAYA) SALAD

Serves 4–5

250 g (9 oz) fresh pineapple
200 g (7 oz) pawpaw (papaya)
75 g (¾ cup, 2½ oz) cheese
(eg Cheshire, mild cheddar,
Caerphilly), grated
¼ teaspoon marjoram, finely chopped
(optional)

Cut pineapple and pawpaw into small cubes (about 1 cm/½ in). Place in a salad bowl. Add cheese and marjoram (if used) to salad. Mix well and serve chilled.

Note: 1. Canned pineapple may be used, but drain off all syrup before use. 2. This salad is a good accompaniment to a very spicy dish or a heavy meat dish, eg a curry (*see* pp. 112–13) or Mexican Stew (*see* p. 136).

BASIL TOMATOES

Serves 4

1 teaspoon basil, finely chopped
1 tablespoon oil
1 teaspoon cider vinegar
350 g (12½ oz) tomatoes
black pepper
1 tablespoon sunflower kernels (seeds)

Mix together basil, oil and vinegar. Set aside for 1 hour. Thinly slice tomatoes and spoon over oil. Chill slightly. Immediately before serving, season with a little freshly ground black pepper. Sprinkle over sunflower kernels.

SPICY TOMATOES

Serves 3–4

200 g (7 oz) tomatoes
1 teaspoon soy sauce
½ teaspoon lemon juice
2 teaspoons oil
black pepper
2 teaspoons chives, finely chopped
2 teaspoons sesame seed, toasted

Thinly slice tomatoes and arrange in a shallow dish. Mix together soy sauce, lemon juice and oil. Season with a little black pepper. Spoon evenly over tomatoes. Mix chives and sesame seed together, sprinkle over tomatoes. Serve at room temperature.

FRUIT RICE SALAD

Serves 3–4

50 g (⅓ cup, 2 oz) brown rice
50 g (⅔ cup, 2 oz) lettuce, shredded
1 banana
50 g (2 oz) grapes (white or black
(green or red))
1 orange

Boil rice until cooked, drain and allow to cool. Shred lettuce and thinly slice banana. Place both in a salad bowl. Halve grapes, remove pips (seeds) and add grapes to bowl. Peel orange and cut into small pieces. Add orange and cooked rice to bowl. Mix well. Serve at room temperature.

SAVOURY RICE

Serves 6–8

200 g (1 cup, 7 oz) white rice
1 teaspoon turmeric
2 teaspoons oil
black pepper
2 green capsicum (sweet peppers)
14 nasturtium flowers (optional)

Boil rice until cooked, rinse in cold water and drain. Allow to cool. Place rice in a bowl. Add turmeric and oil, stir well and season with black pepper. Thinly slice capsicum and cut into small pieces. Add to rice. Chop 12 nasturtium flowers (if used). Add to rice, stir well and garnish with 2 remaining flowers.

WATERCRESS SALAD

Serves 3-4

200 g (7 oz) pawpaw (papaya)
75 g (1 cup, 2½ oz) watercress,
chopped
75 g (¾ cup, 2½ oz) mild cheddar or
Cheshire cheese, grated

Skin pawpaw and cut into small cubes. Mix all ingredients together. Serve very slightly chilled.

Beans

BEANS IN PEANUT (GROUNDNUT) SAUCE

Serves 3-4

150 g (¾ cup, 5½ oz) dried haricot
(navy or pea) beans
250 ml (1 cup, 9 fl oz) Peanut
(Groundnut) Sauce (see sauces,
p. 219)

Soak and boil beans as described in general methods (pp. 22-3). Prepare sauce. Mix into freshly cooked beans. Serve.

Note: This dish is heavy and very nutritious—suitable for a freezing autumn (fall) or winter evening. Serve with plain, freshly cooked vegetables, eg zucchini (courgettes) or leeks.

GREEN HUMMUS

Serves 2

100 g (½ cup, 3½ oz) split peas
4 cloves garlic
1 tablespoon butter
1 tablespoon chives, finely chopped
1 tablespoon lemon juice
salt and black pepper

Soak peas for at least 12 hours. Boil until soft and beginning to go mushy. Drain well, but keep warm. Meanwhile, finely chop garlic. Place in a pan with butter and chives. Melt butter. Gently cook garlic and chives in butter for 2-3 minutes. Mash drained peas. Add to pan containing butter, garlic and chives. Stir well and add lemon juice. Be sure to mix thoroughly. Season with salt and black pepper.

Note: 1. This mixture is quite rich and very strong in garlic, so only small portions are required.
2. The peas need only to be mashed a little—not to a smooth paste.
This is my version of traditional Greek hummus, a very smooth paste made from chickpeas. Chickpeas (garbanzos) haven't always been available so I have adapted the original recipe to fit split peas. It can be served as a course by itself, hot or cold, or as a dip or spread for party snacks.

BIBLE PORK WITH LIMA (BUTTER) BEANS *See* recipe for this dish in 'Pork', p. 116

SPICED DHAL (DAL)

Serves 3

150 g (¾ cup, 5½ oz) red (orange)
lentils
2 cloves garlic
3 teaspoons each of cumin seed
and coriander seed,
finely ground
2 tablespoons butter
2 teaspoons ground ginger
1½ teaspoons turmeric
1½ teaspoons paprika
½ teaspoon Mixed Cake Spice
(see p. 272)*
½ teaspoon ground black pepper
salt

Boil lentils in plenty of water until very soft. Drain well. Mash a little using a fork. Set aside and keep warm.

Finely chop garlic. Gently warm butter in a small pan. Add ground cumin and coriander, and garlic. Add remaining spices (minus salt). Cook gently in butter for 2–3 minutes. This releases the volatile oils which carry the flavour. Stir spicy butter mixture into lentils. Mix well to ensure an even distribution of flavour. Add salt to taste. Serve hot or cold.

Note: 1. Dhal can be a starter to a curry meal or simply a supper dish. Served cold, it can be spread on squares of wholemeal (whole-wheat) bread or toast, or on crackers as a savoury party snack.
2. * Mixed spice can also be used. This consists of 4 parts ground cinnamon, 2 parts ground ginger, 1 part ground nutmeg and 1 part ground cloves.

LENTIL PATTIES

Serves 5

150 g (¾ cup, 5½ oz) red (orange) or
green lentils
2 cloves garlic
2 tablespoons borage, finely chopped
1 teaspoon winter savory,
finely chopped
black pepper
100 g (3½ oz) crushed or kibbled
(cracked, burghul) wheat
2 teaspoons oil
a little beaten egg

Boil lentils in plenty of water until very soft and beginning to turn 'mushy'. Turn into a sieve and drain for 20 minutes—drained liquid will be yellowish and fairly thick. Retain for soup or stock base. Finely chop garlic. Place in a bowl with borage, winter savory and black pepper.

Using a fork, mash lentils a little (they should be quite wet at this stage). Add to bowl. Thoroughly mix with garlic and herbs. Still using a fork, add 80 g (3 oz) of crushed (or kibbled) wheat and oil. Mix well. Stir in a little beaten egg to bind ingredients (¼–½ small egg is all that is required). The mixture will still be quite wet and sticky. Slowly add remaining crushed (or kibbled) wheat until mixture is workable, though still quite wet. Divide into ten portions. Take one portion, mould into a ball and place on a greased baking tray (sheet). Flatten a little to 1½ cm (½ in) thick. Repeat with remaining portions.

Cover and bake at 200°C or 400°F for 15 minutes. Turn patties over halfway through cooking.

Note: These patties can be served with a sauce if you find them too dry. Fresh Tomato Sauce (see sauces, p. 220) makes a good accompaniment. Otherwise, use a plain wholemeal (whole-wheat) sauce (see sauces, p. 218).

Opposite: *Two classic lentil dishes — one from the Middle East, the other India — are brought within the reach of any cook. Spiced Dhal (Dal) and Green Hummus are easy to make and highly nutritious.*

BEANSPROUT PASTIES

Makes 7

FILLING

200 g (7 oz) bean sprouts
1 small onion
150 g (5½ oz) lean (chunk) bacon
1½ tablespoons oil
black pepper
1½-2 teaspoons summer savory,
finely chopped

PASTRY

100 g (½ cup, 4 oz) margarine
250 g (1¾ cups, 9 oz) wholemeal
(whole-wheat) flour
3½-4 tablespoons water
a little beaten egg

FILLING

Boil or steam bean sprouts until just tender. Drain and set aside. Finely chop onion and bacon. Place both in a frying pan (skillet) with oil. Fry gently until onion is tender. Add bean sprouts. Continue frying gently for 3–4 minutes. Remove from heat. Season with black pepper and stir in savory. Set aside to cool.

PASTRY

Rub margarine into flour with fingertips. Add water. Work mixture into a soft dough. Roll out fairly thinly on a well-floured board. Cut pastry into 12 cm (5 in) squares—you should get seven. Divide filling evenly between squares. Taking one square, moisten all edges with a little water. Take one corner, bring it up and over filling, and down to meet opposite corner, making a triangle. Press pastry edges together gently but firmly. Place on a well-greased baking tray (sheet). Repeat with remaining pastry squares. Brush pasties with a little beaten egg. Bake at 200°C or 400°F for 15–20 minutes. Serve hot or cold.

Note: You may have a little too much filling for seven squares. The filling can also double as a savoury pancake or omelette filler.

BEAN DISH

Serves 2–3

100 g (½ cup, 3½ oz) dried haricot
(navy or pea), sugar or red kidney
beans
225 g (8 oz) zucchini (courgettes)
2 large tomatoes
1 onion
1 teaspoon hyssop, finely chopped
1 tablespoon oil
1 tablespoon margarine
1 tablespoon wholemeal
(whole-wheat) flour
200 ml (7 fl oz) milk
black pepper
Parmesan cheese, grated

Soak and cook beans as described on pp. 22–3. Slice zucchini into rounds and set aside. Slice 1 tomato and layer at bottom of an ovenproof dish.

Finely chop onion. Cook gently with hyssop in oil until soft. Stir in cooked beans and sliced zucchini. Mix well. Make a layer of bean mixture over tomato. Make a final layer of second tomato, sliced into rounds.

Prepare a thin sauce by melting margarine in a pan, adding wholemeal flour and slowly adding milk. Season with black pepper. Pour over tomato and bean layers in dish. Cover and bake at 180°C or 350°F for 35 minutes. When cooked, sprinkle liberally with Parmesan cheese. Serve.

Note: Other vegetables can be used in place of the zucchini, eg white (drum head) or green (round head) cabbage, green capsicum (sweet pepper), potato or green (French or runner, string) beans.

TOMATO BEANS

Serves 4–5

1 onion

2 tablespoons oil

1½ teaspoons oregano, finely chopped

pinch each of paprika and cayenne

black pepper

2 cloves garlic

150 ml (2/3 cup, 5½ fl oz) tomato purée (see p. 221)

3 small tomatoes

2 medium green capsicum (sweet peppers)

200 g (2 cups, 7 oz) cooked haricot (navy or pea) beans

Thinly slice onion. Fry gently in oil with oregano, paprika, cayenne, a little black pepper and garlic (finely chopped). When onion is soft and lightly browned, stir in tomato purée. Cook for a further 3 minutes. Remove from heat. When cooled a little, pour half into a blender (liquidiser). Cut tomatoes and 1 capsicum into pieces. Add to blender. Blend for 1 minute or until smooth. Pour mixture back into pan with remaining tomato mixture. Thinly slice second capsicum and add to pan. Bring to boil, cover and simmer for 7–10 minutes until capsicum is tender. Add cooked beans to sauce, stir well and cook for a further 5 minutes to heat thoroughly. Serve hot or cold.

Note: One cup of dried beans when cooked will give the 2 cups required.

HOT TOMATO BEANS

Serves 2–3

100 g (½ cup, 3½ oz) dried beans (eg haricot (navy or pea), sugar)

1 onion

1 tablespoon oil

3 teaspoons oregano, finely chopped

2 tomatoes

2 tablespoons tomato purée (see p. 221)

½ teaspoon paprika

black pepper

¼ teaspoon cayenne

1 sprig of oregano (to garnish)

Soak and boil beans until cooked (*see* general methods, pp. 22–3). Finely chop onion. Sauté in oil. Add oregano and roughly chopped tomatoes. Cook gently for 1–2 minutes, stirring continuously. Add tomato purée, paprika, black pepper and cayenne. Stir well to thoroughly mix ingredients. Cook *very* gently for 10 minutes. Add cooked beans and serve immediately, garnished with sprig of oregano.

Note: This is a simplified version of Tomato Beans (*see* above).

MEXICAN STEW *See* recipe in 'Lamb & goat' (p. 136).

meat & poultry

Meat

The term 'meat' refers to the edible parts of an animal carcass and its edible organs and glands. The quality of a carcass is determined by a number of factors such as:

- age—the older the animal the less tender the meat
- its health and nutritional status—a properly nourished animal has well-developed muscle tissues, organs and glands, and will not carry too much fat
- the post-slaughter hanging period (otherwise known as ageing, holding or ripening)—freshly slaughtered meat is tough.

Following slaughter, proteolytic enzymes (protein-breaking chemicals) go into action and begin to break down the connective tissue between the muscles, muscle bundles and muscle fibres. Hanging may range from two to six weeks for a beef or lamb carcass, but the average is 10–20 days. The meat is hung on hooks or laid on shelves and allowed to 'rest', ideally at a temperature of 2°–4°C or 36°–40°F and 90% humidity.

Smallholders will know the age and health of their beast, but for those buying retail my advice is to find a reliable and competent butcher. Butchery is a skill, and those experienced at their job will have developed an 'eye' for the quality of a carcass and can then advise you. In many countries today, meat is rigorously inspected for disease and then graded for quality. Get to know the grading system of your country and look out for it when buying. With that and your butcher's advice, you should not go wrong.

Within a carcass, meat varies in tenderness and palatability. Perhaps a brief description of the structure of meat will help clarify this. Most of the edible meat on a carcass is muscle. Muscle is composed of microscopic muscle fibres. Each fibre is tubular in shape, elongated at the ends and enclosed by a sheath of tissue. The fibres are grouped into bundles held in place by and surrounded by connective tissue. Many bundles grouped, held together by and surrounded by connective tissue, make up a muscle. Generally speaking, the smaller the muscle, the greater the proportion of connective tissue relative to muscle fibres. Muscle fibre is tender to eat, but connective tissue is tough. Cuts of meat with numerous small muscles include a large proportion of connective tissue and so are the least tender ones, eg neck. The tenderness of a cut of meat is also affected by the amount of exercise to which that muscle or set of muscles is put. For example, the eye muscle of the rib area and the strip muscle of the loin are large muscles (relatively low in connective tissues) and receive very little exercise. They are therefore very tender. Fillet (or tenderloin) is the most tender muscle as it is so large and receives almost no exercise during the entire life of an animal. Even in an old animal, this muscle would be reasonably tender, although perhaps not as palatable (as age affects flavour).

Meat is cooked to render it more palatable and digestible. Meat fibres are made of protein. The effect of heat on protein is to denature (harden) it. (This is easily seen in the case of an egg—a rather liquid, gelatinous protein which sets and hardens when heat is applied.) The aim of the cooking process is to break down the connective tissue between the muscle fibres and fibre bundles and to cook (set or harden) the protein fibres. A well-cooked, tender piece of meat is one where the fibres separate easily when chewed. With the tender cuts of meat, eg steaks where connective tissue is minimal, the cooking process can be fast, eg frying or grilling (broiling) for small cuts, and roasting for large cuts. The less tender cuts, eg shin and neck, need a slow, moist cooking such as stewing or casseroling to break down the connective tissue. Medium-tender cuts, eg brisket of beef, require pot-roasting or braising.

Lastly, a word about fat. Fat reaches a higher temperature than water (or water-based liquids) before vaporising. Fat can therefore maintain the heat required for cooking the meat and should remain *in situ* to maintain moistness. Also, many of the flavourful proteins in meat are water-soluble and might drip out of the meat during cooking. Fat can encapsulate the muscle and prevent loss of these proteins, thus maintaining flavour. It is therefore desirable to have some fat on the carcass and on each piece of meat that is to be cooked. Lean cuts, eg topside, require the addition of fat. Marbling, where small quantities of fat are held between the muscle, is a desirable quality. (The meat appears streaked or dotted with white fat.) The deposition of fats in this pattern develops with age—eg the flesh of veal will never be marbled.

Having briefly covered the theory behind meat quality and cooking techniques, the basic methods of meat cookery are now described separately.

Roasting

Open-Pan Roasting The piece of meat is rubbed evenly all over with fat or oil. It is then weighed and cooking time is calculated. It is placed fat side up in a shallow roasting tin (pan) and is seasoned. The tin is placed in a preheated oven and the meat allowed to cook in its own juices. The meat may be basted several times towards the end of the cooking time.

Alternatively, the tin may be covered with a lid or aluminium foil to maintain moistness.

Spit-roasting Traditionally meat was spit-roasted over an open fire. These days we may use the oven if it includes a spit or a rotisserie. The meat is rubbed evenly all over with fat or oil, seasoned and set on the spit. The instructions given by the oven or rotisserie manufacturer should then be followed.

Seasoning Salt, pepper, spices, garlic and herbs may be used. Spices should be finely ground and herbs finely chopped. They are rubbed into or pressed onto all surfaces of the meat. Garlic is cut into tiny slices. Tiny cuts, evenly spaced, are made in the surface of the meat and a tiny slice of garlic is placed in each. Alternatively, and for a milder flavour, the meat may be rubbed with the cut surface of a garlic clove.

Roasting Times Roasting times for meat can be gauged from the times given below. Alternatively, you can use a meat thermometer. Temperatures for this are given on the right-hand side of the page.

Beef

	Meat Thermometer
Rare—cook at 190°C or 375°F	
35 minutes per kg (16 minutes per lb), plus 10 minutes extra.	60°C (140°F)
Medium—at 180°C or 350°F	
45 minutes per kg (20 minutes per lb), plus 15 minutes extra.	65°–70°C (150°–160°F)
Well done—at 180°C or 350°F	
55–65 minutes per kg (25–30 minutes per lb), plus 20 minutes extra.	77°C (170°F)

Lamb

Pink (medium cooked)—cook at 180°C or 350°F

a. Thin joints, eg shoulder: 35 minutes per kg (16 minutes per lb),
   plus 10 minutes extra.   65°C (147°–150°F)

b. Thick joints, eg leg: 40 minutes per kg (18 minutes per lb),
   plus 10 minutes extra.

Blue (well done)—cook at 180°C or 350°F

a. Thin joint: 45 minutes per kg (20 minutes per lb),
   plus 20 minutes extra.   70°–80°C (160°–175°F)

b. Thick joints: 55 minutes per kg (25 minutes per lb),
   plus 20 minutes extra.

Pork and Veal

Cook at 180°C or 350°F

65 minutes per kg (30 minutes per lb), plus 30 minutes extra.   Pork 85°C (180°–185°F)
                                                                     Veal 77°C (170°F)

Some Traditional Accompaniments to Roast Meat

Beef: • Thin or thick gravy
           • Yorkshire pudding
           • Horseradish sauce
           • Mustard
Pork: • Thin or thick gravy
           • Sage and onion stuffing
           • Apple sauce (*see* recipe for Cilla's Apple Sauce, p. 225).
Lamb: • Thin or thick gravy
           • Mint sauce
Mutton: • Thin or thick gravy
           • Onion sauce
           • Redcurrant jelly
Veal: • Thin or thick gravy
           • Forcemeat balls
           • Bacon rolls

Pot-roasting

Pot-roasting is applied to the medium-tender cuts of meat, eg topside. Firstly, meat is seasoned as described under 'Roasting'. A little fat is heated in a deep pan until hot and the meat added. When the bottom has browned, the meat is turned. This is repeated until each side of the meat has browned, the aim being to harden and seal the outer layer of meat, which will prevent the loss of meat juices and flavour during cooking. At this stage a little water (a few tablespoons) or stock and a few sliced vegetables, eg carrots and onions, may be added. The pot is covered and cooking continues over a low heat, allowing 1 hour 40 minutes per kg (45 minutes per lb), until meat is sufficiently tender. Alternatively, the pot may be placed in the oven at 170°C

or 325°F, again allowing 1 hour 40 minutes per kg (45 minutes per lb). In either case, meat must be basted frequently and turned once or twice during cooking.

Braising

Braising uses more liquid (stock or water) during the cooking process and is applied to less tender cuts of meat. Firstly the meat is seasoned and coated evenly with flour. Fat or oil is heated in a deep pan. The meat is added and browned a little on each side. A few sliced vegetables, eg carrots, onions, tomatoes or leeks, are added plus enough liquid to cover the meat. The pot is covered and set to cook in the oven at 170°–180°C or 325°–350°F, or to simmer gently on top of the stove (cooker) for several hours until the meat is tender.

Alternatively, the flour-coating stage may be omitted, but towards the end of cooking, the lid of the pan should be removed to increase evaporation and thicken the sauce. Stir occasionally after removing the lid. The liquid used may be water, vegetable stock or meat stock. Tomato purée and wine may be added in small quantities for extra flavour.

Seasoning Salt, pepper, finely ground spices or finely chopped herbs may be used. They are rubbed into or sprinkled on the meat before coating with flour or, if omitting this stage, before placing in the pan. A little finely chopped garlic and/or finely chopped herbs may be added to the liquid before it is poured over the meat.

Stewing

Stewing is a slow moist-cooking method applied to tough cuts of meat. The meat is cut into small pieces (approx. 1½ cm (½ in) cubes) which are coated evenly with flour. They are cooked quickly in a little hot fat until browned, removed and set aside. A few sliced vegetables are added to the fat and cooked over a high heat for 1–2 minutes. They are also removed and set aside. A little flour is added to the fat, and liquid (water or stock) is gradually blended in to make a thick sauce. The meat and vegetables are replaced in the pan, and seasoning added. The pan is covered and set on the top of the stove (cooker) to simmer gently or placed in the oven at 170°C or 325°F to cook for about 1½–2½ hours, until meat is tender.

The flour-coating stage and the thin sauce preparation may be omitted. In both cases, the lid of the pan must be removed towards the end of cooking to help evaporation and so thicken the sauce. The stew should be stirred occasionally.

Seasoning Salt and pepper, finely ground spices or finely chopped herbs or garlic are stirred into the stew before cooking.

Boiling

Boiling is used for medium- to large-sized pieces of meat, eg tongue, brisket and particularly those that have been salted, like smoked ham (gammon joints), silverside etc. A large pot of water is brought to the boil. The meat is dropped in, the pan is covered and the meat is simmered gently until tender. Allow 45 minutes per kg (20 minutes per lb), plus 20 minutes extra for beef, veal, mutton and pork; and 55 minutes per kg (25 minutes per lb), plus 25 minutes extra for ham and gammon (smoked ham or bacon). A few sliced vegetables and seasonings may be added to the boiling water with the meat. Salted joints should be soaked in several changes of cold water for 24 hours before cooking.

Seasoning Spices, herbs and garlic may be added to the boiling water, and they may be left whole. If water is to be used for a sauce to accompany meat, it should be strained prior to use. Salt and pepper may also be added, but do not add salt to joints which are already salted.

Grilling (Broiling)

Grilling (broiling) is a fast method of cooking, suitable only for small, tender pieces of meat, eg steak, ham (gammon) steaks (picnic shoulder), chops, bacon, sausages, liver etc. The meat is brushed with a little oil and seasoned. It is placed on greased grill bars or on a greased tray (sheet) and placed under a hot grill (broiler) until cooked. Cooking time will depend on personal preference (whether for rare, medium or well-done steak) and on the thickness of the steaks or chops. The meat should be turned during cooking and may be basted with the juices that drip out. Pork loin chops should always be well cooked, but may curl during cooking. To prevent this, cut the outer rind in several places along its length.

Seasoning Finely chopped herbs and garlic, and finely ground spices are sprinkled on both sides of the meat. This may be done several hours before cooking to allow the meat time to absorb the flavour. The meat may also be marinated (soaked) for several hours in wine or a winy liquid mixture. Before grilling (broiling), the meat must be drained of the marinade. This can be used, together with the cooking juices, to prepare a sauce to accompany the cooked meat.

Frying/Sautéing

Frying/sautéing applies to the same cuts as grilling (broiling). The meat is seasoned and set aside. A little oil or butter is melted in a frying pan (skillet). When quite hot, the meat is added. It is cooked first on one side then the other. The pan may be covered if wished. Generally, frying is a quick process, but with thicker pieces of meat, eg some lamb chump (double loin) chops, sausages and especially thick pork loin chops, the heat may be reduced and the meat cooked quite slowly. Thinly sliced onion, green capsicum (sweet peppers) or other vegetables in small quantities may be cooked with the meat, but allow a little extra oil or butter.

Seasoning Refer to notes under 'Grilling (broiling)'.

Stir-frying

For stir-frying, use only the tender cuts which are normally suitable for grilling (broiling) or frying. Cut the meat into thin strips of about ½–1 cm (¼–½ in) thickness and 4–5 cm (1½–2 in) long. Season well and stir-fry in the usual way (*see* notes on stir-frying on p. 11).

Veal

Strictly speaking, veal should be the meat of an animal no older than three months and may come from a bobby calf, or two- to three-week-old calf. On a smallholding you may wish to raise your calf through to six or even nine months before slaughtering. Butchering is the same as that for beef except that, being a smaller animal, you will not be able to differentiate so well between cuts. Remember that calves have had little or no time to deposit fat on the carcass, so that you will never find marbling in the meat, as you would on beef, or any good thick fat layers that help cook meat and retain flavour. Therefore, it is essential to supply the fat needed either by barding, if roasting, or by adding a good quantity of oil or lard if grilling (broiling) or frying. Braising and stewing, both slow, moist methods of cookery, are often preferred. Several cuts are frequently boned and rolled. These are the hind leg (the rump), shoulder, loin, best end neck (rib) and the breast. Meat containing bone always cooks more quickly than that without, as the bone gets hot and acts as a heat source. Removing the bone in veal ensures a more gentle cooking. Boned veal may be rubbed well all over with lard before rolling and/or spread with a stuffing and rolled and tied. Stuffing is generally a fatty kind such as sausagemeat stuffing (*see* stuffings, p. 230). This helps baste the meat as it cooks and gives it extra flavour. Both alleviate possible dryness and blandness of flavour.

You can substitute veal for beef in any of the recipes given for beef, taking into account the points mentioned above about fat content and flavour.

Mutton

Mutton can be anything from the old ewe that has seen numerous lambing seasons to the adolescent sheep (over 12 months of age), too old to be classed as lamb. The meat of these animals differs tremendously in fat content, flavour and tenderness. Generally, the older the beast, the higher the proportion of fat, the stronger the flavour and the tougher the meat. Suitable cooking methods will depend on which kind of mutton you have. Therefore, you must first of all establish the identity of the animal. All recipes given for lamb may be used for the adolescent and slightly older sheep (18 to 24 months old). Past this age, you will find that the meat requires a longer, more gentle (lower temperature) and moister cooking. Certainly, for the ancient sheep, the only really suitable methods are stewing, boiling and, possibly, braising. Older animals have a stronger flavour. This can be reduced by boiling or stewing in plenty of water or stock, with vegetables. Alternatively, the meat may be highly spiced and flavoured, as in curries. In fact, mutton and the poorer quality cuts of lamb are excellent as curry meats. Before cooking, remove as much fat as you can. If the dish is still too greasy, cool it until the fat solidifies, when it may be removed with ease and the dish reheated as required.

Goat

Young kid meat is very similar to lamb in flavour and may be used in any of the lamb recipes given. It contains a lower proportion of fat, and this may need to be taken into account in roasting and grilling (broiling) recipes. Make sure that the meat is rubbed well with fat (oil, butter or lard, depending on the recipes), and it must be basted frequently. Adolescent kid, 12 months or slightly older, will be stronger in flavour and slightly tougher than lamb, though again it may be used in any of the lamb recipes given. Mature goat can be very strong in flavour and, like the older mutton, is best stewed, boiled or perhaps braised. It is especially suitable for dishes such as curries.

Offal

The previous section described suitable methods of cooking for the cuts of meat from the main carcass. This section takes account of the remainder, eg internal organs, head, feet, tail etc. The economics of smallholding require that there be no waste whatsoever, as in the 'old days' when every centimetre or inch of an animal carcass was valued and used to its utmost advantage. From my childhood days of reading *The Little House on the Prairie* series of books by Laura Ingalls Wilder, I was fascinated to find that even the bladder of the slaughtered homestead pig found a use—as a balloon for the children!

Head

Before using, heads should be thoroughly washed and soaked for several hours in plenty of cold water. Calf's and sheep's head will be skinned, and pig's scalded and scraped. Generally, eyes, eardrums and sometimes nasal passages are removed before cooking. It is easier to work with head halves rather than whole ones. The head is therefore split longitudinally from the nose through to the back of the skull.

Perhaps the best-known use of head is in brawn (or head cheese). Traditionally pig's head is used, but calf's head or beef trimmings may also be used in the proportion of three-quarters pork to one-quarter veal or beef. The jowls from the pig's head are often removed to reduce fattiness of the finished brawn. Boiled pig's head meat is included in liverwurst (liver sausage). In France, calf's head halved or quartered and with the brains removed is boiled and served as a hot or cold hors d'oeuvre with a vinaigrette dressing. It is called, obviously, 'calf's head vinaigrette' or 'tête de veau vinaigrette'. Also in France, boiled ox muzzle or pig's snout thinly sliced, well seasoned and with a vinaigrette sauce is served as a cold hors d'oeuvre or a cold salad. They are known respectively as 'museau de boeuf' and 'museau de porc'. 'La salade Lyonnaise', yet another French hors d'oeuvre, consists of several different cooked meats in separate bowls, each seasoned well with oil, vinegar, shallots (spring onions, scallions) and parsley. The meats may include sliced calf's head, sliced ox muzzle, sheep's or pig's trotters cut into chunks, sliced boiled beef and lightly smoked French cervelat sausage.

Ox cheek is a tough cut, but an economical one for stews and casseroles. A long, slow cooking of up to 5 hours is required. Ponhaws and scrapple are old-fashioned Pennsylvanian dishes of German origin from the early settlers in the United States of America. Pig's head is the basis for both recipes, with the tongue, pig's feet or trotters, tail, skin, heart and all pork trimmings included in scrapple. Boiled sheep's or lamb's head may be used for broths, soups and pie fillings. Pig's head meat may also be included in mincemeat.

Tail

Oxtail is the best-known 'culinary' tail. It is rather tough and strong in flavour and requires a long, slow stewing. Leftover stewed oxtail pieces can be seasoned, buttered and grilled (broiled) under a medium heat until sufficiently hot. Serve with a spicy sauce, selection of chutneys or thin gravy.

Pig's tail can be included in Scrapple (*see* p. 126). A traditional method of eating tail is skewered and roasted over an open fire until well cooked and crispy on the outside. Salt is usually rubbed well into the skin before cooking.

Feet

Pig's feet or trotters should be well shaved; calf's and sheep's should be skinned. In pig's feet, glandular tissue between the toes should be removed and dew claws should have previously been removed. Pig's trotters may be included with the head for making brawn or scrapple, or may be pickled. As already mentioned, boiled and cubed pig's trotter meat may be included in 'la salade Lyonnaise'. Another French method of preparation is 'grilled pig's trotters', otherwise known as 'pieds de porc panés' or 'pieds de porc Sainte Ménéhould'. The trotters are served with plenty of sauce tartare or remoulade. A more elaborate method of preparation involves boning the cooked trotters and stuffing them with chopped pork or sausagemeat (fresh sausage) and truffles. To bind them securely, they are wrapped in pig's caul (the membrane which covers the stomach), and are then grilled (broiled). A rather expensive and lengthy process and one which I have not yet tried. A fine example of how well the French cope with less usual cuts of meat and manage to turn them into interesting and tasty dishes. This one is known as 'pieds de porc truffés'.

For extra flavour in a beef stew or casserole, pig's trotters may be included but removed before serving. Ox (beef or steer) feet may be included in the dish 'tripe à la mode de Caen'. This is a French dish basically consisting of ox tripe, vegetables, cider and brandy. It is cooked for about 12 hours. The full recipe is to be found in Escoffier's *Guide to Modern Cookery*, published by Heinemann in 1956.

Ox foot or calf's foot contains much gelatine which may be extracted by boiling. The resulting meat stock has to be clarified (ie strained), and all fat removed before it is ready for use. It is known as 'aspic jelly'.

Sheep's trotters may be prepared and used in 'la salade Lyonnaise' or may be substituted for pig's trotters in the recipe 'pieds de porc Sainte Ménéhould'.

Tongue

Ox (beef) tongue or calf's tongue may be boiled and pickled. Salted ox tongue may be boiled, skinned and pressed. It is served thinly sliced as a cold salad meat. Tongue is included in many mixed offal (variety meat) dishes.

Mincemeat of the kind we know in the traditional Christmas mince pies was originally a sweet and sour mixture of minced meat. The basic ingredients were minced (ground) meat, suet, fresh and dried fruits (eg apple, nuts, citron), molasses (dark treacle), sugar, spices, brandy or other alcoholic liquor or cider. Minced (ground), boiled ox tongue was sometimes used for the meat ingredient. Pig's tongue may be included in the making of scrapple, ponhaws and liver paste. Lamb's tongue, obviously small and tender, may be boiled or braised. Like ox tongue, it is skinned, pressed and cut into thin slices. Sheep's tongue is used in sausages.

Sweetbreads

There are two types of sweetbread. The stomach sweetbread is an internal organ near the heart called the 'pancreas'. The second type is the neck or throat sweetbread which is called the 'thymus gland'. The latter is believed to be the finest in flavour. Sweetbreads must be treated carefully or they will literally fall apart. First they are soaked for 3 hours in several changes of water. Then they are placed in a saucepan with enough water to cover them, and brought slowly to the boil and allowed to boil for just 2 minutes. The sweetbreads are removed, drained a little and placed in very cold water to cool them quickly. They are then pressed between two plates, the upper one being weighted. Once pressed, they are firm enough to handle and the tubes and rough and horny parts can be removed.

Calf's sweetbreads are reputed to be the best with lamb's a close second. After blanching, they may be braised or thinly sliced and fried, and are usually served with a black butter sauce. Ox (beef or steer) sweetbreads are not popular as they are tough and strong in flavour.

Kidneys

Kidneys straight from the slaughtered animal are covered with a layer of fat and with a thin membrane. Remove both before cooking. (Kidney fat from pigs is said to make excellent lard.) Kidneys should be halved and the core removed before cooking. Ox (beef or steer) kidney is soaked in warm salted water for several hours before cooking. Perhaps one of the best-known English dishes is the ubiquitous steak-and-kidney pie or steak-and-kidney pudding. Ox kidney is most suited to this type of dish requiring a long, slow cooking. In the case of the pie, the steak-and-kidney filling must be cooked separately first. In the pudding, where a suet pastry is used, the meats are added raw and the pudding is steamed for 3–4 hours. I find ox kidney rather too strong in flavour and rarely cook it. Sliced ox kidney may be braised or stewed. Calf's kidney is more tender than that of ox, but is generally treated in the same way, ie soaking followed by stewing or braising. Pig's kidney is strong in flavour and should be skinned, soaked (as for ox kidney) and blanched (boiled) for 1 minute before using. Suitable methods of cooking are grilling, frying, stewing and casseroling.

Lamb's kidney has the most delicate flavour and is tender too. Good for frying or grilling (broiling) or kebabs. It may be soaked prior to use, but needs no blanching. Remove the fine skin and any blood vessels or fat deposits before cooking.

Heart

Rinse hearts in cold water and remove remains of arteries, veins and tendons.

Ox (Beef or steer) Heart I find this very tough and strong in flavour and prefer to set it aside for the cat as it is her favourite dish! However, for those with different tastes, it may be cut up in smallish cubes and stewed or casseroled. A long, slow cooking is suitable.

Calf's Heart This is more tender than ox (beef or steer) heart. We enjoy stuffed braised heart. It may also be pot-roasted.

Pig's Heart This is included in the making of scrapple or it may be stuffed and braised. It is also an ingredient in liverwurst (liver sausage).

Lamb's Heart Quite small and tender and suitable for stuffing and braising (*see* recipe p. 139), or pot-roasting. Sheep's heart is used in Scottish haggis (*see* p. 138).

Stomach or Tripe

The inner lining of ox (beef or steer), calf or sheep stomach is called 'tripe'. Ox tripe is the one most commonly found in butchers' shops. There are two kinds—smooth and honeycomb, which come from the first and second ox stomachs, respectively. The stomachs, when removed after slaughtering, are emptied of their contents, turned inside out and washed thoroughly in several changes of water. The next step is scalding in water at a temperature of about 65°C or 150°F. The inner lining is then scraped and scraped until very white. The next step is boiling for about 3 hours or until tender. The tripe is removed to a large pan of cold water and the fat on the outer layer is scraped off. Following this, the outer membrane is peeled off. The tripe is then ready for cooking or pickling. The most tender tripe comes from calf. Good tripe should be thick, firm, fat and white. It has a very mild flavour, but if cooked carefully with vegetables and herbs can make a tasty dish. It may be stewed, boiled in milk, sliced and deep-fried, or coated with egg and breadcrumbs and grilled (broiled). The latter is a French dish called 'tablier de sapeur' and the tripe is served with a tartare sauce. Another French tripe dish is 'tripe à la mode de Caen', where the tripe is cooked with ox feet—*see* further details of this dish under 'Feet' in this section.

Pig's stomach and intestines are called chitterlings. The stomach may be used as an ingredient of scrapple, cooked sausage or brawn, or as a container or casing for brawn. To prepare a pig's stomach, make a small slit in the small end, empty the stomach contents and turn the stomach inside out. Wash well in plenty of cold water and immerse in almost boiling water to scald. This allows the inner lining to be scraped off. When this has been done, the stomach is ready for use. If the stomach is to be used in one of the meat products, the stomach may be slit right open to aid cleaning and scraping.

Sheep's stomach is used as the casing for Scottish haggis (to prepare the stomach, follow the method for pig's stomach). Haggis is a mixture of heart, lungs (also called 'lights'), liver, oatmeal, suet and herbs. To cook, it may be boiled or baked, or sliced and fried.

Small Intestines

The small intestines of pork and sheep are suitable as sausage casings. Ox (beef or steer) or calf intestines are too thick and tough. The intestines are covered in a layer of fat called 'ruffle fat'. This can be removed easily and in one piece by pulling the fat and the intestines in opposite directions. Next the intestines are turned inside out and the inner mucous layer is completely scraped away. This is a fairly long process and must be done absolutely thoroughly. Several scrapings followed each time by washing in warm water may be needed. When completed, the intestines will be clear with no dull patches.

To help with turning intestines inside out, they should be cut into several lengths. Each is then dealt with separately. One end is turned back on itself. Water is poured into the turned-up area, the weight of which will pull down more intestine. More water is added and the process is continued until the whole length is reversed. Sausage casings may be stored in dry salt until needed. After storing in this way, they must be thoroughly washed inside and out before using.

Liver

Lamb's and calf's livers are thought to be the best. Both are tender and lack the strong flavour associated with pig's and ox (beef or steer) livers. Both may be sliced and grilled (broiled), or fried until just cooked. Sheep's liver is an ingredient in haggis. Pig's liver is usually cooked with other ingredients to tone down the flavour, eg with bacon in a liver-and-bacon casserole, with pork in pâté, or with plenty of herbs and seasonings, as in Peppery Liver (see 'Beef', p. 111).

Ox liver I find much too strong in flavour, and like ox heart, I allow our cat this share of the slaughtered beast! However, it may be used in stews and casseroles together with other meats and is included in liver sausage, though only in a 10–20% proportion by weight. To reduce its strong flavour, it should be sliced thickly and soaked in milk or slightly salted water for several hours.

Brains

Calf's brains are considered the best with lamb's and then sheep's following. They must be soaked in cold water first to remove all traces of blood. Soak for at least 2 hours and change the water several times. The brains are removed, drained and scraped of all their skin, and all tubes and rough parts are removed. They are then soaked in fresh cold water for another ½ hour. Brains may be poached or sliced and gently fried.

Blood

Pig's blood finds a use in black pudding. The blood is mixed with shredded suet, oatmeal, minced onions and plenty of salt and pepper. Other seasonings may be added depending on the locality. The French prefer beetroot (beets) or garlic; the Spanish, fennel; the Germans, thyme and/or marjoram; the Americans, sage; and, in some parts of England, caraway and coriander are used. Pig's intestines are used for the casings. Once prepared, the pudding is boiled until cooked. It can then be stored until required. It is thickly sliced and grilled (broiled) or fried, or it may be eaten cold.

Fat

A large proportion of animal fat can go into the making of sausages. Sausages should contain about one-third by weight of fat. The fat to be used is the leaf fat (which is attached to the diaphragm), back fat, kidney fat and fat trimmings from the cutting of the main carcass.

Fat not used in sausages may be rendered down as lard. Pig's fat is the preferred fat for this purpose. The fat is cut into small pieces and any lean meat is trimmed off and discarded. Skin should also be cut away. The fat is then coarsely ground and placed in a large, heavy-based saucepan (it should only be about half full). The pan is placed over a very low heat to begin melting the fat. As it does so, the heat may be increased to medium, stirring frequently during heating. When rendering is almost complete, small pieces of crackling will float to the surface. You may remove the pan from the heat at this stage, though it is perhaps better to render a little further to evaporate more water and improve storing quality. When cracklings sink to the bottom of the pan, the fat is completely rendered. It is allowed to cool a little and is strained through a double thickness of cheesecloth (muslin) and poured into clean containers. If possible, the lard should be cooled quickly. This makes for a finer grained lard. To store lard successfully, light and air should be avoided. The lard containers should be filled as full as possible, covered with tightly fitting lids and stored in a cool, dark place.

Fat from around the intestines (ruffle fat), fat from around the stomach (caul fat) and any other waste or spare fat trimmings may be rendered down and used for making soap.

Suet is the fat that accumulates around the kidneys of ox (beef or steer) and sheep. It is grated or shredded for use in suet crust pastry and mincemeat, or may be rendered down into lard.

Poultry

This is not the appropriate place to describe methods of killing poultry and I must refer you to Ashbrook's book listed in the Bibliography. However, one point worthy of mention here is that following the kill of any fowl, the brain should be pierced. This relaxes the muscles of the feather follicles and makes plucking an easier task. Also, there is a lessened risk of tearing the skin, which should be avoided for the sake of the appearance of the dressed bird.

Plucking

Plucking is best done soon after killing, while the bird is still warm. The feathers then come away more easily. The following is the 'dry method' and is the most appropriate to anyone plucking small numbers of fowls at home. I like to be properly organised for the plucking and drawing job as it's one I hate. If possible, pluck and draw outside where the breeze will blow away the tiny feathers and the smell.

Place the bird on a table or flat board and have ready a sharp knife, a deep, strong paper bag and a clean pillowcase. Use drawing pins to attach the latter two to your table so that the openings are clear for you to drop in feathers easily. Lay the bird on its back and begin at the breast. Pluck the feathers slightly up and with the 'grain', ie in the direction in which they naturally lay flat. Work over the whole breast down to the vent and up the neck to just below the head. Deposit the soft downy feathers in the pillowcase. Any longer, tougher ones are placed in the paper bag. As you find the feathers becoming larger and tougher, pull up and slightly against the 'grain'. Now work over both legs and the underside of the wings. Again, segregate the soft downy feathers from the tough ones and place in the appropriate receptacle. Once the underside is complete, turn the bird over and pluck this side completely too. The wing tips may be cut off at the first joint and deposited in the paper bag.

When plucking is complete, look over the bird and remove any feather quills that have been missed. Then, to finish the job properly, singe the remaining tiny feathers with a lighted taper, or even a low gas flame. Tie the paper bag closed and bury it in the middle of the compost heap. The pillowcase should be tied tightly with string and thrown with the next wash into the washing machine. Lay it flat to dry. Now you have begun your first feather pillow!

Drawing

Lay the bird on its back and, using a small, sharp knife, cut the skin along the length of the neck on the underside up to the start of the body. Cut off and discard the head. Now lift the skin up and away from the neck bones, using a knife if necessary to cut through the membranes joining skin to neck flesh. Pull or cut out the neck and set aside to make stock. Gently but firmly, pull out the crop, gizzard and windpipe. Leave the neck skin flap intact as this is used later to seal off this end of the carcass. Insert your hand into the neck cavity and, pushing forward, gently but firmly separate the internal organs from the ribcage.

Now turn the bird around (but still on its back) and work at the vent end. Make a horizontal slit just above the vent, but do this very carefully so as not to cut the intestines below. Put your hand through the slit and up into the ribcage of the bird. Gently but firmly feel around and loosen all of the vital organs, then pull them down toward you. Pull out the body contents, which of course will still be attached by the lower end to the vent. Having a clear view, you can now cut the skin around the vent easily without danger of piercing the intestine and contaminating the carcass with faecal matter. Cut away any excess fat, which you will see as lumpy yellow or white masses just inside the rear cavity. Cut off the feet at the hock joint. The feet when thoroughly cleaned may be added to the stock pot or toasted over an open fire until crispy and browned, and then seasoned well. I'm told they are delicious, but I'm afraid I haven't been brave enough to try them myself.

Now remove the oil gland which sits on the top of the tail. The oil from this gland can impart an unsavoury taste to the meat during cooking. Finally, fold the wings and legs neatly in place and secure with string or elastic (rubber) bands.

Ageing

This process is described in general methods of meat cookery and is there referred to as 'hanging'. Poultry is aged by chilling for several hours. You may place the bird in the refrigerator and/or on a bed of ice, turning frequently to ensure an even cooling. Always allow a good circulation of air around the bird and chill as quickly as possible. Ageing time depends on the age and size of the bird and ranges from 4 to 6 hours for an average-sized broiler through to 12 hours for a full-sized turkey. When aged, the bird is ready to cook immediately or may be stored in the deepfreeze.

Offal

Locate the liver lobes and gently detach them, and remove and discard the gall bladder. The liver may be quickly frozen and made into pâté when enough livers have been accumulated, or it may be used, together with the heart, as an ingredient of bread stuffing (*see* stuffings, p. 230). Locate the heart and lungs and set aside with the neck for making stock. Discard the remainder of the inside organs—intestines, windpipe, gizzard and crop.

Trussing

For roasting, the bird is left whole and, to make a compact, neat-looking carcass, it is trussed. If the bird is to be stuffed, do this now from either neck or vent end before trussing begins.

At the neck end, fold the neck skin flap neatly up over the back of the bird, pull the wings up on each side and neatly fold them to hold the skin in place. Use a trussing needle with white string or very strong thread and push through one end of the wing, then through the body and the other wing. Now pass the needle through the other end of the wing, through the body and the other wing back to the original side of the bird. Pull the string taut and tie the two ends of the string.

At the vent end, make a slit 1–2 cm (½–1 in) above the vent hole and push the tail (parson's (pope's) nose) through this slit, which seals off this end of the body cavity. You will note at this stage the importance of having made as small a hole as possible during the drawing process. Now bring the two hock joints up to either side of the tail. Knot string around the tail, then loop firmly around each hock joint. Pull tight and tie.

Jointing

If it is not to be cooked whole, a chicken may be jointed as follows. Cut off the wings at the joint closest to the body. Cut off each leg at its thigh joint (that closest to the body) and, if you wish, each leg may be cut in half at the middle or knee joint. Lay the bird on its back and cut lengthwise through the bird along each side to separate the upper breast from the backbone half. You may now cut the breast meat from the bone or divide the breast half into portions by cutting across or lengthwise along the keel or breast bone. The back may be cut lengthwise along one side of the backbone and/or crosswise into suitably-sized portions.

Boning a Chicken

This takes much practice, so be patient with your failures! Begin by sitting the bird upright on its tail. Using a small, very sharp knife, slice cleanly between flesh and bone. If you hold the flesh up and out with one hand and cut with the knife in the other, you will find the job easier. Always hold the flesh as close as you can to the bone to avoid tearing. Work down and around the carcass until you reach the wing shoulder joint. Work around the joint and stop. Cut off the two end sections of the wing, leaving only the main wing bone. Now return to the shoulder wing joint and cut down and around the bone almost to its end. Cut through the bone, leaving the tip in place. Repeat with the second wing. Having freed the wing flesh, work down and around the body until you reach the legs. For ease of working, pull the skin and flesh down and inside out over the unboned part, rather like pulling off a tight jumper. Cut around the thigh joint, then gradually work down the leg. If it makes it easier, cut through the thigh joint so that you have more manoeuvrability of the leg. Keep slicing flesh from bone until you get to just below the drumstick flesh. Cut right through the bone, leaving the tip of the drumstick bone in place. Repeat with the second leg and continue working down until you reach the tail. Cut through the backbone so that the tail remains with the skin and flesh. Turn the chicken shell right side out. You may now stuff the boned carcass as you wish, sealing off the neck and vent ends by sewing neatly but firmly with strong thread. The wings and legs will be sealed already by the bone tips which have been left in place. Also sew together any mistake holes.

Note: If you find this totally impossible, try making an incision along the length of the backbone and work from there round to the sides, over the wings and legs to the breast. When boning is complete, sew the incision and treat as above.

Roasting

A popular method of cooking, but only applicable to young, tender birds. The meat of chicken, turkey, guinea fowl and wild goose has a tendency to be dry, especially the thicker breast meat. To combat this, the bird may be barded—ie bacon rashers (slices) or fresh pork fat are placed over the breast meat and tied in place with cotton thread (string) (wrapped around the whole carcass). The fat from the bacon melts slowly during cooking and bastes the breast meat.

Alternatively, the bird may be roasted on its side so that the breast meat is in contact with the fatty juices that drip into the pan. The bird must be turned onto its other side halfway through cooking. In both cases, the bird is also rubbed well with softened butter or oil. Domestic goose and duck, ie those bred for the table, tend to be very greasy. No barding is necessary and, especially with goose, the bird should sit on a grid (rack) which holds it above the fatty juices collecting in the pan. Also, the fat collected in the roasting pan is poured off after the first 30 minutes of cooking. A little seasoned stock may then be added to maintain moistness.

Poultry may also be roasted in a pot on the top of the stove. A little butter is melted in the bottom of a very heavy pot (eg cast-ironware) and a few thinly sliced vegetables, eg onion and carrot, are added. They are cooked gently and, when softened, the bird is added. The bird must be turned frequently during cooking and must be cooked over a fairly low heat. Again, with domestic duck and goose it may be necessary to pour off excess fat during cooking.

Roasting may also be done on a spit. The meat is brushed with oil or rubbed with a little softened butter and seasoned before cooking. Roasting temperature for most poultry should be around 200°C or 400°F. Turkey and goose, however, require a longer, slower cooking and an oven temperature of 150°–180°C or 300°–350°F is most suitable. Cooking times are as follows (all weights are oven-ready weights).

Roasting Times Roasting times can be taken from these outlined below. Alternatively, a meat thermometer can be used. Poultry is cooked when the thermometer, inserted into the thickest part of the thigh, reads 85°C (185°F). Also, if you tip the bird and the juices run clear, it is done. If the juices are pink or red, it's not.

Chicken
200°C or 400°F
35 minutes per kg (16 minutes per lb),
plus 10 minutes extra.

Duck
200°C or 400°F
45 minutes per kg (20 minutes per lb).

Goose
180°C or 350°F
55 minutes per kg (25 minutes per lb).

Turkey
170°C or 325°F
3 kg (7 lb): 3 hours
4 kg (9 lb): 3½ hours
5 kg (11 lb): 3¾ hours
6 kg (13 lb): 4¼ hours
7 kg (15½ lb): 4½ hours
8 kg (17½ lb): 4¾ hours
9 kg (20 lb): 5¼ hours
10 kg (22 lb): 6 hours

Seasoning The outside of the meat can be seasoned with a little salt, paprika or finely chopped herbs after the bird has been rubbed all over with oil or butter (and before barding, if this is to be done). Alternatively, herb sprigs and/or a little sliced vegetable, eg onion, may be placed inside the carcass.

A stuffing can be prepared and packed loosely inside the carcass. Forcemeat stuffing is based on fresh breadcrumbs flavoured with chopped onion and herbs. Stuffings based on rice or sausagemeat (fresh sausage) are other popular alternatives. Sausagemeat stuffing is often recommended for large birds, as it helps maintain the meat's moistness. Generally, stuffing is placed in the main body cavity. Two stuffings may be used, one in the neck end and the other in the middle area. When dealing with large birds such as turkey, which have a tendency towards dryness, it is common to prepare a stuffing which is placed between the skin and the breast meat. The skin can be lifted gently from the breast meat to produce a small space in which stuffing can be placed. It should be packed loosely so that the skin does not split during cooking. Our favourite at home was always a sausagemeat (fresh sausage) stuffing over the breast meat. It is high in fat and will automatically baste the poultry meat during cooking.

Some Traditional Accompaniments to Roast Poultry

Gravy A stock is prepared by boiling together in water the poultry giblets and a few vegetables— onion, carrots and finely chopped herbs. The stock should be boiled gently or simmered with the pan covered for 45–60 minutes. It is then strained and gravy is prepared in the usual way, using the giblet stock as the liquid content.

Bread Sauce See recipe in sauces section, p. 219.

Sausages Small cocktail sausages (chipolatas) are most suitable. They should be added to the roasting pan 30 minutes before the end of cooking.

Bacon Rolls Remove rind and cut each rasher (slice) in half. Roll up each half and secure with a wooden cocktail stick (toothpick). Add to roasting dish 30 minutes before end of cooking.

Stuffing As explained in the section on seasoning, it is customary to stuff the cavity of the bird with a stuffing generally based on seasoned breadcrumbs. Two or three different types of stuffing may be used: one kind in the main body cavity, one in the neck and the other under the skin between it and the breast meat. *See* recipes in stuffings, p. 230.

Apple Sauce See recipe in sauces, p. 225.

Casseroling and Stewing

A moist, fairly slow cooking is essential for older birds or for game birds whose age is uncertain. A little butter or oil is heated gently in the bottom of a heavy-based pan. A little chopped onion, herbs and other vegetables (eg carrots, leeks) are added and fried gently until just beginning to soften. The meat, whole or jointed, is added and, with the heat on medium, is browned a little all over. At this stage, excess fat can be poured off. This will be essential for domestic duck and goose, which has very greasy meat. Liquid is then added to the pan to barely cover meat. (The liquid may be vegetable or meat stock, or wine and water.) The pan is covered and cooking continues either on the top of the stove (cooker) over a low heat or in the oven at a low to moderate temperature of 150°–170°C or 300°–325°F. Cooking time will vary according to size and age of bird. A boiling fowl, whole, will take several hours, whereas a smaller, younger bird may take only 1½ hours. When dealing with fatty birds, it is advisable to pour off all liquid into a separate dish. Allow to cool a little when cooking is complete. The fat will solidify and float, and can be skimmed off and the liquid reheated and returned to casserole dish.

Seasoning Salt, black pepper, paprika and/or chopped herbs are added to butter or oil at the same time as vegetables.

Grilling (Broiling) and Barbecuing

Grilling (broiling) and barbecuing are suitable only for young, tender meat in small portions. Young hens, petit poussin (squab, Cornish hens), pigeon or young guinea fowl are halved lengthwise. Quail may be grilled whole, and duck and chicken should be cut into leg and wing portions. The meat is brushed with melted butter or a little oil, and seasoned with salt and finely chopped herbs. It is placed on a grilling grid (rack) or speared onto wooden or metal skewers and grilled or barbecued. Grilling temperature should be moderate and the meat should be turned and basted frequently. Alternatively, the meat can be marinated in a little white wine or orange juice for 1–2 hours before cooking.

Note: Guinea fowl have a tendency to be dry. Baste meat extra well during cooking and serve with a sauce.

Frying/Sautéing

Only small portions of tender meat are suitable for this method. The meat may be brushed with melted butter and coated thinly and evenly with a little flour, or it may be brushed with a little beaten egg and coated with breadcrumbs. A frying batter may also be used if meat is to be deep-fried.

Shallow-frying (Sautéing) Butter or oil is used. It is heated until quite hot and meat pieces are added. Cooking takes place at a fairly high heat to seal the outside of the meat. The pieces should be turned frequently and, when browned a little and evenly, heat is reduced to medium. A slower cooking proceeds until meat is tender—15–20 minutes in all.

Chicken pieces cooked in this way and served with a white sauce thickened with a little egg yolk are the French dish 'poulet fricassé'.

Deep-frying Meat pieces are coated evenly in a frying batter or egg and breadcrumbs, and dropped into deep, hot oil (approx. 190°C or 375°F). Cooking takes 10–15 minutes for white meat, 20–25 minutes for dark meat. If you cut near the bone and juices run clear, it's done.

FRYING BATTER

100 g (3½ oz) plain (all-purpose) flour
½ an egg, beaten
70 ml (2½ fl oz) water
70 ml (2½ fl oz) milk
1 tablespoon oil

Place flour in a bowl. Make a well in centre. Add beaten egg, water, milk and oil to the well. Gradually mix wet and dry ingredients together. Beat for several minutes with a rotary whisk. Use to coat and deep-fry chicken or young rabbit.

Seasoning The meat can be seasoned before being coated or the coating itself can be seasoned before using. Salt, paprika and finely chopped herbs are all suitable.

Boiling

Boiling is usually applied to older, tougher birds. The meat, whole or jointed, is placed in a deep pan. Seasoning and chopped herbs are added, with a small quantity of sliced vegetables (eg onions, carrots). Water is added to completely cover meat. Cooking may take place in a slow oven, or very slowly on top of the stove (cooker) for 2–3 hours, depending on size and age of bird. In both cases, the cooking pot should be tightly covered. The cooked meat is removed, allowed to drain a little and served hot or cold, plain or with a sauce. This is an excellent way of cooking poultry for invalids, young children or those with a more delicate digestion.

A traditional French dish, 'la poule farcie en daube à la berrichonne', shows the French cook's aptitude for turning otherwise dull fare into an interesting and tasty meal. Old laying hens or boiling fowl are used. The bird is boned, stuffed and simmered slowly, together with a calf's foot, in veal stock with plenty of herbs and seasonings. When cooked, the chicken is served cold, coated in the jelly sauce.

Duck can also be boiled. I always remove excess fat from beneath the skin before boiling to reduce fattiness. The resulting stock should be cooled and skimmed before further use.

Stir-frying

Only meat from tender young birds should be used for stir-frying. Cut meat into thin strips about ½–1 cm (¼–½ in) thick and 4–5 cm (1½–2 in) long. Season meat well and stir-fry in usual way, allowing 5–7 minutes for meat to cook (*see* notes on stir-frying, p. 11).

Rabbit

Rabbit meat is an excellent source of protein and is low in fat. Domestic grain-fed rabbits have a fine-textured white meat similar in appearance and flavour to chicken. Young domestic rabbit weighing 1–1½ kg (2–3½ lb) may be shallow fried, deep-fried or stir-fried, roasted or braised. Older rabbit is best stewed or boiled. Wild rabbit is darker in colour, likely to be tougher except when very young and has a more gamey flavour. Very young wild rabbits may be roasted or fried, but overall the best methods are braising, stewing and boiling.

Skinning a Rabbit

Skinning a rabbit is fairly easy and has been likened to pulling off a tight jumper (sweater)! Hang the animal by its right hind leg, belly towards you. You can tie a piece of stout string onto the leg or use the space between the bone and tendon very close to the hock joint to hang the animal from a nail or hook. Now cut off the left hind leg at the hock joint, and the front paws at the first joint. Cut off the head and the tail. Starting at the cut end of the right hind leg, lift the skin from the flesh on the inside of the leg. Using a sharp knife, gently cut through the membranes under the skin. Now using a pair of round-ended scissors, snip the skin down the inside of the leg through to the anus, continuing up the inside of the right hind leg to the hock joint, and cut around the joint. As you cut, use the scissors to lift the skin gently but firmly away from the flesh. Using your sharp knife again, work at the cut end of the left leg, pulling the skin away from the flesh and cutting through the membranes holding the skin and flesh together. Work around the leg until you have about 2 cm (1 in) of skin freed. Then work along the front cut edge of the skin, down the inside of the leg, across the anus and up the inside of the right leg, pulling and separating about 2 cm (1 in) of skin from flesh. Go around the right leg, again down the inside of the leg, but this time working on the rear cut edge, then through to the anus and up to the rear cut edge on the inside of the left leg. Every cut edge of skin should now be well pulled away from the flesh and so, in the next steps of 'unpeeling', will not likely tear as you pull.

Grip the freed skin on each leg and pull firmly downward. You should find that the skin just peels off. Continue 'unpeeling', pulling down firmly right down over the belly, chest, front legs and neck. If you encounter difficult parts, stop and, using your sharp knife, gently but firmly cut through the membranes that are holding flesh and skin together. When pulling, hold the skin as close as is comfortable to the body to prevent tearing. You may later cut the skin up the belly to open it out for drying and tanning if you wish.

Paunching

Lay the animal on a flat board on its back. With sharp scissors, cut from the anus up the middle of the belly to the breastbone. By hand, gently but firmly draw out the body cavity contents. Locate and set aside the heart and liver. Discard the remainder. Wash the rabbit well in cold running water and drain or dry with a cloth.

Jointing

You may roast or braise your rabbit whole, otherwise joint it as follows. Cut off each front leg at the shoulder. Cut off each hind leg at the thigh. On small rabbits these are left whole, but on larger ones cut each hind leg in half at the middle joint. Using scissors, cut around the base of the ribcage, down the side of the body and around to the anus to remove one belly skin flap. Repeat to remove the one on the other side. Discard these. The remaining body section may be cut as you prefer, either lengthwise along the backbone and/or crosswise into sections of a suitable size.

Roasting

You may stuff rabbit with a forcemeat or bread stuffing to enhance its flavour, and then sew belly flaps together again. To improve the appearance of the rabbit, fix front and hind legs in place bent up close to the body, either using skewers or by tying with string. Only 7%

of the total weight of a dressed rabbit comprises fat, compared to chicken which is 14% fat. Therefore, a rabbit must be rubbed thoroughly all over with fat or oil, and is generally barded with strips of fatty bacon or pork fat (ie rashers (slices) are placed over breast meat and tied in place with cotton thread (string) wrapped around the carcass—fat from the bacon melts slowly during cooking and bastes meat). During cooking, rabbit must be basted frequently.

Roasting Times Cook at 180°C or 350°F
Young rabbit of 1–1½ kg (2–3½ lb): 1½–1¾ hours
Older rabbit of 2–3 kg (4½–7 lb): 2–2½ hours

Braising

You may braise young rabbit whole or otherwise joint it. Rub meat thoroughly all over with plenty of oil. Roll in seasoned flour until evenly coated. Pour a little oil in the bottom of a frying pan (skillet). Heat until quite hot. Add rabbit and allow to brown for a minute or two, turning meat to ensure even sealing. Remove to a deep ovenproof dish, season liberally with herbs and, if you wish, add a few vegetables, eg onion, carrot, green capsicum (sweet pepper). Pour a little stock and/or light wine into pan, stir well to remove juices from the pan and pour over meat. The meat should be a quarter to half covered with liquid during cooking. Cover dish tightly. Place in a preheated oven at 170°C or 325°F for 1½–2 hours until tender. The cooking time will depend on the age of the animal and the thickness of the meat. Once or twice during cooking, turn meat over and stir braising sauce. Alternatively, follow these directions, but instead of cooking in the oven, simmer very gently in a pan on top of the stove (cooker).

Note: For extra flavour, you may add one or several of the following: tomatoes—halved or chopped, tomato purée (*see* p. 221), bacon strips, pork strips (belly pork is especially suitable) or cubes of potato.

Frying/Sautéing

Frying/sautéing is only applicable to young, jointed rabbit. Follow the directions given under the frying of poultry, p. 90.

Stewing and Casseroling

Follow directions given for poultry on p. 89, but omit the pouring off of fat. As explained before (see 'Roasting'), rabbit is low in fat and excess fat is not a problem when stewing and casseroling.

Grilling (Broiling) and Barbecuing

Grilling (broiling) and barbecuing are really only suitable for very young domestic rabbits. Season well with herbs and black pepper. Coat well with butter before cooking. When grilling (broiling), you can catch fat and baste frequently, which really is best as rabbit easily becomes dry.

Boiling

You may boil (or even pressure cook) a jointed rabbit until completely tender to use the meat in pies, pasties or similar. Alternatively, cook rabbit until half tender (about 45 minutes). While it is cooking, slice an onion, a carrot and two garlic cloves thinly and fry in plenty of oil. Remove these to a deep ovenproof dish and rinse frying pan (skillet) with a little of the rabbit's boiling water, and a little wine if you wish. When rabbit is half cooked, remove from pan, drain well and place in dish with vegetables. Now follow directions for latter half of 'Braising' on previous page, cooking in the oven at 170°C or 325°F until tender.

Note: Have your ovenproof dish prepared and already hot so that the rabbit is transferred immediately to the oven without being allowed to cool.

Stir-frying

Stir-frying is only suitable for very young domestic rabbit. Cut meat from bones and slice thinly. Stir-fry for several minutes in shallow oil with plenty of herbs and seasonings. Very thinly sliced vegetables may be stir-fried with rabbit for improved flavour. Onion, garlic, green capsicum (sweet pepper), bean sprouts, sliced ginger root and tender greens are suitable.

Beef

BOILED BRISKET

Serves 6

2 tablespoons honey

2½ tablespoons ground coriander

1 boned rolled brisket or *silverside*

(about 1 kg/2¼ lb)

Gently warm honey and stir in coriander. Place brisket in a bowl. Spoon over honey mixture so that each surface is covered. Using the back of a spoon, rub mixture into meat a little. Cover brisket. Set aside in the refrigerator or a cool place for 24 hours. Check brisket once or twice during that time. Spoon over meat any honey mixture that has dribbled off.

Heat a large pan of water. When boiling, drop in brisket. Scrape any dribbled-off honey from bowl and add to water. Cover pan and simmer for 2–2¾ hours or until meat is tender. Remove pan from heat and allow to cool. When cold, remove meat. Drain for a few minutes, slice thinly and serve.

SWEET AND SOUR BEEF IN EGG ROLLS

Serves 3 or 6

SWEET AND SOUR BEEF

1 onion

2 tablespoons oil

500 g (1 lb) brisket (short plate) or
flank of beef

200 ml (7 fl oz) water

1½ tablespoons malt vinegar

2 teaspoons golden syrup
(light treacle)

2 tablespoons tomato purée
(see p. 221)

½ teaspoon lemon balm,
finely chopped

1 teaspoon soy sauce

EGG ROLLS

6 eggs, lightly beaten

6 tablespoons water

3 tablespoons wholemeal
(whole-wheat) flour

margarine

SWEET AND SOUR BEEF

Thinly slice onion. Fry gently in oil until soft. Slice beef into very thin strips. Add to cooked onion. Cook over a high heat for 2 minutes to seal outside of meat. Add water, reduce heat and simmer gently with pan covered for 2 hours. Stir in vinegar, syrup, tomato purée, lemon balm and soy sauce. Continue to simmer with pan uncovered for a further 30 minutes.

EGG ROLLS

Break eggs into a bowl and beat a little. Stir in water and flour. Melt a little margarine in an omelette pan (just enough to coat bottom of pan). When sizzling, add a little egg mixture (one-sixth). Cook egg pancake over a medium heat for several minutes until bottom has browned a little and top has all but set. Now, using a fishslice (spatula), carefully and gently lift pancake and turn it over. Cook on second side for 1 minute.

Spoon a little meat mixture onto one side of pancake. Roll pancake over and over to make a meat roll. Turn onto a warmed plate and set in a warm place. Repeat to make a total of six egg and meat rolls. Serve with freshly boiled plain rice.

Note: This dish may be prepared as a main course: offer two rolls per person, *or* as an hors d'oeuvre: offer one roll per person.

SWEET PEPPER CURRY

Serves 4

1 large onion

6 teaspoons curry powder (see p. 114)

2 teaspoons paprika

2 tablespoons oil

650 g (1½ lb) shin (shank) of beef

300 ml (1¼ cups, 10½ fl oz)
beef stock

2 large green capsicum
(sweet peppers)

2 large red capsicum (sweet peppers)

Slice onion. Place in a heavy-based pan with curry powder, paprika and oil. Fry gently until onion is soft. Cut shin into thin pieces (approx. 2 × 3 × ½ cm (1 × 1¼ × ¼ in)). Reserve bones. When onion is tender, turn heat up to high and add meat. Stirring occasionally, cook at this temperature for 1–2 minutes to seal outside of meat. Add stock and one or two shin bones. Cover and simmer gently for 2 hours. Remove from heat. Set aside for 24 hours.*

The next day, reheat curry until boiling, reduce heat and simmer for 1¾ hours. Cut capsicum into fairly large pieces. Add to curry 30 minutes before the end of cooking. Serve with freshly boiled rice.

Note: 1. *I always partly prepare a curry a day in advance. This gives the flavour time to mature and the rawness is taken from the hot spices.
2. A thin beef stock is preferred and can be prepared by boiling up shin bones in water. The stock should be cooled and skimmed of all fat before using in curry.
3. *See* 'General notes on curries' (pp. 112–14).

WINTER STEW

Serves 3

1 large onion
2 tablespoons oil
1½ teaspoons sage, finely chopped
salt and pepper
400 g (14 oz) stewing steak (eg neck of
beef, shoulder clod roast, chuck roast)
500 ml (2 cups, 17½ fl oz) water
1 tablespoon wine vinegar
1 tablespoon soy sauce
450 g (1 lb) tomatoes
100 g (3½ oz) cauliflower

Thinly slice onion and place in a heavy-based frying pan (skillet) with oil, sage, salt and pepper. Fry gently until onion is soft. Meanwhile, cut beef into thin slices 1–1½ cm (½ in) thick. Be sure to remove all gristle. When onion is cooked, turn heat up to high and add meat. Stirring frequently, cook meat quickly to seal—this takes 2–3 minutes. Remove pan from heat, pour in water and add vinegar and soy sauce. Blend (liquidise) tomatoes until smooth. Add to meat, stirring well. Cover and place in centre of a preheated oven at 140°C or 275°F. Cook for 2½ hours.

Break cauliflower into separate florets. Slice into pieces ½–1 cm (¼–½ in) thick. When meat is cooked, stir cauliflower into stew. Replace in oven for a further 30 minutes. Serve with jacket or boiled new potatoes and freshly cooked vegetables.

Note: 1. I always store tomatoes from summer in the freezer. No preparation is needed other than washing and drying. Just put them in a plastic (polythene) bag, seal and place in freezer. Tomatoes freeze rather like little golfballs and can be removed separately or *en masse*. I find it very useful to have a store of tomatoes readily available for winter meals. When thawed, they are soggy and only useful for soups and stews.
2. A cast-iron dish is most suitable for this recipe and others like it. The dish can be used on the hotplate and transferred straight to the oven.
3. Stir stew once or twice during cooking and check water content—if lid is not tightly fitting, excess evaporation will occur. In that case, add extra water. Final stew should be of medium thickness—neither runny nor stodgy.

KEBABS

Serves 4

600 g (1¼ lb) rump (sirloin or
fillet (tenderloin)) steak
salt and black pepper
2 teaspoons marjoram, finely chopped
2 rashers (slices) bacon
2 green capsicum (sweet peppers)
1 large onion
50 g (2 oz) mushrooms
a little oil

Cut meat into cubes (about 1–1½ cm (½ in)). Season with salt and black pepper. Roll in finely chopped marjoram. Set aside. Cut bacon and capsicum into pieces. Set aside. Peel onion and cut into quarters. Separate each quarter into pieces 2–3 layers in thickness. Remove and discard stalks from mushrooms. Thread each wooden or metal skewer with alternate pieces of prepared ingredients. Brush liberally with oil and either:
• grill (broil) under a fairly high heat for 3–5 minutes, turning frequently during cooking; *or*
• barbecue over hot charcoal for several minutes.
Serve on a bed of rice with a green salad.

Above: *On cold, damp nights, Winter Stew makes a wholesome and warming meal. This meal can be prepared ahead and frozen for later use.*

TOMATO STEAK AND DILL

Serves 4
1 onion
1½ teaspoons dill seed
1½ tablespoons oil
500 g (1 lb) tomatoes
650 g (1½ lb) rump (sirloin or tenderloin) steak
black pepper

Chop onion into thin slices. Together with dill seed, fry gently in oil until onion is soft. Chop tomatoes into small pieces and set aside. Cut steak into thin strips (about 3 cm (1¼ in) long and ½–1 cm (¼–½ in) thick and wide). Add steak to onion. Cook over a high heat, stirring continuously, for 1 minute. Add tomato. Continue cooking quickly, stirring constantly, for a further 2 minutes. Season with black pepper. Serve immediately with rice and/or a green salad.

CORIANDER BEEF

Serves 4

1 large onion
1½ tablespoons oil
1½ tablespoons ground coriander
1½ teaspoons paprika
black pepper
600 g (1¼ lb) blade (chuck) or
braising (round, topside or
rump) steak
3 large tomatoes (400 g/14 oz in
total)
600 ml (2½ cups, 21 fl oz) water
50 g (2 oz) mushrooms
4 tablespoons natural (plain) yoghurt

Thinly slice onion. Place in a heavy-based saucepan with oil, coriander, paprika and a little black pepper. Cook over a medium heat, stirring frequently, until onion is tender. Meanwhile, slice beef into strips 1 cm (½ in) wide and thick and 2 cm (1 in) long. With heat on high, add meat to pan and cook, stirring frequently, for 2 minutes to seal the outside of meat. Chop tomatoes into small pieces. Add tomatoes and water to pan. Cover and boil gently for 1 hour, stirring occasionally. Remove lid from pan and simmer for a further 1¼ hours.

Slice mushrooms, add to pan and simmer for a further 5 minutes. Stir in 2 tablespoons of yoghurt. Pour stew into a warmed serving dish. Trickle remaining 2 tablespoons of yoghurt over top. This is a rather rich dish, so serve with plain cooked vegetables or a simple salad, eg potatoes, coleslaw, green salad.

BARBECUED PORTERHOUSE STEAK

Serves 4

marinade as in Roast Pork Dish
(see p. 121)
4 porterhouse (T-bone) or
sirloin steaks

Prepare marinade and pour over steaks. Leave for at least 2 hours, basting occasionally. Barbecue, grill (broil) or pan-fry steaks in usual way.

GINGER BEEF

Serves 2

1 onion
2 cloves garlic
1 piece of ginger root 1 cm
(½ in) long
1 tablespoon oil
paprika and black pepper
pinch of Chinese five-spice powder
(see p. 365) (optional)
350 g (¾ lb) steak (eg fillet
(tenderloin), T-bone (sirloin))
1 small green capsicum (sweet pepper)
1 tablespoon sherry
2 tablespoons soy sauce

Finely chop onion, garlic and ginger. Fry gently in oil with paprika, pepper and Chinese five-spice powder (if used). Cut steak into thin strips 3 × ½ × ½ cm (1¼ × ¼ × ¼ in). Thinly slice capsicum. Add meat and capsicum to the cooked onion. Cook for 1 minute at a fairly high heat to seal outside of meat. Stir in sherry and soy sauce. Cook on a medium heat for a further 2 minutes. Serve immediately on a bed of freshly boiled rice.

DARK MINCE (GROUND BEEF)

Serves 3–4

1 medium onion

1 tablespoon oil

2 teaspoons turmeric

½ teaspoon paprika

½ teaspoon ground cumin

½ teaspoon French tarragon,
finely chopped

200 g (7 oz) steak mince
(ground beef)

1–1½ tablespoons soy sauce

6 borage leaves, shredded

Finely chop onion. Fry gently in oil until soft. Add turmeric, paprika, cumin seed, tarragon and mince. Cook over a high heat, stirring frequently, for 5 minutes. Add soy sauce and shredded borage. Reduce heat to medium. Cook for further 5 minutes. Serve small helpings only as this dish is rather spicy.

Suggested Servings
- Serve hot with plain boiled rice.
- Serve cold as a starter—a little placed neatly on a lettuce leaf.
- Use to stuff tomatoes, *see* Stuffed Tomatoes (p. 48).
- Use to stuff lettuce leaves, *see* Lettuce Leaf Rolls (p. 100).

Note: Vary quantity of soy sauce according to whether light (Superior Soy) or dark (Soy Superior) soy sauce is used. *See* 'Important notes' (p. 3).

LASAGNE

Serves 5

1 onion

3 cloves garlic, finely chopped

½ teaspoon paprika

pinch of cayenne

black pepper

1 tablespoon oil

2 teaspoons thyme, finely chopped

2 tablespoons oregano, finely chopped

600 g (1¼ lb) steak mince
(ground beef)

300 ml (1¼ cups, 10½ fl oz) tomato
purée, (see p. 221)

75 g (2½ oz) instant (precooked)
lasagne pasta

250 ml (1 cup, 9 fl oz) Basic
Wholemeal (Whole-Wheat) Sauce
(see sauces, p. 218)

2 egg yolks

Slice onion. Place in a large heavy-based frying pan (skillet) with garlic, paprika, cayenne, black pepper and oil. Fry gently until onion is soft. Add thyme, oregano, mince and tomato purée. Stir well and cook gently for 15 minutes. Set aside.

Prepare wholemeal sauce and stir in egg yolks. Cook gently for 2 minutes until sauce has thickened a little more. Remove from heat and set aside. The meat mixture, lasagne and sauce are placed in alternating layers in an ovenproof dish as follows: from bottom to top, one-third mince, one-third sauce, half pasta, one-third mince, one-third sauce, half pasta, one-third mince. Cover dish and bake at 180°C or 350°F for 30 minutes. Pour remaining third of sauce over the top, cover again and return to oven for a further 30 minutes.

STEAK DIVINE

Serves 4

1 large onion

8 sage leaves, finely chopped

2 tablespoons oil

black pepper

500 g (1 lb) steak (eg fillet
(tenderloin))

4 tablespoons tomato purée
(see p. 221)

1 tablespoon cream cheese

Chop onion into thin slices and finely chop sage leaves. Gently fry onion with sage in the oil until onion is slightly browned. Season with black pepper. Cut steak into thin strips (3 × 1 × 1 cm (1¼ × ½ × ½ in)). Add to onion. Keeping heat fairly high, cook for 1 minute, stirring continuously. Add tomato purée, reduce heat a little and continue cooking, stirring all the time, for a further 2 minutes. Remove pan from heat, stir in cream cheese and serve immediately.

STEAK WITH PEPPER SAUCE

Serves 4

2 teaspoons butter

1½ tablespoons wholemeal (whole-
wheat) flour (from which bran has
been sieved)

140 ml (5 fl oz) milk

90 ml (⅓ cup, 3 fl oz) thickened
(double, whipping) cream

salt and black pepper

1 kg (2 lb) steak (eg double fillet, thick
tenderloin)

Prepare basic sauce by melting butter, adding flour and slowly adding milk. Remove from heat. Stir in cream. Season with salt and plenty of black pepper. Cut steak into four even-sized pieces. Season with salt and pepper. Fry, grill (broil) or barbecue in usual way. Serve on a large warmed plate with cream sauce poured over.

Note: For a party snack, cut steak into pieces 2–3 cm (1–1¼ in) square and fry or grill as usual. Cool steak and add to cooled sauce. Stir well until each piece of steak is evenly coated with sauce. Push a cocktail stick (toothpick) into each piece and arrange pieces on a plate.

LETTUCE LEAF ROLLS

Serves 4

Dark Mince (Ground Beef)
(see p. 99)

1 lettuce*

Prepare Dark Mince (Ground Beef) and set aside. Separate lettuce leaves and wash well. Bring a pan of water to boil. Taking one lettuce leaf, drop in boiling water for 15 seconds. Remove and lay on a plate. 'Cook' each leaf the same way. Take one cooked leaf, gently spread out on a plate and place a little mince in the middle. Fold over stalk end, then two sides. Finally, fold over end part of the leaf. Repeat until all lettuce and mince have been used. Serve cold or hot as a starter or as a party snack.

To heat, place lettuce rolls side by side in a shallow greased ovenproof dish, cover with aluminium foil and place in the centre of a preheated oven at 200°C or 400°F for 10 minutes.

Note: * The butterhead (bibb, butterleaf or cabbage lettuce) variety of lettuce is best used here. If using a crisper, firmer lettuce, eg cos (romaine) lettuce, boil each leaf for 30–45 seconds to soften it sufficiently.

Opposite: As its name suggests, Steak Divine is a wonderfully flavoursome way to serve beef.

MOUSSAKA

Serves 5–6

2 medium eggplants (aubergines)
2 tablespoons oil
4 tablespoons water
1 onion
½–1 tablespoon each of oregano and marjoram, finely chopped
2 cloves garlic, finely chopped
250 ml (1 cup, 9 fl oz) tomato purée (see p. 221)
750 g (1¾ lb) steak mince (ground beef)
salt and black pepper
4 large tomatoes (approx. 1 kg/2¼ lb)
2 tablespoons margarine
2 tablespoons wholemeal (whole-wheat) flour
300 ml (1¼ cups, 10½ fl oz) milk
3 egg yolks

Cut one eggplant transversely into thin rounds. Layer at the bottom of an ovenproof dish. Sprinkle with 1 tablespoon of oil and 2 tablespoons of water. Chop onion finely and place in a bowl. Add herbs, garlic, tomato purée, mince and a little salt and black pepper. Blend (liquidise) tomatoes until smooth. Add to bowl. Thoroughly mix all ingredients. Layer over eggplant in ovenproof dish. Cut second eggplant into thin rounds. Layer over meat mixture. Sprinkle with remaining 1 tablespoon of oil and 2 tablespoons of water, cover with a tightly fitting lid and cook in oven at 140°C or 275°F for 1½ hours.

Prepare sauce by melting margarine, mixing in flour and slowly adding milk. Stir in egg yolks. Cook over a gentle heat until sauce thickens further.

When moussaka has cooked, remove from oven, pour sauce over the top, cover and return to oven for a further 30 minutes.

MEATBALLS

Serves 3–4

1 medium onion
1 teaspoon sage, finely chopped
1 tablespoon chives, finely chopped
1 teaspoon thyme, finely chopped
pinch of paprika
black pepper
500 g (1 lb) steak mince (ground beef)
a little beaten egg
500 ml (2 cups, 17½ fl oz) water

Mince or finely chop onion. Place in bowl with sage, chives, thyme, paprika and a little black pepper. Add mince. Using a fork or fingers, thoroughly blend all ingredients. Add a little beaten egg to bind. Take 2–3 teaspoons of mixture, shape into a ball and set aside. Repeat until all mixture has been used. Heat water in a deep saucepan. When boiling, spoon in 12 meatballs, one at a time. With water boiling constantly, allow meatballs to cook for 4 minutes, remove and drain. Repeat until all meatballs are cooked.

Note: 1. Alternatively, the meatballs can be deep-fried.
2. Serve hot with a sauce as a main course, *or* serve cold on cocktail sticks (toothpicks) as a party snack or pre-dinner appetiser. Sauce in a small bowl can be offered as a dip to accompany meatballs, eg Cream Sauce, Thyme Sauce, Mayonnaise (*see* pp. 220, 103, 227 respectively).

MEATBALLS IN THYME SAUCE

Serves 4

Meatballs (see p. 102)

THYME SAUCE

1 teaspoon thyme, finely chopped
2 tablespoons margarine
4½ tablespoons wholemeal
(whole-wheat) flour (from which bran
has been sieved)
350 ml (1½ cups, 12½ fl oz) milk
3 tablespoons meatballs' cooking stock
3 tablespoons thickened (double,
whipping) cream
2 teaspoons chives, finely chopped

MEATBALLS

Make meatballs as given in recipe. Reserve 3 tablespoons of meat stock from cooking for thyme sauce.

THYME SAUCE

Place thyme and margarine in a pan. Heat until sizzling. Add flour and stir well. Remove from heat and gradually blend in milk. Return to heat and stir continuously until sauce thickens. Stir in reserved cooking stock and cream. Stir well.

Add meatballs and set over a gentle heat until meatballs are thoroughly reheated and piping hot. Pour into a warmed ovenproof dish and sprinkle with chives.

Note: Any other sauce can be used in place of Thyme Sauce, eg Onion Sauce, Cream Sauce, Turmeric Sauce (*see* pp. 108, 220, 223 respectively).

PAWPAW (PAPAYA) MINCE (GROUND BEEF)

Serves 2–3

1 large onion
1 tablespoon oil
1 clove garlic, finely chopped
6 French tarragon leaves,
finely chopped
paprika and black pepper
250 g (9 oz) steak mince
(ground beef)
3 tablespoons water
½ small lettuce, shredded
250 g (9 oz) pawpaw (papaya)
1 tablespoon natural (plain) yoghurt
nuts, chopped, or cucumber slices (to
garnish)

Finely chop onion. Fry gently in oil until soft. Add garlic, tarragon, paprika and pepper. Stir in mince, cover and cook at a fairly high heat for 7 minutes. Add water and shredded lettuce, cover and cook for a further 3 minutes. Meanwhile, chop pawpaw into 1 cm (½ in) cubes. Add to mince dish and stir continuously (with pan uncovered now) for 5 minutes. Remove from heat, add yoghurt, stir well and serve garnished with nuts or cucumber.

RISSOLES (BEEF CAKES, HAMBURGERS)

Serves 4

1 large onion
1 teaspoon thyme, finely chopped
1 teaspoon parsley, finely chopped
250 g (9 oz) steak mince
(ground beef)
2 teaspoons oil
salt and black pepper
a little beaten egg
2 tablespoons oil (extra)

Chop or mince onion very finely. Thoroughly mix onion, thyme, parsley, mince, oil and a little salt and black pepper. Finally, add a little beaten egg (¼–½ egg is all that is required). Work mixture with hands. When thoroughly mixed, divide into eight portions. Take one portion, shape into a ball, place on a greased baking tray (sheet) and flatten a little. Repeat with remaining portions. Sprinkle rissoles (beef cakes, hamburgers) evenly with extra oil. Cook under a hot grill (broiler) for 5 minutes. Turn rissoles. Cook for further 5 minutes. Serve hot or cold.

Note: 1. The rissoles can be shallow-fried if preferred.
2. Cream Sauce or a herb sauce may be used to accompany rissoles (*see* sauces, pp. 218–24).

SPAGHETTI BOLOGNESE

Serves 4

MEAT SAUCE

1 large onion
1 tablespoon oil
500 g (1 lb) steak mince (ground beef)
250 ml (1 cup, 9 fl oz) tomato purée
(see p. 221)
1 tablespoon each of oregano, thyme,
finely chopped
4 cloves garlic, finely chopped
1 small chilli (chili pepper), finely
chopped (optional)
1 wineglass red wine
2 large green capsicum
(sweet peppers)
150 g (5½ oz) mushrooms
black pepper

SPAGHETTI

200 g (7 oz) spaghetti
½ teaspoon butter
2 teaspoons thyme, finely chopped
black pepper

MEAT SAUCE

Thinly slice onion. Fry in oil until soft. Add mince, tomato purée, herbs, garlic, chilli (if used) and red wine. Stir well, cover and simmer gently for 1 hour. Thinly slice capsicum and mushrooms, add to meat dish and simmer for a further 15 minutes. Season with black pepper.

SPAGHETTI

Meanwhile, add spaghetti to salted boiling water. Boil until al dente. Drain well and place in a warmed bowl. Add butter and thyme. Season with black pepper. Turn spaghetti well in the bowl to ensure an even coating of butter and herbs.

To serve, pile Bolognese sauce in the middle of a very large round or oval plate. Place spaghetti around Bolognese sauce.

RICE AND CHEESE LAYER

Serves 5

2 large borage leaves, finely chopped

3 cloves garlic

2 medium onions

¼ teaspoon each of marjoram, oregano, sage, rosemary, thyme, finely chopped

1 teaspoon parsley, finely chopped

black pepper

500 g (1 lb) steak mince (ground beef)

45 ml (1½ fl oz) water

300 g (2 cups, 10½ oz) brown rice

150 g (1½ cups, 5½ oz) cheddar cheese, grated

Finely chop borage and garlic. Place in a bowl. Thinly slice onions. Add with herbs to bowl. Season with pepper. Add mince. Thoroughly mix all ingredients. Layer this meat mixture at the bottom of an ovenproof dish, sprinkle over water, cover and cook at 170°C or 325°F for 30 minutes.

Meanwhile, cook rice and drain. Grate cheese and mix into rice. Layer this cheesy rice over meat, cover and return to oven for a further 20 minutes.

TAI TAPU BEEF

Serves 4

600 g (1¼ lb) rib of beef (rump, chuck or round steak)

1½ tablespoons oil

600 ml (2½ cups, 21 fl oz) water

1 teaspoon rosemary, finely chopped

1 teaspoon oregano, finely chopped

2 teaspoons marjoram, finely chopped

2 cloves garlic, finely chopped

black pepper

SAUCE

200 ml (7 fl oz) beef stock

1 onion

¼ teaspoon ground cumin

½ teaspoon turmeric

1 tablespoon soy sauce

2 teaspoons lemon juice

140 ml (5 fl oz) fresh orange juice

1 tablespoon brandy (optional)

125 g (1½ cups, 4½ oz) bean sprouts (optional)

Cut meat into thin strips (about ½–1 cm (¼–½ in) thick and wide and 1½–2 cm (½–1 in) long). Heat oil in a heavy-based saucepan. When quite hot, add beef. Stirring continuously, cook at a high heat for 2 minutes to seal. Add water, rosemary, oregano, marjoram, garlic and a little freshly ground black pepper. Cover pan and simmer for 1¼–1½ hours until beef is tender. When cooked, drain off all liquid into a container, leave meat in pan and set aside.

SAUCE

Measure out 200 ml (7 fl oz) of the liquid from meat. Pour into a separate saucepan (discard remainder or store as beef stock for another recipe). Thinly slice onion and add to liquid. With pan uncovered, bring to boil. Simmer gently until onion is just tender. Add cumin, turmeric, soy sauce, lemon juice, orange juice and brandy.

Pour sauce over meat. With pan uncovered, simmer very gently for 10–12 minutes to allow sauce to thicken. Finally, add bean sprouts (if used). Continue to cook gently for 3 minutes. (If omitting bean sprouts, simmer meat for 15 minutes.)

Note: This dish is quite rich and should be accompanied by a plain vegetable dish or salad, eg lightly steamed green (French or runner, string) beans, leeks, rice or green salad.

BEEF AND POTATO CASSEROLE

Serves 4

500 g (1 lb) potatoes
2 large onions
600 g (1¼ lb) topside (top round) beef
1½ tablespoons oil
3 teaspoons thyme, finely chopped
450 ml (1¾ cups, 16 fl oz) beef stock
salt and black pepper

Cut potatoes into rounds ½–1cm (¼–½ in) thick. Set aside. Thickly slice onions. Set aside. Cut meat into slices ½ cm (¼ in) thick. Heat oil in a frying pan (skillet) Add meat. Cook over a high heat, stirring continuously, for 2–3 minutes to seal. Remove from heat. Set aside. Place ingredients in layers in an ovenproof dish (about 20 cm (8 in) diameter) as follows: from bottom to top, onion, potato, meat (sprinkle with 1½ teaspoons thyme), onion, potato, meat (sprinkle with 1½ teaspoons thyme), potato. Season stock with salt and pepper. Pour over casserole. Cover and bake slowly at 140°C or 275°F for 3¾–4 hours.

ROAST RIB WITH MUSHROOMS

Serves 6–8

3 cloves garlic
1 rib (or forerib) of beef
(1¼–1¾ kg/2¾–4 lb)
salt and black pepper
2 teaspoons thyme, finely chopped
150 ml (⅔ cup, 5½ fl oz) red wine
dripping(s)
8 small onions, peeled and top and
roots removed
1 tablespoon cornflour
(US cornstarch)
200 ml (7 fl oz) water
100 g (3½ oz) mushrooms

Cut garlic into small pieces. Make tiny cuts in surface of meat. Into each, insert a piece of garlic. Season meat all over with a little salt and black pepper. Place in a roasting tin (pan). Sprinkle over thyme. Pour two-thirds of red wine into the bottom of the tin. Cover and set aside to marinate for several hours. Turn meat during this time so that each surface absorbs some of the wine. Add dripping (about 50 g/¼ cup/2 oz) to tin. Roast in usual way at 190°C or 375°F (*see* pp. 73–4). Thirty minutes before the end of cooking, add whole prepared onions to dish. When meat is cooked, place in a warmed serving dish, with onions around meat. Set in a warm place.

To prepare gravy, pour away all but 2 tablespoons of fat from roasting tin. In a separate bowl, carefully blend cornflour, water and remaining wine. Thinly slice mushrooms and add. Place roasting tin on a hotplate. Heat until fat sizzles. Pour in cornflour and mushroom mixture. Stir vigorously to prevent lumps. Reduce heat to low. Cook for 3–4 minutes until mushrooms are tender. This gravy will be quite thick. Serve in a gravy boat or pour over meat immediately before serving.

Above: *Roast Rib with Mushrooms — a rib of beef roasted to perfection and topped with a mouthwatering mushroom sauce.*

ROAST SIRLOIN (STANDING RIB) WITH MARJORAM

Serves 8–9

1 large onion

2 cloves garlic

3 tablespoons cooking oil

salt and black pepper

1½–2 kg (3½–4½ lb) piece of sirloin
(on bone) (standing rib or rib roast)

1 tablespoon marjoram,
finely chopped

dripping(s)

Cut onion into thin slices. Chop garlic into tiny slivers. Mix onion in a bowl with oil. Season with salt and pepper. Place sirloin in a roasting tin (pan). Sprinkle marjoram evenly all over. Pour over oil mixture and add a little dripping—75–125 g (¼–½ cup, 2½–4½ oz). Cover roasting tin and roast in usual way. Remove lid from the tin 30 minutes before the end of cooking to allow meat to brown a little.

Note: This recipe is also suitable for a rolled rib of beef.

SILVERSIDE WITH ONION SAUCE

Serves 6

1 piece fresh silverside (top round
roast) (about 1 kg/2¼ lb)

SAUCE

1 medium onion

270 ml (1 cup, 9 fl oz) milk

1 tablespoon margarine

1 tablespoon wholemeal (whole-wheat)
flour (from which bran has
been sieved)

salt and black pepper

Place silverside in a deep pan, cover with water. Cover pan and bring to boil. Boil gently until silverside is well cooked (2¾ hours per kg/48 minutes per lb).

SAUCE

Slice onion thinly into rounds. Place in a saucepan with milk. Partially cover pan, heat until boiling and boil gently until onion is soft. (When milk first comes to boil, stir well for 1–2 minutes to prevent boiling over. After that the milk froths a lot, but does not spill over.) When onion is tender, set aside. In a separate pan, heat margarine until it sizzles. Stir in flour. Remove from heat. Gradually blend in milk and onion, taking care to avoid lumps. Heat gently, stirring continuously, until sauce thickens. Remove from heat, season with salt and pepper. Set aside.

When silverside is cooked, slice thinly. Arrange slices on a heated serving dish. Reheat onion sauce. Pour evenly over meat.

Alternatives 1. Serve cold, sprinkled with chopped chives, with hot crusty bread.

2. Substitute apple sauce or Cilla's Apple Sauce (*see* sauces, p. 225) for onion sauce. Apple sauce should be served in a separate bowl to sliced meat.

Note: Silverside (like corned beef brisket) is often already salted when purchased. If that is the case, meat should be soaked for 12 hours in several changes of fresh water prior to cooking. Onion sauce may still be prepared, but I do not recommend apple sauce.

BEEF AND RICE

Serves 4

500 g (1 lb) stewing steak (eg chuck
(shoulder))

1 tablespoon oil

4 teaspoons marjoram, finely chopped

black pepper

1 teaspoon paprika

2 cloves garlic, finely chopped

600 ml (2½ cups, 21 fl oz) water

150 ml (⅔ cup, 5½ fl oz) tomato
purée (see p. 221)

50 g (2 oz) mushrooms

200 g (1⅓ cups, 7 oz) brown rice

1 tomato (to garnish)

Cut beef into thin strips (approx. 2 × ½ × ½ cm (1 × ¼ × ¼ in). Heat oil in a heavy-based saucepan. When quite hot, add beef. Cook for 1 minute at a high temperature, stirring continuously, to seal meat. Add marjoram, a little freshly ground black pepper, paprika, garlic, water and tomato purée. Cover pan and simmer for 2–2½ hours until meat is tender. Slice mushrooms. Add 5 minutes before the end of cooking.

Boil rice until tender and drain. Make a ring of rice around the edge of a large serving plate. Pour beef stew into middle. Garnish with sliced tomato.

BEEF OLIVES

Serves 4

1 onion
2 teaspoons rosemary, finely chopped
1 small egg, beaten
170 g (1½ cups, 6 oz) wholemeal
(whole-wheat) breadcrumbs, dried
500 g (1 lb) topside (top round) beef,
thinly sliced
black pepper
225 ml (8 fl oz) red wine
170 ml (⅔ cup, 6 fl oz) water

Finely chop or grate onion. Place in a bowl. Stir in rosemary and beaten egg. Add breadcrumbs. Using a fork, work breadcrumbs into egg and onion mixture. Finally, work with hands and divide mixture into eight portions.

Divide beef into eight portions. Lay one piece of meat flat on a board or working surface, season on both sides with black pepper. Take one portion of breadcrumb mixture. Mould into a sausage shape long enough to fit meat. Place across the middle of the piece of meat. Roll meat around breadcrumb filling. Secure with cotton or two cocktail sticks (toothpicks). Repeat with remaining pieces of beef. Lay beef olives in an ovenproof dish, side by side. Pour over wine and water. Cover and bake at 180°C or 350°F for 1¾–2 hours until beef is tender.

CORNISH PASTIES

Serves 4–8

MEAT FILLING

450 g (1 lb) braising steak (eg skirt or
leg of beef, rump, round or flank)
2 tablespoons wholemeal
(whole-wheat) flour
1 large onion
2 tablespoons oil
400 ml (1⅔ cups, 14 fl oz) water
1 small carrot
¼ teaspoon paprika
2 teaspoons thyme, finely chopped
2 teaspoons soy sauce
black pepper

PASTRY

250 g (1¾ cups, 9 oz) wholemeal
(whole-wheat) flour (from which bran
has been sieved)
150 g (⅔ cup, 5½ oz) margarine
2 teaspoons lemon juice
3 tablespoons water
a little beaten egg

Cut skirt into pieces ½–1 cm (¼–½ in) thick and 1–2 cm (½–1 in) wide and long. Coat evenly with flour. Thinly slice onion. Fry gently in oil until soft. With heat on high, add meat pieces and cook rapidly for 2–3 minutes, stirring continuously to prevent sticking. Pour in water and reduce to very low heat. Chop carrot into small pieces. Add to meat. Also add paprika, thyme, soy sauce and a little black pepper. Mix thoroughly, cover pan and allow to simmer very slowly for 2¾ hours until meat is tender. Remove lid for the last 20–30 minutes of cooking, if necessary, to reduce sauce a little.

TO MAKE PASTIES

Place flour in a bowl and rub in margarine. In a separate bowl, mix lemon juice and water. Make a well in centre of dry ingredients. Pour in liquid. Gradually blend dry and wet ingredients to make a soft dough. Roll out quite thinly. Cut into eight circles using a saucer as a guide. Place a little cooked meat in the centre of each circle. Wet edges with a little water. Fold one half of circle over onto other half—press pastry edges together firmly to seal. Brush with a little beaten egg. Bake at 200°C or 400°F for about 15 minutes until nicely browned.

ASPIC JELLY

3 calf's feet
2 sprigs thyme (each 6-8 cm/
2½-3 in long)
2 sprigs parsley (each 6-8 cm/
2½-3 in long)
1 bay (sweet laurel) leaf
salt and black pepper
3 carrots
1 onion
500 g (1 lb) stewing beef or veal
meat stock or water
a little egg white

Place calf's feet in a deep pan. Add herbs and a little salt and black pepper. Thinly slice carrots and onions. Add to pan. Cut beef into four or six pieces. Also add to pan. Pour over enough meat stock or water to cover ingredients well. Cover with a tightly fitting lid, bring to boil and simmer very, very gently for 3 hours. When cooked, strain liquid into a separate bowl. Discard meat and vegetables. Allow liquid to cool. Skim off all traces of fat from the surface.

Lightly beat a little egg white in a separate pan (2 egg whites per 1½-2 litres (6-8 cups, 2½-3½ UK pints) of liquid. Add cooled liquid (it will now have set to a jelly) to egg white. Mix well. Very gently, heat mixture, beating well, until barely boiling. Maintain at this heat for 10 minutes. (The whites will rise to the surface.) Turn off heat. Leave pan as it is, without stirring, for a further 10 minutes. Pour liquid into a jelly bag and hang over a bowl—the liquid that drains into the bowl should be clear. When set, it will be pure aspic jelly. If jelly is not clear, repeat the process of heating with egg whites followed by straining.

Note: A jelly bag is a very fine-meshed material bag usually used for straining the debris from a fruit jelly, eg apple jelly, crab apple jelly.

Aspic jelly is not much used these days, the convenience of gelatine crystals replacing it. However, gelatine tends to be less tasty and more gluey in texture. A well-prepared aspic jelly is far superior. This recipe will give a fairly mild-tasting jelly. Chicken meat, bones or giblets, a little liver or any similar meat and/or other vegetables can be added to pan before cooking to improve flavour of final jelly.

OXTAIL STEW

Serves 3
1 oxtail
1 tablespoon thyme, finely chopped
1½ teaspoons paprika
black pepper
2 medium onions
2 large carrots
300 ml (1¼ cups, 10½ fl oz) water
300 ml (1¼ cups, 10½ fl oz) red wine

Soak oxtail in cold water for several hours. Wash well in fresh water, cut into pieces and place in an ovenproof dish. Sprinkle over thyme, paprika and black pepper. Slice onion and carrot. Add to dish. Mix together water and wine. Pour over oxtail. Cover and cook in oven at 130°C or 250°F for 3½ hours, stirring two or three times during cooking.

PEPPERY LIVER

Serves 3–4

SAUCE

2 cloves garlic

1 chilli (chili pepper)

2 green capsicum (sweet peppers)

225 ml (1 cup, 8 fl oz) tomato purée
(see p. 221)

2 teaspoons marjoram, finely chopped

1 teaspoon rosemary, finely chopped

1 teaspoon thyme, finely chopped

4 tablespoons red wine

salt and black pepper

LIVER

1 large onion

1½ tablespoons oil

500 g (1 lb) calf's, lamb's or
pig's liver

Parmesan cheese

Finely chop garlic, chilli and capsicum. Place in a saucepan. Add remaining sauce ingredients. Bring to boil and simmer for 30 minutes, stirring occasionally to prevent sticking.

In a large heavy-based frying pan (skillet), gently fry sliced onion in oil until browned. Slice liver thinly (not more than 1 cm (½ in) thick). Place liver slices side by side in frying pan with onion. Cook on a medium heat for 2 minutes. Turn liver slices and cook for a further 2 minutes. Pour over prepared tomato sauce. Simmer gently for 5 minutes. Sprinkle with Parmesan cheese. Serve on a bed of freshly boiled rice.

TONGUE

1 ox's (beef) tongue

coarse (common) salt

Wash tongue in cold water. Dry well on a clean, dry cloth. Rub salt well into tongue, covering entire surface. When white with salt, leave to stand for 10–15 minutes. Again rub salt well into tongue—there should be a thick layer of salt all over. Seal in a plastic (polythene) bag. Store in deepfreeze for at least 2–3 weeks. Remove from freezer and thaw. The tongue may not be frozen solid because of the large quantity of salt. (It will still be fresh as salt acts as a preservative.) Wash under cold running water to remove excess salt. Immerse in a bowl of cold water. Set in refrigerator for 1–2 days. Change water two or three times during that period. Wash tongue again, place in large pan, cover with water and boil for 2½–3 hours, depending on its size. (Test using a skewer as for a roast—meat will feel soft as you push in skewer. When cooked, no bloody juice will emerge.) Drain tongue and cool a little. Reserve stock. Skin tongue. Press into a small dish (eg enamel saucepan with 14 cm (5½ in) diameter). Spoon over some of strained stock. Apply a weight (about 3 kg (6½ lb)). Leave overnight, remove weight and gently turn tongue out of dish. Slice thinly to serve.

Note: Veal tongue can also be used. Allow shorter salting and cooking times.

Sausages

Sausage can contain up to 30% fat and 30% cereal-based filler. (German and Italian sausages contain no cereal at all.) The remaining 40% is lean meat of the tougher cuts. All the carcass trimmings of meat, fat and skin may be used up in sausages. You may omit cereal filler altogether and/or increase fat content. Homemade sausages are easy and satisfying to make and are of a much higher quality than most commercially prepared sausages. The lean meat part may be made up of varying proportions of beef or pork, or even mutton, as you prefer. Season and flavour as you wish. Remember that home-produced sausages require a longer, slower cooking than commercially prepared ones, as they will most likely contain a higher proportion of meat. Sausage casings may be made at home from the intestines of pig or sheep (*see* general notes on offal, pp. 79–84) or may be commercially prepared ones purchased from your local butcher. A recipe for pork sausages can be found on p. 125.

BEEF SAUSAGES (OR BURGERS)

200 g (7 oz) ox (beef) tongue
150 g (5½ oz) ox (beef) heart
200 g (7 oz) ox (beef) or calf's liver
300 g (10½ oz) beef trimmings
(include all rough cuts, some skin
and fatty pieces)
100 g (3½ oz) beef fat
300 g (10½ oz) cracked or kibbled
(burghul) wheat
2-3 tablespoons sage, finely chopped
2-3 teaspoons black pepper
½ teaspoon paprika

Remove and discard gristly parts of upper tongue. Cut into thick slices. Cut away and discard tough skin. Slice heart, removing and discarding any tough tubes. Slice liver, removing and discarding any tough fibrous tissue. (Remember to soak liver in water before using. *See* general notes on offal, pp. 79–84.) Cut beef trimmings into chunks, removing and discarding bone and gristle. Cut fat into chunks, removing and discarding any membranes. Pass all meat and fat together with wheat through a mincer on a very fine setting. Place minced (ground) meats in a bowl. Add sage, black pepper and paprika. Mix thoroughly. Stuff into casings or shape into burgers.

General Notes on Curries

A curry is a meat, fish or vegetable dish flavoured with a medley of spices, notably chillies (chili peppers) (which give the hotness), coriander, turmeric, fenugreek, cumin and paprika. The overall flavour and strength (or degree of hotness) are determined by the proportions of spices used. A recipe for a curry powder or suitable blend of spices is given on p. 114 (this is not the only blend possible of course). Check out recipes for curry powder in other books or experiment yourself to find combinations to suit your palate.

Starters or Appetisers

Due to the spiciness of a curry main course, the meal works rather heavily on the digestive system. Therefore, a light simple starter is best, if indeed you decide to have one at all. My suggestions are as follows:
- Cheese Straws (p. 277),
- Cheese Fondue or Dip (p. 214),
- Stuffed Celery Sticks (p. 58),
- Spiced Dhal (Dal) (p. 66),
- Lentil Patties (p. 66),
- Avocados (pp. 55–6),
- Lettuce Leaf Rolls (p. 100).

Accompaniments to a Main-Course Curry

Offer the following accompaniments to curry in separate bowls. A little of each, approximately several teaspoons, is sufficient per person:
- desiccated (shredded) coconut
- chopped cucumber—plain or dressed in natural (plain) yoghurt
- sliced banana—plain or dressed in natural (plain) yoghurt
- tomato and/or green capsicum (sweet peppers) chopped into tiny pieces
- chopped apple with or without raisins—plain or dressed in natural (plain) yoghurt
- a selection of chutneys.

There are also a range of more ethnic accompaniments, eg raita, chapattis, puris, poppadoms—I have no original recipes and can only direct you to Indian cookery books for these.

Rice

Freshly boiled white (eg basmati) or brown rice is of course the most easy to prepare and the 'safest' with regard to the blending of flavours. Other possibilities for the more adventurous are Peppery Rice or Turmeric Rice—*see* recipes on pp. 44 and 142, respectively.

Dessert

Again, a dessert course should be simple and light, and designed to clean the palate of the spices contained in the curry. My suggestions are:
- fresh fruit salad with or without preserved ginger, eg South Seas Island Salad (p. 294)
- any fresh fruit dish, eg Pears Topped with Cinnamon Cream *or* Bananas in Brandy Sauce (pp. 291 and 284)

- a simple cooked fruit dish, eg Apple Tregear (p. 284)
- mousse, eg lemon- or coffee-flavoured mousse
- baked egg custard (p. 286)
- ice cream served with a fruit purée or fruit syrup.

Planning a Curry Meal

If guests are to be invited, first check on their curry likes and dislikes. People are very individual in their curry tastes, some preferring hot, others medium or mild. If possible, offer two or three curry dishes differing in their spiciness and strength.

CURRY POWDER

4 teaspoons coriander seed, finely ground
2 teaspoons cumin seed, finely ground
¼ teaspoon mustard seed, finely ground
2 cloves, finely ground
2 teaspoons ground turmeric
1 teaspoon ground ginger
½ teaspoon chilli (chili pepper), finely chopped
1 teaspoon ground cinnamon
1 teaspoon fenugreek seed*
¼ teaspoon ground black pepper

In a pestle and mortar, finely grind coriander seed. Transfer to a small bowl. Grind cumin and also add to bowl. Repeat with mustard seed and then cloves. Add remaining ingredients, stir and mix together thoroughly. Store in a screw-top jar.

Note: 1. * Fenugreek seed is very hard so I generally leave it whole as I have found no easy way of grinding it. During cooking it softens quickly and the flavour disperses well.

2. This curry powder is medium hot in strength. The hotness depends on the amount of chilli used. If you use none, you will still have a very tasty curry, but without the heat.

3. You may prefer to grind the spices in an electric coffee grinder or blender (liquidiser).

Pork

BACON JOINT WITH MUSTARD AND TARRAGON SAUCE

Serves 7–10
1 bacon joint (boneless shoulder butt)
(1–1½ kg/2¼–3½ lb)
Mustard and Tarragon Sauce
(see sauces, p. 222)

Bacon joints are always very salty and so need soaking in cold water before cooking. Place pork in an enamel or stainless steel pan. Cover completely with water. Allow to soak for 12–24 hours, changing water once or twice during that period. Once again, re-cover with fresh water, bring to boil and boil gently for 1½ hours. Top up water level as necessary. Remove pork, drain a little, slice thinly and arrange on a serving plate. Set aside in a warm place. Now prepare sauce according to recipe. Pour into a warmed sauce boat or small jug (pitcher). Serve sauce hot or just warm.

Serve sliced bacon and sauce with a green salad or plenty of freshly cooked vegetables.

Alternative • Serve bacon cold, and sauce just warm. Allow bacon joint, when cooked, to cool in boiling water. When completely cold, remove and slice.

SPAGHETTI PORK

Serves 3–4
500 g (1 lb) tomatoes, skinned
(peeled)
3 teaspoons marjoram, finely chopped
150 ml (²/₃ cup, 5½ fl oz) water
½ teaspoon paprika
black pepper
1 onion
500 g (1 lb) belly pork (ground or
sliced shoulder or leg pork) for a
cheap meal, otherwise use a loin cut)*
200 g (7 oz) spaghetti
2 teaspoons butter
1 tablespoon parsley, finely chopped

Place tomatoes in a blender (liquidiser) with marjoram and water. Blend for 1 minute. Pour into a saucepan and add paprika and a little pepper. Thinly slice onion and add to pan. If not minced (ground), cut pork into thin slices (approx. 3 cm (1¼ in) long by ½–1 cm (¼–½ in) thick and wide). Set aside. Heat tomato mixture in pan until boiling. Add pork. Bring to boil again. Reduce heat. Simmer uncovered for 45 minutes.

Boil spaghetti in slightly salted water until al dente. Drain. Mix in butter. Season with a little black pepper. Make a ring of spaghetti around the edge of a large warmed meat plate or dish. Spoon pork into centre. Sprinkle with parsley. Serve.

Note: * Fresh pancetta can also be used, if available. It is generally found in Italian grocery stores or delicatessens.

BIBLE PORK WITH LIMA (BUTTER) BEANS

Serves 4

1 large onion

¼–½ teaspoon dill seed

1 tablespoon oil

1 teaspoon hyssop, finely chopped

4 pork loin chops

2 tablespoons white wine

200 ml (7 fl oz) fresh orange juice

black pepper

200 g (2 cups, 7 oz) lima (butter)
beans, cooked

Finely chop onion. Sauté with dill seed in oil until soft (use a large heavy-based frying pan (skillet)). When soft, add hyssop and place pork loin chops side by side in pan. Cook at medium heat for 3 minutes. Turn and repeat. Pour over wine and orange juice. Season with pepper. Cover and simmer for 5–10 minutes. Turn chops and cook for a further 5 minutes. Add lima beans. Continue simmering until chops are well done and beans are heated through.

Note: Three-quarters of a cup of dried lima beans gives 2 cups when cooked.

LEMON PORK CURRY

Serves 4

1 onion

2 tablespoons oil

2 teaspoons ground coriander

6 teaspoons curry powder (see p. 114)

600 g (1¼ lb) pork (eg knuckle)

300 ml (1¼ cups, 10½ fl oz) water

3 tablespoons lemon balm leaves,
chopped

100 g (½ cup, 3½ oz) raisins

3 tablespoons lemon juice

Thinly slice onion. Place in a heavy-based pan with oil, coriander and curry powder. Fry gently until onion is soft. Meanwhile, cut pork into pieces no thicker than 1½ cm (½ in). Add pork to cooked onion. With heat on high, cook meat for 2 minutes, stirring continuously. Add water, cover, reduce heat and simmer for 30 minutes, stirring occasionally. Add 2 tablespoons of lemon balm, and raisins. Simmer for a further 30 minutes, this time with pan uncovered. Remove from heat. Set aside for 12–24 hours. (I always prepare curry a day before eating to allow the spices time to mature and lose their rawness.) Add remaining lemon balm and lemon juice. Simmer gently with pan covered for 30 minutes.

Note: Refer to 'General notes on curries' (pp. 112–14).

PORK AND WINE

Serves 4–5

2 medium onions

1 tablespoon oil

2 teaspoons sage, finely chopped

salt and black pepper

pinch of paprika

750 g (1¾ lb) pork leg (knuckle,
leg steaks)

150 ml (⅔ cup, 5½ fl oz) white wine

3 tablespoons water

3 large green capsicum
(sweet peppers)

Thinly slice onions. Place in a large saucepan with oil, sage, a little salt and black pepper and paprika. Cook gently until onion is soft. Cut pork into pieces (approx. ½ cm (¼ in) thick, 1 cm (½ in) wide and 3 cm (1¼ in) long). Increase heat to high and add pork pieces. Cook for 2 minutes at this heat, stirring continuously. Add wine and water, cover pan, reduce heat and simmer for 30 minutes. Thinly slice capsicum, add to pan and simmer uncovered for a further 30 minutes (stir occasionally towards the end of cooking). Serve with freshly boiled brown rice or Peppery Rice (*see* p. 44).

SWEET AND SOUR PORK

Serves 2

SAUCE

1 tablespoon brown (demerara, (soft)
light brown) sugar

1 tablespoon malt vinegar

1 tablespoon soy sauce

2 tablespoons tomato purée
(see p. 221)

juice of 1 small orange

MEAT

1 small onion

1 clove garlic

1 piece ginger root, ½ cm (¼ in) long

1 tablespoon oil

300 g (10½ oz) pork (eg fillet half leg)

Blend all sauce ingredients in a bowl. Set aside.

Cut pork into small strips no more than ½–1 cm (¼–½ in) thick and approx. 2 cm (1 in) long. Set aside.

Thinly slice onion and finely chop garlic and ginger. Place in a heavy-based frying pan (skillet) with oil. Cook gently until onion is tender. Now turn heat to maximum and add pork. Cook over this high heat for 2–3 minutes to seal, reduce heat to medium and pour in sauce. Stir well. Cover pan and allow to simmer for 30 minutes, stirring occasionally. Serve with plain rice and a salad or plain stir-fried vegetables.

Note: This is a very rich dish and should be accompanied by plain side dishes. Accompanying courses should be simple and light.

LOIN OF PORK WITH SESAME

Serves 4

1 kg (2¼ lb) pork loin

1 large onion

3 tablespoons lemon juice

5 tablespoons sherry

2 tablespoons water

1 tablespoon sesame seed, toasted

black pepper

3 teaspoons wholemeal (whole-wheat)
flour

1 slice lemon

Place loin in a snugly fitting ovenproof dish. Thinly slice onion and place around meat. In a separate bowl, mix lemon juice, sherry and water and pour over meat. Finally, sprinkle over sesame seed and season with a little black pepper. Cover dish and cook at 180°C or 350°F for 1¾ hours (internal temperature: 85°C (180°–185°F)), basting frequently. Remove from oven and place loin on a heated serving dish. Pour juices into a small pan, carefully blend in flour. Heat, stirring constantly, until sauce thickens. Pour sauce over loin, garnish with slice of lemon and serve.

MUSTARD PORK

Serves 4

1 large onion

6 small sage leaves

1 tablespoon oil

½ teaspoon paprika

600 g (1¼ lb) neck end or blade of
pork (blade or fresh shoulder)

2 tablespoons Dijon/French mustard

650 ml (2⅔ cups, 23 fl oz) water

225 g (3 cups, 8 oz) bean sprouts

Thinly slice onion. Finely chop sage leaves. Gently fry both in oil until onion is soft. Stir in paprika. Cut pork into pieces approx. 3 cm (1¼ in) long and ½–1 cm (¼–½ in) wide and thick. Add pork pieces to onion. Cook over a high heat for 2 minutes to seal, stirring frequently. Stir in mustard and water. Boil gently with pan uncovered for 1 hour. Add bean sprouts, cook for a further 2 minutes. Serve on a bed of freshly boiled rice.

FRUIT PORK CHOPS

Serves 4

2 large (eating) apples

6 small spring onions (scallions),
finely chopped

4 pork chops (loin or rib)

1 teaspoon rosemary, finely chopped

pinch of paprika

black pepper

3 tablespoons white wine or cider or
apple wine

60 ml (¼ cup, 2 fl oz) water

Core apples, cut into thin slices and set aside. Finely chop spring onions. Sprinkle on the bottom of an ovenproof dish. Trim excess fat from chops. Place them side by side in dish on top of onion. Sprinkle chops evenly with rosemary. Season with paprika and black pepper. Layer apples over chops. Pour over wine and water, cover and bake at 180°C or 350°F for 1 hour. Remove from oven several times during cooking and baste with liquid.

PORK CHOPS WITH HYSSOP

Serves 4

1 teaspoon hyssop, finely chopped

1 tablespoon Dijon/French mustard

2 teaspoons brown (demerara, (soft)
light brown) sugar

1 teaspoon cooking oil

salt and black pepper

4 pork chops (eg rib or chump (loin or
shoulder) chops)

Blend together thoroughly hyssop, mustard, brown sugar, oil, salt and pepper. Spread mixture over both sides of pork. Leave for 2 hours. Cook pork under a hot grill (broiler) for 7 minutes. Turn and cook for a further 7–10 minutes until pork is well done.

Note: Few people these days grow hyssop, so if it is unavailable, substitute summer or winter savory or even French tarragon.

PORK CHOPS AND DILL SEED

Serves 4

1 onion

1 tablespoon oil

½ teaspoon thyme, finely chopped

½ teaspoon dill seed

¼ teaspoon paprika

black pepper

1 pinch Chinese five-spice powder
(optional) (see p. 365)

1 small chilli (chili pepper)

1 tablespoon soy sauce

4 pork chops (loin or rib)

Finely chop onion. Fry gently in oil with thyme, dill seed, paprika, black pepper, Chinese five-spice powder (if used) and finely chopped chilli. When onion is soft, stir in soy sauce. Lay chops side by side in pan. On a medium heat, cook for 10–15 minutes. Turn and cook on second side for 10–15 minutes or until chops are well done. (The cooking time will depend on the thickness of chops.)

Opposite: *Pork Chops and Dill Seed — not only are these pork chops wonderfully complemented by the subtle flavour of dill, the sauce also helps to keep them moist and appetising.*

PORK WITH WATERCRESS

Serves 4

700 g (1½ lb) pork fillet (tenderloin)

2 tablespoons oil

2 cloves garlic

75 g (1 cup, 2½ oz) watercress, chopped

225 ml (1 cup, 8 fl oz) red wine

¼ teaspoon cayenne (optional)

4 large peaches or 5 apricots or ½ medium pawpaw (papaya)

2 thin slices (rounds) toast

Cut pork into pieces no more than ½ cm (¼ in) thick and 1 cm (½ in) wide and 2 cm (1 in) long. Heat oil in a pan. When hot, toss in pork and finely chopped garlic. Cook on a high heat for 2 minutes, stirring continuously. Add half of chopped watercress, then red wine and cayenne. Reduce heat. Simmer for 7 minutes.

Meanwhile, slice fruit thinly. When meat is ready add fruit, cover and simmer for 3 minutes. Serve topped with remaining watercress and toast (cut into cubes of ½–1 cm (¼–½ in)).

Note: Fresh fruit is best, but preserved or canned fruit can be used—in which case, drain syrup from fruit and rinse in cold water before using.

ORANGE PORK ROAST

Serves 5

1 piece roasting pork (about 1½ kg/3½ lb)

150 g (½ cup, 5½ oz) dark bitter marmalade

4 tablespoons oil

1 tablespoon lemon balm, chopped

¼ teaspoon ground ginger

300 ml (1¼ cups, 10½ fl oz) water

2 tablespoons brandy (optional)

1 tablespoon wholemeal (whole-wheat) flour

2 tablespoons water (extra)

Place pork in a roasting dish. Blend marmalade and oil. Stir in lemon balm and ginger. Spread over pork to evenly cover all surfaces. Set aside for at least 2 hours. Pour 300 ml (1¼ cups, 10½ fl oz) of water and brandy around meat, cover with a tightly fitting lid and roast in usual way, basting frequently. (*See* notes on roasting times on p. 74.) When cooked, remove roast pork to a hot serving plate. Set aside in a warm place.

In a cup, make a paste of flour and extra water. Carefully blend this paste into roasting liquid. Heat, stirring continuously, until sauce thickens. (This may be done directly in roasting dish or in a saucepan.) Serve a little of the sauce poured over roast and remainder in a gravy boat.

Note: I often use old stock marmalade, especially if it is beginning to crystallise and no longer useful as a preserve. However, a bitter marmalade is essential—if too sweet, the pork's flavour is overwhelmed. If you only have a sweet or semi-sweet marmalade, use only 75 g (¼ cup, 2½ oz).

ROAST PORK DISH

Serves 6–8

4 cloves garlic

1 piece roasting pork
(1½–2 kg/3½–4½ lb) (eg hand (fresh picnic), loin or knuckle (leg fillet end, fresh ham))

3 tablespoons honey or golden syrup (light treacle)

1 teaspoon rosemary, finely chopped

1 tablespoon soy sauce

3 tablespoons white wine

¼–½ teaspoon paprika

black pepper

dripping(s)

200 ml (7 fl oz) water

Cut garlic into tiny slivers. Make small cuts over surface of pork. Into each, place a sliver of garlic. Gently warm honey and rosemary. Blend in soy sauce and white wine. Season with paprika and black pepper. Place pork in an ovenproof dish, pour over sauce, a little at a time, rubbing it in with fingers until all of meat has been covered and sauce is used up. Cover dish and leave to stand for 3 hours. Baste with sauce that has dribbled off and turn meat occasionally. Add dripping (about 100 g/⅓ cup/3½ oz) and water. Roast in usual way, basting frequently. (*See* notes on roasting times on p. 74.)

When meat has cooked, prepare a thin gravy as usual—*see* notes on gravy preparation in 'Sauces and stuffings' (p. 224).

Note: Add extra water during cooking if necessary. If fluid level gets too low, the juices become thick and syrupy and burn easily.

PORK FRIED RICE

Serves 4

3 eggs

1 teaspoon oil

1 onion

1 tablespoon oil (extra)

250 g (9 oz) pawpaw (papaya) or peaches

350 g (12 oz) cooked pork (eg leftovers from a roast), cold

juice of 2 oranges

70 g (1½ cups, 2½ oz) cooked brown rice

paprika and black pepper

15 g (⅓ cup, ½ oz) coconut, freshly grated, or 2 tablespoons coconut, desiccated (shredded)

75 g (½ cup, 2½ oz) raisins

100 ml (3½ fl oz) water

85 g (1 cup, 3 oz) lettuce, shredded

Using 3 eggs and 1 teaspoon of oil, prepare an omelette in usual way (*see* omelette preparation on pp. 180–1). When cooked, cut into small pieces. Set aside, but keep warm. Thinly slice onion, fry gently in extra oil until tender and set aside.

Chop fruit into small pieces and cut meat into thin strips. Add orange juice, rice, meat, paprika and a little black pepper to onion. Cook over a fairly high heat, stirring continuously, for several minutes. Add coconut, raisins and water. Cook for a further 3 minutes. Finally, stir in fruit, lettuce and chopped omelette. Cook over a gentle heat for 2 minutes, turning mixture well to ensure an even heating. Serve immediately.

PACIFIC PORK

Serves 4

1 large onion
1 teaspoon dill seed
1½ tablespoons oil
black pepper
600 g (1¼ lb) cooked pork (eg
leftovers from a roast), cold
2 medium tomatoes, skinned (peeled)
250 g (1½ cups, 9 oz) pineapple rings,
sliced (fresh or canned)
1 small green capsicum (sweet pepper)
6 tablespoons water

Finely chop onion. Place in a frying pan (skillet) with dill seed and oil. Fry gently until onion is soft, season with a little black pepper and set aside. Cut pork into thin strips—no more than 1 cm (½ in) thick. Set aside. Skin (peel) tomatoes and chop into small pieces. Cut pineapple into small cubes. Finely chop capsicum. Add pork and water to onion. Cook over a fairly high heat for 2 minutes, stirring frequently. Add tomato and pineapple, reduce heat and cook gently, stirring frequently, for 4 minutes. Spoon into a hot serving dish and sprinkle with capsicum.

SPARE RIBS WITH PLUMS

Serves 4

1 large onion
2 teaspoons ground coriander
1 tablespoon oil
1 kg (2¼ lb) pork spare ribs (beef may
also be used)
250 ml (1 cup, 9 fl oz) water
400 g (14 oz) red (blue or purple)
plums
3 tablespoons water (extra)
4-6 tablespoons raw (demerara,
turbinado) sugar
250 g (1¼ cups, 9 oz) rice

Finely chop onion. Place in a frying pan (skillet) with coriander and oil. Fry gently until onion is soft. Remove excess fat and gristle from ribs (this is most important). Check meat for thickness (see note below). With heat on high, add meat to onion. Cook quickly for 2 minutes, stirring frequently, to seal. Transfer all contents of frying pan to an ovenproof dish, pour over 250 ml (1 cup, 9 fl oz) of water, cover and cook in oven at 170°C or 325°F for 1 hour. Stir two or three times during cooking.

Prepare plums as follows. Cut plum flesh into quarters, discarding stone (pit). Place in a pan and add extra water. Cook over a gentle heat until plums are tender. Remove from heat and sweeten—amount of sugar required depends on type of plum used: eg Victoria (Santa Rosa) plums are very sweet and only require a little, if any, added sugar. Aim for medium sweetness—neither tart nor too sticky—it's difficult to describe, but as a guide I use small dark-red plums rather like a Kirke's blue plum and sweeten with 4 tablespoons of sugar.

When ribs are ready, stir in plums. Replace in oven for a further 45 minutes. Stir two or three times during cooking. Meanwhile, boil rice until tender. Drain. Make a bed of rice on a large warmed shallow dish. Pile spare ribs on top.

Note: 1. Spare ribs carry a lot of their weight in bone. For large appetites, increase quantity used.
2. Spare ribs vary in thickness and toughness. Remove as much fat as possible and also any gristle. Check that meat is no more than 1½ cm (½ in) thick—slice any thicker parts. This applies in particular to beef spare ribs.

SPICY PORK MEATBALLS

Serves 3–4

MEATBALLS

1 onion

250 g (9 oz) pork mince
(ground pork)

1 teaspoon ground coriander seed

½ egg

paprika and black pepper

2 borage leaves, finely shredded

SAUCE

1 tablespoon margarine

¼ teaspoon thyme, finely chopped

½–1 teaspoon turmeric

2 tablespoons wholemeal (whole-
wheat) flour

250 ml (1 cup, 9 fl oz) milk

2 tablespoons thickened (double,
whipping) cream

black pepper

MEATBALLS

Mince or finely chop onion. Place in a bowl. Add remaining meatball ingredients. Mix thoroughly. Proceed as for Meatballs (*see* p. 102), boiling rather than deep-frying to cook. Set aside.

SAUCE

Gently heat margarine, thyme and turmeric until sizzling. Add flour and stir well. Remove from heat and gradually blend in milk. Return to heat. Cook gently, stirring continuously, until sauce thickens. Cook gently for a further 2 minutes to reduce a little. Stir in cream. Season with a little black pepper.

Add meatballs to sauce. Cook very gently, stirring frequently (but carefully, to avoid breaking meatballs) for 5–10 minutes or until thoroughly heated.

Note: The meatballs and sauce may be placed in a covered ovenproof dish and reheated in the oven at 180°C or 350°F for 20–30 minutes or until thoroughly heated. If for a dinner party, the dish can be prepared well in advance and reheated immediately before serving.

Above: *Spicy Pork Meatballs makes an inexpensive family meal. The accompanying turmeric sauce adds an extra dimension, as well as helping to keep the meatballs tender and moist.*

LIVER AND BACON CASSEROLE

Serves 3

1 large onion
1½ tablespoons oil
¼ teaspoon rosemary, finely chopped
1 tablespoon soy sauce
200 ml (7 fl oz) water
black pepper
250 g (9 oz) pig's liver*
100 g (3½ oz) bacon
300 g (10½ oz) potatoes
100 g (3½ oz) carrots

Thinly slice onion. Fry in oil over a medium heat until browned. Spoon half the onion into a separate bowl, leaving remainder in the frying pan (skillet). Now add rosemary, soy sauce and water. Heat. Simmer gently for 4–5 minutes. Season sauce with a little black pepper. Set aside.

Slice liver into pieces no more than 1 cm (½ in) thick. Cut bacon into lengths of 3–4 cm (1¼–1½ in). Slice potato into rounds no more than ½ cm (¼ in) thick. Thinly slice carrot.

Make layers of casserole ingredients in an ovenproof dish (approx. 16 cm (6 in) diameter and 8 cm (3¼ in) deep). The layers are, from bottom to top: potato, carrot, liver, bacon, onion, potato, carrot, liver, bacon, potato. Finally, pour over sauce, cover with a tightly fitting lid and bake at 180°C or 350°F for 1¼–1½ hours. The liver may still appear pinkish on the outside, but if cut in half, the inside should be light brown. It is important not to overcook liver as it becomes dry, leathery and unpalatable.

Note: * Pig's liver is strongly flavoured and lamb's liver could be substituted.

LIVER PÂTÉ 1

125 g (4½ oz) pork
250 g (9 oz) pig's or calf's liver
1 medium onion
100 g (3½ oz) bacon rashers (slices)
salt and black pepper
1 tablespoon brandy
2 tablespoons thickened (double, whipping) cream
1 teaspoon thyme, finely chopped
pinch of paprika
2 cloves garlic, finely chopped
1 egg

Mince pork, liver, onion and 1 rasher (slice) of bacon on a medium or fine setting. Place in a bowl and season with a little salt and black pepper. Thoroughly mix in brandy, cream, thyme, paprika, garlic and egg. Turn into a well-greased pâté dish, or other straight-sided ovenproof dish, with pâté to a depth of 4–4½ cm (1½–1¾ in). Cut remaining bacon into strips and use these to cover pâté. Cover and bake at 170°C or 325°F for 55 minutes.

PORK SAUSAGES (OR BURGERS)

200 g (7 oz) pork tongue
400 g (14 oz) pork shank (hock,
fresh ham)
300 g (10½ oz) belly pork (bacon
piece) or similar low-quality cut
100 g (3½ oz) fatty pork scraps
(including some kidney fat)
4 cloves garlic
1 tablespoon thyme, finely chopped
¼ teaspoon paprika
black pepper

Prepare pork tongue by removing and discarding any rough gristly parts from upper part. Cut into thick slices. Cut away and discard rough skin. Cut pork shank into pieces, discarding bone but keeping skin. Remove and discard bone and gristle from belly pork. Cut into chunks. Cut pork scraps into chunks, peeling away and discarding excess membranes from kidney fat. Pass all meat and fat through a mincer on a fine setting, including garlic cloves with last lot of meat. Place all minced (ground) meat in a bowl, stir in thyme and season with paprika and plenty of black pepper. Stuff into sausage casings or shape into burgers. For more information about making sausages, *see* p. 112.

BRAWN (or HEAD CHEESE)

Serves 6–8
½ pig's head
1 bay (sweet laurel) leaf
2 teaspoons thyme, finely chopped
2 teaspoons oregano, finely chopped
salt and black pepper
1 small onion
1 teaspoon oil

Wash head well. Remove teeth, eyes, and jowls if wished. Place head in a large pan. Cover with water, bring to boil and boil gently with pan covered for 2 hours. Top up water during cooking if necessary to ensure that head is always covered.

Remove head and allow to cool, retaining cooking stock. Peel off skin and discard. Remove all flesh from bones. Place in a bowl. Weigh meat, then measure liquid required from stock retained—use a proportion of 1 g meat to 1 ml (1 oz to 1 fl oz) stock. Pour measured stock into a blender (liquidiser). Add half the meat. Blend for 1 minute, then pour into a saucepan. Add bay leaf, thyme, oregano. Season well with salt and pepper. Chop remaining meat into very small pieces. Add to pan. Chop onion into tiny pieces, fry in oil until soft. Also add to pan.

Stir contents of pan well. Heat until boiling—allow to boil for 1 minute. Pour into a greased dish or pan (eg 1 kg (2¼ lb) loaf tin (pan)). Leave to cool and set for several hours. Place in the refrigerator and allow to mature for 24 hours. If using a tin container, brawn should be removed before refrigerating—gently ease set brawn out of tin and onto a plate or shallow dish. Cut into slices and garnish with parsley to serve.

Note: Skin, if minced very finely, can be added to brawn or used in sausage.

SCRAPPLE

Serves 8–16
(1 or 2 slices per person)
½ pig's head
2 pig's trotters
1 pig's tongue
250 g (9 oz) pig's lung
1 pig's tail
1 pig's heart
200 g (7 oz) pig's liver
200 g (7 oz) pork trimmings or stewing cuts (eg belly pork, end of neck)
2 handfuls sage leaves
6 cloves garlic
2 medium onions
3 tablesoons chopped chives or garlic (Chinese) chives
150 g (5½ oz) kibbled (cracked, burghul) wheat
200 g (1⅓ cups, 7 oz) cornmeal (polenta), finely ground
100 g (¾ cup, 3½ oz) wholemeal (whole-wheat) flour
½ teaspoon paprika
1 teaspoon ground black pepper

Remove and discard fatty jowls from head. Wash well, especially around teeth, nose and ears. Place in a large pan (a jam pan is ideal). Scrub trotters well and place in pan. Wash tongue well in cold water. Cut away any tough gristly parts from its upper end. Place, whole or halved, in pan. Wash lungs and tail well. Also add to pan. Wash heart. Cut away tough tubes from around the top. Halve or leave whole. Add to pan. Wash liver well, cut away any tough parts and add to pan. Cut pork trimmings into large chunks. Also add to pan.

Completely cover contents of pan with water. Cover and heat. When boiling, reduce heat and allow to simmer for 3 hours. Top up water periodically. The meat must always be submerged. When cooked, remove pan from heat and allow to cool. (This will take several hours.) When cool, sort through and identify pieces. Treat as follows:

Pig's head	Remove meat from bone. Discard ear, teeth, bone and snout.
Lung	Cut off any tough, large tubes and discard them. Cut lung into chunks.
Tail and trotters	Remove and discard both.
Trimmings	Remove and discard bone and gristle. Cut meat into chunks.
Heart	Cut into chunks.
Tongue	Peel off and discard skin. Cut meat into chunks.
Liver	Cut into chunks.

Place meat in a blender (liquidiser). Add 650 ml (2⅔ cups, 23 fl oz) of meat broth. Blend until smooth. (You can mince the meat. If you do, use the finest setting you can.) Pour all but a cupful of blended meat into a large saucepan. Add sage, garlic and onions to remaining meat in blender. Blend until smooth. Pour into pan with rest of meat. Add chives, kibbled wheat, cornmeal, wholemeal flour, paprika and black pepper. Mix thoroughly. Cook over a medium heat, stirring continuously, until bubbling. Simmer gently for about 1 minute, stirring vigorously to prevent sticking. Pour into very well greased bread tins (pans). Allow to cool for about an hour. Cover with aluminium foil. Place in the refrigerator for at least 12 hours.

To serve, gently ease each scrapple loaf from its tin. Cut into slices (8–10 per loaf). Serve as follows:

1. Allow to reach room temperature. Serve as is, for an hors d'oeuvre or cold lunch dish.
2. Fry slices gently on each side. Serve hot with toast for breakfast, lunch or as an hors d'oeuvre.
3. Place slices side by side on a flat dish. Cover with cheese slices. Place in oven at 190°C or 375°F until thoroughly heated. Serve for breakfast, lunch or as an hors d'oeuvre.

Note: 1. The composition of meat can be altered considerably. You could omit some cuts and increase the quantities of others. Meat from other carcasses can be used, eg lamb or beef, and could even substitute the pork entirely. Whatever you choose, you must end up with around 1 kg (2¼ lb) of cooked meat for quantity of seasoning and cereal used.
2. Traditional scrapple is an old Pennsylvanian recipe. There are many variations of this recipe. This one is mine.

Lamb & Goat

ROAST KNUCKLE OF LAMB WITH APRICOTS

Serves 6–8
*1 knuckle (leg) of lamb (about
2 kg/4½ lb)
250 g (¾ cup, 9 oz) apricot jam or
thick sweet apricot purée
3 large sprigs of lemon verbena (5 cm
(2 in) long) or lemon balm (5 cm
(2 in) long) or lemon slices*

Wipe lamb with a clean, dry cloth. Spread jam over meat to evenly coat all surfaces. Place one sprig of lemon verbena, lemon balm or lemon slice on top of roast and the others on each side—they will stick to the jam and remain in place. Wrap lamb tightly in aluminium foil. Place in a roasting tin (pan). Cook at 180°C or 350°F for the set time according to the weight of meat (*see* roasting times, p. 74).

SPICY LAMB CHOPS

Serves 4

½ teaspoon ground cumin

1 teaspoon ground coriander

1 teaspoon turmeric

½ teaspoon paprika

8 lamb chops

1½ tablespoons oil

100 ml (3½ fl oz) white wine

100 ml (3½ fl oz) water

2 teaspoons tomato purée (see p. 221)

Mix cumin, coriander, turmeric and paprika. Rub well into lamb chops. Heat oil in a wide heavy-based frying pan (skillet). When hot, place chops in pan. Cook on a fairly high heat for 1 minute. Turn over. Cook for a further minute. Reduce heat to medium. Pour in white wine, water and tomato purée. Cook for 5–7 minutes, turn chops over and cook for a further 5–7 minutes— depending on thickness of chops. If using thicker loin chops, cover pan during cooking to reduce evaporation or add a little more wine and water towards the end of cooking.

There should be 4 or 5 tablespoons of spicy sauce at the end of cooking. Serve separately in a small jug (pitcher) or spooned over chops.

BARBECUED LAMB CHOPS

Serves 4

4 chump or double loin chops

SAUCE

1 teaspoon winter savory,
finely chopped

2 cloves garlic

1½–2 tablespoons soy sauce

3 teaspoons cider vinegar

1 teaspoon honey or golden syrup
(light treacle)

1 tablespoon oil

¼ teaspoon paprika

black pepper

Finely chop winter savory and garlic. Blend with other sauce ingredients. Warm sauce a little if necessary to blend in honey. Lay chops on a shallow dish or plate and spoon over sauce. Allow to marinate for 2 hours. Turn chops and marinate for a further 2 hours. Remove chops and barbecue as usual.

Measure out 1½ tablespoons sauce and add 3 tablespoons water. Pour into a pan, bring to boil and simmer gently for 2 minutes. Serve as a sauce to accompany chops, but use sparingly as it tends to be strong and salty in flavour and can overpower the flavour of the marinated meat.

ROLLED FILLET OF LAMB
WITH APRICOT STUFFING

Serves 6–8
1 fillet end (loin end of leg) or boned
and rolled baron or saddle of lamb
Rice and Apricot Stuffing (see p. 231)
3 large sprigs of lemon verbena
or lemon balm

Take fillet and locate position of tail. Make a deep incision down side of tail until you reach leg bone. Cut right along length of bone. Carefully cut around bone, separating it from meat, lift out and discard. Carefully cut out any vertebrae. You are left with a large piece of meat, oval in cross-section, with a small cavity towards one end of the oval. The next aim is to open meat out into a rectangle of even thickness. Place knife in bone cavity. Make a second and third incision according to figure A. Stop these incisions part-way through meat and *do not* pass through to skin. Now lay out meat into a rectangle as shown in figure B. Remove as much fat as possible (this is essential), but leave skin intact.

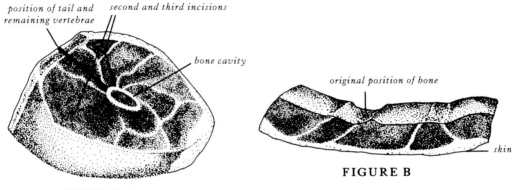

position of tail and remaining vertebrae *second and third incisions* *bone cavity*

FIGURE A

original position of bone *skin*

FIGURE B

Spread stuffing evenly over surface of meat. Starting at a narrow end, roll up meat. Tie firmly in six or seven places along its length with string. Place lemon verbena sprigs over meat. Wrap tightly in aluminium foil. Weigh, place in a shallow roasting tray (pan) and bake in oven at 180°C or 350°F, allowing 45 minutes per kg (20 minutes per lb). If using a meat thermometer, the internal temperature should be 65°C (150°F) for medium, 70°C (160°F) for well done.

To serve, remove meat from foil to a carving plate or board. Cut thick slices, taking care not to break up pattern of meat and stuffing. I find it easier to stand roll up on its end and cut horizontally, lifting slices with a palette knife or fishslice (spatula). Serve juices from around meat separately in a small sauce boat. If excess fat was properly trimmed, the juice will not be greasy.

LAMB WITH BEAN SPROUTS

Serves 4

1 onion

2 tablespoons oil

150 g (5½ oz) potatoes

1 clove garlic

½–1 teaspoon rosemary,
finely chopped

pinch of Chinese five-spice powder
(optional) (see p. 365)

black pepper

300 g (10½ oz) cooked lamb (eg
leftovers from a roast), cold

5 tablespoons white (dry) vermouth or
medium-sweet white wine

125 g (1½ cups, 4½ oz) bean sprouts

Finely chop onion. Fry gently in oil for 2–3 minutes. Peel potatoes and cut into small cubes (approx. 1 cm (½ in)). Finely chop garlic. Add potato, rosemary, garlic and Chinese five-spice powder (if used) to onion. Season with a little black pepper. Cook over a medium heat for 5 minutes, stirring frequently. Cut lamb into small strips (1 × 1 × 2 cm (½ × ½ × 1 in)) and add to pan. Pour in vermouth, stir thoroughly, cover and cook over a medium heat for 7 minutes, stirring occasionally. Add bean sprouts, stir well, cover and cook for a further 5 minutes, stirring occasionally.

Serve with a freshly prepared salad, eg mixed herb, flower, cucumber or a plain green salad.

STUFFED BREAST (FLAP) OF LAMB

Serves 4

½ lamb's breast (flap)

STUFFING

1 apple

1 small onion

½ teaspoon rosemary, finely chopped

50 g (¾ cup, 2 oz) wholemeal (whole-
wheat) breadcrumbs, fresh

1 tablespoon white wine

1 small egg

black pepper

SAUCE

½ teaspoon rosemary, finely chopped

3 tablespoons tomato purée
(see p. 221)

2 tablespoons white wine

5 tablespoons water

2 teaspoons cider vinegar

STUFFING

Grate apple. Grate or finely chop onion. Place both in a bowl. Stir in rosemary and breadcrumbs. Sprinkle over white wine and add beaten egg. Work mixture well with a fork. Season with black pepper.

Cut excess fat from breast meat—it is a fatty cut of meat and not all can be removed, but cut away any thick fatty parts where possible. Next, lay breast on a flat surface. Spread stuffing evenly over it. Roll lengthwise into a sausage shape. Tie in four or five places along its length with white cotton. Place rolled breast in an ovenproof dish in which it fits snugly.

SAUCE

In a small bowl, mix sauce ingredients. Pour over breast. Cover dish with aluminium foil or a lid. Cook in oven at 170°C or 325°F for 1¾ hours. Halfway through cooking, turn breast, cover and replace in oven. Serve with plain boiled rice, or boiled potatoes.

Note: This is a rather rich dish so allow smallish portions only.

Opposite: *Filled with a delicious apple and rosemary stuffing, Rolled Breast (Flap) of Lamb is a tender and succulent version of the traditional roast dinner.*

LAMB CURRY

Serves 3

2 tablespoons oil

1 teaspoon fenugreek seed

½ teaspoon ground ginger

2 teaspoons paprika

1 teaspoon ground cumin

3 teaspoons curry powder (see p. 114)

6 best end of neck cutlets of lamb
or *middle neck (shoulder) cutlets
(rib chops)*

500 g (1 lb) tomatoes

2 onions

200 g (1 cup, 7 oz) white rice

Pour oil into a heavy-based large pan. Add fenugreek seed, ginger, paprika, cumin and curry powder. Heat oil until gently sizzling, stir spices and cook in oil for 1 minute. Trim all excess fat from chops. Place side by side in pan with spices. Cook for 1 minute on each side. Take half of tomatoes and blend (liquidise). Cut onion and remaining tomatoes into thick pieces. Add tomatoes, onions and blended tomato to chops. Stir well, cover and simmer for 1 hour. Stir once or twice during cooking. Remove from heat. Set aside overnight or for at least 12 hours. Simmer gently, uncovered, for 30 minutes. Serve in a warmed serving dish.

Boil rice until tender, drain and serve in a separate bowl.

Note: 1. Please refer to 'General notes on curries' (pp. 112–14).
2. Lamb makes quite a rich curry and is best served with plain boiled rice rather than flavoured rice mentioned in the 'General notes on curries'.
3. Remove any tomato skins which may float to the surface during cooking.

MIDDLE NECK (LAMB SHOULDER) WITH YOGHURT

Serves 3

1 piece middle neck (shoulder) of
lamb, boned (about 500 g/1 lb)

1 large onion

75 g (2½ oz) lean bacon
rashers (slices)

2 teaspoons thyme, finely chopped

½–1 teaspoon winter savory,
finely chopped

3 teaspoons Worcestershire sauce

200 ml (7 fl oz) water

5 tablespoons thick natural (plain)
yoghurt

Trim excess fat from meat—this cut has a large proportion of fat, so you will not be able to remove it all, but do cut away the thicker parts. Place meat, whole, in an ovenproof dish. Thickly slice onion and cut bacon into small squares. Place over and around lamb. In a separate dish, mix thyme, winter savory, Worcestershire sauce and water—pour over meat, cover dish and bake at 150°C or 300°F for 2 hours.

Remove lamb, cut into thin slices and arrange in a heated shallow dish. Strain cooking liquid into a pan. Spoon strained bacon and onion over sliced lamb. Set aside but keep hot.

Skim excess fat from strained liquid—reducing volume by almost one-half. Heat and boil rapidly, uncovered, until reduced in volume to about 65 ml (¼ cup, 2½ fl oz). Remove from heat, allow to cool for a minute or two, then spoon in yoghurt. Mix well. Pour sauce over sliced lamb. Serve immediately with baked potatoes and freshly steamed or boiled vegetables.

Note: This recipe can be adapted for best end of neck (loin, crown roast) in a piece—increase weight used to about 700 g (1½ lb) to allow for bone.

LANCASHIRE LAMB

Serves 6

*1 kg (2¼ lb) middle neck (shoulder)
or scrag end (neck slice, neck) of
lamb, unboned
1½ tablespoons dripping(s) or lard
1 large onion
2 sprigs thyme (each 8 cm (3 in) long)
1 bay (sweet laurel) leaf
1 litre (4 cups, 1¾ UK pints) water
200 g (7 oz) carrots
350 g (12½ oz) potatoes*

PASTRY

*75 g (⅓ cup, 3 oz) margarine
150 g (1¼ cups, 5½ oz) wholemeal
(whole-wheat) flour
1½ tablespoons water*

Trim excess fat from meat and discard—reducing total weight to around 750 g (1¾ lb), including bone. Cut lamb into pieces no thicker than 1½–2 cm (½–1 in). Heat dripping in a large frying pan (skillet). When quite hot, add meat. Cook quickly over a high heat, stirring frequently, until browned all over. Transfer to a deep ovenproof dish, draining off fat (leave fat in pan as it is used later). Thickly slice onion. Add onion, thyme, bay leaf and water to meat. Cover and cook for 2 hours at 150°C or 300°F. Remove from oven and allow to cool for 30–60 minutes. (At this stage, I use the oven's heat for cooking a batch of bread, cakes or a dessert prepared during 2-hour cooking period.)

While lamb is cooling, prepare vegetables. Thickly slice carrots. Reheat fat in frying pan. Cook carrots in fat over a high heat, stirring continuously, until lightly browned. Drain off all fat and set carrots aside. Peel potatoes and cut into thick slices (1–1½ cm/½ in). Set aside in water to prevent discoloration.

When lamb is cool, skim off as much fat as you can and discard. Remove thyme stalks—leaves will have fallen off—and bay leaf. Discard both. Now remove all bone from meat and discard. This messy job involves 'fishing around' in the stew for bony bits of meat. It is not essential and if you prefer to avoid this 'greasy-finger' job, please do. Now add carrot and potato (the latter drained of all water), stir well, cover and replace in oven at 150°C or 300°F for a further hour. While cooking, prepare pastry.

PASTRY

Rub margarine into flour with fingertips. Sprinkle over water. Using a fork, mix well and work into a soft dough. Roll out on a well-floured board to a shape to fit the cooking dish.

When ready, remove lamb from oven. Place pastry over meat and vegetables. Press pastry around edges as best you can (remember the dish is very hot). Place in the oven uncovered, but now at 190°C or 375°F. Cook for 15 minutes. Remove and serve with steamed or boiled vegetables.

LAMB PARCELS

Serves 3

6 mid-loin (double loin) chops, boned
or loin or chump chops, unboned
black pepper
6 small sprigs rosemary
1 large onion
300 g (10½ oz) sausagemeat (fresh
sausage)
¼–½ teaspoon paprika
2 teaspoons rosemary, finely chopped
2 medium tomatoes

Trim excess fat from chops. Season both sides of each with black pepper. Place sprig of rosemary on each. Cut onion into six slices. Place one on each chop. Place sausagemeat in a dish. Add paprika, finely chopped rosemary and season liberally with black pepper. Mix well. Divide into six portions. Take one portion and shape into a ball with hands. Place on a chop and gently flatten to cover meat. Repeat with remaining portions. Cut tomatoes into six thick slices. Place one on each chop. Wrap each chop separately in aluminium foil. Place on a shallow baking tray (sheet). Bake at 190°C or 375°F for 1 hour.

Note: I have kept seasoning of the sausagemeat to a minimum, but you can add other herbs or spices, eg chopped onion, tomato. If you prepare your own sausagemeat (*see* pp. 112, 125), try different kinds for variety.

LAMB AND SPINACH SUPPER

Serves 6

650 g (1½ lb) scrag end of neck (neck
slice, neck) of lamb or other stewing
cut, unboned
2 onions
2 large sprigs rosemary
2 teaspoons butter
50 g (1¼ cups, 1½ oz) spinach or
other greens, eg silverbeet, lettuce,
borage, shredded
8 tablespoons reserved meat stock
salt and black pepper
6 medium potatoes, baked (jacket)*
Hot Tomato Sauce or Fresh Tomato
Sauce (see sauces, pp. 69, 220)

Remove excess fat from meat. Place meat in a large pan. Thickly slice 1 onion. Add with rosemary to pan. Add water to well cover meat, cover with a lid and bring to boil. Reduce heat and simmer for 2 hours. Remove meat from stock. Allow to cool. Reserve stock. Remove meat from bones. Discard bones and fatty parts. Finely chop or mince remaining meat. You should now have around 200 g (7 oz) lean lamb.

Thinly slice second onion. Fry gently in butter until lightly browned. Add spinach. Fry gently for 1 minute. Measure 8 tablespoons of reserved stock and pour into pan. Finally, add lamb. Cook over a medium heat, stirring frequently, until stock has evaporated, but mixture is still moist. Remove from heat, season with salt and black pepper and set aside.

Halve potatoes and scoop out cooked insides, leaving skins intact. Mash potato, add lamb mixture and mix well. Now refill potato skins. Place stuffed potatoes side by side in an ovenproof dish in which they fit snugly. Pour over tomato sauce, cover dish and bake at 180°C or 350°F for 30 minutes.

Note: 1. * The potatoes can be baked at any time. The stuffed potatoes can also can be prepared well in advance of eating—even the day before. Store in a tightly covered container in the refrigerator. Pour over sauce immediately before cooking.
2. Use either sauce, according to preference.

Opposite: Lamb and Spinach Supper — the centres are scooped out of baked potatoes and then mixed with lamb and spinach to make a tasty and nutritious meal.

MEXICAN STEW

Serves 5–6

450 g (1 lb) neck of lamb or scrag end of neck

125 ml (½ cup, 4½ fl oz) red wine

1 large onion

2 cloves garlic

2 red chillies (chili peppers)*

¼ teaspoon each of rosemary, thyme, marjoram, oregano

2 carrots

150 g (1½ cups, 5½ oz) cooked red kidney beans

250 ml (1 cup, 9 fl oz) tomato purée (see p. 221)

Cut lamb into strips 3 cm (1 in) long and 1 cm (½ in) wide and broad. Place in a shallow dish, pour over wine and allow to marinate for 2 hours.

Thinly slice onion and finely chop garlic, chillies and herbs. Slice carrots into thin rounds. Mix together lamb, its marinade and all other ingredients in a heavy ovenproof dish. Cover and cook slowly at 110°C or 225°F for 2 hours.

Note: Three-quarters of a cup of dried beans when cooked will give the 1½ cups required.

* Reduce quantity if preferred.

ROAST SHOULDER OF LAMB

Serves 6

2 cloves garlic

1 shoulder of lamb (about 2 kg/4½ lb)

2 tablespoons soy sauce

½ teaspoon paprika

1 teaspoon turmeric

½ teaspoon ground cumin

½ teaspoon thyme, finely chopped

black pepper

300 ml (1¼ cups, 10½ fl oz) water

3 tablespoons dripping(s) or lard

2 onions

GRAVY

150 ml (⅔ cup, 5½ fl oz) reserved pan juices

150 ml (⅔ cup, 5½ fl oz) water (extra)

2 tablespoons wholemeal (whole-wheat) flour

Cut garlic into thin slices. Make tiny cuts all over surface of lamb. Place a garlic slice in each. Mix soy sauce, paprika, turmeric, cumin, thyme and a little black pepper. Taking a teaspoon at a time, dribble over meat, rubbing in well with fingers. Cover all of the meat in this way. Place in a roasting tin (pan). Leave for 2 hours to allow flavour to penetrate.

Pour 300 ml (1¼ cups, 10½ fl oz) of water into roasting tin. Add dripping or lard. Roast uncovered at 180°C or 350°F (*see* roasting times on p. 74). Baste frequently. Cut onions into quarters. Place around meat for last 30 minutes of cooking. When cooked, remove meat to a heated meat plate and keep hot. Place onions around meat. Reserve pan juices.

GRAVY

Take 150 ml (⅔ cup, 5½ fl oz) of reserved juices. Pour into a saucepan. Add two-thirds of remaining water. Pour rest into a small bowl, blend in wholemeal flour. Add to saucepan. Heat contents of pan, stirring continuously, until gravy thickens. Pour into a hot gravy boat. Serve with meat.

Note: 1. Serve leftovers cold with any remaining gravy (warmed a little). A second batch of gravy can be prepared if needed.

2. Serve cold roast lamb with onion sauce (*see* Silverside with Onion Sauce, p. 108).

3. Use leftover lamb in Lamb with Bean Sprouts (p. 130).

MUTTON WITH MUSTARD

Serves 3

750 g (1¾ lb) stewing mutton
2 teaspoons mustard seed
pinch of paprika
black pepper
1 lamb or mutton trotter
300 g (10½ oz) tomatoes
100 ml (3½ fl oz) water or vegetable
stock
500 g (1 lb) potatoes
3 tablespoons milk
2-4 teaspoons butter
1 tablespoon chives, finely chopped
2-3 tablespoons thick natural (plain)
yoghurt

Remove excess fat from mutton (reducing weight to around 600 g/1¼ lb). Cut meat into small cubes of 1–2 cm (½–1 in). Place in an ovenproof dish. Grind mustard seed and sprinkle over meat. Season with paprika, and black pepper to taste, turning meat to ensure even flavouring. Cut trotter in half and add to dish. Slice tomatoes and layer over meat. Pour in water (or stock), cover dish and cook in oven at 170°C or 325°F for 2¼–2½ hours. When cooked, allow meat to cool for several hours until fat has risen to top and solidified. Scrape off fat, remove trotter halves and any tomato skins, and discard. Spoon meat and all its juices into a saucepan. Set aside.

Peel potatoes, cut into cubes and boil until soft. Reheat meat and juices while finishing potato. Drain potatoes and mash with milk until smooth. Stir in butter and chives. Season with black pepper. Make a ring of potato on a hot serving dish, remove mutton from heat, add yoghurt and pour into potato ring. Serve immediately.

Note: When you add yoghurt, stir once round pan only, so that yoghurt swirls through meat sauce rather than being evenly distributed.

THURSDAY'S MUTTON

Serves 3

750 g (1¾ lb) mutton chops
2 teaspoons white wine vinegar
½–1 tablespoon ground ginger
1½ tablespoons brown (demerara,
(soft) light brown) sugar
2-3 teaspoons rosemary,
finely chopped
¼ teaspoon paprika
1 clove garlic
100 ml (3½ fl oz) water
300 g (2½ cups, 10½ oz) white (drum
head) or green (round head) cabbage,
shredded
50 g (2 oz) egg noodles (the flat ribbon
kind are best)
3 teaspoons butter
1 teaspoon anise seed (aniseed)

Remove and discard excess fat from chops (reducing weight to around 600 g/1¼ lb). Lay chops flat on a plate. Sprinkle with a little vinegar, rubbing well into meat. Turn chops over and repeat. In a small bowl, mix ginger and sugar. Sprinkle half of this mixture evenly over chops, turn over and repeat with remaining mixture. Cover meat and leave for 4 hours. Place chops side by side in a medium-sized frying pan (skillet). Sprinkle in rosemary and paprika. Finely chop garlic. Add to meat. Rinse meat plate with water. Pour this liquid into pan. Cover and heat until boiling, turn chops over. Reduce heat. Simmer very gently for 2½ hours. Turn meat several times during cooking.

Place cabbage in a large pan 15 minutes before meat is cooked. Add water to about 1 cm (½ in) deep. Cook over a high heat (pan uncovered) until tender. At the same time, boil noodles in water until cooked. Heat butter and anise seed in a small pan until sizzling. Set aside. Drain cabbage and noodles, mix together and stir in butter and anise. Spoon onto a flat plate or dish. Heap meat in centre. Serve immediately.

BRAINS WITH MUSHROOMS

Serves 2

1 onion

2 tablespoons oil

paprika

black pepper

½ teaspoon summer savory,
finely chopped

250 g (9 oz) sheep's brains (calf's or
lamb's may also be used)

4 borage leaves, shredded

1 tablespoon soy sauce

125 g (4½ oz) mushrooms, thinly
sliced

Thinly slice onion. Sauté in oil with seasonings and summer savory until soft. Thinly slice brains and shred borage leaves. Add brains, borage leaves and soy sauce to onion, plus a little water to keep moist. On a medium heat, stir continuously until brains are cooked—10–15 minutes (depending on type: calf's can take up to 25 minutes). The brains should be soft, but with every hint of rawness completely gone—take one or two pieces and cut in half to make sure. When almost cooked, add mushrooms, thinly sliced. Continue cooking gently for 2–3 minutes. Check moistness during cooking. Add extra water, a little at a time, if necessary.

Note: You may wish to soak brains in cold water for 1 hour before cooking, and scrape away thin outer skin and remove blood vessels. Leave brains to soak in cold water for another hour. (*See* notes on brains on p. 83.)

HAGGIS

1 sheep's pluck and bag (paunch,
sheep's stomach)

225 g (1½ cups, 8 oz) oatmeal, coarse

2 onions

100 g (3½ oz) suet

½ teaspoon thyme, finely chopped

½ teaspoon sage, finely chopped

salt and black pepper

Wash bag in cold water. Prepare as described for pig's stomach in general methods (p. 82).

Mince 'pluck'. Add toasted oatmeal,* finely chopped onions, grated (shredded) suet, herbs, a little salt and plenty of black pepper. Pack loosely in bag. Sew or bind both openings. Prick all over with a needle to prevent bursting while cooking.

To cook, haggis may be boiled, baked or sliced and fried.

Boiling Immerse prepared haggis in boiling water and boil for 3–4 hours.

Baking Wrap haggis in aluminium foil, place on a baking tray (sheet) and bake at 180°C or 350°F for 1 hour.

Frying Chill well, cut into slices (about 1 cm (½ in) thick) and fry in shallow oil or fat over a medium heat.

I find haggis rather fatty and prefer not to fry it—as a rule I find baking most satisfactory. By wrapping in foil, none of the flavour is lost and fat which accumulates at the bottom of foil can be poured off before serving.

Note: The 'pluck' is the heart, liver and lungs. The 'bag' is the sheep's stomach.

* To toast oatmeal, sprinkle thinly in a heavy-based frying pan (skillet). Heat over a medium heat, stirring or shaking pan frequently, until oatmeal has browned a little.

STUFFED HEARTS

Serves 4

1 medium onion

100 g (1½ cups, 3½ oz) wholemeal (whole-wheat) breadcrumbs, fresh

3 teaspoons thyme, finely chopped

black pepper

4 lamb's hearts

2 rashers (slices) bacon

175 ml (¾ cup, 6 fl oz) red wine

175 ml (¾ cup, 6 fl oz) water

Chop or mince onion until very fine. Place in a mixing bowl. Add breadcrumbs and thyme. Season with black pepper.

Cut away tubes around the two openings into each heart. Rinse hearts in cold water. Taking teaspoonfuls of breadcrumb mixture, stuff both cavities in each heart. Lay side by side in an ovenproof dish. (They should fit quite snugly.) Cut bacon into pieces and place over hearts. Pour over red wine and water, cover tightly and bake at 140°C or 275°F for 1¾ hours.

Note: 1. Beef stock can be used in place of the wine and water.
2. Veal hearts can be used in place of the lamb. Allow about 2¼ hours for cooking. Increase stuffing to approx. 1½ times the quantity given above.

KIDNEYS À LA CRÈME

Serves 4

1 large onion

1 teaspoon thyme, finely chopped

2 tablespoons oil

4 lamb's kidneys

4 tablespoons brandy

100 g (3½ oz) mushrooms

100 ml (3½ fl oz) (single, light) cream

black pepper

Finely slice onion. Sauté with thyme in oil until onion is browned a little and soft. Slice kidneys thinly (about ½ cm (¼ in) thick). Add to cooked onion. Pour in brandy. Cook at a fairly high heat, stirring continuously, for 2 minutes. Reduce heat a little. Add thinly sliced mushrooms. Pour in cream. Stir well, cover pan and allow to cook very gently for a further 2–3 minutes until kidney is cooked. Test by cutting a piece of kidney in half—there should be no rawness, but meat should not be dry. Season with black pepper and serve.

MOUNTAIN GOAT CURRY

Serves 3–4

500 g (1 lb) lean goat meat (any stewing cut will do)

150 g (5½ oz) cream cheese

3 teaspoons curry powder (see p. 114)

2 teaspoons dill seed

5 tablespoons oil

1 tablespoon thick-set natural (plain) yoghurt

150-200 ml (²/3-³/4 cup, 5½-7 fl oz) water

200 g (1 cup, 7 oz) rice

350 g (12 oz) eggplant (aubergine)

½ teaspoon cumin seed, crushed

Cut meat into cubes of 1½-2 cm (1 in). Place in a bowl. In a separate bowl, mix cream cheese, curry powder and dill seed. Add meat to mixture, coating thoroughly. Set aside for at least 12 hours. Heat 1 tablespoon of oil in a pan. When hot, add meat, stirring continuously. Cook for 2 minutes to seal. Reduce heat, stir in yoghurt and add water. Cover pan and cook very gently for 2½ hours. Half an hour before cooked, put rice in a pan of water to boil. Cut eggplant into thin strips. Fry gently in a large frying pan (skillet) with 4 tablespoons of oil and cumin seed. When eggplant is tender, make a ring of it around the edge of a shallow dish. Pour in curry. Drain rice well and serve both dishes.

GOAT CHOPS WITH
CUCUMBER AND POTATO SAUCE

Serves 3–4

300 g (10½ oz) cucumber

6 teaspoons butter

500 g (1 lb) goat chops (any lean frying type)

4 cloves garlic

black pepper

250 g (9 oz) potatoes

4 tablespoons thickened (double, whipping) cream

6 teaspoons chives, finely chopped

2 tablespoons thick-set natural (plain) yoghurt

Thinly slice cucumber (peel first if necessary). Layer half over the bottom of an ovenproof dish. Heat butter until just melted. Spoon 2 teaspoons evenly over cucumber. Lay chops side by side on top of cucumber. Finely chop garlic. Sprinkle evenly over meat. Season with a little black pepper. Now layer remaining cucumber evenly over meat. Spoon remaining butter evenly over top. Cover dish and cook at 170°C or 325°F for 2 hours. Half an hour before meat is cooked, peel potatoes, cut into cubes and boil until tender. Drain well and press through a sieve. Using a fork, evenly blend in cream. Stir in chives and yoghurt. Season with a little black pepper. If necessary, reheat potato mixture very gently in a pan on the stove (cooker). Spoon into a small heated serving dish. Remove meat from oven. Serve at the table with potato sauce. (Spoon sauce as it is too thick to pour easily.)

Poultry & Game

BASIC CHICKEN STEW

Serves 4

1 medium chicken

1 onion

100 g (3½ oz) carrot

300 g (10½ oz) potatoes

2 teaspoons thyme, finely chopped

1 bay (sweet laurel) leaf

½ teaspoon rosemary, finely chopped

1 teaspoon sage, finely chopped

2 teaspoons oregano, finely chopped

1 tablespoon chives, finely chopped

black pepper

100 g (3½ oz) button mushrooms (optional)

Joint chicken. Cut carcass into quarters. Place meat, bones and giblets in a saucepan. Add *just* enough water to cover. Cover and bring to boil. Reduce heat. Simmer for 30 minutes.* Thinly slice onion and carrot. Thickly slice potatoes. Set vegetables aside (potatoes must be set in water to prevent discoloration).

Remove giblets and carcass. Discard bones and giblets (remove any meat remaining on chicken bones and replace in pan). Add onion, carrot, potatoes, thyme, bay leaf, rosemary, sage, oregano and chives to pan. Season with plenty of black pepper. Cover and boil gently for 45–50 minutes. Thinly slice mushrooms (if used), add to stew and simmer uncovered for 5 minutes.

Note: 1. Mushrooms must be young and white—mature mushrooms with black spores will cause discoloration.
2. This recipe can be adapted to make use of chicken carcasses from which main portions have been removed—eg where used for barbecuing or in another recipe. In this case, 3–4 carcasses will provide sufficient meat for four servings.
3. * If preferred, stew can be cooled and skimmed of all fat at this stage.

BARBECUED CHICKEN IN MARINADE

Serves 4–8

8 chicken pieces (portions) (wings, legs)

MARINADE

½ teaspoon rosemary, finely chopped

1 tablespoon oil

6 tablespoons fresh orange juice

pinch of paprika

In a small bowl, blend marinade ingredients. Lay chicken pieces in a shallow dish. Spoon over marinade. Allow chicken to marinate for 2–4 hours, turning meat and basting three or four times. Remove chicken pieces and barbecue as usual.

CHICKEN POT

Serves 8

1½ kg (3½ lb) chicken pieces, (eg legs, wings or breast)

1 onion

2 small carrots

2 large tomatoes

2 cloves garlic

4 tablespoons tomato purée (see p. 221)

200 ml (7 fl oz) water or chicken stock

200 ml (7 fl oz) white wine

1 teaspoon paprika

black pepper and cayenne

1 teaspoon French tarragon, finely chopped

2 large green capsicum (sweet peppers)

2 rashers (slices) bacon

Place chicken pieces in a large, deep casserole dish. Thinly slice onion, carrots, tomatoes and garlic. Add to dish. In a separate bowl, mix tomato purée, water (or stock), wine, paprika, black pepper, cayenne and French tarragon. Pour over chicken and vegetables. Cover dish and bake at 180°C or 350°F for 1¾ hours. Thinly slice capsicum and cut bacon into small pieces. Add to chicken dish, cover and cook at 180°C or 350°F for a further 30 minutes.

COLD CHICKEN IN TARRAGON SAUCE

Serves 6

6 chicken pieces (portions), cooked

1 quantity Tarragon Sauce (see sauces, p. 223)

2 slices lemon

Arrange chicken pieces in a shallow dish or on a plate, pour over Tarragon Sauce and garnish with lemon slices.

CHICKEN CURRY

Serves 3–4

1 medium onion

1½ tablespoons oil

1 tablespoon curry powder
(see p. 114)

½ teaspoon turmeric

3 teaspoons ground coriander

750 g (1¾ lb) tomatoes, skinned
(peeled)

500 g (1 lb) chicken pieces (portions)

1 large green capsicum (sweet pepper)

Thinly slice onion. Place in a frying pan (skillet) with oil. Add curry powder, turmeric and coriander. Fry gently until onion is soft. Skin (peel) tomatoes. Blend (liquidise) until smooth. Pour into frying pan with onions. Simmer, to reduce a little, for 10 minutes. Place chicken pieces in a deep casserole dish. Slice capsicum and place over chicken. Pour over tomato sauce, cover and cook at 170°C or 325°F for 2 hours. Serve with freshly boiled plain rice or Turmeric Rice (*see* below).

Alternative Add 75 g (½ cup, 2½ oz) raisins before oven cooking.

Note: For further notes on curry main-course accompaniments, hors d'oeuvres and desserts *see* 'General notes on curries' (pp. 112–14).

FRUITY CHICKEN CURRY

Serves 4

1 medium chicken

1 onion

2 tablespoons oil

4 teaspoons curry powder (see p. 114)

½–1 teaspoon paprika

250 ml (1 cup, 9 fl oz) water

300 g (10½ oz) eating (dessert) apples

50 g (⅓ cup, 2 oz) sultanas (golden raisins)

juice of 1 orange

Joint chicken. Discard carcass and giblets (these may be boiled up for chicken stock). Thinly slice onion. Place in a deep heavy-based frying pan (skillet) with oil, curry powder and paprika. Fry gently until onion is soft. Add chicken pieces. Cook over a medium heat for 3–4 minutes, stirring frequently and turning chicken. Pour in water, cover and simmer for 1 hour. Stir frequently during cooking. Turn chicken pieces several times to ensure an even cooking. Core apples, but do not peel. Cut into thickish slices. Add apple slices, sultanas and orange juice to chicken, stir well and continue to simmer with pan covered for a further 15 minutes. Serve with Turmeric Rice (*see* following recipe) or plain boiled rice if preferred.

TURMERIC RICE

Serves 3–4

200 g (1 cup, 7 oz) white rice*

1 teaspoon turmeric

1 teaspoon butter

50 g (⅓ cup, 2 oz) raisins

salt and black pepper

Boil rice until tender. Rinse well with fresh boiling water and drain well. Thoroughly mix in turmeric and butter. Stir in raisins, season with a little salt and black pepper. Serve.

Note: * Basmati rice is ideal. The grains of this rice are small but long.

Opposite: *Fruity Chicken Curry, served here with Turmeric Rice, makes a wholesome and spicy meal for cold winter nights.*

CHICKEN SALAD

Serves 3

*1½ teaspoons lemon balm,
finely chopped*

2 teaspoons mayonnaise (see p. 227)

*75 g (⅔ cup, 2½ oz) white (drum
head) cabbage, finely shredded*

125 g (4½ oz) cooked chicken, cold

*100 g (3½ oz) grapes (white or black
(green or red))*

Mix together lemon balm and mayonnaise. Allow to stand for at least 30 minutes to draw flavour from herb. Finely shred cabbage. Cut chicken into thin strips. Cut grapes in half and scoop out pips (seeds). Mix chicken, cabbage and grapes in a bowl, add mayonnaise and stir well. Serve as an hors d'oeuvre or as a cold lunch dish.

Alternative Mix in 1 rasher (slice) of cold cooked bacon cut
into tiny pieces.

Note: * To prepare mayonnaise, follow recipe on p. 227, but omit garlic.

CHICKEN IN MAYONNAISE

Serves 5–6

*½ teaspoon French tarragon,
finely chopped*

3 tablespoons mayonnaise (see p. 227)

1 tablespoon cider vinegar

paprika and black pepper

300 g (10½ oz) cooked chicken, cold

*75 g (1 cup, 2½ oz) lettuce,
finely shredded*

*5–6 whole lettuce leaves or 5–6 slices
wholemeal (whole-wheat) bread*

Mix tarragon, mayonnaise and cider vinegar. Add a pinch of paprika and a little freshly ground black pepper. Set aside for at least 30 minutes to draw flavour from tarragon. Cut chicken into small pieces and finely shred lettuce. Place both in a salad bowl, add mayonnaise dressing and mix thoroughly. Serve each portion on a lettuce leaf or a thin slice of wholemeal bread as an hors d'oeuvre or a lunch dish.

Note: 1. Small portions only are required as this dish is rather rich.
2. * To prepare mayonnaise, follow recipe in sauces (p. 227), omitting garlic.

CHICKEN WITH GINGER

Serves 4

1 medium chicken

1 large onion

2 green capsicum (sweet peppers)

2 cloves garlic

*6 tablespoons tomato purée
(see p. 221)*

1 teaspoon ground ginger

2 tablespoons sherry (optional)

½ teaspoon paprika

*1 teaspoon French tarragon,
finely chopped*

Joint chicken and place chicken pieces (portions), carcass and giblets in a large pan. Add enough water to well cover chicken. Cover pan with a lid. Bring to boil, reduce heat and simmer for 45 minutes. Remove chicken pieces and 300 ml (1¼ cups, 10½ fl oz) of cooking liquid to a second pan (discard carcass and giblets, but retain stock for use in soups, stews, sauces etc). Thinly slice onion and capsicum. Finely chop garlic. Add these and remaining ingredients to second pan. Bring to boil, reduce heat and simmer uncovered for 15 minutes. Serve with plain boiled rice and a salad.

CHICKEN WITH NOODLES

Serves 6
1 boiling (stewing) chicken*
1 onion
1 bay (sweet laurel) leaf
*3 sprigs thyme (approx. 5 cm
(2 in) long)*
*1 sprig oregano (approx. 7 cm
(2¾ in) long)*

SAUCE
*750 ml (3 cups, 27 fl oz) of reserved
cooking stock, skimmed*
1½ teaspoons thyme, finely chopped
salt and black pepper
2 onions
2 tomatoes

NOODLES
*500 ml (2 cups, 17½ fl oz) of reserved
cooking stock, skimmed*
100 g (3½ oz) egg noodles

Place chicken and its giblets into a deep pan. Cut onion into quarters. Add to pan with herbs. Add water to well cover chicken, cover with a lid and bring to boil. Simmer gently for 3½ hours. Top up water during cooking as necessary. Remove chicken. Set aside to cool. Strain stock and allow to cool (discard giblets, herbs and onion). When cool, remove all chicken meat from bones. Break or cut into pieces (portions) (remove and discard skin too if preferred). When stock is cool, skim as much fat as possible from surface and discard.

SAUCE
Measure out 750 ml (3 cups, 27 fl oz) of skimmed stock. Pour into a pan. Add thyme and season with salt and pepper. Thinly slice onions, cut tomatoes into small pieces and add both to pan. Bring to boil. Boil uncovered for 30 minutes. Reduce to a gentle simmer and add chicken pieces. Cover pan and allow to cook very gently while preparing noodles.

NOODLES
Measure 500 ml (2 cups, 17½ fl oz) of original chicken stock into a pan. Bring to boil. Add noodles and cook until al dente. Drain (retaining liquid). Stir noodles into chicken. Spoon onto a large meat plate or large shallow dish. Serve with a green salad or stir-fried vegetables.

Alternative Boil chicken as described in first section. Remove, cool and joint meat. Use for Chicken in Tarragon Sauce (p. 141), Chicken in Mayonnaise (p. 144), Salisbury Chicken (below) or Chicken Salad (p. 144).

Note: * This recipe is most suitable for old laying hens which are far too tough for roasting. The remaining stock and that from the cooked noodles should be saved for a soup—it really is delicious.

SALISBURY CHICKEN

Serves 4
¼ teaspoon paprika
¼ teaspoon dill seed
2 tablespoons mayonnaise (see p. 227)
200 g (7 oz) cooked chicken, cold
2 teaspoons medium-dry sherry
1 teaspoon soy sauce
black pepper

Stir paprika and dill seed into mayonnaise. Allow to stand for at least 1 hour. Very finely chop or mince chicken. Place in a bowl. Add prepared mayonnaise, sherry and soy sauce. Season with a little black pepper.

Note: 1. This dish can be served as a party snack—spread thinly on crackers or thin squares of wholemeal (whole-wheat) toast; *or* as an hors d'oeuvre, served on a lettuce leaf or a thin piece of toast. Only offer small portions as this dish is very rich.
2. * To prepare mayonnaise, follow recipe on p. 227, omitting garlic.

WHOLE CHICKEN WITH ORANGE

Serves 4

1 roasting chicken (about 1½ kg/
3½ lb)

1 small onion

1 orange

200 ml (7 fl oz) water

1 teaspoon paprika

2 teaspoons French tarragon,
finely chopped

Place chicken in a roasting dish (pan) or ovenproof casserole. Peel and quarter onion, placing quarters inside chicken carcass. Squeeze juice from orange. Pour over chicken breast and legs, rubbing in a little with fingers. Pour water around base of chicken. Finally, sprinkle with paprika and tarragon. Cover and bake at 200°C or 400°F for 1–1½ hours, depending on size of chicken (see roasting times for poultry on p. 88). Baste several times during cooking.

DUCK WITH ORANGE SAUCE

Serves 4–5

1 duck (1½-2 kg/3½-4½ lb)

1 onion

2 oranges

2 teaspoons thyme, finely chopped

½ teaspoon paprika

salt

250 ml (1 cup, 9 fl oz) water

2 slices of orange (to garnish)

SAUCE

1 tablespoon butter

1 level tablespoon cornflour
(US cornstarch)

100 ml (3½ fl oz) water

juice of 1 orange

1 tablespoon golden syrup (light
treacle)

Wash duck in cold water, drain and place in an ovenproof dish or casserole. Peel onion and cut into quarters. Place inside duck carcass. Take a half of 1 orange, peel and cut into thick slices. Also place inside duck carcass. Squeeze juice from remaining 1½ oranges. Pour slowly over duck, rubbing into meat a little. Sprinkle duck with thyme, paprika and a little salt. Pour water into cooking dish, cover and cook at 170°C or 325°F for 2 hours. Baste four or five times during cooking.

SAUCE

To avoid lumps, use a little of the water to mix cornflour to a smooth paste. Melt butter in pan until sizzling. Quickly stir cornflour paste into melted butter. Remove from heat. Blend in remaining water and orange juice. Return to heat. Stirring continuously, bring to boil. Reduce heat and cook very gently for 1–2 minutes. Remove from heat. Stir in syrup (sauce 1).

Take 3 tablespoons of sauce 1. Place in a separate dish. Add 1 tablespoon of juices from around cooked duck. Stir and blend well (sauce 2).

Remove duck from dish. Place on a warmed meat platter or shallow dish. Spoon sauce 2 over duck. Garnish with orange slices. Serve sauce 1 at table in a warmed jug (pitcher).

Opposite: *This classic dish, Duck with Orange Sauce, is ideal for special family occasions or when entertaining friends.*

APIA DUCK

Serves 4–5
1 onion
2 tablespoons oil
600 g (1¼ lb) boned duck, boiled
1 teaspoon thyme, finely chopped
¼ teaspoon paprika
black pepper
2 bananas
200 g (7 oz) pawpaw (papaya)
50 g (¾ cup, 2½ oz) lettuce, shredded
50 g (⅓ cup, 2 oz) raisins

Thinly slice onion. Fry gently in oil until soft. Cut meat into thin slices. Add duck, thyme, paprika and a little black pepper to onion. Cook over a medium heat, stirring well, for 2 minutes. Slice bananas, add to pan, stir well and continue cooking for a further minute. Chop pawpaw into small pieces (1–1½ cm (½ in) cubes). Add pawpaw, lettuce and raisins to pan. Cook very gently for a further 3 minutes, stirring frequently.
Alternative Add 2 tablespoons natural (plain) yoghurt just before serving. Stir in or leave as covering sauce.

Note: 1. This dish can be served on a bed of shredded lettuce and accompanied by Melba toast or hot herb bread for supper *or* as an hors d'oeuvre.
2. White duck meat such as Muscovy is best for this dish.

GOOSE WITH APPLES

Serves 6
1 goose
1 small eating (dessert) apple
2 quantities of Apple and Onion Stuffing (see *stuffings*, p. 231)
salt
¼–½ teaspoon mace, ground
Cilla's Apple Sauce
(see *sauces*, p. 225)

Starting at rear of bird, above cavity made to remove entrails, separate skin from flesh. Proceed forward, gently lifting skin from breast meat to form a cavity on either side of breast bone. You may find the skin firmly attached along the breast bone—leave intact. At rear of bird, at entrance to gut cavity, you will find on most domestic geese quantities of subcutaneous (below-skin) fat—much of this can be cut away and discarded, but save two pieces and cut into strips. Tuck these fat strips inside cavities just made, along each side of breast bone. These will release fat during cooking and automatically baste breast meat. Now thinly slice apple. Place slices one layer thick over breast meat inside cavity. The breast meat when cooked will be moist from fat-basting, but the greasiness is tempered by the acidity of the apples. Stuff body cavity with Apple and Onion Stuffing. Close cavity with skin flaps. Sprinkle whole goose with a little salt and mace. Rub into skin well. Place in a roasting tin (pan), cover tightly with aluminium foil or a lid and cook at 200°C or 400°F allowing 55 minutes per kg (25 minutes per lb).

After half an hour of cooking, baste goose well, drain excess fat from roasting tin and replace in oven. Baste frequently during remaining cooking period. Serve with Cilla's Apple Sauce.

Note: For a thin sauce to accompany meat, warm several tablespoons of apple jelly with a small quantity of meat juices. Thicken with a teaspoon or two of cornflour (US cornstarch).

YOUNG MALLARD WITH
LEMON AND SHERRY SAUCE

Serves 4–5

*2 young mallard (500-600 g/
1-1¼ lb each)*

1 onion

3 slices lemon

4 lemon balm leaves

rind of 1 lemon, grated

5 tablespoons lemon juice

*1 tablespoon lemon balm leaves,
finely chopped*

350 ml (12 fl oz) water

black pepper

4 tablespoons medium-dry sherry

5 teaspoons cornflour (US cornstarch)

1 tablespoon granulated sugar

Wash ducklings well. Place in a deep ovenproof dish. Peel onion and cut off two thick slices. Place one inside each duckling carcass cavity with half a slice of lemon and 2 lemon balm leaves. Thinly slice remaining onion. Place in a bowl. Add grated lemon rind, lemon juice, finely chopped lemon balm and water. Season with black pepper. Pour over duckling, cover with a tightly fitting lid and cook in oven at 180°C or 350°F for 1¼ hours. Baste often. Turn ducklings at least once during cooking so that every part of bird sits in liquid at some stage.

Remove ducklings from dish and joint them. Reserve cooking liquid. Place meat in a warmed shallow ovenproof dish. Set aside but keep hot. Pour sherry into a small bowl. Carefully blend in cornflour. Add sugar. Heat ducklings' cooking liquid until simmering. Slowly add sherry mixture, stirring continuously. Continue heating until sauce thickens. Pour sauce over duckling meat. Serve garnished with remaining lemon slices.

LIVER PÂTÉ 2

*2 tablespoons mixed herbs, eg thyme,
sage, marjoram, rosemary and lemon
thyme or lemon balm, finely chopped*

3 cloves garlic

400 ml (1⅔ cups, 14 fl oz) milk

100 g (3½ oz) apple

1 onion

2 tablespoons margarine

*2 tablespoons wholemeal (whole-
wheat) flour*

350 g (12 oz) chicken or pig's liver

pinch of paprika

black pepper

2 eggs

Place herbs, garlic and milk in a blender (liquidiser). Cut apple into quarters and core. Skin and quarter onion. Place apple and onion in blender. Blend for 30 seconds. Prepare sauce by melting margarine, adding flour and slowly adding about 150 ml (⅔ cup, 5½ fl oz) of milk mixture. Cook sauce gently for 1 minute to reduce a little. Set aside.

Cut liver into thin strips. Place in blender with remaining milk mixture. Blend for 30–40 seconds. Pour this mixture slowly into sauce, stirring well to blend thoroughly. Season with paprika and black pepper. Break eggs into mixture, beat a little and pour into a well-greased ovenproof dish (approx. 20 cm (8 in) in diameter). Cover and bake at 180°C or 350°F for 1½ hours. Remove and allow to cool. Place in refrigerator. This pâté tastes best if eaten the next day. Serve with thin slices of freshly toasted wholemeal (whole-wheat) or rye bread.

Guinea Fowl

Guinea fowl is rather like chicken, but has a gamey flavour reminiscent of its relative, the pheasant. Any of the preceding chicken recipes may be used. As extras, I offer the following two recipes. Remember that guinea fowl meat tends to be dry—particularly breast meat. To counteract this, always brush well with oil before cooking. When cooking a whole fowl, place carcass breast side down in the cooking dish. *See* notes on roasting poultry (pp. 87–9).

GUINEA FOWL BAKED IN YOGHURT

Serves 4–6

6 pieces (portions) guinea fowl
(eg legs, wings or breast)
2 tablespoons oil
1 teaspoon caraway seed
½ teaspoon paprika
black pepper
200 g (7 oz) natural (plain) yoghurt
50 g (½ cup, 2 oz) cheddar cheese,
grated
25 g (⅓ cup, ¾ oz) wholemeal
(whole-wheat) breadcrumbs, fresh

Brush each piece of guinea fowl liberally with oil to coat all surfaces. Place side by side in an ovenproof dish. Sprinkle caraway and paprika evenly over meat. Season with a little black pepper. Spoon yoghurt evenly over top. Cover with a lid or aluminium foil. Bake at 190°C or 375°F for 1 hour.* Grate cheese into a small bowl. Stir in breadcrumbs. Spread evenly over guinea fowl, re-cover and replace in oven for 10 minutes.

Note: 1. For this dish I use 1 guinea fowl of around 1½ kg (3½ lb). I remove legs, wings and breast meat for use, which then serves four. The carcass may be used for a soup or stock in Basic Chicken Stew (see p. 140). If you prefer, use 6 guinea fowl legs or 6 guinea fowl breasts in this recipe, which then serves six.
2. * After cooking for 1 hour, yoghurt will have curdled and separated, but this does not matter.

GUINEA FOWL FOR REUBEN

Serves 4–6

1 guinea fowl (about 1½ kg/3½ lb)
2 tablespoons oil
1 cardamom pod
100 ml (3½ fl oz) white wine
150 g (½ cup, 5½ oz) dark honey
(eg Jamaican, Manuka, English)
1 tablespoon ground ginger

Brush guinea fowl evenly all over with oil. Place breast side down in a deep snugly fitting ovenproof dish. Remove seeds from cardamom pod and crush a little. Gently warm wine and honey. Stir in cardamom and ginger. Pour over fowl, cover with a lid and bake at 200°C or 400°F. Allow 35 minutes per kg (16 minutes per lb), plus 15 minutes. Baste frequently and, halfway through cooking, turn fowl onto other side of breast.

ROAST TURKEY

Serves 8–10

1 turkey (about 4 kg/9 lb)
Sausagemeat (Fresh Sausage)
Stuffing (see stuffings p. 230)
Bread Stuffing for Poultry
(see stuffings, p. 231)
4 small onions
3 tablespoons oil
2 teaspoons thyme, finely chopped
2 teaspoons parsley, finely chopped
black pepper
6 rashers (slices) bacon
125 g (½ cup, 4½ oz) lard
Bread Sauce (see sauces, p. 219)

Wash turkey well, inside and out. Drain. Pat dry with a clean cloth or paper towels (absorbent kitchen paper). Working at neck end, place one hand in body cavity. Pushing forward with fingers, gently but firmly lift skin away from breast meat on one side. Continue pushing and separating as far back as possible, then down to leg and wing, and up to breast bone. Take half of Sausagemeat (Fresh Sausage) Stuffing. Pack into cavity to cover breast meat. Now repeat with other side of breast. Stuff with remaining sausagemeat. Divide bread stuffing into four portions and shape each into a ball. Place stuffing and onions (peeled) inside body cavity. Truss turkey in usual way or simply pull loose neck skin up to seal off body cavity, fold it over back and sew in place or secure with cotton thread (string).

In a small bowl, mix oil, thyme and parsley. Season with black pepper. Rub this oil and herb mixture evenly all over turkey. Cut bacon rashers into halves. Place side by side over turkey to cover whole breast area. Tie each in place with cotton thread. Melt lard in a roasting tin (pan). Place turkey in tin, breast side up. Cover tightly with aluminium foil. Bake at 170°C or 325°F for 3½ hours. Baste frequently during cooking. Thirty minutes before the end of cooking, remove foil to allow turkey to brown. Serve with Bread Sauce.

Note: *See following recipe for making use of cold leftover turkey.*

TURKEY AND LOVAGE PIE

Serves 6

PASTRY

75 g (1/3 cup, 3 oz) margarine

*150 g (1 1/4 cups, 5 1/2 oz) wholemeal
(whole-wheat) flour*

2 tablespoons water

FILLING

350 ml (1 1/2 cups, 12 1/2 fl oz) milk

1 medium onion

1 tablespoon oil

*2 tablespoons wholemeal
(whole-wheat) flour (extra)*

3-4 teaspoons lovage, finely chopped

200 g (7 oz) cooked turkey, cold

PASTRY

Rub margarine into flour with fingertips. Sprinkle over water. Using a fork, work mixture into a soft dough. Roll out on a well-floured board. Use pastry to line a greased pie dish (plate) (18 cm (7 in) diameter).

FILLING

Pour milk into a saucepan, bring to boil. Stir well to stop boiling over. Reduce heat. Boil gently for 15 minutes (uncovered). Set aside.

Finely chop onion. Fry in oil over a medium heat until browned a little. Stir in extra flour and lovage. Remove from heat. Gradually blend in milk. Return to heat. Stir constantly until sauce thickens. Chop turkey into small pieces. Stir into sauce. Spoon mixture into pastry case (shell). Bake pie at 200°C or 400°F for 25–30 minutes.*

Note: Chicken or duck can be used in place of turkey.

* This pie can also be baked with a top. In this case, double the amount of pastry.

DEEP-FRIED RABBIT WITH SOUR SAUCE

Serves 4

8 rabbit hind legs

Sour Sauce (see p. 170)

Make three times quantity given in recipe for Sour Sauce. Cut hind legs of rabbit at middle joint. Deep-fry pieces as required. Serve immediately with sauce in a separate bowl.

Note: Refer to notes on rabbit for details of deep-frying (*see* p. 93).

RABBIT BRAISED IN HOT CHILLI SAUCE

Serves 5–6

1 rabbit (1 1/4 kg/2 3/4 lb)

4 tablespoons oil

2 teaspoons dill seed

1/4 teaspoon paprika

400 ml (1 2/3 cups, 14 fl oz) water

*4 tablespoons tomato purée
(see p. 221)*

4 cloves garlic

2 chillies (chili peppers)

300 g (1 1/2 cups, 10 1/2 oz) white rice

Joint rabbit. Heat oil in a large deep pan. Add rabbit pieces (portions), keeping oil hot. Turn meat frequently to seal outside. Cook for 5 minutes. Remove from heat. Add dill seed, paprika, water and tomato purée. Finely chop garlic and chillies. Add to dish. Mix thoroughly. Spoon into a large ovenproof dish or casserole. Be sure to scrape pan clean. Cover with a tightly fitting lid. Place in hot oven at 170°C or 325°F for 2 1/2 hours. Stir mixture two or three times during cooking. Top up with a little extra water if necessary. Just before rabbit is cooked, boil rice until tender. Serve rabbit and rice in separate bowls.

RABBIT AND NOODLES

Serves 6

350 g (12½ oz) cooked rabbit, boned
2 tablespoons margarine
2 cloves garlic
2 tablespoons wholemeal
(whole-wheat) flour
200 ml (7 fl oz) milk
2 teaspoons marjoram, finely chopped
100 g (3½ oz) egg noodles
black pepper
1 large tomato
1 medium-sized green capsicum
(sweet pepper)
1 tablespoon butter
150 g (1¼ cups, 5½ oz) dried wholemeal (whole-wheat) breadcrumbs,
finely ground

Cut meat into strips. Set aside. Heat margarine in a large, heavy-based saucepan. When sizzling, add finely chopped garlic and cook for 1 minute. Stir in flour. Remove from heat. Blend in milk. Cook gently, stirring continuously, until sauce thickens. Remove from heat. Add marjoram and rabbit. Mix thoroughly.

Boil noodles until al dente, drain and add to rabbit and sauce. Mix thoroughly. Season with black pepper. Spoon into an oven-proof dish. Now chop tomato and capsicum into small pieces. Place in a small pan. Add butter and cook gently until capsicum is tender. Remove from heat, add the breadcrumbs and mix thoroughly. Spread over rabbit mixture. Bake at 180°C or 350°F for 30 minutes.

RABBIT AND LEEK CASSEROLE

Serves 4–5

1 rabbit (1–1¼ kg/2¼–2¾ lb)
salt and black pepper
pinch of paprika
250 g (9 oz) leeks
100 g (3½ oz) carrots
300 ml (1¼ cups, 10½ fl oz)
vegetable or chicken stock
3 tablespoons sherry
1 teaspoon French tarragon,
finely chopped

Joint rabbit. Season each piece (portion) with a little salt and black pepper and a sprinkling of paprika. Place in a deep casserole. Cut leeks and carrots into thin rounds. Place over and around meat. In a separate bowl, mix stock, sherry and tarragon. Pour into casserole, cover with a tightly fitting lid and cook in the oven at 180°C or 350°F for 2½ hours.

FRIED RABBIT WITH
SWEET SESAME SAUCE

Serves 4–5

600 g (1¼ lb) rabbit legs

1 egg, beaten

100 g (¾ cup, 3½ oz) dried whole-meal (whole-wheat) breadcrumbs, finely ground

150 g (⅔ cup, 5½ oz) butter

4 tablespoons fresh orange juice

SAUCE

2 tablespoons butter

3 tablespoons sesame seed

3 tablespoons pawpaw (papaya) jam (see p. 323)

8 tablespoons thick natural (plain) yoghurt

2 teaspoons cornflour (US cornstarch)

2 teaspoons lemon juice

4 tablespoons thickened (double, whipping) cream, whipped

Take hind legs of rabbit and cut at middle joint. For larger thigh joints, you may need to open meat out to reduce its thickness. Cut down to bone and along length to open meat out flat. Cut flattened piece in half. Leave bone intact in one half or remove, as you wish. Cut front legs at second joint. Wash all pieces well and dry thoroughly. Beat egg and pour into shallow dish. Place breadcrumbs on a large plate. Coat pieces of rabbit evenly in egg. Roll in breadcrumbs until evenly coated. Set aside.

I find it best to fry the rabbit in two batches. Sort out thickest pieces to cook first. Place 100 g (3½ oz) butter in a heavy-based frying pan (skillet). Heat until sizzling. Keeping heat on high, add rabbit pieces. Cook for 2–3 minutes. Now cover pan, reduce heat to low. Cook gently until meat is cooked right through (15–20 minutes). Turn meat during cooking as necessary. Test if cooked by cutting open thickest piece. When ready, remove meat to a warmed serving dish and keep hot. Add remaining 50 g (2 oz) butter to pan. Cook rest of rabbit. Reduce cooking time by 5 minutes, as these pieces are thinner.

SAUCE

While rabbit is cooking, prepare sauce. Melt butter in a small pan, add sesame seeds and cook gently for several minutes until seeds have browned slightly. Remove from heat. Add jam. Mix thoroughly. Mix in yoghurt. Mix cornflour and lemon juice in a small cup. When smooth, stir into sauce. Heat very gently, stirring continuously, until sauce thickens fully. Remove from heat, allow to cool for 1 minute, fold in cream. Serve sauce warm but not hot.

Sprinkle orange juice over rabbit and serve as follows:

- Place cooked rabbit pieces on a plate and pour sauce over.
- Serve sauce in a sauce boat or small jug (pitcher). Offer individual servings of rabbit.
- Offer a very small sauce-filled bowl to each person. The rabbit is eaten with fingers and dipped into sauce. Herb bread should be served with meal. Finger bowls of rose-scented water (to prepare, *see* p. 374) are also offered. Fresh, light salads should follow. (This is our favourite serving method.)

Note: If pawpaw (papaya) jam is unavailable, try peach or apricot jam, or a marmalade or jelly, eg rosehip, redcurrant or rowanberry. Light-coloured fruits are best, so avoid mulberries, blackberries (brambles), blackcurrants.

ROAST RABBIT WITH APPLE
AND LEMON SAUCE

Serves 5–6

1 rabbit (1¼–1½ kg/2¾–3½ lb)

3 lemons

250 g (1 cup, 9 oz) butter

3 teaspoons mint, finely chopped

3 tablespoons lemon juice

400 g (14 oz) eating (dessert) apples

2 teaspoons cornflour (US cornstarch)

a little water

8 tablespoons thickened (double, whipping) cream

3-4 teaspoons thick natural (plain) yoghurt

Prepare rabbit as for roasting (*see* pp. 92–3). Place in an oven-proof dish into which it fits snugly. Take 1 lemon and cut into quarters. Place two quarters around rabbit. Set other two quarters aside. Finely grate rind of other 2 lemons and squeeze juice. Place grated rind in a small pan. Add 150 g (⅔ cup, 5½ oz) butter and 2 teaspoons of mint. Heat gently until butter has melted. Stir in lemon juice. Pour over rabbit, cover and cook at 180°C or 350°F for 1½ hours. Baste frequently during cooking.

Thirty minutes before rabbit is cooked, prepare sauce. Peel and core apples. Cut into small cubes (½–1 cm/¼–½ in). Place in a pan with remaining butter. Cook very gently until apple is tender, but not mushy. To avoid lumps, mix cornflour with just enough water to make a smooth paste. Stir cornflour paste into apple. Allow to cook for about 30 seconds. Remove from heat. Gradually blend in cream. When smooth, add remaining mint. Cook very gently until sauce thickens. Remove from heat. Gradually blend in yoghurt. Reheat very gently if necessary.

To serve, remove cooked rabbit to a hot meat plate, leaving behind roasting juices. Pour hot apple sauce over rabbit. Garnish with two remaining lemon quarters. Alternatively, serve rabbit in its roasting juices, garnished with two remaining lemon quarters. Serve apple sauce in a separate bowl.

fish

Fish is an excellent source of protein and minerals, in particular iodine. It is becoming quite expensive now if compared to meat, but in many countries today it is still possible to catch your own. My husband and I gorged ourselves on fish when we lived on Western Samoa in the Pacific. The market was beside the sea and the boats drew up to the wharf with the fish and shellfish which were sold there and then, ungutted and often still wriggling! Fish of all colours and sizes were brought in. Our favourite was bonito—a tuna fish. The flesh is pink when raw, but turns brownish in colour when cooked, and the texture becomes rather meaty. Our favourite dish was stir-fried bonito with a sweet and sour sauce. It was superb. Another fish we thoroughly enjoyed was parrotfish, so called because the skin is bright turquoise in colour and the mouth is horny and shaped just like that of a parrot. This fish we preferred raw. It sounds awful, but in fact is delicious—details of preparation are given later.

Lobsters (crawfish, rock lobsters) and crabs were so cheap they quickly became market-day 'musts'. In all, we preferred these plain—ie just boiled. The flavour of fresh lobster or crab is enough in itself, needing no seasoning and no sauce. Not far from town were mudflats in which resided tiny shellfish whose local name was *tuangane*—these were rather like tiny scallops. The local womenfolk would plait small baskets of coconut leaves and then go out and dig for *tuangane* to fill the baskets. They sold the harvest of their labour in the market or more often by the side of the road. We placed the *tuangane* in boiling water to open the shells and ate them raw, plain or with a little sauce or mayonnaise—they were delicious.

Preparation of Fish

Fish if bought whole, ie uncleaned, or if personally caught, is said to be 'green'. First it has to be descaled and gutted.

Scaling

The fish is held by the tail and scraped towards the head. The back of the knife is a good tool to use. You are actually scraping 'against the grain', as it were, and scales will pop out of place and can be washed off under cold running water. The largest fish scales I have ever seen are those of the parrotfish. They were easy to see and easy to remove. Take care to do a thorough job on fish with tiny scales. A little extra effort makes all the difference.

Gutting

Round Fish The point of a sharp knife is pushed into the belly of the fish just under the operculum (or gill slit). The knife cuts along the line of the belly to the vent, just before the tail fin. The entrails may be gently scraped out. The fish is washed well in cold water.

Flat Fish The gut of a flat fish is just behind the head. A semi-circular cut is made behind the head on the upper surface (the dark side). The gut cavity will be seen and entrails may be gently scraped out and fish washed well in cold water.

Skinning

It is not always necessary to skin fish, it really depends on how the fish is to be cooked and on personal preference. For grilling (broiling), the skin may be left on, also for baking whole. It is more usual to leave the skin on round fish.

Round Fish Cut skin behind the operculum from the back to the belly. With one hand holding the head, use other hand to pull skin gently but firmly away from the head. It should come away neatly in one piece. If necessary, use a very sharp knife to slit skin along the line of the backbone. Also take care with skin in areas where the ventral fins are situated—you may get tearing here. Cut off skin at the tail. Repeat on the other side.

It is also possible to remove skin once the fish has been filleted. In this case, lay fillet down on a flat surface, skin down and flesh uppermost. Starting at the pointed end of fillet and using a sharp knife, gently separate skin and flesh. Grasping skin with one hand and a sharp knife in the other, cut between skin and flesh—ie with knife held at something like a 45° angle with the blade turned downwards towards skin, gently cut between skin and flesh. It sounds rather complicated, but is in fact quite an easy task. The important thing is to keep the knife blade at the correct angle, so that it does not cut through the flesh nor slice through the skin, but cuts nicely between them.

Flat Fish Lay fish dark side up. Make a small cut in skin just in front of tail. Now with tail in one hand, grasp cut skin and gently but firmly pull away from tail. The skin should come away in one sheet. The underneath or lighter skin may be removed or left in place according to preference.

Filleting

Round Fish Cut off head just behind operculum. From this cut end you will be able to see the backbone. Begin filleting at this cut end. The aim is to slice between the backbone and flesh, so that no bones get left behind in the fillet, and little or no flesh is left on the backbone that will be discarded. Take cutting slowly. Carefully control the angle of the blade so that, as nearly as possible, it lies parallel to the backbone. Use a slicing motion and gradually cut right through to tail. Cut off this fillet and set aside. Now, starting again at the head end and exercising the same care as before, cut under backbone to free fillet underneath: cut it off at tail. Examine both fillets closely. Remove any remaining bones with tweezers.

Flat Fish These give four fillets. First, cut along the line of and through to the backbone from behind head to right in front of tail. Cut behind head in a curve as though you were about to cut off the head, but in fact cut through only half the thickness of the fish. Using this cut as the starting place, insert knife and with a slicing motion cut horizontally just above bones to separate flesh from bones. Continue until just before tail. Cut this fillet off at tail. Turn fish around and remove second fillet. Turn fish over and remove remaining two fillets in the same way. Inspect all fillets. Remove any remaining bones with tweezers.

Boning

Large Round Fish This applies to salmon and salmon trout. First they must be cooked either by poaching or by slow baking (wrapped tightly in aluminium foil) in the oven. (*See* later notes on cooking methods.) When cooked, lay fish flat on a board and skin as described for round fish. Now cut transversely through the backbone just behind head and just in front of tail. Using a sharp knife, cut carefully along the line of the backbone. Ease out backbone slowly and carefully so as not to break the flesh.

Small Round Fish This applies to smaller fish such as herrings and mackerel. Often fish for smoking, such as trout, are boned in this way. The flesh remaining is in one flat piece and not folded over in the middle. Gut fish first, then cut off head and tail. Open fish out from the belly. Press flat onto a board with skin uppermost. Feel for backbone. Press well along backbone to loosen it. Now turn fish over. With a pointed knife, carefully ease backbone and rib bones from flesh. Check fish carefully. Remove any remaining bones with tweezers. The fish may now be folded back into its original shape, cut into two fillets or left flat as described for smoked trout.

Steaks and Cutlets

Instead of filleting, round fish may be cut transversely into steaks or cutlets. The skin is left intact and the bones left in place. Cutlets come from the middle part of the fish. There will be a gap or hole at the bottom, which is the gut cavity. Steaks are cut from the tail end beyond the gut cavity, so they are complete with no hole or gap at the bottom.

Methods of Cooking
Grilling (Broiling)

Grilling (broiling) is suitable for small round or flat fish which are grilled (broiled) whole, or for fillets and steaks.

Brush fish with a little olive oil. If whole fish are used or fillets with skin on, make several incisions in skin at regular intervals to prevent skin bursting and to allow a more even cooking—of particular importance with whole fish. Season with a little salt and black pepper and, if wished, a sprinkling of finely chopped herbs. Grill (broil) under a medium heat. Turn once during cooking and baste frequently. Fillets will take 4 to 5 minutes and 10 to 15 minutes for steaks, cutlets and whole fish. When sufficiently cooked, flesh will be white (or pale pink for salmon and salmon trout) and will separate easily into flakes when a round-bladed knife is gently pushed into it. Take particular care with exposed flesh (where skin has been removed), as there is a tendency for it to dry out and harden on the surface. Control this with grill (broiler) temperature, amount of basting and distance of fish from the grill element.

Special care must be taken if grilling (broiling) sole. Elizabeth David says it should be skinned on both sides and grilled under a low to medium heat, basting frequently. Alternatively, sole may be marinated in a little lemon juice for 30 to 60 minutes, brushed well with olive oil and sprinkled with breadcrumbs. This will protect the fish from drying out.

Fish kebabs may be prepared using cubes of fish fillet and shellfish such as scallops, prawns (shrimp) and mussels. The fish may be marinated in lemon juice, white wine or a sauce before cooking. It is then threaded on metal or wooden skewers, brushed with a little oil and grilled (broiled) under a medium heat for 15 minutes. Kebabs should be turned and basted frequently.

Poaching or Boiling

Poaching or boiling is suitable for whole fish, small or large, or for cutlets and fillets. The fish is simmered slowly in liquid either on top of the stove (cooker) in a saucepan or in a covered dish in the oven at 180°C or 350°F. The liquid may be milk, fish stock or water, and is usually seasoned with herbs (eg bay (sweet laurel) leaf), lemon juice, onions and black peppercorns. The fish is cooked when flakes separate easily.

A traditional French fish stock used in particular for salmon and salmon trout is Court Bouillon and is prepared as follows.

COURT BOUILLON

2 carrots
3 spring onions (scallions) (white and green parts)
1 small sprig lovage (5 cm/2 in long) or pinch of celery seed
1 bay (sweet laurel) leaf
3 parsley sprigs (3-4 cm /1¼-1½ in long)
4 tablespoons lemon juice
250 ml (1 cup, 9 fl oz) dry white wine
salt and black pepper
1 small sprig fennel (approx. 5 cm/2 in long)
850 ml (3½ cups, 1½ UK pints) water

Thinly chop carrots, spring onions and lovage (if used). Place in a pan with white wine, celery seed (if used), lemon juice, bay leaf and water. Finely chop parsley and fennel. Add to pan. Season with a little salt and black pepper. Cover pan and bring to boil. Reduce heat and simmer gently for 15 minutes. Strain through a fairly fine mesh and use as required. This recipe was adapted from that in *The Cookery Year* published by the Reader's Digest Association.

Steaming

For steaming, the fish is placed on a plate or shallow dish. It is seasoned with a little salt and black pepper, and chopped herbs if wished. A small knob of butter is placed in the middle of the fish and a few tablespoons of milk or water are poured over. A second plate is placed on top. The plates are then placed over a pan of boiling water. The heat from the rising steam cooks the fish.

This method is suitable for thin pieces of fish such as fillets, thin steaks or cutlets. Cooking time is around 10 minutes depending on the thickness of the fish. Fish cooked in this way is very easily digested and is therefore excellent invalid fare—as my mother knew well. Now I hate steamed fish—it reminds me so much of those awful childhood illnesses, chicken pox, measles and the like. Don't be put off though, it is an excellent way of cooking fish simply, so that its fine flavour comes through totally unadulterated.

Frying/Sautéing

Always fry or sauté fish in clean fresh-tasting vegetable oil. Olive oil is reputed to be the best for flavour, with peanut oil coming a close second. One of the important points to note with all fish to be fried is that it must be thoroughly dry on the outside. Paper towels (absorbent kitchen paper) or a cloth will do the job nicely. If fish is wet on the outside, a high temperature on the surface of the fish will not be achieved immediately. The fish will then have a chance to absorb the oil before the outside is sealed, and the result will be soggy, oily fish. If a batter or breadcrumbs are used, they will not stick in place, but will fall away during cooking.

A second point worth mentioning is that the oil must always be hot when fish is added. If too cool, soggy, oily fish will again be the result. If too hot, the outside of the fish will be overcooked before the inside is ready. The correct temperature is approx. 180°C or 356°F. To test, drop in a small cube of fresh bread. It should cook to a golden brown in 40–60 seconds.

Shallow-frying (Sautéing)

- Dust fish lightly with flour that has been seasoned with salt, black pepper and a little finely chopped herbs; *or*
- Brush liberally with beaten egg using a pastry brush. Sprinkle evenly all over with breadcrumbs. Medium-ground oatmeal may be used in place of breadcrumbs.

The depth of oil need be only ½–1 cm (¼–½ in). Heat oil and, when hot enough, gently lay fish flat in the pan. Cook over a moderate to high heat for about 10 minutes, depending on the thickness of the fish. The fish should be turned over halfway through cooking. Drain well on paper towels (absorbent kitchen paper) before serving.

Deep-frying

- Dust with flour—*see* notes under 'Shallow-frying (sautéing)' above.
- Coat with egg and breadcrumbs—*see* notes under 'Shallow-frying (sautéing)' above.
- Coat with batter. Dust fish with a little flour, dip into batter and place straight into hot fat. It will puff up with the heat and cook into a crisp, golden-brown casing.

CRISPY BATTER

1 egg yolk, lightly beaten
5-6 tablespoons milk
1 tablespoon oil or *(single, light)*
cream
100 g (¾ cup, 3½ oz) plain
(all-purpose) flour
2 egg whites

Beat yolk a little. Beat in milk and oil or cream. Place flour in a bowl and make a well in centre. Pour in liquid. Gradually mix together, avoiding lumps. Just before using, whisk whites and fold into mixture.

Note: This batter is also suitable for coating fruit slices, comfrey leaves, elderflower heads, poultry and rabbit.

Baking

Baking is suitable for whole fish, large or small, or for fillets, cutlets or steaks.

Whole Fish Brush fish all over the outside with melted butter or olive oil. To season, sprinkle with salt, black pepper and finely chopped herbs. Alternatively, place a sprig of fresh herbs, eg fennel, inside body cavity. The fish may be stuffed with a breadcrumb mixture flavoured with chopped vegetables and herbs, if wished. It is then wrapped tightly in aluminium foil and placed in the centre of a preheated oven. Large fish, eg salmon and salmon trout, should be slowly baked at around 150°C or 300°F. Smaller fish, eg trout, are baked at 180°C or 350°F. *See* recipe for Stuffed Trout (p. 172).

Fillets, Steaks and Cutlets The fish is placed in a shallow ovenproof dish, dotted with two or three knobs of butter and seasoned with salt, and finely chopped herbs. Several tablespoons of milk or water are poured over. The dish is covered and placed in a preheated oven at 180°C or 350°F. Cooking time is quite short—10–15 minutes, depending on the thickness of the fish. Baste two or three times during cooking.

   Fillets may be spread with a stuffing, rolled and secured with cotton thread (string) or cocktail sticks (toothpicks). In this case, the fish will stand out well above the added liquid. It is therefore essential to cover the dish tightly with aluminium foil or a lid. Baste several times during cooking.

Stir-frying

Stir-frying is an Asian method of fish cookery and particularly suited to oily rather than white fish. The fish is cut into pieces of 3–4 cm (1¼–1½ in) long and 1 cm (½ in) thick and broad. A very small amount of oil is poured into a heavy-based frying pan (skillet) or wok—just enough to lightly oil the surface. When oil is almost smoking, the fish is added and stirred continuously. The heat should be kept fairly high. The fish cooks in just 2–3 minutes. Finely chopped vegetables, spring onions (scallions), tomatoes, green peas, etc may be added with the fish. Towards the end of cooking, a sauce—sweet and sour sauce, tomato sauce, lime or lemon juice or wine—may be added. My husband used to prepare a superb sweet and sour fish dish using the bonito which I mentioned earlier.

Seasoning Season the oil with spices and chopped herbs or marinate the fish pieces first in wine or fruit juice. Fresh ginger, finely chopped, goes surprisingly well with stir-fried fish. I thought it would completely mask the delicate fish flavour, but not so.

Eating Raw

As I mentioned earlier, raw fish is surprisingly good and was a favourite of ours when we lived in Western Samoa. Only white fish (eg parrotfish) should be used.

   We called this fish dish 'Ota'. First the flesh is cut into cubes of about 1–1½ cm (½ in).

It is placed in a bowl and fresh lime (or lemon) juice added. Use plenty of juice so that each piece of fish gets a thorough soaking. Place bowl in the refrigerator for 12–18 hours. Stir fish several times during soaking. Just before serving, pour off the juice, reserving about one-quarter. Prepare fresh coconut cream (*see* p. 166). Mix with reserved juice. Pour over fish, toss well and serve chilled.

COCONUT CREAM

1 ripe coconut

Take coconut and extract flesh. Grate or chop flesh very finely. Place in a bowl. Pour over a little warm water. Allow to stand for 1 minute. Spoon grated coconut into a muslin (heavy cheesecloth) bag, hold over a clean bowl and squeeze and squeeze. The liquid that comes out is coconut cream. Repeat until all coconut has been squeezed. The water in which coconut was soaked may be mixed into coconut cream or discarded (it can be added to a curry or simply drunk). The thickness of the coconut cream is determined by the amount of water used for soaking. For the fish dish Ota (p. 164), prepare a fairly thick cream, about the thickness of thickened (double, whipping) cream.

Fish

FRIDAY PIE

Serves 6

PASTRY
75 g (⅓ cup, 3 oz) margarine
150 g (1¼ cups, 5½ oz) wholemeal (whole-wheat) flour
2 tablespoons water

FILLING
200 g (7 oz) bream (red bream, scup, porgy), snapper or tarahiki fillets or other white fish
1½ tablespoons oil
1½ teaspoons dill seed
125 ml (½ cup, 4½ fl oz) Basic Wholemeal (Whole-Wheat) Sauce (see sauces, p. 218)
3 large eggs, separated
black pepper

PASTRY
Rub margarine into flour with fingertips, sprinkle water over mixture. Using a fork, work into a soft dough. Roll out on a floured board. Use pastry to line a shallow greased pie dish (plate) 20 cm (8 in) in diameter.

FILLING
Cut fish into small pieces. Heat oil. When quite hot, add dill seed and fish. Cook over a fairly high heat, stirring constantly, until fish is well cooked. (It will flake when gently pressed with a round-ended knife.) Remove from heat. Set aside.

Prepare sauce according to recipe (prepare half the quantity given). Separate egg yolks from whites. Beat yolks into sauce, stir in cooked fish and season with black pepper. Whisk egg whites until stiff. Fold into fish mixture. Pour into pastry case (shell). Bake at 190°C or 375°F for 25 minutes.

SOUTHBRIDGE FISH

Serves 4–8

250 g (9 oz) cauliflower
300 g (10½ oz) cooked white fish
(eg cod, hake, tarahiki, John Dory,
snapper)
4 medium-sized French sorrel leaves
100 g (1 cup, 3½ oz) cheese
(eg cheddar), grated
250 ml (1 cup, 9 fl oz) Basic Wholemeal (Whole-Wheat) Sauce
(see sauces, p. 218)
salt and black pepper
pinch of paprika
2 teaspoons butter
50 g (1 cup, 2 oz) wholemeal (whole-
wheat) breadcrumbs, fresh

Break cauliflower into tiny florets. Steam, stir-fry or boil until tender. Set aside. Flake fish and set aside. Shred sorrel leaves and grate three-quarters of cheese. Warm wholemeal sauce a little. Add cheese and sorrel. Stir until cheese has melted. Season with salt, pepper and paprika. Add fish and cauliflower. Stir gently to mix all ingredients, but take care not to break up fish and cauliflower pieces. Spoon into a shallow ovenproof dish 20 cm (8 in) in diameter.

In a saucepan, gently heat butter until just melted. Add breadcrumbs. Grate remaining cheese and add to pan. Mix well. Spoon evenly over fish and cauliflower. Place in preheated oven at 180°C or 350°F for 15–20 minutes until thoroughly heated.

Alternatives
- Make a cooked rice and grated cheese layer over fish in place of breadcrumb mixture. Cover dish with aluminium foil and bake for 20–25 minutes.
- Make a cooked vegetable and grated cheese layer in place of breadcrumb mixture, eg sliced green (French or runner, string) beans, sliced potato or sliced fresh tomato.
- Omit breadcrumbs and butter. Sprinkle with grated cheese.
- Omit breadcrumb and cheese layer entirely and leave plain.
- Substitute 1 tablespoon of finely chopped chives for sorrel.

FISH PÂTÉ

Serves 4

100 g (3½ oz) fish fillets (white or
oily, eg haddock, mullet, mackerel,
tarahiki, kahawai)
2 tablespoons butter
2 teaspoons lemon thyme,
finely chopped
2 teaspoons parsley, finely chopped
100 g (3½ oz) cream cheese
3 teaspoons dry white wine
black pepper
4 fresh lettuce leaves

Chop fish into tiny pieces. Set aside. Heat butter in a small pan. When sizzling, add fish, lemon thyme and parsley. Cook over a medium heat, stirring constantly, for several minutes until fish is cooked. Remove from heat. Set aside to cool. Mash fish until well broken into small pieces. Add cream cheese, wine and a little black pepper. Continue mashing and mixing until evenly blended. Place a little pâté on each lettuce leaf. Serve with Melba toast or hot crusty bread as an hors d'oeuvre.

Note: Fish pâté may also be served spread on bread or crackers as a party nibble or pre-dinner appetiser; *or* as a dip—served with thin fingers of toast, carrot sticks or cheese straws.

ROSEMARY FISH TRIANGLES

Serves 4–8

PASTRY

125 g (½ cup, 4½ oz) margarine
250 g (1¾ cups, 9 oz) wholemeal
(whole-wheat) flour
3½ tablespoons water

FILLING

100 g (3½ oz) fish fillets (eg cod,
trout, tarahiki, snapper)
250 ml (1 cup, 9 fl oz) milk
50 g (2 oz) butter
100 g (½ cup, 3½ oz) carrot, grated
1½-2 teaspoons rosemary,
finely chopped
2 tablespoons wholemeal (whole-
wheat) flour
1 egg
salt and black pepper

PASTRY

Rub margarine into flour with fingertips. Sprinkle water over mixture. Using a fork, work into a soft dough. Roll out on a floured board. Cut pastry into eight squares of 12 cm (5 in).

FILLING

Cut fish into small cubes of 1–1½ cm (½ in). Place in a small pan with milk. Bring to boil. Reduce heat and simmer for 5 minutes. Remove from heat. Drain milk into a small bowl. Set milk and fish aside separately. Melt butter in a pan. When sizzling, add carrot and rosemary. Cook over a gentle heat, stirring frequently, until carrot is tender. Stir in flour, remove from heat and gradually blend in milk. Heat gently, stirring constantly, until sauce thickens. Allow to cook for a further 2 minutes to reduce a little. Remove from heat, break egg into sauce and beat thoroughly. Return to heat. Cook gently, stirring vigorously, until it thickens further. Remove from heat, stir in fish and season with salt and black pepper. Set aside until cool.

Divide filling into eight portions. Place one portion on each square. Take one square, moisten edges with a little cold water and fold pastry over to make a triangle. Press pastry edges together firmly. Place triangle on a well-greased baking tray (sheet). Brush with a little beaten egg white. Repeat with remaining squares. Bake in oven at 200°C or 400°F for 20 minutes.

PINEAPPLE FISH

Serves 4

300 g (10½ oz) oily fish fillets (eg
mackerel, trevally, tuna, mullet)
200 g (7 oz) tomatoes
1 tablespoon oil
1 tablespoon lemon balm,
finely chopped
500 g (1 lb) fresh pineapple, peeled
and diced
1 banana
2 teaspoons coconut, desiccated
(shredded) (optional)

Cut fish into small cubes of 1–1½ cm (½ in). Set aside. Skin (peel) tomatoes, chop into tiny pieces and set aside. Heat oil in an enamel or stainless steel pan. Add fish and lemon balm. Cook over a fairly high heat, stirring constantly, for 3–4 minutes. Add tomatoes. Cook gently for 5 minutes, stirring frequently. Cut pineapple into cubes of 1–1½ cm (½ in). Add to fish. Cook for a further 3 minutes, stirring frequently. Serve topped with sliced banana and, if wished, a sprinkling of desiccated (shredded) coconut.

Note: It is essential to use fresh fish and fresh pineapple for the correct blending of flavours.

Opposite: *A delicious and unusual way to serve fish, Rosemary Fish Triangles will appeal to everyone.*

FISH WITH BASIL

Serves 4–5

1 medium onion

1 tablespoon oil

3–4 teaspoons basil, finely chopped

3 tablespoons tomato purée

(see p. 221)

black pepper

250 g (9 oz) tomatoes

50 g (2 oz) egg noodles

150 g (5½ oz) white fish fillets (eg haddock, hake, cod, tarahiki, hoki)

1½ tablespoons butter or margarine

2 tablespoons wholemeal (whole-wheat) flour

250 ml (1 cup, 9 fl oz) milk

3 egg yolks

Thinly slice onion. Fry gently in oil until tender. Remove from heat. Add basil and tomato purée. Season with a little black pepper. Blend (liquidise) tomatoes until smooth (skin (peel) first if you prefer), add to pan and mix thoroughly. Bring to boil, reduce heat and boil gently, uncovered, for 5 minutes. Set aside. Boil noodles until al dente, drain and add to tomato mixture. Cut fish into small cubes of 1–1½ cm (½ in). Add tomatoes and noodles. Mix well. Spoon into a shallow ovenproof dish 20 cm (8 in) in diameter and 4–5 cm (1½–2 in) deep.

In a small pan, heat butter until sizzling, stir in flour and remove from heat. Gradually blend in milk. Return to heat. Stirring constantly, heat gently until sauce thickens. Add egg yolks, beat sauce well and continue heating very gently until it thickens further. Layer sauce over tomato and fish mixture. Bake at 200°C or 400°F for 25–30 minutes.

POLYNESIAN FISH

Serves 4

SAUCE

200 g (7 oz) potato
2 tablespoons oil
100 ml (3½ fl oz) tomato purée
(see p. 221)
2 teaspoons fresh ginger,
finely chopped
1 teaspoon soy sauce
2 teaspoons cider vinegar
2 teaspoons ground coriander
paprika and black pepper
100 ml (3½ fl oz) white wine
100 ml (3½ fl oz) water
1 clove garlic, finely chopped

FISH

400 g (14 oz) oily fish fillets (eg
mackerel, trevally, tuna, mullet)
1-2 tablespoons oil
1 tablespoon coconut, desiccated
(shredded) (optional)

SAUCE

Peel potato. Cut into thin strips (approx. 1 cm/½ in wide, 3 cm/1¼ in long and 3–4 mm/¼ in thick). Heat 2 tablespoons of oil. When quite hot, add potato. Cook over a high heat, stirring frequently, until potato is beginning to brown. Add remaining sauce ingredients. Mix well. Simmer gently (uncovered), stirring frequently, for 5 minutes. Remove from heat. Set aside but keep warm.

FISH

Cut fish into strips (approx. 3 cm/1¼ in long and 1 cm/½ in wide and thick). Stir-fry in oil. Add sauce to fish. Continue cooking for a further minute or two until thoroughly heated. Spoon into a heated serving dish. Sprinkle with coconut if used. Serve with plain boiled rice and/or stir-fried vegetables.

Note: Sweet potato (kumara) or bamboo shoots can be used in place of potato.

DEEP-FRIED FISH WITH SOUR SAUCE

Serves 4

4 portions white fish in breadcrumbs
(eg sole or plaice, snapper or
gurnard fillets)

SAUCE

1 tablespoon natural (plain) yoghurt
1 tablespoon sour (dairy sour) cream
1 teaspoon salad burnet,
finely chopped

Thoroughly blend all sauce ingredients. Spoon into a small dish or sauce boat. Set aside for at least 1 hour to draw flavour from fresh herb. Stir thoroughly before using.

For details of preparing and cooking fish, *see* pp. 158–65.

The sauce is served at the table with the fish, as with the traditional sauce tartare.

Note: Sour Sauce can also be used to accompany baked or steamed fish.

FISH AND CARAWAY SOUFFLÉ *See* recipe under soufflés (pp. 204–5).

SARDINE-STUFFED EGGPLANT (AUBERGINE) *See* recipe in 'Hot vegetable dishes' (p. 33).

SWEET AND SOUR FISH

Serves 4

SAUCE

¾ tablespoon wholemeal (whole-wheat) flour

2 tablespoons water

1 clove garlic

1½ tablespoons soy sauce

1 tablespoon brown ((soft) light brown) sugar

1½ tablespoons wine vinegar

1 tablespoon tomato sauce (ketchup) (see p. 338)

1 tablespoon dry sherry

¼ teaspoon chilli (chili pepper), finely chopped (optional)

½ tablespoon fresh ginger, finely chopped

FISH

400 g (14 oz) mackerel fillets or any other oily fish (eg trevally, tuna, mullet)

½-1 tablespoon oil

SAUCE

In a bowl, blend flour and water until smooth. Finely chop garlic. Add to bowl, with all remaining sauce ingredients. Pour into a small pan. Heat gently, stirring continuously, until sauce thickens. Set aside but keep warm.

FISH

Cut fish into cubes (1–1½ cm/½ in). Heat oil in a heavy-based frying pan (skillet) or wok until very hot. Add fish and stir-fry until just cooked. Pour sauce over fish, stir well and continue heating for ½–1 minute, until thoroughly heated. Spoon into a hot serving dish. Serve immediately with plain boiled rice.

FISH WITH CARAWAY AND RICE

Serves 3

200 g (7 oz) white fish fillets

50 g (⅓ cup, 2 oz) brown rice

1 green capsicum (sweet pepper)

2-3 tablespoons whole almonds (optional)

2 tablespoons oil

2 teaspoons caraway seed

4 tablespoons orange juice

2 teaspoons lemon juice

black pepper

2 tablespoons (single, light) cream

3 wedges lemon

Cut fish into small cubes of 3 cm (1¼ in). Set aside. Cook rice until tender. Set aside but keep hot. Thinly slice capsicum and chop nuts (if used) into small pieces. Place oil in a large frying pan (skillet). Set over a medium heat. When oil is hot, add capsicum, caraway seed and nuts. Cook, stirring frequently, for 2–3 minutes. Add fish and, stirring continuously, cook over medium heat for a further few minutes until outside of fish pieces is well sealed. Stir in orange and lemon juice. Allow to cook, stirring frequently, until juices have all but evaporated. Remove from heat, season with black pepper, mix in rice and stir in cream. Turn onto a warmed dish. Serve with lemon wedges.

STUFFED TROUT

Serves 4

50 g (1 cup, 2 oz) wholemeal (whole-wheat) breadcrumbs, fresh
salt and black pepper
1 teaspoon French tarragon, finely chopped
100 ml (3½ fl oz) white wine
1 medium onion
100 g (3½ oz) mushrooms
4 trout
100 ml (3½ fl oz) water

In a bowl, mix breadcrumbs, salt, a pinch of black pepper, tarragon and 2 tablespoons of white wine. Finely chop onion and mushrooms. Add to bowl. Mix ingredients well. Set aside.

Gut trout and wash well in cold water. Take one-quarter of breadcrumb mixture. Use it to stuff 1 trout. Tie trout with cotton thread (string) in two places along its length. Repeat with remaining trout. Place side by side in an ovenproof dish. Pour over water and remaining white wine. Season with a little salt. Cover and bake at 180°C or 350°F for 25–30 minutes. Baste twice during cooking.

STUFFED TROUT WITH APRICOT FILLING

Serves 6

6 trout
1 quantity Rice and Apricot Stuffing (see stuffings, p. 231)

Gut trout, wash well and pat dry with a clean cloth or paper towels (absorbent kitchen paper). Stuff each trout as full as possible with stuffing. Tie in at least three places around belly with cotton thread (string). Wrap each separately in aluminium foil. Place fish side by side in a shallow ovenproof dish. Bake at 180°C or 350°F for 25–30 minutes.

TROUT BAKED WITH YOGHURT

Serves 4

4 whole trout
2 small oranges
black pepper
½ teaspoon ground mace
8 tablespoons natural (plain) yoghurt

Wash trout well and dry with a clean cloth or paper towels (absorbent kitchen paper). Place side by side in a shallow ovenproof dish. Thinly slice oranges. Set aside four slices for garnish. Divide remaining orange slices among the 4 fish. Place slices neatly inside gut cavity so that they overlap—they will, of course, protrude from the cavity. Sprinkle a little black pepper over each fish. In a small bowl, mix mace and yoghurt. Spoon evenly over fish, except heads. Cover with a lid or aluminium foil. Bake at 200°C or 400°F for 20 minutes. Serve in dish straight from oven, garnished with orange slices.

OMELETTE WITH RAINY DAY FILLER *See* savoury omelette section (p. 196) for this recipe.

Opposite: *For special occasions, Stuffed Trout with Apricot Filling makes an impressive, but simple to make, main course — especially if the trout has been freshly caught.*

PRAWNS (SHRIMP) AND ASPARAGUS WITH FENNEL SAUCE

Serves 3–4

500 g (1 lb) whole prawns (shrimp)

250 g (9 oz) asparagus

SAUCE

2 cloves garlic

½ small green capsicum (sweet pepper)

1 tablespoon butter

1½–2 teaspoons fennel leaf, finely chopped

2 teaspoons garlic (Chinese) chives, chopped

3 tablespoons thickened (double, whipping) cream

2 egg yolks

2 tablespoons cream cheese

pinch of paprika

black pepper

½–1 tablespoon lemon juice

TO PREPARE PRAWNS

Plunge prawns into boiling water. Boil for 3 minutes. Remove from heat. Allow prawns to cool in water. Serve warm or cold, but not hot.

SAUCE

Very finely chop garlic and capsicum. Gently heat butter in pan until sizzling. Stir in garlic, capsicum, fennel and garlic chives. Cook for 2–3 minutes. Remove from heat. Stir in cream. Beating vigorously, add egg yolks. Heat sauce very gently until thickened. Remove from heat, add cream cheese and stir until thoroughly blended into sauce. Season with paprika and a little black pepper. Finally, add lemon juice. Mix thoroughly. Pour into small individual serving dishes. Serve warm or cold.

Plunge asparagus into boiling water. Boil rapidly for a few minutes until tender. Drain and set aside. Serve warm or cold. The prawns and asparagus are eaten with the fingers at the table, using the sauce as a dip.

Note: Other shellfish can be prawns, eg scallops, crayfish, used instead of lobster (rock lobster) or mussels. Adjust quantities as necessary, remembering that of 500 g (1 lb) of prawns used, a third to a half is head and shell.

Remember to offer finger bowls of scented water to all guests. *See* Scented Pelargoniums/Geraniums (p. 374) for instructions.

ALAFUA FISH

Serves 2–3

100 ml (3½ fl oz) thin (single, light) cream

2 tablespoons coconut, desiccated (shredded)

1 tablespoon chives, finely chopped

black pepper

200 g (7 oz) oily fish fillets (eg trout, bonito)

2 teaspoons butter

Pour cream into a small pan. Add coconut and chives. Season with a little black pepper. Warm very, very gently for 15 minutes—it must not bubble at all (the aim is to soften coconut and draw out flavour). Cut fish into small cubes of 1–1½ cm (½ in). Heat butter in a shallow frying pan (skillet). When gently sizzling, add fish. Cook over a medium heat, stirring frequently, until well cooked. Pour in coconut sauce, stir thoroughly and immediately remove from heat (again, do not allow to bubble). Spoon into a piping hot serving dish. Serve with boiled white rice, boiled sliced red sweet potato (kumara, yam) or baked sweet potato.

Note: Allow only small portions of the fish as it is rather rich.

TUNA FISH KEDGEREE

Serves 3–4
1 medium onion
1½ tablespoons oil*
125 g (⅔–¾ cup, 4½ oz) rice (white
or brown)
175 g (6 oz) tuna fish, cooked
1 teaspoon lemon juice (optional)
salt and black pepper

Finely chop onion. Fry gently in oil until tender and lightly browned. Boil rice until tender, drain and set aside. Flake tuna fish. Add to cooked onion. Cook over a very gentle heat for 1 minute, stirring well. Add rice and lemon juice. Cook very gently for several minutes until thoroughly heated. Season with salt and pepper. Spoon into a hot shallow serving dish. Serve immediately.

Note: * If using canned tuna, excess oil can be drained from fish and used to fry onion.

WHITEBAIT FRIED WITH SAGE

Serves 3
50 g (½ cup, 2 oz) wholemeal (whole-
wheat) flour
1 small handful sage leaves
200 g (7 oz) whitebait
oil for deep-frying
3 lemon wedges

Pass flour and sage leaves through a grinder (I use my coffee grinder) until you have a fine powder. Rinse whitebait under running water. Drain away excess liquid. Spread flour over a flat plate. Taking a small handful at a time, roll whitebait in flour until evenly coated. Repeat until all whitebait are flour-coated. Be gentle as they bruise and fragment easily. Deep-fry whitebait for several minutes. Drain well to remove excess oil. Place on a hot serving dish. Serve with lemon wedges.

eggs &

dairy
PRODUCTS

Eggs

Eggs always seem to me to be one of nature's finest miracles—a neat little packet of nutritious goodness in a wrapping so well designed that cooking may be done with or without it. For the smallholder, eggs are fairly easily produced and provide a constant, even source of protein throughout the year. It seems a pity therefore that egg cookery generally is so limited. Dr William Kitchener, writing in *The Cook's Oracle* around 1821, observed: 'They reckon 685 ways of dressing eggs in the French kitchen . . .' With that in mind, it does seem a shame that in most homes, hotels and restaurants, eggs take third place after meat and fish and that there is such a limited variety of egg dishes. So cooks, please read Elizabeth David's *French Provincial Cooking* (see Bibliography). She has written an excellent chapter describing basic methods of egg cookery and offers interesting and varied recipes based around each basic method. I don't wish to repeat or rewrite her information. Her writing style is superb and it really is worthwhile getting hold of a copy. The basic methods of cookery as as follows.

Boiling

I assume that everyone has their own preferred method here. Of particular interest are 'oeufs mollets', ie softboiled eggs where the white has just cooked and the yolk is still runny. When cooked to this stage, the eggs are removed from the hot water and plunged into cold water. They are tapped gently all over with the handle of a knife until well cracked and then carefully shelled. These eggs are used a lot in French luncheon and hors d'oeuvre dishes served hot or cold, with or without a sauce. Elizabeth David gives a recipe for 'oeufs mollets à la Crécy'. My version is Suppertime Eggs. 'Oeufs mollets' are also pleasant eaten barely warm, sprinkled with a little parsley and freshly ground black pepper, and with a little vinaigrette dressing.

When hard-boiling eggs, immediately they are cooked, plunge them into cold water to cool quickly and to prevent discoloration. Hard-boiled eggs may be included in mixed salads, or may be halved and stuffed. Chopped hard-boiled egg and a little finely chopped chives may be included in potato salad dressed with mayonnaise.

Poaching

For poaching, an egg poacher may be used or the eggs may be cooked in a saucepan of water. The water should be fairly deep, about 6 cm (2½ in) at least for 1 or 2 eggs. A tablespoon or two of vinegar is added and a pinch of salt. The egg is broken into a small cup or on a saucer. When water is boiling, it is stirred vigorously to produce a kind of whirlpool. The egg is then slid in. It will at first whizz around in the water, but will gradually lose momentum. Very carefully, and without touching egg, stir again to keep the water circling. When water has reached boiling point again, reduce heat to keep it boiling evenly, but not too rapidly. Once the white can be seen to be done, remove egg with a gravy (slotted) spoon. Serve.

Elizabeth David offers a few more suggestions for cooking good poached eggs. One is that eggs a few days old are best. She says the whites should be in such a condition that they coagulate nicely without disintegrating, going 'ropey' or separating completely from the yolk. She also makes the suggestion that the egg, while still in its shell, may be momentarily immersed in boiling water. This is supposed to coagulate a thin outer layer of white which keeps the egg in a neat parcel during the later stages of poaching.

My favourite here is 'boring old' standard poached eggs on toast—the way my mother always prepared them. Friday evening in my early teens was swimming at the local baths (swimming pool). I remember in particular dark, chilly winter evenings, arriving home tired and ravenous after my exercise, to flop in front of a roaring fire back in the cosy, easy environment of home and to be presented with poached eggs on toast seasoned just with a little salt. How delicious they always were . . .

Coddling

Egg coddlers are small, round containers with screw-top lids. Each is of a size to just contain one egg (minus shell). A little melted butter is placed in the coddler and an egg is broken into it. The top is screwed in place. The coddler is carefully lowered into a shallow pan of gently boiling water, which should come no more than one-half or two-thirds the way up the sides of the coddler. Cooking time takes 3–4 minutes. Coddled eggs should be fairly soft, rather like 'oeufs mollets', ie the white just set but the yolk still runny. The eggs are served in their container. One can buy pretty little porcelain egg coddlers which look delightful at the table.

In order to vary this egg dish, a little sauce may be poured over the eggs when cooking is completed and immediately before serving. Alternatively, a little sauce may be poured over the egg just as the white is beginning to set. In this case, it is easier to leave the lid of the coddler off during cooking. A thin cream sauce with or without herbs, a little thin tomato sauce or a little meat sauce may be used.

Alternatively, eggs may be prepared in a similar manner in an uncovered ramekin dish (soufflé cup), ie a small metal, china or earthenware dish large enough to contain an individual serving.

Frying

Eggs may be shallow- or deep-fried. When shallow-fried, a cast-iron frying pan (skillet) with a lid is best. It maintains the heat evenly and allows the eggs to cook alone without having to spoon hot fat over the top. I find less oil or butter is needed with a cast-iron pan (ie one kept in a well-oiled or greased condition), so that the eggs are less fatty. Fried eggs should never have brown, frizzled edges. This indicates too high a cooking temperature, as the outer edges have to be overdone in order for the yolk to be cooked. However, neither should the fried egg be greasy and limp.

Alternatively, the eggs may be cooked in the French way, called 'oeuf sur le plat'. One or two eggs are broken into a small dish containing a little melted butter. The dish is covered and cooking is done either directly on top of the stove or in a moderate oven for several minutes.

Eggs may be deep-fried in hot oil in much the same way as chips. Take care here with the temperature. Too low, and the egg becomes greasy; too high, and it becomes frizzled and overcooked on the outside. When cooked, the eggs should be removed with a gravy (slotted) spoon and allowed to drain of excess oil on paper towels (absorbent kitchen paper) or a cloth.

Scrambling

Scrambling eggs is hardly worth describing since everybody has their own method of preparation. However, the most important point is that eggs will continue to cook and harden even when removed from the heat or the pan. Overcooked scrambled egg is appalling—hard egg surrounded by watery juice. Therefore, remove your pan from the heat just before egg is ready, ie when it is still at the soft creamy stage. A further note worth mentioning is that cooking should be done over a moderate heat. If too high, the eggs will be spoiled. The Norwegians are lovers of scrambled egg cooked with fresh cream flavoured with chopped chives and seasoned with a little salt. When cooked, it is cooled and used as a base or part base for open sandwiches (usually known as 'Danish open sandwiches', but very popular in Norway). Working in the kitchens of Oslo Airport restaurant, it was my job every other day to prepare eggs in this way. I was horrified the first time I was assigned this job. Breaking 6 dozen eggs was a task in itself! Never before or since have I prepared such enormous quantities of scrambled egg!

Omelettes

I love preparing omelettes—I love the way an omelette grows and grows in the pan and enjoy the final part of flipping over one half of the omelette so that it sits like a semi-circular yellow and brown cushion, with perhaps a hint of filling peeping from the sides. My method is easy and straightforward, yet I never feel totally at ease without my own favourite pan. An omelette pan should have sloping sides and a flat base, and should be a nonstick kind—not one with a chemical nonstick coating, but one which you know doesn't tend to cling to the food. Much less butter is needed with a nonstick kind and the omelette is therefore less greasy.

First break eggs into a bowl. Add seasonings and herbs if wished. Do not stir or break yolks and whites. Next, heat a little butter or margarine in a pan—just enough to evenly and thinly coat the bottom. When it is just beginning to turn colour, beat eggs in the bowl to thoroughly mix white and yolks and, in doing so, incorporate a little air. You will see this as large air bubbles in the mixture. Beating takes only 10 or 20 seconds. Pour egg mixture into the pan— it will immediately set on the bottom. Allow egg to set a little on the sides. Taking a spatula (palette knife) or small fishslice, push a little of the edge towards the middle. At the same time, tilt the pan towards the edge you are pushing so that liquid egg runs into the exposed part of the pan. Repeat in various places around the edge of the omelette. The result will be an omelette which is evenly 'puffed up' all over. When the top is not quite set but the underneath has browned, remove the pan from heat. Flip half of the omelette over on to the other half and gently slide onto a warmed dish or plate. Serve immediately.

If adding filling, prepare it in advance. Spread evenly over the top of omelette when top is barely set. This allows it to mix a little with the egg and to warm a little. Proceed as above.

Note: Cooking should always take place over a fairly high heat. The size of the pan is quite important. I find mine, which has a base diameter of 18 cm (7 in), is ideal for 4 eggs. The diameter of the pan should match that of the heat source so that the omelette cooks evenly throughout.

An alternative, which is perhaps considered the more correct way of serving an omelette, is to fold it over into thirds and, when easing it out of the pan, to flip it over so that the folded-over edges are underneath.

Omelettes may be savoury or sweet. In the latter case, a little caster (superfine) sugar in place of seasoning is added to eggs before cooking. A sweet omelette may be spread with jam, fruit purée or fruit syrup during final stages of cooking, or may be served with a thin sweet sauce such as brandy sauce, fruit syrup or maple syrup.

Soufflés

Like omelettes, I enjoy cooking soufflés. I don't find it a difficult task, but do enjoy the concentration and the care needed to get it just right.

Basic Soufflés Contrary to popular belief, a soufflé dish does not have to be china or glass and straight-sided. Traditional French soufflé dishes were made of metal and were oval in shape.
The ingredients for a plain soufflé are as follows. (Please refer to recipe section for details.)

2 level tablespoons butter or *margarine*
2 level tablespoons wholemeal (whole-wheat) flour
300 ml (1¼ cups, 10½ fl oz) milk
5 medium eggs, separated

- A sauce is prepared from butter (or margarine), flour and milk. The thickness of the sauce is important in the later stage of folding in whites. If too thick, it will 'squash' air from the whisked white resulting in a heavy soufflé. If too thin, the two cannot be mixed thoroughly—the soufflé will be variable in texture and will cook unevenly.
- The eggs are now separated. This is done with utmost care. The success of the soufflé depends to a large extent on the whisked egg white. If any egg yolk is included with the white, or if the bowl and whisk are greasy, the whites will not whisk up to the same lightness. However, whisking egg white is not done at this stage—it must be done immediately before the soufflé is to be cooked.
- When sauce has cooked, remove from heat. Set aside. Beat egg yolks well. Stir into sauce with any seasonings and herbs, or, if soufflé is sweet, a little caster (superfine) sugar.
- The sauce is then allowed to cool until just warm. If wished, the soufflé preparations may now be put aside for several hours until soufflé is to be cooked.
- Whisk egg whites until stiff, ie until they stand into peaks, but still appear creamy on top. When overwhisked, whites will begin to look dryish on the surface and will begin to crack or become divided by deep fissures. Elizabeth David suggests that perhaps the best test is when the mixture forms peaks which remain attached to the whisk without flopping as the whisk is slowly pulled up and out of the mixture. In any case, this stage is critical and eventually after successes and failures one gets a 'feel' for when whites are done.
- Taking a little at a time, fold egg whites into cooked sauce. This must be done thoroughly but with a light hand in order to achieve evenness throughout soufflé. So, with a little egg white on top and using a metal spoon, lift sauce mixture up and over egg white, turning spoon over as you do so.

Repeat several times. Add more egg white and repeat. If folding in correctly, sauce mixture will become light and airy and increase in volume as it becomes mixed with whites. If done incorrectly, air is knocked out of egg white. The sauce does not appreciably increase in volume and already feels heavy.

- Slowly and carefully pour into a well-greased soufflé dish (approx. 18 cm (7 in) in diameter and 8 cm (3¼ in) deep). Place in centre of a preheated oven at 180°C or 350°F. Cooking takes about 25 minutes. The soufflé should be well risen and browned on top, and inside should be moist but not runny. A soufflé must be taken from the oven straight to the table as it will begin to shrink immediately it is taken from the oven.

Note: If making a sweet soufflé, you can dust greased soufflé dish with raw (demerara, turbinado) sugar. The molasses in sugar has a lower melting point than the soufflé, and will form a light crust around mixture, holding soufflé as it rises.

Alternatively, individual soufflés may be cooked in small dishes. Cook at 170°C or 325°F. Cooking time depends largely on the size of cooking dish and depth or thickness of soufflé.

Soufflés may be flavoured with grated cheese, chopped herbs (eg chives, sorrel or marjoram), small pieces of cooked bacon or smoked fish, or chopped tomato. There are, of course, many possibilities. The main point worth remembering is that added ingredients must be in small pieces, otherwise the soufflé will not be strong enough to hold the pieces and they will sink to the bottom. Chopped cooked fruit or a little fruit purée may be added to the sauce just before addition of the yolks. Sweet soufflés may be served with a thin fruit sauce or syrup.

Cold Soufflés Eggs form one of the basic ingredients, but these cold soufflés are not cooked. Whisked egg white provides the air and lightness, but gelatine is used to set the mixture. In the true sense of the word these are not soufflés at all. A soufflé of this type is also called a 'mousse'. It may be sweet or savoury.

Quiches and Flans

Eggs form one of the basic ingredients of quiches and flans, but I do not wish to set down any basic rule of thumb for their preparation. Please refer to the individual recipes.

Dairy Products

Goats are, I am happy to say, one of the loves of my life. I find them fascinating, intelligent, mischievous, full of character, productive and thoroughly irresistible. So when we began smallfarming, goats were a must. Of course, goat's milk was the 'by-product'! I loved it and learned to do a lot with it—my learning is the substance of this section.

Later, when smallfarming in Western Samoa with meat-, rather than milk-producing goats, I took over a friendly milking cow called Lisa from some friends who were leaving. She yielded two huge buckets of milk a day, was also thoroughly naughty, spoiled and charming, and we loved her. So I extended my goat's milk recipes to make use of Lisa's generous milk production. The hard cheese recipe works with cow's milk, but even the enthusiastic dairy cook will need to pay scrupulous attention to detail.

For the reader interested in dairy-farming, I have included sections of an article entitled 'Goat Dairy Products' that I originally wrote for the magazine of the New Zealand Association of Small Farmers—cowherds excuse the continual reference to goats (as I said, the recipes do work with cow's milk too).

'Goat Dairy Products'

For smallfarmers interested in supplying, at least in part, their own dairy products, goats can be the answer. The cow requires rich pasture and plenty of it! The goat, having a slightly different digestive system to either cow or sheep, primarily requires fibre and will feed well on gorse, brambles, dock, thistles and hawthorn. They are browsers rather than grazers and enjoy a vast selection of grasses, weeds, shrubs, bushes, tree leaves and barks. In fact, what is usually termed 'scrub land' (waste land) is often ideal for the goat—do not, however, fall into the trap of thinking a goat eats tin cans, can be kept on a 60 cm (2 ft) length of chain and visited once a week. Tethering, once the animal has got used to it, is fine so long as the chain has two swivels, is at least 3–6 m (10–20 ft) long and allows access to water, and shelter from wind and rain (they hate to get wet). Exercise is also a must. Occasional tethering together with periods of free range is the best. Goats love company and are best kept in pairs at least.

However, the main aim of this article was not to lecture in goat management, but to talk about the use I have made of goat dairy products. The management side is far better described in *Goat Husbandry* by David McKenzie (*see* Bibliography).

Milk

Milk yield in the goat reaches a peak two months after kidding and from there on steadily declines over a lactation of some 15 months. Factors affecting yield are numerous and include age, number of kiddings, diet and udder structure. Yield can be anything from ½–5 litres (1–9 UK pints, 1¼–10½ US pints) daily. With my two goats, both first kidders, I was receiving 5.7–6.8 litres (10–12 UK pints, 12–14 US pints) a day immediately after weaning the kids, at six to eight weeks.

The milking was done in an old hay shed using only two saucepans and several Agee jars (large canning jars)—everything was sterilised before each milking. Keeping equipment, milking hands and udders clean, I could store the milk unpasteurised for up to a week in the refrigerator. Since goats may carry tuberculosis and/or brucellosis (though they may be more resistant than cattle), it is wise to have the milk tested regularly by your local branch of the government's agricultural department. Your veterinarian can arrange this for you.

However, 5.7–6.8 litres (10–12 UK pints, 12–14 US pints) was far more than two people and a dog could drink, so it was time to start thinking of other uses for the milk! Once again, David McKenzie's book was most useful and I have adapted his and other ideas to my own circumstances. The remainder of this article will be confined to describing how to produce yoghurt and cottage cheese—two of the easiest dairy products—as well as cheese, cream and butter production. Goat's milk makes really excellent dairy products so that the results are well worth the effort. A word of warning—keep everything as clean and sterile as possible or you may be rewarded with a very 'goaty' product!

Butter

Thickened (double, heavy) cream is used to make butter. In order to get flavour, some degree of souring of the cream is necessary. Under commercial production, cream is pasteurised and inoculated with the required bacterium. At home, provided all processes leading up to butter production have been hygienic, all that is required is natural souring, ie the cream, which is still warm from the separator, is placed in a warm place, eg the airing cupboard or the warm area at the top back of the refrigerator, for 24 to 36 hours. Butter is made by agitating soured cream so that fat globules collide and stick together. As churning proceeds, butter grains will form which gradually get larger and larger—the remaining fluid being buttermilk. As churning proceeds, a definite change in tone can be heard. The churn should be only two-thirds full at the most and churns are often marked with the optimum speed of revolution. Metal churns, though not so decorative in the kitchen, are far more practical for maintaining hygienic conditions.

The Stages of Butter-making

1. Scald churn with boiling water. This cleans the churn immediately before use and also prevents butter from sticking to sides.
2. Pour tepid cream into churn—it should be between one-third and two-thirds full.
3. Churn until grains the size of mustard seeds form.
4. Add 180 ml (¾ cup, 6½ fl oz) of tepid water per 500 ml (2 cups, 17½ fl oz) of cream. Continue churning until butter particles are the size of peas.
5. Drain off buttermilk.
6. Add 180 ml (¾ cup, 6½ fl oz) of tepid water per 500 ml (2 cups, 17½ fl oz) of original cream used. Churn for a few seconds to wash butter and drain off fluid (this is not buttermilk and is best discarded—hens, dogs and pigs love it).
7. Repeat stage 6 until washing water is clear.
8. Gather butter into one mass and remove to a wooden board.
9. With board tilted to aid draining, work butter with butter pats (wooden spatulas) to draw out remaining fluid. This last step is of absolute importance. It is time-consuming, but rather like bread-dough kneading, I find it a mind-calming job. If the board and spatulas are dry before beginning, you will find they absorb quite a lot of water from the butter and your job is made easier.
10. When required butter consistency is reached, the butter is ready.

11. Store in a cool place. As this butter contains no preservative, it will not store at room temperature for more than a few days.

Note: 1. If you wish to salt butter, add a little to cream before churning or sprinkle a little over butter as you work it at stage 9.

2. If you wish to colour butter, add food colouring to cream before churning. Carrots may be used to give colour—grate 1 large carrot per 500 ml (2 cups, 17½ fl oz) of cream. Add to warm cream. Allow to stand for 5–10 minutes then strain through muslin (heavy cheesecloth), squeezing well to release carrot juice into cream. Discard carrot. Proceed as usual.

3. For smaller quantities of cream, use a rotary egg whisk in place of butter churn. I find it best to deal with no more than 250 ml (1 cup, 9 fl oz) at a time. This method works, but I find it more difficult to work the butter free of fluid in the cleaning (at stage 6). This leaves butter wetter, which makes it a more difficult and lengthy process at stage 9.

Cream

Cream is easy to produce from goat's milk using a hand separator, which is fairly easy and cheap to buy. As goat's milk contains smaller fat globules than cow's milk, the setting of the separator has to be adjusted. The yield of thick cream (for whipping) can be as much as 450 ml (1¾ cups, 16 fl oz) per 4½ litres (8 UK pints, 9½ US pints) of milk. I save up milk yields from several days in covered containers in the refrigerator, and just before passing it through the separator, warm it to 30°C or 90°F. Providing all equipment is clean, the cream will store untainted for a period of one week in a covered container in the refrigerator. Make sure your separator is washed thoroughly with washing soda or dairy detergent immediately after using, as ordinary cleaning agents may leave a sticky surface which will spoil the next batch of cream.

SOUR (DAIRY SOUR) CREAM

500 ml (2 cups, 17½ fl oz) thick (double, whipping) cream
2 teaspoons commercial (dairy sour) cream

Warm cream to blood heat (use your finger to test). Stir in thoroughly 2 teaspoons of commercially prepared sour cream. Pour into a warmed vacuum flask. Leave until sufficiently thick—this may take several days.

NATURAL (PLAIN) YOGHURT

METHOD 1
1 litre (4 cups, 1¾ UK pints) milk
4 tablespoons natural (plain) yoghurt

METHOD 1
Heat milk until boiling, stirring well to prevent boiling over. Reduce heat and simmer uncovered until reduced in volume by one half. Allow to cool until just above blood heat (test with your little finger—the milk should feel hot but easily bearable). Add yoghurt and beat milk a little, using a fork or small whisk to ensure an even distribution. Pour into a warmed vacuum flask and leave for 24 hours. Remove yoghurt from flask and store in refrigerator.

METHOD 2

750 ml (3 cups, 26½ fl oz) milk
4 tablespoons skim (skimmed, nonfat)
milk powder
4 tablespoons natural (plain) yoghurt

METHOD 2

Heat milk until boiling, stirring well to prevent boiling over. Reduce heat and allow to simmer uncovered for 20 minutes. Remove from heat. Set aside to cool until just above blood heat—test for temperature with your little finger (*see* explanation in method 1). Spoon 6 tablespoons of milk into a small bowl. Thoroughly mix in milk powder and yoghurt. Add to milk in pan. Mix thoroughly. Retest temperature at this stage. Reheat if necessary—it is essential, however, if this is done, to stir continuously whilst heating and on no account to let temperature rise above that of blood heat, otherwise you risk killing the yoghurt bacterium (commonly referred to as 'bug'). Pour into a warmed vacuum flask and leave for 24 hours. When ready, remove from the flask and store in the refrigerator.

Note: 1. Always wash out vacuum flask carefully and sterilise with boiling water before using again for yoghurt.

2. Four tablespoons of this yoghurt may be used to prepare more yoghurt.

Cheesemaking

COTTAGE CHEESE

METHOD 1

500 ml (2 cups, 17½ fl oz) whole
(full-cream) or skim (skimmed,
nonfat) milk
1 teaspoon commercial rennet*

METHOD 1

Bring milk (whole milk is best) to body temperature. Remove from heat source. Stir in 1 teaspoon of commercial rennet and leave to curdle. Strain curds through muslin (cheesecloth) for several hours.

METHOD 2

juice of 1 or 2 lemons
500 ml (2 cups, 17½ fl oz) milk

METHOD 2

Add juice of 1 or 2 lemons to milk. Heat gently and slowly until milk curdles—temperature may be fairly high when this happens. The curds formed are smaller than those of method 1 and require finer meshed cloth for straining. Several layers of muslin (cheesecloth) will suffice.

Note: 1. Cottage cheese may be eaten plain, or made into a tasty dip by adding herbs, spices and/or flavourings—*see* Stuffed Celery Sticks (p. 58). Cottage cheese made by method 1 makes a good accompaniment to fruit and puddings.

2. * Junket tablets may be used in place of liquid rennet.

Hard Cheese

As a child, I read avidly the Laura Ingalls Wilder series, *Little House on the Prairie* and others, and was inspired by Ma and Laura's ability to make what sounded like good cheese even under the primitive conditions of the 'Wild West'. The cheesemaking-at-home ideal was epitomised in *Heidi* with descriptions of Grandfather and Heidi sitting round a roaring fire, halfway up a Swiss mountain, toasting goat's milk cheese on long forks—I had to try this myself.

After reading several articles on commercial cheese production, the whole process sounded so complicated that I wasn't at all sure I'd be able to make cheese at home. The principles of cheesemaking, in simple terms, are as follows: warmed milk is inoculated with a bacterium ('the starter') and curdled by the addition of rennet, which coagulates the protein. Cheese is made by separating the protein and fatty curds from the whey or liquid portion, compressing them and leaving them to mature. Maturing involves the action of the bacteria on the solidified protein. In simple terms, the type, taste and texture of a cheese is entirely dependent on the milk used, and on the chemical activity that occurs within the compressed curds (each bacterium has its own specific mode of chemical activity). Some cheese may take long periods of time to complete the maturing process. Feta cheese, which uses sheep's milk, takes two years.

The recipe I finally decided to use is very basic and uses only materials which are readily available at home. It may be a good idea to invest in a cooking thermometer if you don't already have one.

The Stages of Hard Cheesemaking

1. Warm 3 litres (5¼ UK pints, 6¼ US pints) of goat's milk to blood heat (use the finger test). This is best done in a double boiler, ie a pan sitting inside a larger pan containing water, sitting over heat source.
2. Remove milk from heat source. Stir in 2 teaspoons of 'starter' and 1–2 teaspoons of rennet. The starter can be procured from the local cheese factory or may be cultured buttermilk or yoghurt. For convenience, I use yoghurt.
3. When milk has curdled (about 5 minutes), cut curds: with a knife, cut solid mass of curd into vertical strips about 2½ cm (1 in) thick. Cut again, perpendicular to the first plane of cutting so that you have a mass of 2½ cm (1 in) thick 'rods'. By hand, gently turn curds on their side and cut again. The aim of this process is to produce, as near as possible, 2½ cm (1 in) cubes of curd from which whey can drain more easily.
4. Leave cut curds to rest for 10–15 minutes.
5. With milk pan again in its double boiler, warm curds to 38°C or 100°F, stirring gently all the time with a wooden spoon. Sometimes the temperature may go a little above this with little effect—as long as it is not hot enough to kill the bacterium, all is well. Warming should be done fairly slowly, about 20–25 minutes to reach required temperature. During this warming, whey is slowly driven out of curds. It is a matter of experience knowing when curds are ready for draining—they start to go stringy and, if pressed between finger

and thumb, will begin to feel almost rubbery or springy. The cheese should be neither too dry nor too wet, so this stage is fairly critical—if curds are too wet, working them in the next stage will seem 'sloshy'. If too dry, they will feel like rubber.

6. Drain off excess whey. It is sometimes necessary at this stage to let curds rest for 10–15 minutes and allow more whey to drain out. To the drained curds, add 2 teaspoons of table salt. Work this well into the curds with your hands.

7. Line a cheese hoop (*see* below) with muslin (cheesecloth). Press salted curds well down into it. Place on a grooved or slightly tilted surface so that whey may drain away freely. Put 'follower' (*see* below) in position. Weight with a 5–7 kg (11–15 lb) weight for 24 hours.

    Cheese Hoop and Follower   I use a straight-sided margarine container with the bottom cut out. The bottom is used as the 'follower', ie it sits on top of curds in hoop and acts as a flat surface on which to place the heavy weight. It also distributes weight evenly across curds. Any straight-sided, open-ended cylinder may be used as a hoop. The size really depends on the amount of curds you have. Obviously you don't want to end up with a 'pancake' of cheese by using too large a hoop.

8. After 24 hours, remove cheese from hoop. Carefully peel off muslin (cheesecloth). It may be necessary to trim round the edges of the cheese if it is irregular in shape. Place in a cool airy cupboard or shelf (meat safes are ideal).

9. Turn cheese every day until a thin rind has formed all over cheese.

10. Paint on a thin layer of paraffin wax—this stops cheese drying out.

11. Store in a cool airy cupboard for 1–2 months.

This cheese varies a little in texture and taste, but is delicious! It is quite strong though, so be prepared for something with a little more body than commercially manufactured cheese. Until you get the feel for the correct consistency of the curds, you may find that your cheese does not melt well. Initially, I found that my cheese was fine if grated and used in sauces or in pizzas, but was useless for toasted (grilled, broiled) cheese sandwiches. In thick slices on a piece of bread it could not be reduced to the gooey mass my husband loves! With experience, I have corrected this, though I still find that it does not melt quite so readily as cow's milk cheese— perhaps that's how Grandfather and Heidi managed to keep the cheese on their forks when toasting it over a fire!

Eggs

CURRIED STUFFED EGGS

Serves 2–4

4 eggs, hard-boiled
¼ teaspoon turmeric
½ teaspoon curry powder (see p. 114)
4 teaspoons cottage cheese, sieved (strained)
4 teaspoons thickened (double, whipping) cream
1 large sprig parsley

Shell eggs and halve them lengthwise. Scoop yolks into a bowl and mash well. Add turmeric, curry powder, cottage cheese and cream. Mix thoroughly. Cut a thin slice from bottom of each egg white 'shell' so that they will sit steadily on a plate. Fill with curried yolk mixture. Garnish each with a tiny sprig of parsley.

EGGS WITH ORANGE SAUCE

Serves 6

½ tablespoon butter or margarine
1 tablespoon wholemeal (whole-wheat) flour (from which bran has been sieved)
rind of 1 orange, grated
3 tablespoons milk
3 tablespoons fresh orange juice
1½ tablespoons thickened (double, whipping) cream
3 eggs, hard-boiled
2 teaspoons lemon balm, finely chopped
6 lettuce leaves

Prepare orange sauce as follows. Heat butter in a small pan. When sizzling, stir in flour and orange rind. Remove from heat and gradually blend in milk and orange juice. Heat sauce gently, beating thoroughly to avoid curdling, until it thickens. Remove from heat, stir in cream and set aside to cool a little.

Halve eggs lengthwise. Scoop out yolks into a small bowl. Add lemon balm and 2 tablespoons of orange sauce. Using a fork, mash yolks and thoroughly blend three ingredients together. Refill the eggs with this mixture. Place a lettuce leaf on each of six plates, place a stuffed egg half on each leaf and pour over a little of the sauce.

BAKED EGG CUSTARD *See* recipe under 'Desserts' (p. 286).

COFFEE MOUSSE *See* recipe under 'Desserts' (p. 287).

CHOCOLATE MOUSSE *See* recipe under 'Desserts' (p. 283).

EGG ROLLS These are rather like a cross between a pancake and an omelette. Suitable fillings may be taken from either of those recipes. Ingredients for and full details of the preparation are to be found in the recipe Sweet and Sour Beef in Egg Rolls (p. 95).

ROSEMARY NOODLES AND EGGS

Serves 4–5

3 cloves garlic

1 medium onion

½ tablespoon oil

75 g (2½ oz) egg noodles

200 g (7 oz) tomatoes, skinned
(peeled)

100 g (1 cup, 3½ oz) mature
(sharp) cheddar cheese, grated

3 tablespoons tomato purée
(see p. 221)

3 eggs

75 ml (⅓ cup, 2½ fl oz) milk

1 teaspoon rosemary, finely chopped

black pepper

Finely chop garlic and onion and fry gently in oil until tender. Set aside.

Boil noodles in salted water until al dente. Drain well and add to onion. Chop tomatoes into tiny pieces. Grate cheese. Add cheese and tomatoes to onion and noodles. Mix well. Spoon mixture into a greased ovenproof dish approx. 18 cm (7 in) in diameter.

In a separate bowl, beat tomato purée, eggs and milk. Stir in rosemary and season with black pepper. Pour over noodle mixture in bowl. Bake in the oven at 180°C or 350°F for 40 minutes.

SATURDAY EGGS

Serves 3

1 quantity Mushroom Cream Sauce
(see sauces, p. 222)

50 g (1 cup, 2 oz) borage or other
greens (eg lettuce, spinach, comfrey,
beet leaves), finely shredded

3 tablespoons water

½ tablespoon margarine

3 eggs

black pepper

1 tablespoon parsley, finely chopped

Prepare Mushroom Cream Sauce. Set aside. Finely shred borage (or other). Place in a pan with water and margarine. Cook over a high heat with pan uncovered, stirring frequently, until all water has evaporated and greens are tender. Remove from heat. Spread borage as a layer on the bottom of a shallow ovenproof dish, 18 cm (7 in) in diameter. Make three depressions in this layer and into each carefully break an egg. Sprinkle with black pepper. Pour sauce over top, taking care not to break egg yolks. Cook in the oven at 200°C or 400°F for 10–12 minutes. Serve sprinkled with parsley.

SUPPERTIME EGGS

Serves 3–4

250 ml (1 cup, 9 fl oz) Basic
Wholemeal (Whole-Wheat) Sauce
(see sauces, p. 218)

½ teaspoon tarragon, finely chopped

salt and black pepper

3 eggs, hard-boiled

150 g (¾ cup, 5½ oz) carrots, grated

½ tablespoon margarine

Parmesan cheese

Prepare sauce, add tarragon and season with salt and black pepper. Set aside but keep warm. Place eggs in a pan in water and boil for 6 minutes. Meanwhile, grate carrot. Boil in a little water with margarine until just tender. Drain and layer at the bottom of a warmed ovenproof dish. Shell eggs and cut in half lengthwise. Arrange eggs, yolk side down, on top of carrot. Pour tarragon sauce evenly over eggs, sprinkle with Parmesan cheese and place in a hot oven for 5 minutes or under a medium–hot grill (broiler) for 5 minutes until thoroughly heated.

Note: This is a modified version of a French recipe, 'oeufs mollets à la Crécy'.

ENGLISH EGG BREAD

Serves 2

2 eggs

3 teaspoons marjoram, finely chopped

paprika

salt and black pepper

2 slices wholemeal (whole-wheat)
bread

1 tablespoon oil

Break eggs into a bowl. Add marjoram, paprika, salt and pepper. Beat well. Pour onto a plate or shallow dish. Place bread slices side by side on plate, pressing down lightly into beaten egg. Leave for several minutes. Turn bread slices over and again press down lightly. Leave for 3–4 minutes. The bread should have soaked up egg and be evenly saturated. Heat oil in a frying pan (skillet). When hot, carefully lift bread slices into pan so that they sit side by side. Allow to cook for 2 minutes. Turn over and cook for a further 2 minutes. The egg should be well set and lightly browned on both sides of bread. Serve at breakfast, lunch or supper, just plain or as below.

Alternatives Serve egg bread topped with one or several of the following: sliced fresh tomato; sliced tomato, then placed under a hot grill (broiler) for a few minutes; slices of salami; a rasher (slice) of cooked bacon; grated cheese; grated cheese, then melted under a hot grill; sardines; anchovies; cooked sausage; lightly fried mushrooms.

SWEET AND SOUR EGGS

Serves 2–3

SAUCE

4 cloves garlic

2 teaspoons fresh ginger,
finely chopped

1 teaspoon oil

2 tablespoons tomato purée
(see p. 221)

6 tablespoons chicken stock

1 tablespoon golden syrup
(light treacle)

2 teaspoons cider vinegar

EGG MIXTURE

2 tablespoons water

½ tablespoon wholemeal (whole-
wheat) flour

1 tablespoon chives, finely chopped

4 eggs

2 teaspoons oil

SAUCE

Finely chop garlic. Place in a small stainless steel or enamel pan with ginger and oil. Fry gently for several minutes. Add remaining sauce ingredients. Simmer for 10 minutes, stirring occasionally. Set aside but keep warm.

EGG MIXTURE

Add water, flour and ½ tablespoon of chives to a bowl. Beat well. Add eggs and beat a little until evenly blended with flour and water. Spoon oil into a heavy-based frying pan (skillet) and heat until very hot. Pour in eggs, reduce heat to low and allow mixture to cook uncovered and undisturbed until just set. Remove from heat. With egg still in pan, cut into small squares. Pour sauce over egg, toss well and turn into a hot serving dish. Sprinkle with remaining chives.

Note: This may be served on a bed of plain boiled rice or stir-fried bean sprouts; with stir-fried vegetables or alone as the first course of a Chinese meal.

Opposite: Omelettes are quick and easy to prepare — the ideal meal for when time is short, and one with almost endless variations. Here a freshly cooked Tomato and Onion Omelette lies on a plate ready to eat, with a Fresh Basil Omelette still in the pan.

Omelettes

Omelettes are quick and easy to prepare. They are suitable for breakfast, lunch or supper and may be sweet or savoury. Basic omelette preparation is dealt with on pp. 180–1.

This section deals with the flavouring of omelettes. Firstly, the eggs themselves may be flavoured with spices and/or herbs before cooking. Secondly, a filling may be prepared—the omelette is prepared as usual and *just* as it is cooked, the filling is spread over the top. The omelette is then folded over on itself and served immediately. A suitable filling may be something quite simple such as grated cheese or something a little more elaborate such as Summer Savory Mix. For the less simple fillings, it is best if they are hot or at least warm when used.

Savoury Omelettes

Some suggestions for savoury flavourings follow (all quantities are sufficient for a *four*-egg omelette, which serves two).

Flavouring the Eggs
One or more of the following may be beaten together with the eggs before cooking:
- pinch of paprika
- pinch of cayenne
- pinch of dill seed
- ¼–½ teaspoon finely chopped herbs (mild-flavoured ones are best), eg French tarragon, marjoram, summer savory, lemon balm, chives, sage, oregano, fennel
- 1 tablespoon of finely chopped 'greens', eg borage, French sorrel, salad burnet, spinach.

Simple Fillings
One or more of the following are suitable:
- 75 g (¾ cup, 2½ oz) grated cheese
- 2 tomatoes, chopped into tiny pieces
- 1 small green capsicum (sweet pepper), chopped into tiny pieces
- 50 g (2 oz) cooked or cured meat, eg ham, salami, pork or chicken—cut into tiny cubes
- 50–75 g (2–3 oz) cooked vegetables, eg green (French or runner, string) beans, corn (maize) kernels, zucchini (courgettes), potatoes, onions—thinly sliced. One or a mixture of several may be used, eg potato and onion
- 50 g (2 oz) mushrooms, thinly sliced and raw, or lightly fried
- 1–2 tablespoons thinly sliced spring onions (scallions)
- 2–3 tablespoons finely shredded lettuce and tender herbs and flowers, eg watercress and nasturtium flowers.

Filling Mixes
These are the more elaborate fillings. A few examples are given in the following recipes and it is hoped that the enthusiastic cook will expand on them.

SUMMER SAVORY MIX

50 g (½ cup, 2 oz) mature (sharp)
cheddar cheese, grated
25 g (1 oz) (chunk) bacon (optional)
1 teaspoon oil
100 g (⅔ cup, 3½ oz) green (French
or runner, string) beans
1 tablespoon margarine
1 tablespoon cornflour
(US cornstarch)
40 ml (1½ fl oz) milk
80 ml (⅓ cup, 3 fl oz) white wine
black pepper
½ teaspoon summer savory,
finely chopped

Grate cheese and set aside. Cut bacon into tiny pieces. Fry gently in oil until cooked. Drain well on paper towels (absorbent kitchen paper). Set aside. Cut beans into tiny pieces and steam, stir-fry or boil until tender. Set aside. To avoid lumps in sauce, mix cornflour and a little of the milk to a smooth paste. Heat margarine in a pan. When sizzling, add cornflour paste. Remove from heat. Carefully blend in remaining milk and then white wine. Cook gently, stirring continuously, until sauce thickens. Remove from heat, add cheese and stir until well blended. Season with summer savory and a little black pepper. Stir in beans and bacon. Set to warm over a very gentle heat while preparing omelette.

LEMON CHICKEN

1 small onion
½ tablespoon oil
1 teaspoon wholemeal (whole-wheat)
flour
3 tablespoons (single, light) cream
salt and black pepper
pinch of paprika
100 g (3½ oz) chicken, cooked
25 g (1 oz) apple, diced
25 g (⅓ cup, 1 oz) French sorrel,
shredded
2 teaspoons lemon juice

Thinly slice onion. Fry gently in oil until tender and lightly browned. Remove from heat and stir in flour. Carefully blend in cream, avoiding lumps. Return to heat. Cook very gently until mixture thickens a little. Season with salt, pepper and paprika. Set aside. Cut chicken into small pieces and dice apple. Add apple, chicken, sorrel and lemon juice to onion sauce mixture. Reheat and cook gently for 2 minutes while preparing omelette.

Note: To flavour beaten egg, add 1 teaspoon of finely chopped lemon balm leaves and a little salt and black pepper.

CREAMY FRENCH SORREL   *See* recipe on p. 46. Prepare half the quantity given there.

BEAN AND CORN FILLER   *See* Bean and Corn Pie on p. 25. Prepare half the quantity for pie filling.

CHICKEN IN MAYONNAISE FILLER   *See* recipe on p. 144. Prepare only one-quarter of given quantity per four-egg omelette

Other recipes may be used as fillers, eg Dark Mince (Ground Beef) (p. 99), Ginger Beef (p. 98), Brown Rice Salad (p. 62), Hot Tomato Beans (p. 69), Steak Divine (p. 100), Kidneys à la Crème (p. 139). Prepare about one-quarter of quantity of each recipe.

RAINY DAY FILLER

250 g (9 oz) potatoes
3 teaspoons salad burnet,
finely chopped*
pinch of paprika
1 teaspoon dill seed
1 can sardines in oil (125 g/
4 oz size)
salt and black pepper

Peel potatoes. Steam or boil until just tender. Cool a little, cut into small pieces and set aside. Drain oil from sardines. Measure 1 tablespoon of it into a heavy-based frying pan (skillet). Discard remaining oil. Add salad burnet, paprika and dill seed to oil. Cook gently for 3–4 minutes. Chop sardines into small pieces. Add sardines and potatoes to dill seed and oil mixture. Season with a little salt and plenty of black pepper. Mix thoroughly. Set aside in a warm place while preparing omelette.

Note: 1. * In place of salad burnet, any other greens can be used, eg borage, French sorrel, fat-hen, dandelion, chickweed, spinach, lettuce. With milder tasting greens, such as lettuce, the quantity may be increased.
2. The eggs can be flavoured with a little dill seed or finely chopped greens.

TWO-CHEESE FILLING

100 g (3½ oz) feta cheese
25 g (¼ cup, 1 oz) mild cheddar
cheese, grated
90 ml (⅓ cup, 3 fl oz) natural (plain)
yoghurt
50 g (⅓ cup, 2 oz) raisins
2 teaspoons salad burnet,
finely chopped
a little salt and paprika

Cut feta cheese into small cubes. Grate cheddar cheese. Place both in a bowl, add remaining ingredients and mix well. Allow to reach room temperature before using.

Sweet Omelettes

Two teaspoons of caster (superfine) or icing (powdered) sugar are beaten into the 4 eggs immediately before cooking the omelette. The omelette may be flavoured as follows.

Flavouring the Eggs
One of the following may be beaten together with eggs before cooking:
- ½–1 teaspoon finely chopped lemon balm
- 1 teaspoon finely chopped borage flowers
- 1–2 teaspoons chopped marigold (calendula) petals.

Simple Fillings
One of the following may be suitable:
- sliced fresh fruit, 25–50 g (¼–½ cup, 1–2 oz) per omelette—eg banana, apricot
- fruit purée, 60–125 ml (¼–½ cup, 2–4 fl oz) and only slightly sweetened
- jam, syrup or honey—2–3 tablespoons are sufficient.

BRANDIED PEACHES

3 medium peaches
1 quantity Brandy Sauce
(see sauces, p. 227)

Cut peaches into small pieces or slices and add to sauce. Spread over omelette when cooked and fold over in usual way.

Note: Any fresh fruit can be used, eg sliced bananas, diced apple or a mixture of fruit.

LEMON GRAPES

125 g (4½ oz) sweet grapes, seeded
25 g (¼ cup, 1 oz) raisins or dates,
chopped (optional)
1 quantity Lemon Honey Sauce (see
sauces, p. 226)

Halve grapes and remove pips (seeds). Place in a bowl with raisins. Stir in sauce and spoon over cooked omelette.

HONEYED BANANA AND ALMOND

1 tablespoon honey
1 teaspoon lemon balm,
finely chopped
2 teaspoons almonds, flaked
2 bananas

Gently warm honey and lemon balm for several minutes. Remove from heat and allow to cool. Immediately before using, add almonds and thinly sliced bananas. Spoon over omelette.

Pancakes

BASIC PANCAKE BATTER

Makes 6
250 ml (1 cup, 9 fl oz) milk
100 g (¾ cup, 3½ oz) wholemeal
(whole-wheat) flour
1 egg
4-5 teaspoons oil

Pour half the milk into a jug (pitcher). Carefully blend in wholemeal flour, avoiding lumps. Beat in remaining milk and egg. Spoon ½–1 teaspoon oil (just enough to coat bottom of pan) into a frying pan (skillet) approx. 18 cm (7 in) in diameter. Heat over a high heat. When oil is very hot (almost smoking), pour in a little batter (one-sixth). Cook over a high heat until top has just set. Turn pancake, using a spatula (palette knife) or fishslice. Cook for a further 1–2 minutes on second side until lightly browned. Ease pancake onto a plate and set aside. Store in a warm place while cooking next pancake. Repeat process until six pancakes in all have been cooked.

Pancakes are served rolled up into a sausage shape. They may be plain or, more usually, flavoured in one or more of the following ways:

- The batter may be flavoured before cooking with herbs or spices.
- A filling may be prepared and spread evenly over cooked pancake. The pancake is then rolled up and served.
- A sauce may be prepared and poured over rolled-up pancakes immediately before serving.

Pancakes may be sweet or savoury and served hot or cold. Allow one or two pancakes per person—depending on the other courses and appetite. Suggestions for flavourings are as follows:

Flavouring the Batter Refer to 'Omelettes' (pp. 194, 196) for suitable flavourings for batter. Quantities given there will be sufficient for the basic pancake batter recipe.

Fillings Again refer to 'Omelettes', both savoury and sweet, for suitable fillings. Double the quantities given there will be sufficient for the basic pancake batter recipe.

Sauces Sauces may be sweet or savoury, but should be kept thin and light as the pancakes themselves are rather filling. Examples are Brandy Sauce (p. 227) or Lemon Honey Sauce (p. 226) for sweetness; or Yoghurt Sauce (p. 224), Mushroom Cream Sauce (p. 222) for savoury pancakes.

One, two or all three of the above methods of flavouring may be used at any one time. A selection of our particular favourites follows, which the reader may use as a starting point for experimenting with different combinations.

Savoury Pancakes

Savoury pancakes make delicious first courses, or may be served as luncheon or supper dishes. Some tasty recipe suggestions are given below.

CHEESY PANCAKES

Makes 6
SAUCE
½ tablespoon margarine
1 tablespoon wholemeal (whole-wheat) flour
150 ml (⅔ cup, 5½ fl oz) milk
30 g (¼ cup, 1 oz) cheddar cheese, grated
pinch of paprika
150 g (1 cup, 5½ oz) green (French or runner, string) beans, cooked
100 g (3½ oz) bacon, cooked
1 quantity Basic Pancake Batter (see p. 197)

Prepare sauce in usual way (*see* Basic Wholemeal (Whole-Wheat) Sauce on p. 218 if in doubt). Stir in cheese and paprika. Set aside but keep hot.

Chop beans and bacon into tiny pieces, mix together and set aside. Prepare pancakes in usual way. Divide bean and bacon mixture into six. Place a portion on each pancake. Roll each pancake in a sausage shape. Place pancake rolls side by side in a shallow dish. Pour over cheesy sauce. Place in a moderate oven at 180°C or 350°F for 10 minutes until thoroughly heated.

HERB PANCAKES

Makes 6

FILLING

150 g (5½ oz) potato, cooked
2 tablespoons herb greens (a mixture
of French sorrel, salad burnet and
chickweed), shredded
90 ml (⅓ cup, 3 fl oz) natural (plain)
yoghurt
salt and black pepper
1 teaspoon marigold (calendula)
petals or nasturtium flowers, finely
chopped

PANCAKES

1 quantity Basic Pancake Batter (see
p. 197)
1 teaspoon summer savory,
finely chopped
1 tablespoon parsley, finely chopped
(to garnish)

Chop potato into tiny pieces. Place in a bowl. Add remaining filling ingredients and mix thoroughly. Divide into six portions and set aside.

Beat summer savory into pancake batter, prepare six pancakes in usual way and allow to cool. Spread one portion of filler on each pancake and roll up. Serve cold sprinkled with parsley.

TARRAGON PANCAKES

Makes 6

½ teaspoon French tarragon,
finely chopped
1 quantity Basic Pancake Batter (see
p. 197)
Rainy Day Filler (see p. 196)

Beat tarragon into pancake batter. Set aside. Prepare filling and set aside in a warm place. Prepare pancakes as usual. Divide filling into six portions, spread each pancake with filling and roll up. Serve immediately.

Note: Rainy Day Filler is rather heavy, so do not use a double quantity as suggested in the notes on p. 196.

DILL AND EGGPLANT (AUBERGINE) FILLER

Makes 6

1 large onion
2 teaspoons dill seed
3-4 tablespoons oil
200 g (7 oz) eggplant (aubergine)
black pepper
1 quantity Basic Pancake Batter (see
p. 197)
100 g (3½ oz) cream cheese
1 teaspoon parsley, finely chopped

Thinly slice onion and place in a frying pan (skillet) with dill seed and oil. Cut eggplant into small pieces (½–1 cm/¼–½ in cubes). Add to pan. Fry gently until onion and eggplant are tender. Season with black pepper and remove to a warm dish. Set aside and keep warm.

Prepare pancakes in usual way. Thoroughly mix cream cheese and parsley into eggplant mixture. Divide into six portions. Place one portion on each pancake, roll up and either serve immediately or serve cold.

DILL AND MUSHROOM FILLER

1 large onion
2 teaspoons dill seed
2 tablespoons oil
200 g (7 oz) mushrooms*
black pepper
1 quantity Basic Pancake Batter (see p. 197)
100 g (3½ oz) cream cheese
1 teaspoon parsley, finely chopped

Thinly slice onion. Place in a frying pan (skillet) with dill seed and oil. Thinly slice mushrooms. Add to pan. Fry gently until onion and mushrooms are tender. Season with black pepper and remove to a warm dish. Set aside and keep warm.

Prepare pancakes in usual way. Thoroughly mix cream cheese and parsley into mushroom mixture. Divide into six portions. Place one portion on each pancake, roll up and either serve immediately or serve cold.

Note: * Use young mushrooms which will not blacken the mixture with their fungal spores.

Sweet Pancakes

Sweet pancakes are an ideal dessert choice, especially in the winter. They are quick and easy to make, and will always be a success with both family and guests. Pancakes can be filled with fresh fruit, eg blueberries (bilberries) or strawberries, and smothered in freshly whipped cream. They are also delicious served plain, with lemon juice and sugar sprinkled over them. The following recipes provide some more tempting ways to prepare them.

APPLE PANCAKES

Makes 6
1 quantity Basic Pancake Batter (see p. 197)
1 tablespoon sesame seed, toasted (optional)
180 ml (¾ cup, 6½ fl oz) apple purée, sweetened
150 ml (⅔ cup, 5½ fl oz) thickened (double, whipping) cream
1 tablespoon honey
1 teaspoon crystallised (candied) angelica, chopped

Prepare pancakes in usual way. Allow to cool. Immediately before using, stir sesame seed (if used) into apple purée. Spread each pancake with apple mixture, roll up and arrange on a serving plate. Whip cream until thick and pile over pancakes. Dribble honey over top and sprinkle with angelica.

<u>TUNA MIX</u> Follow recipe for Tuna Fish Kedgeree (p. 175). The pancakes may be served hot or cold.

FRESH FRUIT PANCAKES

Makes 6
4 medium-sized apricots
1 quantity Lemon Honey Sauce (see sauces, p. 226)
1 quantity Basic Pancake Batter (see p. 197)
150 ml (2/3 cup, 5½ fl oz) thickened (double, whipping) cream
6 crystallised (sugared) violets or *6 pieces of crystallised (candied) angelica*

Chop apricot flesh into small pieces and mix thoroughly with sauce. Prepare pancakes as usual and allow to cool. Spread each with a little of the fruit mixture, roll up and place on individual plates or dishes. Whip cream until thick and pile a little over each pancake (I pile the cream lengthwise along the top of the roll). Decorate each with a violet flower or piece of angelica and serve.

LEMON PANCAKES

Makes 6
1 quantity Basic Pancake Batter (see p. 197)
2 quantities Lemon Honey Sauce (see sauces, p. 226)
2 lemon slices (to garnish)

Prepare pancakes in usual way, roll up each and place side by side in a warmed shallow dish. Warm sauce and pour over pancakes. Garnish with lemon slices. Serve immediately.

NEW YEAR'S PLUM DELIGHT

Makes 6
6 red plums (sweet and ripe)
200 g (7 oz) cream cheese
a little sugar
1 quantity Basic Pancake Batter (see p. 197)
4 tablespoons honey

Cut plum flesh into tiny pieces. Place in a bowl. Add cream cheese. Mix thoroughly. Sweeten to taste. Prepare pancakes in usual way. While still warm, spread each with a portion of plum mixture. Roll up and place side by side on a heated shallow dish. Gently heat honey until quite hot. Dribble evenly over pancakes. Serve immediately.

RAISIN PANCAKES

Makes 6
3 tablespoons honey
1 teaspoon lemon juice
100 g (½ cup, 3½ oz) raisins
1 quantity Basic Pancake Batter (see p. 197)

Gently warm honey and lemon juice. When thoroughly mixed, add raisins. Set aside and allow to cool. Prepare pancakes as usual. Spread each with a little of the honey mixture. Roll up and serve immediately.

HONEYED ROSEMARY PANCAKES

Makes 6
3 tablespoons clear honey
½-1 teaspoon rosemary,
finely chopped
1 quantity Basic Pancake Batter
(see p. 197)

Gently heat honey and rosemary until quite hot but not boiling. Set aside and allow to cool slowly until warm. Prepare pancakes as usual. Spread each with 2 teaspoons of honey mixture. Roll up and serve immediately.

BUCKWHEAT PIKELETS (DROP SCONES, PANCAKES)

Makes 12-14
2 eggs
3 tablespoons milk
100 g (¾ cup, 3½ oz) buckwheat
flour*
1½ tablespoons sugar
¼-½ teaspoon ground cinnamon
1 teaspoon baking powder
a little oil

Beat eggs and milk in a bowl. Gradually beat in flour. Add sugar, cinnamon and baking powder. Mix thoroughly. Heat a little oil (enough to shallowly cover bottom) in a heavy-based frying pan (skillet). When very hot, drop in tablespoonfuls of mixture (batter), evenly spaced in pan. The mixture will spread a little as it cooks to make neat little round pikelets. Cook for a minute or two until lightly browned. Turn pikelets and cook on other side until lightly browned. Lift gently onto a warmed plate, add a little more oil to pan and cook a second batch. Repeat until mixture has all been used.

Note: Serve sweet or savoury as follows: butter warm pikelets and serve with jam or honey; *or* serve with a slice of cheese and eat plain or lightly toasted under a hot grill (broiler).

   * In place of buckwheat flour, 80 g (⅔ cup, 3 oz) of plain (all-purpose) flour or wholemeal (whole-wheat) flour can be used.

Batters

THICK BATTER

100 g (¾ cup, 3½ oz) plain
(all-purpose) flour
2 teaspoons oil
4-5 tablespoons milk
2 eggs

Place flour in a bowl. Make a well in centre. Add oil, milk and eggs to well. Gradually mix wet and dry ingredients together. Beat for several minutes with a rotary whisk. Use to coat and deep-fry fruit (eg apple, pineapple or banana slices) or greens (eg comfrey or spinach leaves).

Opposite: *Pancakes are a simple but delicious meal which can be made with a variety of tempting toppings.*

BASIC BATTER

75 g (²/₃ cup, 2½ oz) plain
(all-purpose) flour
250 ml (1 cup, 8 fl oz) milk
1 egg

Place flour in a bowl, make a well in centre and pour in milk. Gradually mix ingredients together thoroughly. Add egg and beat well for several minutes.

YORKSHIRE PUDDING

75 g (²/₃ cup, 2½ oz) plain
(all-purpose) flour
250 ml (1 cup, 8 fl oz) milk
1 egg

Yorkshire pudding traditionally accompanies roast beef. Prepare Basic Batter as above. Set aside. Place 2 tablespoons of fat from roasting meat in a small ovenproof dish or tin (pan) (eg a 1 kg/2¼ lb bread tin). Pour batter into dish. Bake beside roast beef at 200°C or 400°F for 35–40 minutes, or until set and golden brown.

Soufflés

BASIC SOUFFLÉ RECIPE

2 tablespoons margarine
2 tablespoons wholemeal
(whole-wheat) flour
300 ml (1¼ cups, 10½ fl oz) milk
5 eggs, separated

Before beginning, carefully read notes on soufflé preparation (*see* pp. 182–3).

Heat margarine in a saucepan until sizzling, stir in flour. Remove from heat. Gradually blend in milk. Return to heat. Cook gently, stirring continuously, until sauce thickens. Cook for a further 3 minutes to reduce a little. Set aside to cool slightly.

Separate eggs, beat yolks into cooled sauce. Whisk whites until they are stiff and form peaks. Gradually fold egg whites into sauce mixture. Carefully pour into a well-greased ovenproof dish approx. 18 cm (7 in) in diameter and 8 cm (3 in) deep. Bake at 180°C or 350°F for 25 minutes.

Savoury Soufflés Season the sauce with *black pepper, salt* and a little *paprika* and further flavouring of your choice as follows:

Cheese Soufflé—Add *100 g (1 cup, 3½ oz) grated mature (sharp) cheese* to hot sauce and stir until melted and thoroughly blended. *One teaspoon finely chopped sage* may also be added to the sauce for variation in flavour.

French Sorrel Soufflé—Add *30–75 g (¼–½ cup, 1–2½ oz) finely shredded French sorrel* to thickened sauce. Cook sauce further to reduce it.

CRISPY BATTER *See* recipe under fish cookery, p. 163.

Herb Soufflé—Add *1-2 tablespoons finely chopped herbs* or *herb seeds* to thickened sauce. For a finer flavour, herbs may be steeped in warmed milk for ½-1 hour prior to use. Suitable herbs are: marjoram, chives, lemon balm, oregano, dill seed (½-1 tablespoon), toasted sesame seed (use any *one* of these).

Fish and Caraway Soufflé—Add *1½-2 teaspoons caraway seed* plus *100 g (3½ oz) flaked cooked fish*, eg tuna or salmon, to sauce before adding egg white.

Prawn (Shrimp) Soufflé—Add *100 g (3½ oz) chopped prawns (shrimp)* and *2 teaspoons finely chopped fennel leaves* to sauce before adding egg white.

Sweet Soufflés The soufflé sauce is sweetened with 2-3 tablespoons granulated sugar while it is still hot, before the eggs are added. If preferred, the wholemeal (whole-wheat) flour may be sieved to remove the bran prior to its use in the sauce.
  Variations on a basic sweet soufflé are as follows:

Vanilla Soufflé—Gently heat milk with a *vanilla pod* for 5-10 minutes. Remove pod and use milk as usual in the recipe. Alternatively, flavour sweetened sauce with a few drops of vanilla essence (extract), then proceed as usual.
  Another method of making a vanilla soufflé is to keep a vanilla bean in a container of raw (demerara, turbinado) sugar. The bean will impart its flavour to the sugar. Make soufflé as usual, also dusting greased soufflé dish with vanilla-flavoured sugar (*see* p. 376). The result is delicious.

APPLE AND SPICE SOUFFLÉ

Serves 6
500 g (1 lb) apples
a little water
½ teaspoon ground allspice
2 tablespoons brown ((soft) light brown) sugar

SOUFFLÉ
1 tablespoon magarine
1 tablespoon wholemeal (whole-wheat) flour
150 ml (⅔ cup, 5½ fl oz) milk
2 teaspoons granulated sugar
¼ teaspoon vanilla essence (extract)
3 eggs, separated

Peel and core apples. Cut into slices. Place in a saucepan with just enough water to cover bottom of pan. Cook over a medium heat until apple slices are tender. Drain well, discarding juice (use to prepare a fruit cordial). Layer apple on bottom of a shallow ovenproof dish—a pie dish (plate) or quiche dish (pan) is suitable—20 cm (8 in) in diameter and 4-5 cm (1½-2 in) deep. Sprinkle with allspice and brown sugar. Set aside.
  Prepare soufflé mixture as for Basic Soufflé Recipe opposite. Flavour sauce with sugar and vanilla essence before you add stiffly beaten egg white. Spoon evenly over apples. Bake at 180°C or 350°F for 20 minutes. Serve immediately.
Alternatives • Add 50 g (⅓ cup, 2 oz) of raisins to apple before spooning over soufflé mixture.
  • Other fruit may be used instead of apples, eg fresh peach slices, 5 medium to large peaches or 500 g (1 lb) of stewed apricots—well drained of juice.

Note: I use Granny Smith apples for this recipe. If you wish, cooking apples can be used, but extra sugar may be required.

ORANGE SPICE SOUFFLÉ

Serves 6

1 tablespoon honey

1 teaspoon butter

½ teaspoon ground cinnamon

rind of 1 orange, grated

200 g (1¼ cups, 7 oz) raisins

SOUFFLÉ

1 tablespoon margarine

1 tablespoon wholemeal (whole-wheat) flour

150 ml (²⁄₃ cup, 5½ fl oz) milk

3 tablespoons fresh orange juice

1 tablespoon raw (demerara) sugar

3 eggs, separated

Gently warm honey and butter until melted and thoroughly blended. Remove from heat. Stir in cinnamon and orange rind. Finally, mix in raisins. Spread mixture evenly over base of a shallow ovenproof dish, eg a quiche dish (pan) approx. 20 cm (8 in) in diameter.

Prepare soufflé according to Basic Soufflé Recipe (p. 204), adding orange juice and sugar to thickened sauce before adding egg yolks. Layer prepared soufflé mixture over raisins. Bake at 180°C or 350°F for 25 minutes.

Above: *Orange Spice Soufflé can be served in individual soufflé pans for that extra special touch.*

Opposite: *Serve Savoury Apple Pasties (top) and Cheese Balls (bottom) as hors d'oeuvres at a party — they make wonderful finger food.*

Cheese

SAVOURY APPLE PASTIES

Makes 6

FILLING
50 g (¼ cup, 2 oz) white rice
100 g (1 cup, 3½ oz) mature (sharp)
cheese, grated
50 g (⅓ cup, 2 oz) raisins
1 teaspoon caraway seed
1 large eating (dessert) apple

PASTRY
100 g (4 oz) margarine
250 g (1¾ cups, 9 oz) wholemeal
(whole-wheat) flour
3½–4 tablespoons water
a little beaten egg

FILLING
Boil rice until tender. Drain well and place in a bowl. Add cheese, raisins and caraway seed to bowl. Grate apple (do not peel) and add to bowl—you need about 125 g (4½ oz). Thoroughly mix all ingredients in the bowl. Set aside.

PASTRY
Rub margarine into flour with fingertips. Add water. Work mixture into a soft dough. Roll out fairly thinly on a well-floured board. Using a saucer as a guide, cut pastry into six circles. Divide filling evenly between circles.* Taking one circle, moisten edges with a little water. Bring opposite sides up over filling to meet at top. Press edges together gently but firmly. Place on a well-greased baking tray (sheet). Repeat with remaining pastry squares. Brush with a little beaten egg. Bake at 200°C or 400°F for 15–20 minutes. Serve hot or cold.

Note: * You may find you have a little too much filling for the six circles.

MARY'S MACARONI CHEESE

Serves 3–4
1 large onion
pinch of paprika
1 teaspoon sage, finely chopped
250 ml (1 cup, 9 fl oz) milk
1 tablespoon margarine
6 tablespoons milk (extra)
2 tablespoons wholemeal (whole-
wheat) flour
75 g (¾ cup, 2½ oz) mature (sharp)
cheese, grated
2 tomatoes
½ small green capsicum (sweet
pepper) (optional)
salt and black pepper
150 g (1 cup, 5½ oz) wholemeal
(whole-wheat) macaroni

Thinly slice onion and place in a pan. Add paprika, sage and 250 ml (1 cup, 9 fl oz) of milk. Heat until simmering. Stir several times to prevent boiling over. Cover and cook gently for 5 minutes until onion is tender. Remove from heat and stir in margarine. In a small bowl, blend 6 tablespoons of milk and flour until smooth. Add to milk and onion. Heat, stirring continuously, until sauce thickens. Now add grated cheese. Stir until it has melted and is thoroughly blended with sauce. Remove from heat and set aside. Cut 1 tomato and capsicum (if used) into tiny pieces. Add both to sauce. Season with salt and black pepper. Set aside but keep warm.

Boil macaroni until al dente. Drain well. Add to cheese sauce. Mix well. Pour into an ovenproof dish. Slice remaining tomato on top of macaroni cheese. Place uncovered in a hot oven for 5–10 minutes until thoroughly heated.

MALCOLM'S MACARONI CHEESE

Serves 2
1 tablespoon margarine
1½ tablespoons wholemeal (whole-wheat) flour
200 ml (7 fl oz) milk
3 tablespoons white wine
1 clove garlic
1 chilli (chili pepper)
1 teaspoon each of sage, thyme, marjoram, finely chopped
black pepper
50 g (½ cup, 2 oz) cheddar cheese, grated
100 g (¾ cup, 3½ oz) macaroni
2 tablespoons cheddar cheese, grated (extra)

Heat margarine in a pan until sizzling. Stir in flour. Remove from heat. Blend in milk and white wine. Finely chop garlic and chilli. Add these, plus sage, thyme, marjoram and a little black pepper, to sauce. Heat sauce gently, stirring continuously, until it thickens. Allow to simmer very gently for a further 2 minutes to reduce a little. Remove from heat. Add 50 g (½ cup, 2 oz) of cheese. Stir until thoroughly blended with sauce. Set aside but keep warm.

Cook macaroni in boiling water until al dente. Drain, add to sauce and mix well. Pour into a warmed ovenproof dish. Sprinkle with extra cheese. Place under a medium grill (broiler) until thoroughly heated.

CHEESE BALLS

Makes approximately 14
50 g (½ cup, 2 oz) cheddar cheese, grated
50 g (2 oz) cream cheese
1 teaspoon marjoram, finely chopped
black pepper
pinch of cayenne (optional)
pinch of paprika
1½ tablespoons sesame seed, toasted

Place all ingredients (except sesame seed) in a small bowl. Mash and mix well until thoroughly blended. Take 2 teaspoons of mixture. Roll between fingers to form a small ball. Repeat until all mixture has been used. Spread sesame seed on a small plate. Roll each ball in seed until evenly coated. Pierce each with a cocktail stick (toothpick), arrange on a plate and place in refrigerator to chill. Serve as a pre-dinner appetiser or party snack.

CHEESY LEEK AND BACON PIE *See* recipe under 'Hot vegetable dishes' (p. 35).

CHEESECAKE *See* recipe under 'Desserts' (p. 283).

CHEESE, CARROT AND CARAWAY PASTIES *See* recipe under 'Hot vegetable dishes' (p. 30).

GRILLED (BROILED) CHEESY VEGETABLES *See* recipe under 'Hot vegetable dishes' (p. 26).

PIZZA 1

Serves 4–6

BASE

75-80 g (½-⅔ cup, 2½-3 oz) wholemeal (whole-wheat) flour
1½ teaspoons caraway seed
3 tablespoons water
½ teaspoon granulated sugar
¼ teaspoon dried yeast (active dry
yeast)
1 tablespoon olive oil

TOPPING

500 g (1 lb) tomatoes, skinned
(peeled)
4 cloves garlic, finely chopped
2 tablespoons olive oil
black pepper
2 teaspoons basil, finely chopped
125 ml (½ cup, 4½ fl oz) milk
1 tablespoon wholemeal (whole-wheat)
flour
1 egg yolk
100 g (1 cup, 3½ oz) mature (sharp)
cheese, grated

BASE

Mix flour and caraway seed in a small mixing bowl. Make a well in centre. Warm water to just above blood temperature, pour into a small plastic cup and stir in sugar and yeast (I suggest plastic as it absorbs little heat from the water—with such a small quantity of water it is important to maintain warmth, but an alternative would be to use an ordinary cup standing in a small dish of hot water). Allow yeasty mixture to stand until frothy on top. Pour into well in flour, add oil and gradually mix wet and dry ingredients into a dough. Roll dough into a circle to fill a 25–28 cm (10–11 in) pizza pan or into a rectangle 15 × 30 cm (6 × 12 in). Place on a well-oiled pizza pan or well-oiled baking tray (sheet). Set in a warm place to prove (rise) for 1 hour (it should almost double in thickness during this time). Meanwhile, prepare topping.

TOPPING

Skin (peel) tomatoes. Chop into tiny pieces. Place tomatoes, garlic and oil in a pan. Bring to boil. Boil gently for 20 minutes, stirring frequently, to reduce and thicken. Remove from heat, season liberally with black pepper, stir in basil and set aside. In a separate pan, add milk and flour. Beat until smooth. Heat gently, stirring continuously, until sauce thickens. Add egg yolk. Continue heating gently until it thickens further. Set aside.

Place risen base in oven to bake at 200°C or 400°F for 5 minutes. Remove. Spread evenly with tomato mixture. Mix cheese into flour and egg sauce. Spread evenly over tomato mixture. Apply cheesy sauce in small quantities, evenly placed across pizza. Spread gently with a palette knife or spatula. Replace in oven at 200°C or 400°F for 10–12 minutes.

Alternatives This recipe is a basic pizza. Add toppings to suit your own taste, eg:

- Place thin slices of *salami* or cooked *sausage* over pizza after spreading with cheese mixture.
- Decorate finished pizza with *anchovies* or *sardines*.
- Add 1 cooked *sausage*, chopped into small pieces, to tomato mixture before spreading over base.
- Add 50 g (2 oz) of lightly fried *mushrooms* to tomato mixture before spreading over base (use young button mushrooms to avoid discoloration).

- Add 100 g (3½ oz) of lightly fried chopped *bacon* to tomato mixture before spreading over base.
- Mix 50 g (2 oz) of chopped *ham* into cheesy sauce before spreading over tomato layer.
- Decorate finished pizza with thin slices of fresh *tomato, zucchini (courgette), cucumber* or *olive*.
- Mix 2 tablespoons of toasted *sesame seed* and/or 1 tablespoon of finely chopped *herbs* with cheese mixture before spreading over pizza.

Note: One cup of grated cheese can be used instead of cheesy sauce.

Below: *Pizza always seems to be a favourite with children, and can be a tempting and nutritious treat for adults as well.*

PIZZA 2

Serves 4–6

BASE

100 ml (3½ fl oz) water
½ teaspoon dried yeast (active dry yeast)
½ teaspoon sugar
150 g (1¼ cups, 5½ oz) wholemeal (whole-wheat) flour
1 teaspoon oil

TOPPING

1 onion
1 clove garlic
1 tablespoon oil
450 g (1 lb) tomatoes, skinned (peeled)
1 tablespoon marjoram, finely chopped
1 tablespoon oregano, finely chopped
1 teaspoon paprika
black pepper
1 large green capsicum (sweet pepper)
1 tablespoon tomato sauce (ketchup) (see p. 338) (optional)
100 g (1 cup, 3½ oz) cheddar cheese, grated

1 teaspoon oil (extra)
1 teaspoon water

BASE

Warm 100 ml (3½ fl oz) water to blood heat. Stir in yeast and sugar. Set aside in a warm place until frothy on top. Place half of flour in a bowl. Make a well in centre. Pour in yeast liquid and 1 teaspoon oil. Gradually mix wet and dry ingredients. Add remaining flour, a little at a time. Work mixture into a soft dough—use a fork initially, but as dough becomes drier, use hands. Knead for several minutes. Place in a greased bowl. Cover with a damp cloth. Set aside in a warm place to prove (rise) for 1 hour. Remove from bowl. Knead for 2 minutes. Roll out on a floured board to fit a pizza pan 25–28 cm (10–11 in) in diameter or a baking tray (sheet) (15 × 30 cm (6 × 12 in)). Place on a well-oiled pizza pan or baking tray. Cover with a damp cloth. Set aside in a warm place to rise for 20–25 minutes. Bake at 200°C or 400°F for 5 minutes. Meanwhile, prepare topping.

TOPPING

Finely chop onion and garlic. Fry gently in oil until lightly browned. Skin (peel) tomatoes and blend (liquidise) or finely chop. Add tomatoes, marjoram, oregano, paprika and plenty of black pepper to onion. Heat mixture, stirring well, until boiling. Reduce heat and simmer uncovered for 10 minutes, stirring frequently. Thinly slice capsicum. Add capsicum and tomato sauce to pan. Simmer uncovered, stirring frequently, for a further 10 minutes or until sauce is sufficiently thick. Set aside.

Bake pizza base at 200°C or 400°F for 5 minutes.

In a small cup, mix extra oil and 1 teaspoon water. Brush over cooked pizza base. Spread tomato mixture evenly over top, sprinkle with grated cheese and bake at 200°C or 400°F for 7–10 minutes.

Alternatives See notes following Pizza 1.

Cheese & Eggs

CHEESE AND ONION PUDDING

Serves 6

1 large onion

1 tablespoon oil

125 ml (½ cup, 4½ fl oz) milk

50 g (½ cup, 3½ oz) wholemeal
(whole-wheat) flour

75 g (¾ cup, 3½ oz) mature
(sharp) cheese, grated

pinch of cayenne

3 teaspoons summer savory,
finely chopped

3 eggs

black pepper

Thinly slice onion. Fry gently in oil until tender. Layer on bottom of a greased quiche or pie dish (plate) approx. 20 cm (8 in) in diameter. Pour milk into a bowl, add flour and, using a fork, beat until smooth. Add cheese with cayenne, summer savory and eggs to bowl. Beat mixture for 2–3 minutes, season with black pepper and pour into quiche dish. Bake at 150°C or 300°F for 25 minutes. Serve hot straight from oven (it is also good cold, but will sink as it cools and become rather heavy).

CHEESE AND POTATO CAKES

Makes about 10

150 g (5½ oz) cooked potato, cold

1 egg

3 tablespoons wholemeal (whole-
wheat) flour

100 g (1 cup, 3½ oz) cheese, grated

2 teaspoons marjoram, finely chopped

pinch of paprika

salt and black pepper

1 tablespoon oil

In a bowl, mash potato until smooth. Add egg and flour. Mix well. Add cheese, marjoram, paprika and a little salt and black pepper. Blend thoroughly. Take a tablespoon of mixture. Using hands, form into a small ball. Gently flatten into a scone (biscuit) shape 1–2 cm (½–1 in) thick. Repeat until all mixture has been used—about ten potato cakes. Pour ½ tablespoon oil into a heavy-based frying pan (skillet) and heat. When quite hot, place potato cakes side by side in pan. Cook over a low heat for 10 minutes. Add second ½ tablespoon oil, turn cakes over and cook for a further 10 minutes. Serve hot or cold as a picnic nibble, hors d'oeuvre or party snack.

CHEESE FONDUE OR DIP

2 tablespoons butter
2 tablespoons wholemeal (whole-
wheat) flour (from which bran
has been sieved)
3 tablespoons milk
125 ml (½ cup, 4½ fl oz)
medium-dry white wine
1 egg
1 teaspoon summer savory,
finely chopped (optional)
pinch of paprika
50 g (½ cup, 2 oz) mature
(sharp) cheddar cheese, grated

Melt butter in a pan. When sizzling, stir in flour. Remove from heat. Carefully blend in first milk and then wine. Return to heat. Cook gently, stirring continuously, until sauce thickens. Simmer gently for a further 2 minutes to reduce a little. Remove from heat, add egg and beat vigorously. Now cook, gently beating continuously, until sauce thickens further (take care to beat thoroughly to avoid curdling). Remove from heat, add savory (if used), a little paprika and cheese. Stir until cheese has melted and is thoroughly blended with sauce.

Note: This dish may be served:
1. as a fondue—keep hot over a small flame. Offer bread cubes, and small pieces of fresh vegetable, eg carrot sticks, cauliflower florets, to dip. Serves 2.
2. as a dip—for a party snack or pre-dinner appetiser. Offer bread or toasted bread fingers, crackers or fresh vegetable pieces to dip.

WELSH RAREBIT

Serves 2–3

50 g (2 oz) bacon rashers (slices)
1 teaspoon oil
1 medium tomato
1 large egg
80 g (¾ cup, 3 oz) cheese, grated
¼ teaspoon French tarragon,
finely chopped
2 tablespoons dry white wine
pinch of paprika
3 slices toast

Cut bacon into small pieces. Fry lightly in oil. Drain and set aside. Chop tomato into small pieces. Set aside. Break egg into a saucepan and beat a little. Stir in cheese, tarragon, wine, paprika and bacon. Mix thoroughly. Heat gently, stirring continuously, until mixture thickens to consistency of a thick sauce. Add tomato and stir well. Spread evenly over three slices of toast. Place under a hot grill (broiler) for 1–2 minutes until sizzling.

CHEESE AND EGG PIE

Serves 6

PASTRY

75 g (⅓ cup, 3 oz) margarine
150 g (1¼ cups, 5½ oz) wholemeal
(whole-wheat) flour
1 teaspoon thyme, finely chopped
2 tablespoons water

FILLING

1 small onion
1 teaspoon sage, finely chopped
¼ teaspoon paprika
black pepper and salt
2-3 tablespoons milk
5 eggs
100 g (1 cup, 3½ oz) mature
(sharp) cheddar cheese, grated

PASTRY

Rub margarine into flour with fingertips until finely distributed. Stir in chopped thyme. Sprinkle in water and work with a knife to form a dough (it should be moist, but not sticky). Shape into a ball, using fingers. Roll out on a floured board. Line a greased shallow pie or flan dish (quiche pan) approx. 18 cm (7 in) in diameter with pastry.

FILLING

Finely chop onion and place in a bowl. Add sage, paprika, black pepper, salt and milk. Break eggs into bowl. Beat, using a fork, until eggs, onion and seasonings are well mixed. Add cheese to eggs and again beat mixture well, using a fork. Pour filling into pastry-lined dish. Bake at 180°C or 350°F for 25–30 minutes or until set. Serve hot or cold.

sauces &

stuffings

There are many variations possible on the following recipes. I have provided a number of alternatives, using these recipes as bases, but you may wish to experiment with ideas of your own as you go along.

Savoury Sauces

BASIC WHOLEMEAL (WHOLE-WHEAT) SAUCE

1 tablespoon butter or margarine
2 tablespoons wholemeal (whole-wheat) flour
250 ml (1 cup, 9 fl oz) milk

Gently heat butter until sizzling and stir in flour. Remove from heat and gradually blend in milk, avoiding lumps. Return to heat. Cook gently, stirring continuously, until sauce thickens.

Note: 1. The sauce can be seasoned with a little salt, black pepper, paprika and/or cayenne.
2. For a smooth sauce, use wholemeal flour from which bran has been sieved.
3. This recipe gives a quantity of sauce equal to 250 ml (1 cup, 9 fl oz).

RICH WHOLEMEAL (WHOLE-WHEAT) SAUCE

1 tablespoon butter or margarine
2 tablespoons wholemeal (whole-wheat) flour
250 ml (1 cup, 9 fl oz) milk plus
1-2 tablespoons skim (skimmed, non-fat) milk powder
or
350 ml (1½ cups, 12½ fl oz) milk

Blend 1-2 tablespoons of skim milk powder into cup of milk before using in sauce. Alternatively, measure 350 ml (1½ cups, 12½ fl oz) of milk into a pan. Boil gently until reduced to 250 ml (1 cup, 9 fl oz). Proceed to make sauce in usual way, as given for Basic Whole-Wheat Sauce (p. 218).

These two recipes may be used as a base for other sauces. Examples are as follows:

Rich Rosemary Sauce Add *½ teaspoon finely chopped rosemary* to butter before adding any other ingredients. Use *2 tablespoons (single, light) cream* in place of 2 tablespoons milk.

Cheese Sauce Add *50-75 g (½-¾ cup, 2-3 oz) mature (sharp) grated cheddar cheese* to sauce after it has thickened. Remove from heat. Stir well until cheese has melted and is thoroughly mixed in.
Note: The addition of ½ teaspoon of finely chopped sage, a little paprika and/or a little cayenne make tasty variations.

Indian Sauce Add *½ teaspoon curry powder* to sizzling butter before adding flour. Stir *1 teaspoon of sweet chutney*, eg banana or mango, into thickened sauce. (*See* Indian Okra 1 on pp. 38-9.)

French Sorrel Sauce Add *50 g (⅓ cup, 2 oz) shredded French sorrel* to thickened sauce and cook very gently, stirring continuously, for a further 1–2 minutes.

Herb Sauce Add any *one* of the following herbs to butter before adding flour: 1 teaspoon finely chopped thyme; ½ teaspoon finely chopped sage; 2 teaspoons finely chopped lemon balm leaves; ½–1 teaspoon finely chopped oregano; ½ teaspoon finely chopped rosemary; or 2 teaspoons finely chopped chervil.

Peanut (Groundnut) Sauce Add *3 teaspoons peanut (groundnut) butter* to thickened sauce. Stir well until thoroughly blended. (*See* Leeks in Peanut (Groundnut) Sauce on p. 36.)

Lemon Sauce Prepare basic sauce using wholemeal (whole-wheat) flour from which bran has been sieved. While still hot, add *1 tablespoon raw (demerara, turbinado) sugar* and stir well. Allow sauce to cool. Stir in *grated rind of 2 medium lemons*. Gradually blend in *juice of 2 medium lemons*, taking care to avoid curdling. (*See* Beetroot (Beets) with Lemon Sauce on p. 57.)

BREAD SAUCE

1 tablespoon wholemeal (whole-wheat) flour
225 ml (¾–1 cup, 8 fl oz) milk
pinch of paprika
pinch of cinnamon, ground (optional)
¼–½ teaspoon coriander, ground (optional)
1 bay (sweet laurel) leaf
1 medium onion
black pepper
50 g (2 oz) bread (wholemeal (whole-wheat) or part wholemeal)

Beat flour into 2 tablespoons milk, avoiding lumps. Set aside. Pour remaining milk into a saucepan. Add paprika, cinnamon, coriander (if used) and bay leaf. Thinly slice onion and add to pan. Bring to boil. Simmer, stirring frequently, until onion is tender. Remove from heat. Slowly pour in flour and milk mixture, beating well to avoid lumps. Return to heat. Cook gently, stirring constantly, until sauce thickens. Simmer gently for a further 2–3 minutes to reduce a little. Remove from heat. Season with a little black pepper. Crumble bread or cut into tiny cubes of ½–1 cm (¼–½ in) and stir into sauce. Pour sauce into a small dish. Serve hot or cold.

Note: 1. Stale bread can be used, but if very dry, it should be sprinkled with a little of the milk before using to soften it.
2. Bread sauce traditionally accompanies roast turkey, but can also be used with a piece of boiled beef, silverside or brisket.

CREAM SAUCE

2 teaspoons butter
1½ tablespoons wholemeal (whole-wheat) flour (from which bran has been sieved)
140 ml (⅔ cup, 5 fl oz) milk
90 ml (⅓ cup, 3 fl oz) thickened (double, whipping) cream

Prepare a sauce in usual way with butter, flour and milk. When sauce thickens, cook gently for a further minute to reduce a little. Remove from heat and stir in cream. Serve hot or cold, savoury or sweet.

SAVOURY CREAM SAUCE

2 teaspoons butter
1½ tablespoons wholemeal (whole-wheat) flour (from which bran has been sieved)
140 ml (⅔ cup, 5 fl oz) milk
90 ml (⅓ cup, 3 fl oz) thickened (double, whipping) cream
seasoning to taste (see method)

This sauce is a good accompaniment for meat, fish or vegetables. Make as for Cream Sauce (above) and season with one or more of the following: salt and black pepper (*see* Steak with Pepper Sauce, p. 100); pinch of paprika; pinch of cayenne or 1 teaspoon finely chopped herbs, eg thyme, rosemary, salad burnet.

FRESH TOMATO SAUCE

1 medium onion
1 clove garlic (optional)
2 tablespoons oil
2 teaspoons oregano, finely chopped
400 g (14 oz) tomatoes, skinned (peeled)
¼–½ teaspoon paprika
salt and black pepper

Chop onion and garlic (if used) into tiny pieces. Place in a pan with oil and oregano. Fry gently until onion is soft, but not browned. Skin (peel) tomatoes. Blend (liquidise) for 1 minute. Add to cooked onion. Stir well. Allow to simmer uncovered for 20–25 minutes, stirring occasionally. Remove from heat. Press tomato mixture through a fine sieve. Season with paprika, salt and plenty of black pepper. Reheat if necessary. Serve.

Alternative Method After blending tomato, press through a fine sieve. Add sieved tomato liquid to cooked onion. Simmer gently with pan uncovered until required thickness is reached. Serve without further sieving.

Note: 1. Use well-ripened red tomatoes for a good colour and flavour.
2. Do not confuse with bottled or preserved tomato sauce (ketchup)—like that bought commercially—*see* recipe for this on p. 338.

Opposite: *The success of many meals lies in the sauce they are served with. Fresh Tomato Sauce (bottom) can lift the flavour of many dishes, while Basic Wholemeal (Whole-Wheat) Sauce is often the foundation of traditional sauces.*

TOMATO PURÉE

750 g (1¾ lb) tomatoes

Halve tomatoes, place in a blender (liquidiser) and blend for 1 minute. Pour into a saucepan, bring to boil and simmer uncovered for 30 minutes. Stir frequently to prevent sticking. Remove from heat. Press through a sieve to remove seeds and skin. This recipe makes about 250 ml (1 cup, 9 fl oz) of purée.

Note: 1. Use ripe red tomatoes.
2. As purée simmers, it will splash—take care to avoid burns.

MUSTARD AND TARRAGON SAUCE

1 tablespoon margarine
½ teaspoon French tarragon,
finely chopped
2 tablespoons wholemeal (whole-
wheat) flour
140 ml (²⁄₃ cup, 5 fl oz) milk
2 tablespoons (single, light) cream
1 tablespoon Dijon/French mustard
black pepper

Gently heat margarine until sizzling. Add tarragon, followed by flour. Stir well, remove from heat and gradually blend in milk. Return to heat. Cook gently, stirring continuously, until sauce thickens. Finally, stir in cream and mustard. Season with a little black pepper. Serve hot or cold with ham steaks (gammon, picnic shoulder), ham, boiled bacon joint, pork or beef.

LEMON BUTTER SAUCE

rind of ½ lemon, finely grated
25 g (1 oz) butter
2 teaspoons fresh lemon juice

Gently warm all ingredients in an enamel or stainless steel pan. Serve with freshly steamed or boiled vegetables—pour sauce over the vegetables and mix thoroughly. (This quantity of sauce is sufficient for 150–200 g (5–7 oz) of vegetables.)

MUSHROOM CREAM SAUCE

75 g (2½ oz) mushrooms
1 tablespoon butter
2 teaspoons wholemeal (whole-wheat)
flour
3 tablespoons milk
3½ tablespoons thickened (double,
whipping) cream

Chop mushrooms into tiny pieces. Place in a pan with the butter. Cook gently for several minutes until mushrooms are tender. Add flour and stir thoroughly. Remove from heat. Carefully blend in milk, avoiding lumps. Return to heat. Cook gently until sauce thickens well. Remove from heat. Add cream, mixing thoroughly. Pour over a freshly cooked whole cauliflower, broccoli, Brussels sprouts, zucchini (courgettes) or carrots; *or* serve with grilled (broiled) meat, poultry or fish.

BARBECUE SAUCE *See* recipe for Barbecued Lamb Chops on p. 128. The sauce may be used as a marinade for lamb, pork or beef that is to be grilled (broiled), fried or barbecued.

HOT TOMATO SAUCE The preparation of this sauce is described in Hot Tomato Beans on p. 69. The sauce may also be served with vegetables, meat, poultry or fish.

THYME SAUCE *See* Meatballs in Thyme Sauce on p. 103.

ONION SAUCE *See* Silverside with Onion Sauce on p. 108.

MINT SAUCE

2 teaspoons cider vinegar
2 teaspoons malt vinegar
1 teaspoon brown ((soft) light brown)
sugar
2 teaspoons honey
1 teaspoon mint leaves, finely chopped

Mix together all ingredients, warming a little to dissolve sugar and thoroughly blend in honey. Serve as a traditional accompaniment to roast lamb; *or* as a dressing on cooked and cooled beetroot (beets) served as a salad.

TARRAGON SAUCE

1 small onion
140 ml (²/₃ cup, 5 fl oz) white wine
140 ml (½ cup, 5 fl oz) milk
1 tablespoon butter
½–1 teaspoon French tarragon,
finely chopped
2 tablespoons wholemeal (whole-wheat) flour (from which bran has
been sieved)
140 ml (²/₃ cup, 5 fl oz) thickened
(double, whipping) cream
black pepper

Thinly slice onion. Place in an enamel or stainless steel pan with wine. Simmer gently, with pan uncovered, until onion is tender. Remove from heat. Set aside to cool (most of wine will have evaporated—with only 2–3 tablespoons remaining). When cool, pour onion and wine into a blender (liquidiser). Add milk. Blend until smooth. Set aside.

Gently heat butter until it sizzles, add tarragon and stir in flour. Remove from heat. Gradually blend in onion mixture. Return to heat. Cook gently, stirring continuously, until sauce thickens. Allow to simmer for several minutes, still stirring, to reduce a little. Set aside. When quite cool, add cream. Beat sauce until smooth and well blended. Season with a little black pepper. Use as desired—this sauce is most suitable with cold, cooked poultry (*see* Cold Chicken in Tarragon Sauce on p. 141).

TURMERIC SAUCE

1 tablespoon margarine
½ teaspoon rosemary, finely chopped
½ teaspoon turmeric, ground
1 small clove garlic
pinch of cayenne
2 tablespoons wholemeal (whole-wheat) flour
250 ml (1 cup, 9 fl oz) milk
2 tablespoons white wine
black pepper

Place margarine, rosemary, turmeric, finely chopped garlic and cayenne in a saucepan. Heat until margarine sizzles. Stir in wholemeal flour. Remove from heat. Slowly blend in milk. Return to heat. Stirring continuously, cook until sauce thickens. Continue to cook for a further minute to reduce a little. Remove from heat, cover and set aside for 30 minutes. Stir in white wine. Reheat sauce until almost boiling. Season with black pepper. (*See* Cauliflower with Turmeric Sauce on p. 32.)

YOGHURT SAUCE

1 tablespoon margarine
1 tablespoon wholemeal (whole-wheat)
flour (from which bran has been
sieved)
100 ml (3½ fl oz) milk
4 tablespoons natural (plain) yoghurt
salt and black pepper

Gently heat margarine in a saucepan until sizzling. Stir in flour, remove from heat and carefully blend in milk. Return to heat. Stirring continuously, heat gently until sauce thickens. Remove from heat. Blend in yoghurt. Season with salt and black pepper.

Note: 1. Serve sauce hot, poured over freshly cooked vegetables, eg leeks, carrots. Alternatively, use cold in place of mayonnaise as a dressing for cold potato salad. For extra flavour, add a little finely chopped spring onion (scallion) and/or finely chopped chives.
2. For extra flavour add 1 teaspoon finely chopped herbs, eg chives, thyme, marjoram or lemon balm, to margarine before blending in flour.

GRAVY

Gravy is the most usual sauce served with roast meat. It is prepared using a little of the liquid fat from around the roast meat, plus water or vegetable stock, and flour to thicken. A little wine, spirits (brandy, sherry), soy sauce, Worcestershire sauce, tomato purée or commercially prepared gravy browning may be added for extra flavour. Basic gravy is prepared as follows:

2-4 tablespoons fat from around
roast
1½ tablespoons cornflour
(US cornstarch)
250 ml (1 cup, 9 fl oz) water or
vegetable stock

Remove roast meat from roasting dish (pan). Pour away all but 2–4 tablespoons of liquid fat. In a small bowl, mix cornflour to a smooth paste with a little of the water or stock. Gradually mix in remaining water or stock. Place roasting dish over heat. When fat is beginning to sizzle, pour cornflour and water in. Stir gravy vigorously until the sauce thickens. Simmer for several minutes to reduce a little, stirring frequently. Flavour as preferred (see above). Serve over meat or separately in a serving jug (pitcher).

Note: 1. In place of cornflour, 2 tablespoons of wholemeal (whole-wheat) flour may be used.
2. If vegetables to accompany meat are boiled, liquid remaining after cooking may be used in place of plain water.

Sweet Sauces

CILLA'S APPLE SAUCE

500 g (1 lb) cooking apples
a little water
½ teaspoon sage, finely chopped
granulated sugar (to taste)

Peel and core apples, chop into small pieces and place in a saucepan with water—a few tablespoons should be sufficient. Cook over a medium heat, stirring frequently, until apples are very soft. Remove from heat. Mash to a pulp using a fork or potato masher. While still warm, stir in sage and a little sugar to taste (apples should remain a little tart so don't overdo sugar). Spoon into a bowl and allow to cool. Stir once or twice to evenly distribute sage flavour, which will be drawn out by heat of the apples. Serve as an accompaniment to roast pork, boiled (unsalted) silverside or roast duck.

Note: In place of cooking apples, the Granny Smith variety of eating (dessert) apples can be used. In this case, omit sugar.

CUSTARD SAUCE

2 tablespoons butter or margarine
1 tablespoon cornflour
(US cornstarch)
190 ml (¾ cup, 6½ fl oz) milk
1 tablespoon granulated sugar
1 egg yolk

Mix cornflour with a little of the milk to make a smooth paste. Gently heat butter until sizzling. Stir cornflour paste into butter. Remove from heat. Carefully blend in remaining milk, avoiding lumps. Return to heat. Heat gently, stirring constantly, until sauce thickens. Remove from heat. Add sugar and egg yolk. Mix well. Return to heat. Cook very gently for a further ½–1 minute, stirring constantly, until sauce thickens a little more. Serve hot or cold.

Note: Before using milk, warm it gently for a few minutes with a vanilla pod immersed in it. When sufficiently flavoured, remove pod; *or* a few drops of vanilla essence (extract) may be added to finished sauce.

CHOCOLATE SAUCE 1

2 tablespoons butter or margarine
1 tablespoon cornflour
(US cornstarch)
190 ml (¾ cup, 6½ fl oz) milk
1 tablespoon granulated sugar
1 egg yolk
2 teaspoons cocoa powder
50 g (2 oz) dark bitter (plain, semisweet) chocolate

Follow recipe as for Custard Sauce, above, but at the very end, when sauce has thickened but is still hot, stir in cocoa and chocolate (broken into small pieces). Beat well until cocoa and chocolate are thoroughly blended. Serve hot or cold.

CHOCOLATE SAUCE 2

2 tablespoons butter or margarine
2 tablespoons wholemeal (whole-wheat) flour (from which bran has been sieved)
2 tablespoons cocoa powder
250 ml (1 cup, 9 fl oz) milk
2 tablespoons brown ((soft) light brown) sugar

Gently heat butter until sizzling. Remove from heat. Stir in flour and cocoa. Carefully blend in milk a little at a time. Reheat gently, stirring continuously, until sauce thickens. Remove from heat, add sugar and stir until dissolved.

Note: For a richer sauce, add *50 g (1 oz) grated dark (plain, semisweet) chocolate* with sugar. Beat well until both are evenly blended with sauce.

LEMON HONEY SAUCE

1 teaspoon lemon balm, finely chopped
2 tablespoons honey
1 tablespoon lemon juice

Blend all ingredients over a very gentle heat. Maintain at a warm temperature for 5 minutes to draw flavour from lemon balm. Allow to cool to room temperature.

BRANDY SAUCE

2 teaspoons brown ((soft) light brown)
sugar
1 tablespoon golden syrup
(light treacle)
1½-2 tablespoons brandy

Heat sugar and syrup very gently in a pan, stirring well, until sugar has dissolved. Remove from heat and add brandy, mixing well to blend thoroughly.

SWEET CREAM SAUCE

2 teaspoons butter
1½ tablespoons wholemeal (whole-
wheat) flour (from which bran has
been sieved)
1 tablespoon caster (superfine) sugar
or honey
140 ml (²/₃ cup, 5 fl oz) milk
90 ml (¹/₃ cup, 3 fl oz) thickened
(double, whipping) cream

Prepare sauce in usual way with butter, flour, sugar and milk (*see* p. 220). When sauce thickens, cook gently for a further minute to reduce a little. Remove from heat and stir in cream. Serve with fresh or stewed fruit or a dessert, eg Raspberry Pudding (p. 290).

EASY FRUIT SAUCE

1 tablespoon fruit jelly or *jam*
1 tablespoon water

Gently warm jelly and water, stirring constantly, until well mixed. Use hot or cold as a sweet sauce.

Note: Always use jelly or jam made from pure fruit—store-bought preserves sometimes contain a considerable amount of non-fruit filler.

Salad Dressings

MAYONNAISE

1 egg
3 cloves garlic (optional)
150 ml (²/₃ cup, 5½ fl oz) oil
½ teaspoon cider vinegar
pinch of cayenne
pinch of paprika
black pepper and salt

Break egg into a blender (liquidiser). Add garlic (if used). Blend for 30 seconds. The next stage of adding oil must be taken very slowly to prevent curdling. Add a little oil, blend, add a little more, blend again and so on, until all oil has been added. The mayonnaise should be thick, pale yellow and creamy. Pour into a small bowl. Gradually beat in cider vinegar. Season with a little cayenne, paprika, black pepper and salt.

Note: Use good-quality oil, eg sunflower, safflower (Mexican saffron) or olive.

PLAIN SALAD DRESSING

3 tablespoons oil
2 teaspoons cider vinegar
salt and black pepper
pinch of paprika (optional)

Using a fork, beat together oil and vinegar in a small bowl. Season with salt and pepper and a sprinkling of paprika (if used).

Alternatives • Add ½ teaspoon finely chopped herbs to vinegar 30 minutes before use. Proceed as above.

• Use herb vinegar, eg thyme or tarragon vinegar, in place of plain cider vinegar.

Note: Use good-quality oil, eg sunflower, safflower (Mexican saffron) or olive.

FRENCH DRESSING

2 cloves garlic
3 teaspoons fresh lemon juice
3 tablespoons oil
pinch of paprika
salt and black pepper

Very finely chop or crush garlic. Mix with lemon juice. Using a fork, gradually beat in oil. Season with paprika, salt and black pepper. Ideally, allow to stand for 20–30 minutes before using. Beat again and use.

Alternative Add ½ teaspoon finely chopped herbs, eg French tarragon, to lemon juice. Allow to stand for 10–20 minutes before using. Proceed as above.

Note: Use good-quality oil, eg sunflower, safflower (Mexican saffron) or olive.

VINAIGRETTE DRESSING OR SAUCE

3 tablespoons spring onion (scallion), finely chopped
1 tablespoon parsley, finely chopped
¼ teaspoon ground mustard seed
3 teaspoons white wine vinegar or herb-flavoured vinegar
paprika
25 g (1 oz) capers*
140 ml (²/₃ cup, 5 fl oz) olive oil
salt and black pepper

Place spring onion, parsley, ground mustard, paprika and vinegar in a bowl. Finely chop capers and add. Beat in oil, a little at a time. When all oil has been thoroughly mixed, season with a little salt and black pepper.

Note: * Pickled nasturtium seeds can be substituted for capers. (See recipe, p. 340.)

SPICY SAUCE   *See* recipe for Spicy Leeks on p. 61.

FRENCH MUSTARD DRESSING   *See* recipe for Val's Mushrooms on p. 62.

ORANGE DRESSING

rind of ½ orange, finely grated
2 tablespoons fresh sweet orange juice
½ tablespoon oil

Thoroughly blend all ingredients and use, eg in Brown Rice Salad (p. 62).

HONEYED LEMON DRESSING

2 tablespoons fresh lemon juice
3 teaspoons honey
2 tablespoons oil

Gently warm all ingredients, mixing thoroughly. Allow to cool and use, eg in a mixed greens salad.

Above: *Whether it be for meat or poultry, using the best fresh ingredients is essential. The result will be a subtle but wonderful flavour permeating the finished roast.*

Stuffings

SAGE AND ONION STUFFING

1 small onion
45 g (¾ cup, 1½ oz) wholemeal
(whole-wheat) breadcrumbs, fresh
2 teaspoons sage, finely chopped
salt and black pepper
2 teaspoons dripping(s) or lard
½ egg

Finely chop onion, almost to a pulp. Place in a bowl. Add breadcrumbs, sage and seasonings. Mix well. Melt dripping. Mix with egg in a separate bowl. Stir into breadcrumbs, working mixture with a fork or hands until thoroughly mixed.

Note: 1. To stuff poultry, eg turkey or chicken, pack stuffing loosely inside carcass of bird, then truss as usual.
2. To accompany roast pork: spoon stuffing into a small greased bowl, pressing down only slightly, so that it lies 3–4 cm (1¼–1½ in) deep. Cover with a lid or aluminium foil. Bake at 180°C or 350°F for 20 minutes.

MUSHROOM AND TARRAGON STUFFING

1 medium onion
100 g (3½ oz) mushrooms
50 g (1 cup, 2 oz) wholemeal (whole-wheat) breadcrumbs, fresh
1 teaspoon French tarragon, finely chopped
2 tablespoons white wine
a little black pepper

Finely chop onion and mushrooms. Place in a bowl. Add all remaining ingredients. Mix thoroughly. Use to stuff whole fish that are to be baked (*see* Stuffed Trout on p. 172) or poultry (*see* notes for stuffing poultry on pp. 88–9).

Note: If preferred, half an egg may be mixed in to bind ingredients.

SAUSAGEMEAT (FRESH SAUSAGE) STUFFING

1 small onion
100 g (3½ oz) lean (chunk) bacon
50 g (1 cup, 2 oz) wholemeal (whole-wheat) breadcrumbs, fresh
1 teaspoon ground coriander
¼ teaspoon paprika
2 teaspoons winter savory, finely chopped
½ egg
350 g (12½ oz) sausagemeat (fresh sausage)
black pepper

Chop onion and bacon into tiny pieces. Place in a bowl. Add breadcrumbs, coriander, paprika and winter savory. Mix well. Add egg and sausagemeat, season with black pepper and, using a fork or hands, evenly blend ingredients together. Use to stuff a roasting fowl, placing sausagemeat in body cavity or, in the case of turkey and similar fowl where meat has a tendency to be dry, place between skin and the breast meat—*see* notes on stuffing poultry on pp. 88–9.

BREAD STUFFING FOR POULTRY

liver and heart from bird to be stuffed
2 teaspoons butter
1 medium onion
1 small egg
1 teaspoon brandy
1 tablespoon white wine
¼-½ teaspoon paprika
2 teaspoons thyme, finely chopped
2 teaspoons parsley, finely chopped
salt and black pepper
*175 g (3 cups, 6 oz) wholemeal
(whole-wheat) breadcrumbs, fresh*

Chop liver and heart into very tiny pieces. Fry gently in butter until just cooked. Place in a bowl with all the juices from frying pan (skillet). Chop onion into tiny pieces—almost a pulp—and add to bowl. Stir in egg, brandy, wine, paprika, thyme and parsley. Season with a little salt and black pepper. Finally, add breadcrumbs and, using a fork or hands, mix thoroughly. Use to stuff body cavity of a roasting bird, such as chicken or turkey. In the latter case, I form the stuffing into four balls which are placed inside the cavity together with three or four small, peeled, whole onions.

RICE AND APRICOT STUFFING

150 g (¾ cup, 5½ oz) white rice
1 very small onion
1 tablespoon oil
*2 teaspoons lemon balm,
finely chopped*
100 g (⅔ cup, 3½ oz) dried apricots
*50 g (⅓ cup, 2 oz) sultanas (golden
raisins)*
pinch of ground cinnamon
*2 teaspoons apricot jam or sweetened
apricot purée*

Boil rice until tender. Drain and set aside. Finely chop onion. Place in a frying pan (skillet) with oil and lemon balm. Fry gently until onion is soft, but not brown. Remove from heat. Set aside.

Chop apricots into tiny pieces. Add with sultanas, cinnamon, jam and rice to pan. Mix thoroughly. Use to stuff poultry; whole fish that is to be baked; boned meat, eg knuckle (shin) of lamb that is to be rolled and roasted or vegetables, eg marrow (summer or yellow squash) that is to be baked.

APPLE AND ONION STUFFING

1 medium-sized eating (dessert) apple
1 very small onion
*50 g (1 cup, 2 oz) wholemeal (whole-
wheat) breadcrumbs, fresh*
*½-1 teaspoon rosemary,
finely chopped*
1 tablespoon white wine
½ medium egg

Grate apple and grate or finely chop onion. Place both in a bowl. Mix in breadcrumbs and rosemary. Add wine and beaten egg. Using a fork, mix well, binding mixture together. Bake in a small covered dish at 180°C or 350°F for 45 minutes. Serve with roast pork, lamb or use to stuff poultry, especially duck, or other meat as in Stuffed Breast (Flap) of Lamb (see p. 130).

Savoury Butter

A savoury butter is a butter flavoured with a savoury ingredient such as finely chopped herbs, crushed herb seed or spices. I offer three recipes, but in fact any savoury flavouring may be added in any quantity, to suit personal taste.

Savoury butter can be served with crackers, fresh bread, Melba toast or savoury scones (biscuits). It is also used in the preparation of hot 'garlic bread' or 'herb bread'. A thickly sliced loaf of bread of any type, but commonly long French bread (*baguette*), is used. Our favourite is hot herb bread with Thyme Butter.

Savoury butter may also be used as a sauce for freshly steamed or boiled vegetables. The butter is gently melted and thoroughly mixed into cooked vegetables.

Note: If dried herbs are to be used, moisten with a tiny quantity of boiling water. Allow to stand for 10–15 minutes before using.

THYME BUTTER

1-1½ teaspoons thyme, finely chopped
50 g (2 oz) butter

Using a fork, thoroughly blend ingredients. Ideally, allow to stand at room temperature for at least 1 hour. Work again before using. The thyme flavour is slowly drawn from the herb. The longer you allow the butter to stand before using, the better it will taste.

LEMON BUTTER

rind of ½ lemon, grated
1 teaspoon fresh lemon juice
1½-2 teaspoons lemon balm,
finely chopped
50 g (2 oz) butter

Thoroughly blend ingredients, working mixture with a fork. Ideally, allow to stand for at least 1 hour and work again before using. As with Thyme Butter above, the longer lemon balm flavour is allowed to permeate butter, the better it will be.

MIXED HERB BUTTER

¼ teaspoon each of salad burnet
and rosemary, finely chopped
½ teaspoon each of thyme and lemon
balm, finely chopped
50 g (2 oz) butter

Using a fork, blend all ingredients. Ideally, butter should be allowed to stand for 1 hour before using, to allow the full flavour of herbs to permeate.

Flavoured Vinegar
Herb Vinegar

Herb vinegar is vinegar flavoured with a certain herb or combination of herbs. A herb vinegar can be used for culinary, cosmetic or medicinal purposes. Only the first use is considered here.

Preparation Take *one small handful of fresh herb* (or about 40 g (⅓ cup, 1½ oz), loosely packed). Place in an enamel or stainless steel pan. Pour *500 ml (2 cups, 17½ fl oz) vinegar* over herb, cover pan and heat until almost boiling. Remove from heat. Allow to stand for 12–24 hours. Strain vinegar into a glass bottle or jar (discarding spent herbs), add a few sprigs of fresh herb and cap tightly. Set aside for 1–2 weeks, then use as desired.

One or a combination of several of these herbs may be used:

basil	lemon verbena	summer savory
French tarragon	mint	thyme
garlic	peppermint	winter savory
lemon balm	rosemary	
lemon grass	sage	

Note: 1. Any good-quality vinegar may be used. I prefer to use white wine vinegar, or cider vinegar.
2. Dried herbs may be used in place of fresh herbs, but only if good quality. Use 3 tablespoons dried herb per 500 ml (2 cups, 17½ fl oz) vinegar.
3. For garlic vinegar, use either green leaves or cloves in approximately the following quantities per 500 ml (2 cups, 17½ fl oz) vinegar: 2 tablespoons chopped greens or 3 finely chopped cloves.

Uses Herb vinegar can be used in almost any recipe that requires vinegar. Since the aim is to enhance the flavour, it is important to check the compatibility of the herb flavour and the dish itself. Herb vinegar is useful in marinades, sauces, salad dressings and preserves.

Spiced Vinegar

Spiced vinegar is a vinegar flavoured with herb seeds or spices. It is used in particular to enhance the flavour of sauces, chutneys and pickles.

Preparation Pour *500 ml (2 cups, 17½ fl oz) vinegar* into an enamel or stainless steel pan. Add 1–2 tablespoons of seed or spice—whole or crushed. Cover and heat until almost boiling. Remove from heat and allow to stand for several hours. Strain vinegar into a glass bottle or jar. Use as desired (it is ready for immediate use). If preferred, vinegar may remain unstrained, but it must be remembered that flavour will increase in strength over time.

One or a combination of several of these seeds and spices may be used:

allspice	chillies (chili peppers)	dill seed
anise seed (aniseed, sweet cumin)	cinnamon (sticks or quills)	fennel seed
black peppercorns	cloves	ginger (chopped root)
celery seed	coriander seed	mustard seed

Note: *See* recipe for Pickled Onions on p. 340 as an example of the use of spiced vinegar.

bread

'Man cannot live by bread alone', goes the familiar saying, but cereal grains form the staple food of most cultures in the world. Seventy per cent of the world's total harvested land is for cereals (approx. 1 billion hectares/2.5 billion acres). The three most important cereals are maize (corn), wheat and rice.

The success of cereals as a major food source is attributable to several factors:
- They have adapted well to the wide variety of soils, climates and environments around the world.
- They are quite hardy with regard to disease.
- They are efficient in the transfer of the sun's energy into a food form available to humans.
- They are annuals and so produce a crop each year.
- They are relatively easily harvested.
- They are easily stored.
- They may also be used as a source of food for livestock, which in turn produce either milk or meat.

The way the grain is converted into a palatable food varies between cultures and, of course, according to the adopted grain. Some examples are:
- *rice*—simply hulled and boiled (China)
- *tortillas*—pounded maize (corn) kernels mixed with water, flattened into a kind of pancake and then baked or fried (Mexico)
- *chapattis*—barley meal 'pancakes' of India
- *oatcakes*—oatmeal flour, fat and water biscuits baked on a hotplate or in the oven (Scotland)
- *sadza/nsima*—maize (corn) meal and water 'porridge' (Zimbabwe and other parts of Africa)
- *couscous*—a crushed wheat dish (North Africa)
- unleavened (unrisen) barley flour bread (mentioned in the Bible and the manna of the Israelites) or leavened (risen) wheat flour bread, popular since Ancient Egypt.

The cereal grain is a neat package of nutrients—protein, fibre, carbohydrate, fats, vitamins and minerals. The complement of these 'ingredients' varies between grains.

Some mention must be made of protein. We now know that proteins are built from smaller units called amino acids which are chemically linked together. There are 20 commonly occurring amino acids in nature, and proteins vary according to their complement of amino acids. Of the amino acids, nine are termed 'essential' to humans, ie they must be taken into the body in the food eaten. The remaining acids are called 'non-essential', since the human body is capable of manufacturing them, given that the correct building blocks are available. The essential ones are lysine, isoleucine, leucine, histidine, methionine, phenylalanine, threonine, tryptophan and valine (arginine is also 'essential' for children).

Cereal proteins are likely to be low in lysine, tryptophan or methionine. In order to ensure the correct amino acid intake, one must either eat a variety of grains or accept protein from another source, eg eggs, fish, milk, cheese, meat or beans. Maize (corn) and wheat, for example, are both low in lysine and tryptophan. Cereal grains also vary in their complement of vitamins and minerals, eg maize is very low in nicotinic acid (one of the vitamin B complex) and people relying on maize as a dietary mainstay must find another source of the compound or suffer a deficiency (pellagra). As cereals in one form or another make up the bulk of our diet, it would seem sensible to eat a variety of them wherever possible. Most are available in the developed parts of the world.

I found that once I began using different grains and flours in my cooking, I became inquisitive with regard to their origin and history. A trip to the local university library was made and the following is the summary of my reading. I have included soya bean (soybean), lupin and buckwheat which are not members of the cereal family (Graminae), but the flour of which can be used for baking. (Pea flour is used in Indian cookery in particular.)

Note: Please refer to breadmaking section (p. 246) for further explanations on leavened and unleavened bread and the glutenaceous nature of cereal protein.

Cereals & Grains
Wheat (Triticum species)

Triticum turgidum—poulard, rivet, English wheat

T. monococcum—einkorn

T. aegilopoides—wild wheat

T. diococcum—emmer

T. diococcoides—wild emmer

T. aestivum—bread wheat

T. durum—macaroni wheat

T. polonicum—macaroni wheat

As is obvious from the list above, there are many varieties of wheat. However, the main ones of commercial value are few. *Triticum aestivum* is used for bread wheat and *T. durum* for pasta and semolina. (In Mediterranean areas, *T. polonicum* is also occasionally grown for pasta.)

Einkorn is still grown today on some small peasant-owned plots. Although it generally yields a poor harvest, it will grow in poor rocky ground where no other wheat will survive. Remains of emmer and einkorn wheat found in Iraq date back about nine millennia. Bread-wheat cultivation in the Nile Valley, India, China and possibly England dates back as far as around 5000 BC. Archaeologists have confirmed that wheat flour baked into unleavened bread was produced by the people of the Near East in 2500 BC. The Egyptians were also master bakers, and remains of leavened wheat bread have been found in Egyptian tombs, probably dating back to 2000 BC.

Bread wheat can be classified into two types: hard and soft. There are varieties of both which may be planted in the spring or autumn (fall), gaining the name of spring and winter wheat, respectively.

Hard wheats contain a higher proportion of protein than soft wheats (a distinction which was appreciated as far back as Roman times). Hard wheat grows well in areas of limited rainfall, eg the prairies of Canada, the USA, the Ukraine, China and Argentina. It contains 12–16% protein. Hard wheat is largely used for human consumption in the form of bread. Due to its high protein content, hard wheat bakes into a better bread which retains moisture and is relatively long-lasting. *Triticum durum* is classed as a hard wheat. It has a high gluten content and is most suitable for spaghetti, macaroni, other pastas and semolina. Major growing areas are North Dakota in the USA, southern Europe and central and western India.

Soft wheat prefers a less harsh, but moister climate typical of most of Europe and east of the Mississippi in the USA. Protein content ranges between 8 and 11%. Most of the world's soft wheat harvest goes into livestock feeds. For human consumption, it is suitable in particular for pastries and 'fancy' breads, eg French bread. Europe imports considerable quantities of hard wheat to blend with its home-produced soft wheat for 'regular' bread production.

The wheat grain has four important main parts.

- The *pericarp* is the outer layer of the wheat grain. It is a fibrous, protective outer layer and offers little in the way of nutrition to humans other than its value as fibre in the diet.
- The *aleurone* layer contains protein and also minerals.
- The *endosperm* is mostly starch.
- The *embryo* has a high proportion of oils and vitamins (particularly vitamin B).

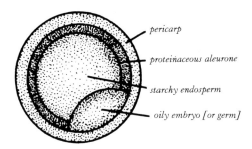

Note: This simplified grain structure is typical of the cereal family.

The embryo constitutes 6%, the pericarp 5%, the aleurone 3–4% and the endosperm 82–86% of the total weight of the wheat grain.

The milling process goes roughly as follows. The grain is moistened, or tempered, to help prevent fragmentation during milling. It is then passed between corrugated rollers which break or slightly crush the grain, thus separating the husk, embryo and grain. As it emerges from the roller, sifting is done to separate each of the three portions and also any unbroken grain (the latter is passed through the rollers again). The grain pieces, which are called middlings, pass through four or five sets of rollers with successively finer corrugations. Sifting occurs after each rolling to separate the various sections. The final wheat middling is rather like a granular flour. This is then passed through reduction rollers—these are smooth-surfaced rollers which grind the middlings into a fine flour. There are several sets of rollers and sifting occurs after each rolling to separate embryo and husk debris from the flour.

The final process is that of bleaching by the use of chemicals to produce the white flour that we are familiar with in stores and supermarkets. Unfortunately, because the embryo and also some of the aleurone layer are removed, nutritionally important vitamins and minerals are lost. For example, 84% of the total thiamine content is lost during milling.

Of course, without the type of milling which produces our white flour, we would be unable to produce the fancy cakes and pastries which delight our palate. Though nutritionally superior, wholemeal (whole-wheat) flour is far less versatile. As wholemeal flour has a lower proportion of gluten, it is often mixed with white flour (1:1) in all types of baking. This helps cakes etc to rise and lightens their texture while still giving the flavour of wholemeal. However, as the proteins of wheat are glutenaceous, both types of flour are excellent for making leavened bread.

Maize (Corn) (Zea mays)

Maize (corn) is one of the world's three most important cereals of today and also one of the oldest, having been under cultivation for thousands of years. It is thought to have originated

in Mexico and from there spread south to the Andean regions of South America and north into North America, where it became an important crop of the American Indians. Maize pollen some 80 000 years old has been found near Mexico City. The maize plant, however, unlike our other cultivated cereals, looks totally different today from that of the wild form. Genetic selection for chosen characteristics has produced a plant which would be unable to survive in the wild. Without constant supervision and husbandry, maize in its present form is unsustainable. It has been adapted to suit a variety of environments and climates and has been adopted by several cultures. Maize was introduced into northern New Zealand around 1772, and although Maori cultivation of other crops was well established at the time, maize was quickly adopted. A favourite way of eating maize was to rot the ear in water for six months or more. The kernels, which were of course partly decomposed at this stage, were then crushed and boiled with milk and sugar to make a kind of porridge. Alternatively, the kernels were fried in fat. This method of cooking was also used in Peru.

Maize often grows well where rice will not and in parts of Eastern Asia, although rice is the preferred cereal, maize is accepted. In Indonesia, either the 'green' ears are roasted over a fire or the kernels are removed, crushed and made into a kind of pudding. Crushed or pounded maize is the mainstay cereal in many parts of Africa where it is boiled with water into a kind of porridge called *sadza* in Zimbabwe, *nsima* in Malawi. Mexicans, of course, use pounded maize meal (cornmeal, polenta) to make tortillas, tamale, pinoles and mush.

There are three main types of maize of importance commercially today. They are:
- field corns
- sweetcorns
- popcorns.

Field Corns These can be further divided into:
- *Flint Corns*—the kernels are hard and starchy and were the ones grown by the North American Indians at the time of the arrival of the first Europeans.
- *Dent Corns*—the kernels are hard and starchy, capped with soft starch. These kind are high yielding and are of importance in the commercial cornbelts of the USA today.
- *Flour Corns*—the kernels are made up of soft starch and are therefore suitable for peasant-farming areas where the kernels are to be ground or pounded by hand.

Sweetcorns The kernels are sugary rather than starchy and are suitable for eating fresh as a raw or lightly boiled vegetable.

Popcorns These are characterised by a type of kernel which bursts open on heating.

Maize has a fairly high percentage of protein, but is low in lysine and tryptophan which are essential amino acids. Maize therefore cannot be relied on as the only protein source. Also, the proteins are not glutenous, making maize unsuitable for leavened bread unless it is mixed with a cereal containing glutenous protein, like wheat. Maize does have application throughout the food industry, eg as cornflour (US cornstarch) used as a thickening agent. Products of maize are used also in other industries—cornflour may be hydrolysed to corn sugar, syrup and gum-like polymers which are used for adhesives.

Rice (Oryza sativa)

Rice is also one of the world's three most important grains. It has been estimated that 60% of the world's population survives with rice as the staple food. In Asia, consumption of 100–200 kilograms (220–440 pounds) of rice per person per year is not uncommon.

Rice first appeared in South-East Asia and is known to have been under cultivation since 3000 BC. Rice is classified by the length of the grain into three broad categories: long, medium and short. It may also be classified according to the type of protein it contains, glutenous or non-glutenous. The latter is the most important since 'fluffy' and not sticky rice is preferred when cooked.

- *Long-grain* rice is non-glutenous and is the rice most grown in South-East Asia.
- *Medium-grain* rice is the one most frequently grown in America. (The USA produces only 1% of the world's rice harvest.)
- *Short-grain* rice is rather glutenous and starchy and is grown in Japan as it is better adapted to a northern climate.

When the hulls of rice are removed you have brown rice, a rice preferred by most 'health-food' enthusiasts. Further processing into white rice involves the polishing of the grain to remove the outer brown layer. This layer is rich in protein and thiamine (vitamin B), so white rice is nutritionally inferior to brown rice.

Rice flour may be mixed with wheat flour to make biscuits, eg shortbread. Rice grain may be fermented into an alcoholic drink, eg *arak* from Indonesia or *sake* from Japan.

Wild Rice (Zizania aquatica)

Wild rice is not a major crop, but I have seen it on sale in many places all over the world. It is becoming increasingly popular as a 'designer' rice in today's Western cuisine. As expected from its Latin name, it grows in water—mostly ponds and slow-moving streams. Traditionally it is harvested from canoes. It is now grown under supervised cultivation and mechanically harvested. Nutritionally equal to rice, it is something of a novelty. However, although still more expensive than ordinary rice, it is becoming cheaper and more readily available.

It is always best to soak this grain in plenty of cold water before cooking to save on fuel and cooking time. Rather nice in flavour, I would describe it as nutty or almost pleasantly woody. There is definitely plenty of fibre if you buy it as I did at the 'brown' stage, ie hulled but unpolished.

Oats (Avena sativa)

Oats originated in Europe and grow well only in a fairly moist, temperate climate. This cereal is high in protein, fat, fibre, minerals and vitamins. Certainly the Scots have thrived in their freezing northern climate on a basic diet of oat porridge!

Today oats are produced chiefly in the USA, Russia, Canada, Poland, Germany and France, and are used for both animal and human consumption. Oatmeal is ground-hulled grains. Similar in texture to cornmeal (polenta), oatmeal is beige/fawn in colour. It is possible to purchase fine-, medium- and coarse-ground oatmeal. Rolled oats (oatflakes) require a little more processing. First the grains are heat dried, then they are cooled and passed between rollers. This breaks the hull from the grain which is removed. The hulled grain (which still retains the embryo and some bran layers) is cut into uniformly sized pieces (halves or quarters). These are steamed to kill lipases (enzymes which cause the breakdown of fats, giving a rancid smell and flavour). As oats are rich in fat, steaming improves the shelf-life of the final oat product. The oat pieces are then passed between rollers which flatten them into uniform-sized flakes. This is the 1-minute, quick-cooking rolled oat. The old-fashioned 5-minute rolled oat is the whole oat kernel (ie uncut, steamed and rolled). Oatflour used in baby foods and some ready-to-eat cereals are ground rolled oats.

Although oats are rich in protein, it is not of the glutenin type so oats are of no use for bread and cakes. The most popular use is in oatcakes (really oat biscuits (cookies)). It is possible to use oats for breadmaking if they are mixed with a strong wheat flour in no more than a 50% proportion—the bread is heavy but delicious!

Barley (Hordeum vulgare)

Barley is the world's fourth most important grain and is probably one of its oldest. Originating from the Middle East, it is thought to have been domesticated 9000 years ago and is equal in age of cultivation only to emmer wheat. The Ukraine and Russia are leading barley producers, as are France and the UK. Barley is grown in significant quantities in Canada, the USA, Turkey, India and Morocco. Most of the grain harvested goes directly into livestock feeds. About one-third is used to produce malt and only a small percentage is taken for the making of pearl barley (for soups), and for flour.

Malt is produced as follows. The whole barley grains are soaked in water and allowed to sprout under strictly controlled conditions of temperature, humidity and atmosphere. The young sprouts that grow from the grain contain an enzyme called amylase, which is important in fermentation and the brewing of beer. When the enzyme level in the barley sprouts is maximal, further growth is stopped by heating and drying. Malt is not only used for brewing beer, but has extensive uses elsewhere in the food industry. For example, it is used in confectionary, coffee substitutes, breakfast cereals, icings, malted milk, infant food, malt flours and medicinal syrups. Malt also has application in various other industries.

Pearl barley is produced by dehulling the grain and polishing to remove the outer proteinaceous aleurone layers—rather like the polishing of rice. Barley flour is used widely in Asian countries, notably India, where it is used to make chapattis—a type of wholegrain 'pancake'.

Barley flour is not suitable for breadmaking for two reasons. It is low in protein, and barley protein is non-glutenous. Varieties low in protein but high in starch are grown as they are better for malting. Mixed with wheat flour, barley can be made into bread, but it is crumbly in texture

and rather heavy. Barley flour is easily digested and often used in cookery for invalids, babies and children.

Note: 'Patent barley flour' is that made from pearl barley. Ordinary barley flour is from hulled grain.

Rye (Secale cereale)

Rye is probably a fairly recently cultivated cereal—it was certainly known to the Greeks and Romans, but there is no evidence to show that it was used by the Egyptians or by the Swiss Lake Dwellers (the latter are amongst the earliest farmers of the world). Rye originates from eastern Europe and Asia Minor. *Secale monatanum* and *S. anatolicum*, wild varieties, are still to be found there today. *Secale cereale* is the only cultivated species and is generally grown on land unsuitable for other crops. It grows well on poor, rather acid soil and likes a fairly cool, dry climate. Most of the world's rye harvest is for pasture or hay, or grain for stock feed. The protein in rye is partly glutenous, containing gliadin but not glutenin. It is possible to use it for leavened bread, although it will not give as light a bread as wheat. It is traditionally used in the making of black bread, a rather heavy, bitter bread—popular in Germany, Poland and Russia. Molasses gives the dark colour.

Pumpernickel bread should be completely rye flour. Homemade rye bread which has 50% or more of rye flour will naturally be heavy in texture. Rye flour is also good for making biscuits (cookies) or crackers.

Millet

There are many varieties of millet, the most common ones being:

- *Setaria italica*—foxtail
- *Pennisetum glaucum*—cat tail (pearl, Indian)
- *Eleusine coracana*—finger
- *Panicum miliaceum*—proso (broomcorn, hog)
- *Panicum ramosum*—browntop
- *Echinochloa frumentacea*—barnyard
- *Digitaria* species—finger

Millet has been cultivated and eaten for thousands of years. Foxtail was used by the primitive peoples of the Tehuacán Valley, Mexico, 7000 years ago. Finger is another millet of ancient use, probably originally from North-East Africa. An important crop for human and animal consumption, millet is found in China, the Balkans, Africa, India, southern parts of Russia and Japan.

In India, unleavened millet flour bread has been known since prehistoric times. In Ethiopia, millet flour pancakes called *injara* are traditional fare. Fermented millet grain may also be made into a kind of beer. In some parts of southern Africa, this beer has importance at special ceremonies, eg it may be poured over the floor of a newly made mud hut in a kind of blessing and opening ceremony. In most developed nations, it is little used for human food. Its more popular use is as a chick or bird seed. It is commonly sold in pet shops.

Sorghum (Sorghum bicolor *or* S. vulgare)

There are many types or cultivars of *Sorghum bicolor* of agricultural importance all over the world. Sorghum probably originates from North-East Africa, but spread with the early movement of people into Asia, where it has been a grain of some importance for both animal and human consumption. (It was known in Egypt before the time of Christ.) In Africa, the pulverised grain is made into a kind of porridge or mush. It is also fermented to make beer. In India, sorghum grain is eaten entire, boiled or stir-fried in place of rice. Sorghum flour is also used to make unleavened bread. In other parts of Asia, sorghum flour is used to make flat pancakes rather like the Mexican cornmeal (polenta) tortillas.

For animal food, sorghum may be used as forage, for silage or for grain feeding. Being a fairly small grain, sorghum is not easy to process and does not compete with wheat, maize or rice, except in areas where these other grains will not grow.

Buckwheat (Fagopyrum esculentum)

Originally from central Asia and northern Europe, this plant of the Polygonaceae family has been a staple food in China for over 1000 years. Migration westward gradually introduced buckwheat into eastern Europe and Mediterranean countries. It is well adapted to poor soils, and can be grown where little else will give a good harvest. Buckwheat is a very versatile crop. The young leaves and shoots may be used as animal forage or for human consumption.

They may also be used as a green manure to help feed and improve the soil. At the flowering stage, it is an excellent food for bees. Buckwheat honey is said to have a particularly agreeable flavour and aroma, and is especially popular in Russia. Finally, at the seed or grain stage, it may be used for animal or human consumption.

In the USA and the UK, most of the harvested grain goes into animal and especially poultry foods. The seed testa, however, is very hard and must be removed or broken to aid digestibility. It is then mixed with other grains.

As a human food, it is most popular in northern and eastern Europe, India and Southeast Asia (Hindus are allowed to eat buckwheat on fast days). In Asia, *Polygonum cymosum* (Chinese perennial buckwheat) and *P. tartaricum* (rough buckwheat) are also grown and eaten. The Russian army is fed a ration of buckwheat groats (hulled grain) cooked in butter or oil. Blinis and piroshkis, two well-known Russian dishes, are made from buckwheat flour. This flour is widely used in Russia and eastern Europe today, and is particularly found in Jewish and Polish cuisines.

In Japan, buckwheat goes by the name of *soba*. The whole grain is steamed and dried. It may be further cooked by boiling to produce a kind of porridge, or may be baked into a kind of cake called a *manju*. The flour of buckwheat is used to make *soba-neri*-bread, or *soba-kiri*, rather like macaroni. In Germany, the grain is often added to soups and puddings. Buckwheat flour pancakes are popular in the Netherlands. In America, a national dish is buckwheat cakes, which are cooked on a gridiron and served hot with maple syrup.

Buckwheat proteins are not predominantly glutenous, though there are enough to bake into a fairly good yeasted bread. The flour is best used in cakes and biscuits (cookies) where it gives a dark, almost violet, colour to the mixture.

Soya Bean (Soybean) (Glycine max)

The soya bean (soybean) is not a plant of the Graminae family, but I have included it as soya bean flour may be purchased and used for baking bread, scones (biscuits) and biscuits (cookies).

Soya beans, which are of the Leguminosae family, have been under cultivation in China for thousands of years. They were mentioned in a document written by Sheng Nung in 2838 BC. Held in high regard in Ancient China, soya beans were classed as one of the five sacred grains, thought vital to Chinese civilisation.

Soya beans have a particularly high protein and oil content. The former is rich in the amino acid lysine, which is low in most cereals. The oil may be removed and used for cooking oils and margarines, or used in industry—eg paint, linoleum and varnish production. The bean left after oil removal is used largely in animal foods, but also in human foods, eg potted meats, soups, confectionery, bread, cakes, crackers, biscuits (cookies).

Soya bean carbohydrate is non-starchy and so is suitable for diabetics. Soya bean flours vary in their content of protein and oil. Those containing oils will have been heat-treated to kill the lipase enzymes which would otherwise cause the flour to go rancid. Those with low or no oil will have been prepared from soya bean flakes produced after the removal of oil, eg for cooking oils and margarines. Full-fat flours are prepared first by steaming the whole bean. Cracking, dehulling and finally grinding follow.

Lupin (Lupinus *species)*

Another plant of the Leguminosae family native to southern Europe, the Mediterranean and West Asia, lupins have been cultivated and used as animal fodder and for human consumption since the time of Ancient Egypt. Their prime value is that they will grow in light, sandy soil not suited to other crops. Secondly, they have a very high protein content. (It is to be noted, however, that some species of lupin in the mature seed state are poisonous.) Those non-poisonous species most commonly used are the white lupin (*Lupinus albus*); the blue (sundial) lupin (*L. perennis*) and the yellow lupin (*L. luteus*).

The main disadvantage with lupins is their unpalatability—there are sweet and bitter varieties. Research has been carried out in New Zealand to find new, more palatable varieties. Investigation is also being made into the possible uses of lupin seeds in the commercial food industry for human consumption—lupin flour biscuits (cookies) and pastry, lupin protein for TVP (textured vegetable protein or meat substitute).

It is possible to purchase lupin flour in some health-food stores. I found its flavour rather strong and not terribly acceptable unless masked by another flavour, like strong cheese. Everything I made with the flour came out rather heavy and crumbly in texture, so I suspect the proteins to be non-glutenous and unsuitable for breadmaking.

Breadmaking

'He is rich who doesn't want for bread.'
St Jerome, AD 388

Bread as a basic food item has been around for thousands of years. Initially, it was unleavened (unrisen), but cooking techniques improved over the years and methods of rising bread were discovered. The resulting leavened bread generally became the more popular of the two, though in some areas of the Middle East unleavened bread is still preferred. Unleavened bread is a basic water and cereal-flour mixture baked over a hot fire or in an oven. Leavened bread is again a basic cereal-flour and water mixture, but with a rising agent added. The rising agent produces a gas, the gas is warmed and, by the law of nature, rises. As it does so, it carries with it the mixture in which it is contained. As more heat is applied (during cooking), the proteins in the dough harden, maintaining the risen state of the mixture. The result is a bread permeated by tiny air pockets. The texture and taste of leavened bread are much different from those of unleavened bread. Most usually the rising agent is yeast, but in soda breads, bicarbonate of soda (baking soda) is used. In either case, the gas produced is carbon dioxide.

The type of protein in the cereal grain determines its suitability for leavened bread. Those most suited are called glutenous proteins and are classified into two groups: gliadens and glutenins. Both have the quality of becoming gluey or sticky when water is added, producing a pliable or elastic dough. The importance of this quality is twofold. Firstly, it is possible to knead the dough. (This improves the texture of the final product—*see* 'The stages of breadmaking', pp. 247–8.) Secondly, as the carbon dioxide is rising and escaping the dough, the protein is able to stretch upward. Non-glutenous proteins would tend to allow gas to escape without the dough being pulled upward.

Wheat is the most suitable cereal for making leavened bread, as it contains the highest proportion of glutenous proteins. I find bread baked by most commercial bakers today sadly disappointing: it is papery in texture and bland in flavour. As time went by, fewer and fewer of the old-style bakeries with good old-fashioned yeasty bread were to be found. Fortunately, these old-style bakeries are currently enjoying a resurgence in popularity. However, it was as a dissatisfied customer that I first turned my hand to breadmaking. I found to my surprise that it wasn't nearly as complicated as I had thought. Having mastered white bread reasonably comfortably, I then turned to wholemeal (whole-wheat) bread. After much experimenting, I found to my delight that it was even simpler to make and that the time-consuming kneading process could be considerably reduced.

Over the years many people have asked about breadmaking—they are obviously keen to give it a go, but are put off by the myth that it is too difficult for the ordinary cook. Nonsense! There is nothing as satisfying as a thick slice of home-baked bread and butter. Almost like a piece of history when you think of those early Egyptian bakers busily discovering the techniques of leavened breadmaking!

The Stages of Breadmaking

1. *Activating the Yeast* Yeast is a living organism which is purchased fresh or dried. In the former case, it usually comes in little cubes and must be kept in the refrigerator. In the latter case, it comes in sealed packets or in jars and again I advise keeping it in the refrigerator. If in packets, these must be kept dry. When purchased, the yeast is dormant and must be activated before it is useful in breadmaking. In simple terms, this means feeding it with sugar—it will then become active and reproduce asexually by a process known as 'budding'. A by-product of budding is carbon dioxide which is the baker's chief rising agent.

   Fresh (Compressed) Yeast This has a soft, fudge-like texture. Mash it together with the sugar in a small bowl. Stir well and you will find the mixture first becomes a thick paste and then a thick liquid. It is now ready to use. This is called 'creaming the yeast'.

   Dried (Baker's) Yeast Mix the yeast and sugar together and stir into a little warm liquid. Set in a warm place. The mixture is ready to use when very frothy on top.

   Killing the Yeast It is important to keep the yeast alive during the preparation stages of breadmaking. This means taking care over temperature. Yeast, like any living organism, is killed if temperatures get too high. Liquids may be given the 'little finger test'. Dip your little finger in and if liquid feels hot, but comfortable enough to keep it there for a minute or so, the temperature is correct. Use commonsense with warm places for proving (rising). Warm but not hot is the rule. Place bowls and tins on a wooden board to insulate from hot metal surfaces if necessary.

2. *Making the Dough* Place half of flour in a large mixing bowl. Add yeasty liquid and any other liquid (also warmed) in recipe. Stir well. The result will be a thick, pasty mixture. Using a fork to mix, gradually add remaining flour. As a dough forms and mixture gets drier, put fork aside and work by hand. The dough should be soft and pliable, but not sticky.

3. *Kneading* Gluten is produced when the cereal proteins are mixed with water. Gluten is naturally pliable, but its quality can be much improved by working it. This is called kneading. It is difficult to explain the technique of kneading and it would be better to actually watch a baker at work. However, the following may perhaps get the reader started.

Shape dough into a large ball. Using both hands, push down and away—a motion which squashes and stretches at the same time. Take edge furthest from you, pull it up and fold it over, pushing it down into edge nearest you. Turn dough through 90°. Repeat pushing away folding over and pressing down. When kneading is done correctly, you will feel dough becoming smoother, softer and more pliable. Continue kneading for about 10 minutes (longer for beginners who will, of course, be slower).

4. *Proving (Rising)* Shape kneaded dough into a ball. Place in an oiled or greased bowl and cover with a damp cloth. Set in a warm place. Leave until dough has doubled in bulk—anything up to 2 hours. (Take care to ensure temperatures do not get too high.) This stage allows gluten to rest and yeast to continue to react. As carbon dioxide tries to escape mixture, the dough will be pulled upward and outward, increasing its bulk.

5. *Kneading* Knead dough as described in stage 3 for 5 minutes. There is a tendency for gas bubbles to accumulate in one spot resulting in caverns in the finished product. Kneading at this stage breaks gas pockets into small ones and distributes them evenly throughout dough. When done correctly, kneading will incorporate air into dough which can also act as a rising agent.

6. *Proving (Rising)* Repeat as for stage 4. Doubling in bulk should not take as long this time.

7. *Kneading* Repeat as for stage 5.

8. *Shaping* Shape dough to approximate dimensions of container in which bread is to be cooked; or, for buns, divide and shape accordingly. All containers or baking trays (sheets) must be well greased. Use butter or margarine to grease tins. Oil is not as effective, especially if you are regularly baking in the same tins. Place dough in tin (pan) and press down lightly.

9. *Rising* Cover tin with a damp cloth. Set aside to allow dough to rise for last time. It may not double in bulk this time. Allow 20–30 minutes.

10. *Cooking* Always cook bread at a high temperature. Around 200°C or 400°F is ideal. A 1 kg (2¼ lb) loaf takes 30–40 minutes. To test a loaf, turn tin (pan) over and tap bottom. The loaf should slip out easily. Tap bottom of loaf—if it sounds hollow, it is cooked. If not, return loaf to tin and replace in oven for a further 5 minutes. Retest.

Note: It is possible to omit stages 6 and 7. It is a matter of time and preference. Obviously the more work that goes in, the better the quality of the finished product.

Wholegrain Bread

Wholegrain doughs cannot be treated in the same way as white flour bread. The proportion of gluten is low or may be asbent, as in the case of oatflour. The dough, therefore, is less pliable and more difficult to work. However, less work is needed as wholegrain doughs seem to maintain an even texture and even distribution of air bubbles. Gentle handling is essential: wholegrain dough will not spring back into shape after kneading and punching and pummelling in the same way as white flour dough. I restrict the kneading and proving (rising) stages to a minimum.

The dough must be kept warm at all times. Remember that the yeast has a more difficult job rising non-glutenous doughs which do not stretch easily. Keeping the dough warm maintains the yeast at peak activity and peak carbon dioxide production. Flour, liquids, bowls and kneading boards should all be warmed a little before use. Preparation goes as follows:

1. *Activating the Yeast* Refer to 'The stages of breadmaking', p. 247.

2. *Making the Dough* Refer to 'The stages of breadmaking', p. 247.

3. *Kneading* Refer to 'The stages of breadmaking', p. 248. Handle dough gently and knead only for 3–5 minutes.

4. *Shaping the Dough* Gently shape dough to fit container in which it is to cook. Grease container well, put dough in and press down lightly.

5. *Proving (Rising)* Cover container with a damp cloth and set in a warm place to rise. Gluten-containing doughs should be allowed to double in bulk. Others, like oat and barley, will probably not double. Allow 1–1½ hours for this proving (rising).

6. *Cooking* Refer to 'The stages of breadmaking' on p. 248.

Note: If using wholemeal (whole-wheat) or rye flour, extra proving (rising) and kneading stages may be included between stages 3 and 4.

Sweet & Savoury Bread

The following recipes offer a fairly wide variety of breads, both savoury and sweet. I usually flavour my bread with either fresh herbs or aromatic seeds. I've offered suggestions for suitable flavourings as a note at the bottom of each recipe. Breads may also be topped with seeds for decoration, eg poppy or caraway seeds. Readers may choose their own as preferred.

Throughout the recipes I refer to a 1 kg (2¼ lb) loaf tin (pan), except in one or two recipes where a 500 g (1 lb) tin is more suitable. The one I use has the following dimensions: base, 18 × 9 cm (7 × 3½ in); sides, 7 cm (2¾ in) deep; top, 21 × 12 cm (8¼ × 4¾ in). The sides are sloping—hence the larger top dimensions than the base (bottom).

Serving Bread

Serve hot or cold. To reheat bread, wrap tightly in aluminium foil. Place in a hot oven for 10–15 minutes. Bread may be served simply buttered, with a preserve or honey, or with a savoury butter (*see* p. 232). Bread to be served hot may be sliced and spread with butter or savoury butter *before* reheating. The butter and flavourings are absorbed into the bread.

BASIC WHITE BREAD

400 g (3¼ cups, 14 oz) plain (all-purpose) white flour
1 teaspoon dried (baker's) yeast (active dry yeast) or *3 teaspoons (1 (0.06 oz) cake) fresh (compressed) yeast*
1 teaspoon granulated sugar
250 ml (1 cup, 9 fl oz) water (or 125 ml (½ cup, 4½ fl oz) water and 125 ml (½ cup, 4½ fl oz) milk)

Activate yeast as described in stage 1 on p. 247. Proceed through stages 2–10 as described. Omit 6 and 7 if you wish. This mixture makes 1 loaf approx. 1 kg (2¼ lb) in weight.

BASIC WHOLEMEAL (WHOLE-WHEAT) BREAD

400-425 g (3¼-3½ cups, 14-15 oz) wholemeal (whole-wheat) flour
300 ml (1¼ cups, 10½ fl oz) water (warm)
1 teaspoon dried (baker's) yeast (active dry yeast)
1 teaspoon granulated sugar

Follow stages as for wholegrain bread on p. 249. This quantity makes 1 loaf of approx. 1 kg (2¼ lb).

MALT AND RAISIN BREAD

1 teaspoon dried (baker's) yeast (active dry yeast)
1 teaspoon granulated sugar
375-400 g (2¾-3 cups, 13-14 oz) wholemeal (whole-wheat) flour
180 ml (¾ cup, 6½ fl oz) water
150 g (1 cup, 5½ oz) raisins
3 tablespoons malt (extract)

For details of following stages, see 'Wholegrain bread' (p. 249).
Stage 1: Proceed as described.
Stage 2: Place half of flour in a large mixing bowl. Stir in raisins. Make a well in centre. Warm malt a little and pour into well. Also add yeast liquid. Thoroughly mix dry and wet ingredients. Proceed as described.
Stage 3: Knead.
Stage 4: Shape dough—use a well-greased 1 kg (2¼ lb) loaf tin (pan).
Stage 5: Prove (rise).
Stage 6: Bake at 190°C or 375°F for 30–35 minutes.
Note: To improve the appearance of finished loaf, brush top with a little well-beaten egg 15 minutes before the end of cooking.

Opposite: Cornmeal (polenta) makes a delicious quickbread, slightly nutty in flavour.

CORN (POLENTA) BREAD

150 g (1 cup, 5½ oz) cornmeal
(polenta), finely ground
125 g (1 cup, 4½ oz) wholemeal
(whole-wheat) flour
2 rounded teaspoons baking powder
50 g (2 oz) margarine
175 ml (⅔–¾ cup, 6 fl oz) milk
1 egg

Mix cornmeal, flour and baking powder in a bowl. Melt margarine in a pan, remove from heat, stir in milk and beat in egg. Add liquid to dry ingredients. Mix thoroughly. Spoon into a well-greased 1 kg (2¼ lb) loaf tin (pan). Bake at 180°C or 350°F for 35–40 minutes.

BRAN BREAD

100 g (2 cups, 3½ oz) bran
50 g (½ cup, 2 oz) wholemeal
(whole-wheat) flour
1 tablespoon raw (demerara,
turbinado) sugar (optional)
4 teaspoons baking powder
50 g (2 oz) margarine
3 tablespoons milk
2 eggs

Mix bran, flour, sugar (if used) and baking powder in a bowl. Make a well in the centre. Gently melt margarine in a saucepan, remove from heat and stir in milk. Add eggs and beat well. Pour into well in the dry ingredients. Thoroughly mix the wet and dry ingredients. Spoon into a well-greased small loaf tin (pan) (500 g (1 lb) size). Bake at 200°C or 400°F for 25 minutes.

GOLDEN WHEATGERM BREAD

350 g (2²/₃ cups, 12½ oz) wholemeal
(wholewheat) flour
50 g (½ cup, 2 oz) wheatgerm
1 teaspoon dried (baker's) yeast
(active dry yeast)
1 teaspoon granulated sugar
250 ml (1 cup, 9 fl oz) water

Follow method described for wholegrain bread on p. 249. Allow 1¼–1½ hours for stage 5 proving (rising). Use a 1 kg (2¼ lb) loaf tin (pan). Bake at 190°C or 375°F for 25–30 minutes until well cooked and golden brown.

PLAIN BARLEY BREAD

250–275 g (2–2¼ cups, 9–10 oz)
barley flour
200 g (1½ cups, 7 oz) wholemeal
(whole-wheat) flour (from which bran
has been sieved)
1 teaspoon dried (baker's) yeast
(active dry yeast)
1 teaspoon granulated sugar
300 ml (1¼ cups, 11 fl oz) water

Follow stages 1–6 as described for wholegrain bread on p. 249.
Stage 5: Proving (rising) should take 1–1¼ hours.
Stage 6: Bake at 190°C or 375°F for 35 minutes. (Use a 1 kg (2¼ lb) loaf tin (pan).)

Alternatives   • Add 2–3 teaspoons of caraway seeds to flour before making into a dough.
  • Add 2 teaspoons of anise seed (aniseed) to flour before making into a dough.

COCONUT FARE

75 g (²/₃ cup, 2½ oz) wholemeal
(wholewheat) flour
100 g (2 cups, 3½ oz) bran
50 g (²/₃ cup, 2 oz) coconut, desiccated
(shredded)
4 teaspoons baking powder
2 tablespoons golden syrup (light
treacle or light corn syrup) or honey
50 g (2 oz) margarine
150 ml (²/₃ cup, 5½ fl oz) milk
1 egg, separated

Mix flour, bran, coconut and baking powder in a large bowl. Heat syrup (or honey) and margarine in a saucepan until margarine has melted, remove from heat and stir in milk. Separate egg yolk from white. Add yolk to milk mixture. Beat well. Add this liquid to dry ingredients. Mix thoroughly. Whisk egg white until stiff. Carefully fold into the loaf mixture (batter). Spoon into a well-greased 1 kg (2¼ lb) loaf tin (pan). Bake at 180°C or 350°F for 30 minutes.

APRICOT ROLL

BREAD

200 g (1½ cups, 7 oz) wholemeal (whole-wheat) flour

225 g (1¾ cups, 8 oz) plain (all-purpose) flour

100 ml (3½ fl oz) water

200 ml (7 fl oz) milk

1 teaspoon dried (baker's) yeast (active dry yeast)

1 tablespoon raw (demerara, turbinado) sugar

1 tablespoon oil

FILLING

3 tablespoons honey

1 tablespoon brown (demerara, (soft) light brown) sugar

1 teaspoon lemon balm, finely chopped

1 teaspoon rosemary, finely chopped

100 g (¾ cup, 3½ oz) apricots, chopped

50 g (¼ cup, 2 oz) sultanas (golden raisins)

BREAD

Mix together two flours. Place half of flour in a large mixing bowl. Set aside remaining half. Pour water and milk into a saucepan. Warm gently until it reaches blood heat. Remove from heat. Stir in yeast and sugar. Set aside until frothy on top. Make a well in centre of flour in bowl, pour in yeast mixture and add oil. Mix dry and wet ingredients together using a fork. Beat a little. Add remaining flour, a little at a time, working well between additions. While dough is still wet, continue to use a fork, but when mixture is drier, use hands and knead in remaining flour. Knead for a few more minutes. Roll dough into a ball, place in an oiled or greased bowl, cover with a damp cloth and set in a warm place to prove (rise) for 1 hour. Remove dough from bowl, knead for 3 minutes and again set to prove as above for 1 hour. Remove dough from bowl and knead for 1 minute. Roll out on a well-floured board (use white flour here) into a rectangle approx. 30 × 18 cm (12 × 7 in).

FILLING

Gently heat honey, brown sugar, lemon balm and rosemary. Stir well. When thoroughly blended, remove from heat. Set aside. Chop apricots into tiny pieces. Add apricots and sultanas to honey and herbs. Mix well. Spread mixture evenly over rectangle of dough, leaving free a margin of 2 cm (1 in) along one of the short sides. Starting at the opposite short side, very carefully roll dough over and over into a sausage shape. Moisten margin with a little water to seal this edge onto the dough roll. Place roll in a well-greased 1 kg (2¼ lb) baking tin (pan). Cover with a damp cloth and set in a warm place to prove (rise) for 30 minutes. Bake at 190°C or 375°F for 25–30 minutes.

Note: For details of kneading and proving (rising), refer to notes under 'The stages of breadmaking' (pp. 247–8).

BRAN AND MALT LOAF

125 g (1 cup, 4½ oz) wholemeal (whole-wheat) flour

100 g (2 cups, 3½ oz) bran

4 teaspoons baking powder

2 tablespoons malt (extract)

130 ml (½ cup, 4½ fl oz) milk

1 egg

Mix flour, bran and baking powder in a bowl. Gently heat malt in a pan. Remove from heat, stir in milk and beat in egg. Pour liquid into dry ingredients. Mix thoroughly and spoon into a well-greased 1 kg (2¼ lb) loaf tin (pan). Bake at 180°C or 350°F for 30 minutes.

MIXED HERB BREAD

*400 g (3 cups, 14 oz) wholemeal
(whole-wheat) flour*
3 teaspoons costmary, finely chopped
3 teaspoons sage, finely chopped
*2 teaspoons lemon balm leaves, finely
chopped*
*1 teaspoon dried (baker's) yeast
(active dry yeast)*
1 teaspoon granulated sugar
300 ml (1¼ cups, 10½ fl oz) water

Evenly mix together herbs and flour before using. Proceed as described under 'Wholegrain bread' (p. 249). Use a well-greased 1 kg (2¼ lb) loaf tin (pan).

SWEET ORANGE LOAF

*1 teaspoon dried (baker's) yeast
(active dry yeast)*
1 teaspoon granulated sugar
*350 g (2⅔ cups, 12½ oz) wholemeal
(whole-wheat) flour*
130 ml (½ cup, 4½ fl oz) water
6 tablespoons orange juice
*3 tablespoons brown ((soft) light
brown) sugar*
rind of 2 oranges, grated

Proceed as described under 'Wholegrain bread' (p. 249), adding orange juice, brown sugar and grated rind at stage 2. Proving (rising) (stage 5) takes 2 hours. Bake at 190°C or 375°F for 30–35 minutes. Use a well-greased 1 kg (2¼ lb) loaf tin (pan).

Alternative Add 3 teaspoons finely chopped lemon balm for extra flavour.

SAMUEL'S BREAD

75 g (⅔ cup, 2½ oz) rye flour
*75 g (⅔ cup, 2½ oz) wholemeal
(whole-wheat) flour*
*150 g (1 cup, 5½ oz) oatmeal,
medium ground*
*1 tablespoon raw (demerara,
turbinado) sugar*
50 g (⅓ cup, 2 oz) raisins
*3 teaspoons bicarbonate of soda
(baking soda)*
1 teaspoon cream of tartar
180 ml (¾ cup, 6½ fl oz) milk

Mix together thoroughly rye and wholemeal flour, oatmeal, sugar, raisins, bicarbonate of soda and cream of tartar. Make a well in centre of dry ingredients, pour in milk and carefully blend wet and dry ingredients. Spoon into a well-greased 1 kg (2¼ lb) loaf tin (pan). Bake at 200°C or 400°F for 20 minutes.

Note: This bread is delicious simply buttered, as a breakfast or tea bread.

Opposite: One of the essences of farmhouse cooking seems to be the smell and taste of freshly baked bread. Mixed Herb Bread and Sweet Orange Loaf fresh from the oven and ready to eat are almost irresistible.

MALT TEA LOAF

225 g (1⅔ cups, 8 oz) wholemeal (whole-wheat) flour
2½ teaspoons baking powder
100 g (⅔ cup, 3½ oz) sultanas (golden raisins)
2 tablespoons malt (extract)
2 tablespoons golden syrup (light treacle)
100 ml (3½ fl oz) milk
1 egg

Mix flour, baking powder and sultanas in a bowl. Heat malt and syrup in a pan. Remove from heat, stir in milk and beat in egg. Add liquid to dry ingredients. Mix thoroughly and spoon into a well-greased 1 kg (2¼ lb) loaf tin (pan). Bake at 180°C or 350°F for 30 minutes. When cold, slice and serve buttered.

EGG AND MILK BREAD

200 ml (7 fl oz) milk
1 teaspoon dried (baker's) yeast (active dry yeast)
1 teaspoon granulated sugar
425 g (3½ cups, 15 oz) plain (all-purpose) flour
2 eggs, beaten
a little beaten egg (to glaze)

Heat milk until warm. Stir in yeast and sugar. Set aside in a warm place until very frothy on top. Sift half of flour into a large mixing bowl. Make a well in centre and pour in yeast mixture. Beat eggs in a separate bowl. Add to well. Gradually blend wet and dry ingredients. Beat well. Gradually add remaining flour, initially working mixture with a fork. As dough becomes drier, you will find using the hands more effective. Remove dough from bowl. Knead for 3 minutes on a floured board. Place dough in a well-greased bowl, cover with a damp cloth and set in a warm place to prove (rise) for 1¼ hours or until doubled in bulk.

Remove, knead for further 3 minutes and replace as before to prove for a further hour. Remove, knead for 1 minute, then divide the dough into three. Roll each third into a sausage shape 25–30 cm (10–12 in) long. Plait the three lengths together, place on a well-greased baking tray (sheet), cover with a cloth and set in a warm place to rise for 20 minutes. Brush lightly with a little beaten egg. Bake in the centre of a preheated oven at 200°C or 400°F for 18–20 minutes.

Alternative Caraway Bread—Stir 2 tablespoons caraway seed into flour before using.

Note: If necessary, moisten ends of the bread 'sausages' to bind them together.

LOVAGE AND
CREAM CHEESE ROLLS

Makes 10

FILLING

20 g (¾ oz) onion, raw
1½ teaspoons lovage, finely chopped
75 g (2½ oz) cream cheese
pinch of paprika
black pepper

BREAD

1 teaspoon dried (baker's) yeast
(active dry yeast)
1 teaspoon granulated sugar
425 g (3¼ cups, 15 oz) wholemeal
(whole-wheat) flour
300 ml (1¼ cups, 11 fl oz) water

FILLING

Chop onion into tiny pieces. Place in a bowl with lovage and cream cheese. Evenly blend together. Season with paprika and a little black pepper. Set aside.

BREAD

Prepare dough as described under 'The stages of breadmaking' (pp. 247–8). Using flour, water, yeast and sugar, take the stages as follows:

Stage 1: Activate yeast.
Stage 2: Make dough.
Stage 3: Knead.
Stage 4: Prove (rise)—this takes 1 hour.
Stage 5: Knead.
Stage 6: Shape dough—divide into ten equal portions. Work each into a ball.

Fill each bun with a little cream cheese mixture as follows. Take a ball of dough, hold in one hand and press thumb of other hand into centre to form a small cavity. Using forefinger and thumb, press and pull dough up around cavity to form a kind of bowl (rather similar to clay work). Spoon a little (one-tenth) cream cheese mixture into 'bowl'. Pull sides of bowl over the top to meet each other. Press together, sealing off cavity. Roll bun around between hands a little so that it resumes its ball shape. Place on a well-greased baking tray (sheet). Repeat with remaining nine portions of dough.

Stage 7: Rising—allow 20 minutes for this.
Stage 8: Bake at 200°C or 400°F until browned on top and well cooked (around 15–20 minutes).

Note: 1. The buns will have a hollow cavity inside and cream cheese will have been partly absorbed by bread.
2. Serve hot straight from oven. They can be reheated if necessary by wrapping tightly in aluminium foil and placing in a hot oven for 10–15 minutes.
3. Serve cold, plain.
4. Serve cold, split and spread or filled with cottage cheese, grated cheddar cheese, tomato and lettuce, or grated carrot.

OATMEAL AND ROSEMARY BREAD

1 teaspoon dried (baker's) yeast
(active dry yeast)
2 teaspoons granulated sugar
250 ml (1 cup, 9 fl oz) water
2 tablespoons honey
1 teaspoon rosemary, finely chopped
300 g (2 cups, 10½ oz) oatmeal*,
finely ground
200 g (1⅔ cups, 7 oz) plain
(all-purpose) flour

Mix yeast, sugar and a little of water (warmed) to activate yeast (*see* p. 247). Pour remaining water into a saucepan. Heat gently until just above blood heat. Stir in honey and rosemary. Mix half the oatmeal and half the flour in a large mixing bowl. Make a well in centre. Pour in activated yeast, and water, honey and rosemary mixture. Using a fork, thoroughly blend wet and dry ingredients. Still using a fork, gradually add remaining flour and oatmeal until a dough is formed. Place dough on a floured board and knead for 3 minutes. Form into a ball, place in a well-greased bowl, cover with a damp cloth and put to prove (rise) in a warm place for 1½ hours.

Remove from bowl. Knead for 3 minutes. Shape to fit a well-greased 1 kg (2¼ lb) loaf tin (pan). Place in tin. Cover with a damp cloth. Set in a warm place to prove until almost doubled in bulk—1–1¼ hours. Bake at 190°C or 375°F for 30 minutes.

Note: 1. * Porridge oatflakes (rolled oats, regular oatmeal) may be used if they are finely ground. (I put them through the coffee grinder.)
2. Owing to the high proportion of non-glutenous flour (ie oatmeal), this bread will be heavy.
3. Serve as a sweet breakfast bread or as a tea bread.

WINTER LOAF

250 g (1¾ cups, 9 oz) wholemeal
(whole-wheat) flour
150 g (1¼ cups, 5½ oz) plain
(all-purpose) flour
1 teaspoon dried (baker's) yeast
(active dry yeast)
1 teaspoon granulated sugar
2 tablespoons molasses (dark treacle)
250 ml (1 cup, 9 fl oz) water

Mix together thoroughly the wholemeal and white flour. Now refer to 'Wholegrain bread' (p. 249). Follow each stage as described, adding molasses at stage 2, together with warm water and activated yeast. Use a well-greased 1 kg (2¼ lb) loaf tin (pan). Bake at 190°C or 375°F for 30 minutes.

Note: This bread is delicious cut into thick slices and served with hot soup.

YOGHURT BREAD

1 teaspoon dried (baker's) yeast
(active dry yeast)
1 teaspoon granulated sugar
6 tablespoons natural (plain) yoghurt
375 g (2¾ cups, 13 oz) wholemeal
(whole-wheat) flour
150 ml (²/3 cup, 5½ fl oz) water

Proceed as described under 'Wholegrain bread' (p. 249), adding yoghurt with yeast liquid at stage 2. Proving (rising) (stage 5) takes 1½ hours. Bake at 190°C or 375°F for 30 minutes. Use a well-greased 1kg (2¼ lb) loaf tin (pan).

Alternative Add 1 tablespoon dill seed to yoghurt before using. Allow to stand for at least 1 hour to draw the flavour from seeds.

SPICE AND RAISIN LOAF

1 teaspoon dried (baker's) yeast
(active dry yeast)
1 teaspoon granulated sugar
230 ml (8 fl oz) water
350-375 g (2²/3-2¾ cups,
12½-13 oz) wholemeal
(whole-wheat) flour*
2 tablespoons raw (demerara,
turbinado) sugar
¼ teaspoon ground ginger
2 teaspoons ground cinnamon
200 g (1¼ cups, 7 oz) raisins

For details of following stages, refer to 'Wholegrain bread' (p. 249).

Stage 1: Activate yeast with 1 teaspoon sugar in warmed water.

Stage 2: Mix together half of the flour, the raw sugar, ginger, cinnamon and raisins in a large mixing bowl. Proceed as described.

Stage 3: Knead.

Stage 4: Shape dough—use a well-greased 1 kg (2¼ lb) loaf tin (pan).

Stage 5: Prove (rise)—this will take around 2 hours.

Stage 6: Bake at 190°C or 375°F for 35 minutes.

Note: 1. * I use wholemeal (whole-wheat) flour from which bran has been sieved. The loaf is lighter and I believe the flavours blend more satisfactorily. However, this is only a personal preference, so leave bran in if you wish.
2. To improve the appearance of finished loaf, brush top with a little well-beaten egg 15 minutes before the end of cooking.

RYE BREAD

325 g (2½ cups, 12 oz) wholemeal (whole-wheat) flour (from which bran has been sieved)
150 g (1¼ cups, 5½ oz) rye flour
1 teaspoon dried (baker's) yeast (active dry yeast)
1 teaspoon granulated sugar
200 ml (7 fl oz) water
100 ml (3½ fl oz) milk

Follow the stages of breadmaking as described under 'Wholegrain bread' (p. 249).

Stage 1: Activate yeast.
Stage 2: Make dough.
Stage 3: Knead—3 minutes.
Stage 4: Prove (rise)—1 hour.
Stage 5: Knead—3 minutes.
Stage 6: Shape dough (use a well-greased 1 kg (2¼ lb) loaf tin (pan)).
Stage 7: Prove—1 hour 20 minutes.
Stage 8: Cook at 190°C or 375°F for 30–35 minutes.

Note: 1. Rye flour makes a rather gummy dough which is difficult to work and which bakes into a very heavy, close-textured bread. It is therefore better to mix it with wheat flour—either high gluten white or wholemeal (whole-wheat). This recipe gives a medium-textured bread. The proportion of rye flour may be increased, but with a consequently heavier bread.
2. This bread may be flavoured with herbs or seeds, eg 1 tablespoon finely chopped rosemary; ½–1 tablespoon caraway seed; ½ tablespoon ground coriander seed or ½ tablespoon celery seed.

DARK RYE BREAD

200 g (1½ cups, 7 oz) rye flour
175-200 g (1⅓-1½ cups, 6-7 oz) wholemeal (whole-wheat) flour (from which bran has been sieved)
1 teaspoon dried (baker's) yeast (active dry yeast)
1 teaspoon granulated sugar
2 tablespoons molasses (dark treacle)
1 tablespoon oil
180 ml (¾ cup, 6½ fl oz) water

For details of following stages, refer to 'Wholegrain bread' (p. 249).

Stage 1: Activate yeast with sugar in warmed water.
Stage 2: Place rye flour in a large mixing bowl. Make a well in centre. Warm molasses a little. Pour molasses and oil into well. Add yeast liquid. Thoroughly mix wet and dry ingredients. Work dough a little.
Stage 3: Knead—3 minutes.
Stage 4: Prove (rise)—1 hour.
Stage 5: Knead—2–3 minutes.
Stage 6: Shape dough (use a well-greased 1 kg (2¼ lb) loaf tin (pan)).
Stage 7: Prove—this will take 1½–2 hours.
Stage 8: Bake at 190°C or 375°F for 30–35 minutes.

Alternatives • Add 1–2 teaspoons caraway seed to rye flour in stage 2.
• Add ½ cup (2½ oz) raisins to rye flour in stage 2.

THREE-CEREAL BREAD

200 g (1²/₃ cups, 7 oz) barley flour
200 g (1²/₃ cups, 7 oz) plain
(all-purpose) flour
150 g (1 cup, 5½ oz) oatmeal,
medium ground
50 g (2 oz) butter or margarine
2½ tablespoons honey
3 eggs
2 teaspoons bicarbonate of soda
(baking soda)
¼ teaspoon cream of tartar

Mix together the two flours and oatmeal. Gently heat butter until just melted. Remove from heat, stir in honey and allow to cool a little. Add eggs and beat well. Stir in bicarbonate of soda and cream of tartar. Make a well in centre of dry ingredients. Pour in liquid. Gradually mix wet and dry ingredients together to make a soft dough. Knead for 1–2 minutes. Place in a well-greased 1 kg (2¼ lb) loaf tin (pan). Bake at 200°C or 400°F for 30 minutes.

WHOLEMEAL (WHOLE-WHEAT) FRENCH LOAVES

1 teaspoon dried (baker's) yeast
(active dry yeast)
1 teaspoon granulated sugar
400 g (3 cups, 14 oz) wholemeal
(whole-wheat) flour
300 ml (1¼ cups, 10½ fl oz) water
a little egg white, beaten

Prepare the loaves according to the stages given below. Refer to 'Wholegrain bread' (p. 249) for details.

Stage 1: Activate yeast.

Stage 2: Make dough.

Stage 3: Knead.

Stage 4: Prove (rise).

Stage 5: Knead.

Stage 6: Shape dough and divide in half. Roll each half into a sausage shape approx. 25 cm (10 in) long. Place side by side on a greased baking tray (sheet).

Stage 7: Prove.

Stage 8: Bake at 200°C or 400°F for 20–25 minutes. Five minutes before the end of cooking, brush each loaf with a little beaten egg white.

cakes & desserts

Generally I use a basic cake mixture (batter) as given for Plain Cake below, and add flavouring, eg grated orange peel plus orange juice; lemon peel and juice; cocoa or instant coffee powder; dried mixed fruit; chopped glacé (candied) cherries or chopped sweet herbs, eg lemon thyme, lemon balm, tansy or rosemary. For most of these variations, I sieve bran out of wholemeal (whole-wheat) flour before weighing. The bran adds a nutty flavour which is pleasant in plain cake or with a dried fruit addition, but is not compatible with other flavours such as coffee or orange.

Cakes

PLAIN CAKE (BASIC MIXTURE/BATTER)

175 g (approx. ¾ cup, 6 oz) margarine
175 g (¾ cup, 6 oz) raw (demerara, turbinado) sugar
300 g (2½ cups, 10½ oz) wholemeal (whole-wheat) flour
180 ml (¾ cup, 6½ fl oz) water
3 eggs, separated
3 rounded teaspoons baking powder

Heat margarine in a saucepan until just melted. Remove from heat, add sugar and beat well. Add several tablespoons of flour and beat well. Add a little water and beat well. Repeat with alternate additions of flour and water until about half of each has been used. Separate eggs, beat yolks well, add to cake mixture (batter) and beat. Repeat with alternate additions of flour and water, beating well after each addition until all has been used. Stir in baking powder. Whisk egg whites until stiff. Fold into mixture. Spoon into a greased and lined deep round cake tin (pan) (approx. 20 × 8 cm (8 × 3¼ in)).* Bake in the centre of a preheated oven at 150°–170°C or 300°–325°F for 55–60 minutes.

Note: 1. When using wholemeal flour, thorough beating between additions of ingredients is essential to prevent heaviness.
2. * If this size cake tin is unavailable, you can use a 23 × 5 cm (9 × 2 in) tin.

Plain Cake Variations

Chocolate Cake To the basic cake mixture (batter), add *5 tablespoons cocoa powder* and an *extra 1 tablespoon water*.

Herb Cake Use *1–2 tablespoons finely chopped herbs*, according to taste. Heat 180 ml (¾ cup, 6½ fl oz) of water until boiling. Pour over chopped herbs. Cover and allow to cool. When tepid, use in cake mixture (batter) as usual. Steeping herbs draws out the flavour, resulting in a more thoroughly and evenly flavoured cake. My favourite is lemon thyme herb cake.

Coffee Cake Add *2 tablespoons instant coffee* to basic cake mixture (batter). If using coffee granules, these must be dissolved in the warmed water. Alternatively, use 180 ml (¾ cup, 6½ fl oz) black coffee in place of water.

Citrus Cake Add *grated rind of 2 oranges and juice of 1 orange* (lemon rind and juice may also be used) to basic cake mixture (batter). *See also* Orange Sandwich Cake (p. 271).

Fruit Cake Add *250-300 g (1½-1¾ cups, 9-10½ oz) dried fruit*, eg raisins, currants, sultanas (golden raisins) or a mixture of these. If fruit is very dry, add an extra tablespoon of water.

Cherry Cake Add *200 g (1 cup, 7 oz) glacé (candied) cherries* or *cooked fresh cherries* to basic cake mixture (batter). Halve or quarter them and dust with a little plain (all-purpose) flour before adding, to prevent them settling at the bottom of the mixture.

Decorating

If you wish to decorate any of the cakes mentioned above, refer to the toppings and glazes used in the following recipes.

APPLE CAKE

175 g (approx. ¾ cup, 6 oz) margarine
175 g (¾ cup, 6 oz) granulated sugar
180 ml (¾ cup, 6½ fl oz) water
3 teaspoons ground cinnamon
50 g (½ cup, 2 oz) wheat germ
3 eggs, separated
250 g (1¾ cups, 9 oz) wholemeal (whole-wheat) flour
500 g (1 lb) apples (eg Granny Smiths, Coxe's orange pippins, Greenings)
4 teaspoons baking powder

Gently heat margarine until melted and stir in sugar. Add water, cinnamon and wheat germ. Beat a little. Separate eggs, add yolks to cake mixture (batter) and beat. Gradually add flour, beating well between additions. Set mixture aside. Take a round cake tin (pan) of about 23 cm (9 in) diameter with a removable base. Grease well. Line base with greased parchment paper.

Peel apples, quarter, cut away and discard cores. Take one quarter, cut into thin slices lengthwise and arrange in a circular pattern in the bottom of the cake tin. Repeat until the tin is decorated with apple slices one layer thick. Chop remaining apple into tiny pieces. Stir into cake mixture. Thoroughly mix in baking powder. Whisk egg whites until stiff. Carefully fold into mixture. Spoon into cake tin. Bake at 150°C or 300°F for 1 hour—the cake should be moist, but still well cooked at the centre. Leave in the tin until cold. Turn out upside down onto a large plate. Carefully remove tin and parchment paper (the top of the cake is now decorated with apple slices).

Alternative In place of wheat germ, I often use kibbled (cracked, burghul) wheat—the flavour of the cake is nutty and the texture much heavier and wetter. (We really enjoy moist cake, but if preferred, you can reduce quantity of water to 160 ml (2/3 cup, 5½ fl oz).)

Note: This cake can be served as a teatime cake or as a dessert.

BANANA LOAF

100 g (3½ oz) margarine
100 g (½ cup, 3½ oz) granulated sugar
75 g (⅔ cup, 2½ oz) nuts (eg walnuts, peanuts (groundnuts), hazelnuts), finely chopped
2 teaspoons ground cinnamon
450 g (1 lb) bananas
2 eggs, beaten
200 g (1½ cups, 7 oz) wholemeal (whole-wheat) flour
2 teaspoons baking powder

Cream margarine and sugar together. Add nuts and cinnamon. Mix well. Peel bananas and mash well. Stir into cake mixture (batter). Break eggs into a separate bowl and beat well. Add eggs and flour, a little at a time and alternately, mixing well between additions. Thoroughly mix in baking powder. Spoon into a well-greased 1 kg (2¼ lb) loaf tin (pan). Bake at 170°C or 325°F for 50 minutes.

CARAWAY SEED CAKES

Makes 18
CAKE
100 g (3½ oz) margarine
100 g (½ cup, 3½ oz) raw (demerara, turbinado) sugar
1–1½ teaspoons caraway seed
130 ml (½ cup, 4½ fl oz) water
175 g (1⅓ cups, 6 oz) wholemeal (whole-wheat) flour
1 egg, beaten
2 teaspoons baking powder

FROSTING
2 tablespoons raw (demerara, turbinado) sugar
3 tablespoons water
75 g (½ cup, 2½ oz) icing (powdered) sugar
almond essence (extract)
1 tablespoon top of the milk or thin (single, light) cream
½–1 teaspoon caraway seed

CAKE
Melt margarine and sugar in a saucepan over a gentle heat. Remove from heat. Stir in caraway seed and water. Add half of the flour, a little at a time, mixing well between additions. Break egg into a separate bowl. Beat well. Add to cake mixture (batter). Beat well. Add remaining flour, again a little at a time, beating well between additions. Finally, stir in baking powder. Spoon into small well-greased patty tins (cupcake pans) or paper cupcake cases. Bake at 190°C or 375°F for 15–20 minutes or until lightly browned and firm. Cool on a wire rack.

FROSTING
Heat raw sugar and water in a small pan until boiling. Stirring frequently, boil gently for 5 minutes. Remove from heat and add icing sugar, a little at a time, working well between additions. When about half of the sugar has been added, stir in almond essence and top of the milk. Continue to add remaining icing sugar. Spread a little frosting over the top of each cake. Sprinkle with a few caraway seeds to decorate.

Note: This cake mixture is rather wet so it is best to support paper cupcake cases by placing them in patty tins (pans) or close together on a baking tray (sheet).

Opposite: Perfect for afternoon tea with friends and family, Apple Cake and iced Caraway Seed Cakes make tasty snacks at any time of the day.

CARROT CAKE

200 g (7 oz) margarine
175 g (¾ cup, 6 oz) raw (demerara, turbinado) sugar
200 g (²/3 cup, 7 oz) golden syrup (light treacle)
125 ml (½ cup, 4½ fl oz) milk
350 g (2²/3 cups, 12½ oz) wholemeal (whole-wheat) flour
150 g (¾ cup, 5½ oz) carrot, grated
3 eggs, beaten
2½ teaspoons baking powder

Melt margarine, sugar and syrup gently in a saucepan. Stir in milk. Place flour in a mixing bowl. Stir in carrot. Make a well in the centre, pour in liquid and gradually incorporate flour. Mix well. Add beaten eggs. Beat mixture (batter) well. Finally, stir in baking powder. Pour mixture into a well-greased baking tin (pan) (approx. 21 × 17 × 5 cm (8¼ × 6¾ × 2 in)). Bake at 170°C or 325°F for 50 minutes until firm.

Alternatives • *Sticky Dark Gingerbread*—Substitute dark (black) treacle (molasses) for syrup and (soft) dark brown (Barbados) sugar for raw sugar. Add 4 teaspoons ground ginger (or to taste) and ½ teaspoon cinnamon. Omit carrot. Method as above.

• *Pumpkin (Winter Squash) Cake*—Substitute 200 g (7 oz) lightly boiled mashed pumpkin (winter or Crown Prince squash) for carrot. Proceed as above, but bake at 150°C or 300°F for 1 hour.

CHOCOLATE CUPCAKES

Makes 18–20

100 g (3½ oz) margarine
100 g (⅔ cup, 3½ oz) (soft) dark brown (Barbados) sugar
2 teaspoons molasses (dark (black) treacle)
8 tablespoons water
175 g (1⅓ cups, 6 oz) wholemeal (whole-wheat) flour
1 egg, beaten
6 teaspoons cocoa powder
1½ teaspoons baking powder
100 g (3½ oz) (sweet or dark) cooking (sweetened baking) chocolate
flaked almonds (to decorate)

Melt margarine and sugar in a large pan. Remove from heat. Stir in molasses and water. Add half of the flour, a little at a time, stirring well after each addition. Beat egg, add to cake mixture (batter) and beat mixture well. Add remainder of flour gradually, again beating well between additions. Finally, stir in cocoa and baking powder. Mix thoroughly. Spoon into paper cupcake cases or greased patty tins (cupcake pans). Bake at 190°C or 375°F until firm but not dry—about 15 minutes. Allow to cool before covering with chocolate.

Break cooking chocolate into small pieces. Melt gently in a bowl over a pan of hot water. Spoon a teaspoon of melted chocolate over each cake. Decorate with 1 or 2 pieces of flaked almond.

CHOCOLATE YOGHURT CAKE

CAKE

200 g (7 oz) margarine
100 g (⅔ cup, 3½ oz) brown ((soft) light brown) sugar
100 g (½ cup, 3½ oz) raw (demerara, turbinado) sugar
4 large eggs
50 g (½ cup, 2 oz) cocoa powder
250 ml (1 cup, 9 fl oz) natural (plain) yoghurt
350 g (2⅔ cups, 12½ oz) wholemeal (whole-wheat) flour
4 teaspoons baking powder

TOPPING

100 g (3½ oz) butter
125 g (¾ cup, 4½ oz) icing (powdered) sugar
1 tablespoon cocoa powder
75 g (2½ oz) dark (plain, semisweet) chocolate
1 tablespoon chocolate vermicelli (sprinkles) (optional)
2 violet flowers, crystallised (sugared) (optional)

CAKE

Cream margarine and both sugars until light and fluffy. Add 2 eggs and beat mixture (batter) well. Now add cocoa and beat well. Spoon in half of the yoghurt. Gradually blend yoghurt and cake mixture together. Add half of the flour and mix well. Add remaining 2 eggs and beat. Add remaining yoghurt and beat. Finally, add remaining flour and baking powder. Beat thoroughly. Spoon into a well-greased round cake tin (pan) (approx. 23 cm (9 in) diameter). Bake at 150°C or 300°F for 50 minutes. Leave in tin until cool.

TOPPING

Cream butter and sugar. Thoroughly blend in cocoa. Melt chocolate in a bowl set in a pan of hot water. Beat melted chocolate into butter mixture. Allow to cool a little and use to coat top of the cake. Sprinkle over chocolate vermicelli (if used) to decorate. Place two violet flowers (if used) in the centre of the cake.

MALCOLM'S CHOCOLATE CAKE

CAKE

125 g (½ cup, 4½ oz) margarine

100 g (⅔ cup, 3½ oz) (soft) dark brown (Barbados) sugar

125 g (⅓ cup, 4½ oz) molasses (dark (black) treacle)

2 eggs, beaten

100 g (¾ cup, 3½ oz) wholemeal (whole-wheat) flour

3 tablespoons cocoa powder

2 teaspoons baking powder

DECORATION

3 tablespoons thickened (double, whipping) cream

150 g (5½ oz) (sweet or dark) cooking (sweetened baking) chocolate

2 glacé (candied) cherries

CAKE

Cream margarine and sugar. Add molasses. Mix in thoroughly. Beat eggs in a separate bowl, add to cake mixture (batter) and beat well (the mixture may curdle a little at this stage, but this is all right). Add flour a little at a time, mixing well between additions. Finally, stir in cocoa and baking powder. Mix thoroughly. Turn into a well-greased loaf tin (pan) (1 kg (2¼ lb) size). Bake at 170°C or 325°F for 35 minutes. Cool thoroughly before decorating.

DECORATION

Whip cream until light and fluffy. Set aside. Melt chocolate in a small pan set in a bowl of hot water. Fold in cream, taking care to keep melted chocolate warm. When thoroughly blended, pour over the cake. Spread evenly to cover top and sides. Using a knife, make swirling patterns in the chocolate. Halve cherries and use to decorate the top of the cake.

COFFEE AND NUT CAKE

CAKE

100 g (3½ oz) margarine

100 g (⅔ cup, 3½ oz) brown ((soft) light brown) sugar

100 ml (3½ fl oz) milk

125 g (1 cup, 4½ oz) wholemeal (whole-wheat) flour

100 g (¾ cup, 3½ oz) nuts, finely chopped

1½ tablespoons instant coffee

2 teaspoons baking powder

4 eggs, beaten

COFFEE CREAM

150 ml (⅔ cup, 5½ fl oz) thickened (double, whipping) cream

2 teaspoons instant coffee

1 tablespoon caster (superfine) or icing (powdered) sugar

¼ cup (1 oz) nuts, chopped (optional)

CAKE

Cream margarine and sugar. Add milk and flour alternately in small quantities. Beat mixture (batter) well between additions. Stir in nuts, coffee and baking powder. Mix thoroughly. Finally, break eggs into a separate bowl. Beat well. Add to cake mixture and beat well. Pour mixture into a well-greased 22 × 17 × 5 cm (8½ × 6½ × 2 in) cake tin (pan). Bake at 150°C or 300°F for 30 minutes until browned and set.

COFFEE CREAM

Whip cream until stiff. Thoroughly mix in coffee, sugar and nuts. Spread over the top of the cooled cake.

Note: This cake can be eaten plain or with coffee cream spread on top. Serve as a teatime cake or a dessert.

If using coffee granules, they must be dissolved in the warmed milk before adding to mixture.

OATMEAL CAKE

CAKE

200 g (7 oz) margarine
175 g (¾ cup, 6 oz) granulated sugar
150 g (½ cup, 5½ oz) golden syrup
(light treacle)
350 g (2⅓ cups, 12½ oz) oatmeal,
medium ground
3 large eggs, beaten
200 g (1½ cups, 7 oz) wholemeal
(whole-wheat) flour
3 teaspoons baking powder

LEMON GLAZE

2 tablespoons fresh lemon juice
2 tablespoons water
3 tablespoons granulated sugar
1 tablespoon honey
¼ teaspoon gelatine crystals (powder)
2 slices of lemon, fresh or crystallised
(candied)

CAKE

Gently heat margarine and sugar in a large pan until melted. Remove from heat and stir in syrup. Add oatmeal and mix thoroughly. In a separate bowl, beat eggs with an egg-beater until frothy on top. Stir eggs into cake mixture (batter). Finally, add flour and baking powder. Mix thoroughly. Pour into a well-lined and greased cake tin (pan) (22 × 17 × 5 cm (8½ × 6½ × 2 in)). Bake at 150°C or 300°F for 50 minutes.

LEMON GLAZE

Add lemon juice, water, sugar and honey to a small pan. Bring to the boil. Boil gently for 8–10 minutes, stirring frequently. Remove from heat. Add gelatine crystals. Mix thoroughly. Allow to cool for 1 minute. Pour glaze over cake, spreading evenly with a warmed knife if necessary. Garnish with lemon slices—crystallised are best, but fresh will do (though, of course, will not last as long).

Alternatives This cake is based on the Carrot Cake on p. 267, but offers an alternative to using purely wheat flour. Flavourings may be added, eg 2 teaspoons mixed spice;* 4 teaspoons ground ginger; 1 tablespoon finely chopped herbs, eg lemon thyme, rosemary or 1 tablespoon aromatic seeds, eg anise, caraway.

Note: * Mixed spice is 4 parts cinnamon, 2 parts ground ginger, 1 part ground nutmeg and 1 part ground cloves. (*See also* Mixed Cake Spice, p. 272.)

SESAME CAKES

Makes 16

200 g (2¼ cups, 7 oz) rolled oats
(regular oatmeal), finely ground
100 g (¾ cup, 3½ oz) barley flour
100 g (3½ oz) margarine
50 g (⅓ cup, 2 oz) brown ((soft) light
brown) sugar
4 tablespoons sesame seed, toasted
4 teaspoons baking powder
80 ml (⅓ cup, 3 fl oz) milk

Mix ground oats and barley flour in a bowl. Rub in margarine with fingertips. Stir in sugar, sesame seed and baking powder. Make a well in centre of dry ingredients and pour in milk. Mix thoroughly. Spoon into well-greased patty tins (cupcake pans). Bake at 190°C or 375°F for 15 minutes.

Note: 1. These are very crumbly but delicious (increase quantity of barley flour to 125 g (1 cup, 4½ oz) for a less crumbly mixture). They can be served plain or with whipped cream.
2. To grind rolled oats, pass through a coffee or similar grinder until almost as fine as flour. I have always used rolled oats, as in all the countries we have lived, I have not had easy access to fine-ground oatmeal—I assume the result is the same with either.
3. Wholemeal (whole-wheat) flour can be used in place of barley flour, but the flavour is not nearly as good and the texture is much heavier. When using wholemeal flour, double the quantity of milk used.

ORANGE SANDWICH CAKE

CAKE

175 g (6 oz) margarine

175 g (¾ cup, 6 oz) raw (demerara, turbinado) sugar

100 ml (3½ fl oz) water

rind of 2 oranges, grated

5 tablespoons orange juice

250 g (1¾ cups, 9 oz) wholemeal (whole-wheat) flour (from which bran has been sieved)

3 eggs, separated

3 rounded teaspoons baking powder

CREAM FILLING

75 g (⅓ cup, 3 oz) margarine

100 g (⅔ cup, 3½ oz) icing (powdered) sugar

1 tablespoon orange juice

rind of 1 orange, grated

3 tablespoons thickened (double, whipping) cream

a little icing (powdered) sugar (to decorate)

CAKE

Gently heat margarine until melted, remove from heat, add sugar and beat well. Stir in water, orange rind and orange juice. Gradually add flour, beating well between additions. Separate eggs and beat yolks. Add yolks to cake mixture (batter). Beat well. Thoroughly mix in baking powder. Whisk egg whites until stiff. Fold into cake mixture. Spoon into 2 well-greased and floured sandwich (round, layer) tins (pans). Bake at 190°C or 375°F for 20 minutes. Remove from oven, cool a little and gently ease from tins. Allow to cool further until cold.

CREAM FILLING

Cream margarine and icing sugar until light and fluffy. Add orange rind. Gradually add orange juice, mixing well between additions. Whisk cream until stiff. Stir into filling mixture. When the cake has cooled, spread one cake with filling and gently place the other cake on top. Sprinkle with a little icing sugar to decorate.

Alternative Substitute lemon rind and lemon juice for the orange given in this recipe.

Note: The lightness of this cake depends on the amount of air incorporated during preparation. Beating the mixture thoroughly at all stages is essential.

SWEET SOYA CAKES

Makes 9

2 teaspoons baking powder

150 g (1¼ cups, 5½ oz) soya (soy) flour*

50 g (2 oz) margarine

2 tablespoons golden syrup (light treacle)

1 tablespoon milk

1 egg

lemon glaze (to decorate) (see p. 270)

angelica, crystallised (candied) (to decorate)

CAKE

Mix baking powder and flour in a bowl. Melt margarine. Remove from heat and stir in syrup. Add milk and egg. Beat well. Stir into flour and mix well. (The mixture will be very moist.) Spoon into well-greased patty tins (cupcake pans). Bake at 200°C or 400°F for 10–12 minutes until browned, but still moist.

LEMON GLAZE WITH ANGELICA

Prepare glaze according to recipe under Oatmeal Cake (p. 00)— prepare half quantity only. While still hot, spoon a little glaze over each cake. Decorate with a small piece of crystallised angelica (*see* notes under angelica, pp. 354–5, to make your own).

Note: * If you find these cakes too heavy, you can use a half and half mixture of soya flour and plain (all-purpose) flour. This gives a lighter texture.

MIXED CAKE SPICE

4 teaspoons ground coriander

4 teaspoons ground cinnamon

1 teaspoon ground allspice (optional)

½ teaspoon ground nutmeg

½ teaspoon ground ginger

Thoroughly mix all ingredients. Store in a screw-top jar and use as required. Use in all recipes requiring Mixed Cake Spice.

Scones (Biscuits)

BASIC WHOLEMEAL (WHOLE-WHEAT) SCONES (BISCUITS)

Makes 10

3 teaspoons baking powder

200-225 g (1½-1⅔ cups, 7-8 oz) wholemeal (whole-wheat) flour

50 g (2 oz) margarine

2 tablespoons oil

100 ml (3½ fl oz) milk

Mix baking powder and flour in a bowl. Melt margarine in a pan. Stir in oil and milk. Make a well in the flour, pour in liquid and, using a fork, gradually mix flour into liquid—dough will be quite moist. Work (knead) for a minute. Roll out (1-1½ cm (½ in) thick) on a floured board and cut into rounds with a pastry (cookie) cutter. Place on a well-greased baking tray (sheet). Bake at 190°-200°C or 375°-400°F for 15 minutes.

Alternatives • Add 2 teaspoons finely chopped herbs, eg sage, lemon thyme, lemon balm, bergamot (bee balm).

• Add 2 teaspoons aromatic seeds, eg caraway, roasted sesame, dill.

• Add 50 g (½ cup, 2 oz) grated cheddar cheese with a pinch of paprika (and cayenne if wished).

BANANA SCONES (BISCUITS)

Makes 8-9

2 ripe bananas

2 tablespoons honey or golden syrup (light treacle)

50 g (⅓ cup, 2 oz) raisins or sultanas (golden raisins)

100 g (¾ cup, 3½ oz) wholemeal (whole-wheat) flour

2 teaspoons baking powder

2 teaspoons milk

Mash bananas and blend with honey. Add raisins and stir well. Gradually add flour, blending carefully to avoid lumps. Finally, work in baking powder and milk—the mixture will be sticky and moist. Spoon into well-greased patty tins (cupcake pans). Bake at 200°C or 400°F for 15 minutes.

SWEET BARLEY SCONES (BISCUITS)

Makes 10

100 g (¾ cup, 3½ oz) barley flour
100 g (¾ cup, 3½ oz) wholemeal
(whole-wheat) flour
2 teaspoons baking powder
1 tablespoon oil
1 tablespoon golden syrup
(light treacle)
60 ml (¼ cup, 2 fl oz) milk

Mix two flours and baking powder in a bowl. In a separate bowl, carefully blend oil and syrup over a gentle heat. Gradually mix in milk. When thoroughly blended, pour into a well in the dry ingredients. Mix into a soft dough, roll out (1–1½ cm (½ in) thick) on a floured board and cut into rounds with a pastry (cookie) cutter. Place on a well-greased baking tray (sheet). Bake at 200°C or 400°F for 10 minutes until lightly browned, but still moist.

SAVOURY BARLEY SCONES (BISCUITS)

Makes 9

100 g (¾ cup, 3½ oz) barley flour
75 g (⅔ cup, 2½ oz) wholemeal
(whole-wheat) flour (from which bran
has been sieved)
2 teaspoons baking powder
50 g (½ cup, 2 oz) cheddar cheese,
grated
50 g (2 oz) margarine
4 tablespoons milk

Place barley flour, wholemeal flour and baking powder in a mixing bowl. Mix thoroughly. Stir in grated cheese. Melt margarine in a small pan. Add milk. Make a well in dry ingredients. Pour in melted margarine and milk. Using a fork, gradually incorporate flour into liquid. Work dough a little until smooth. Roll out (1–1½ cm (½ in) thick) on a floured board. Cut into rounds with a pastry (cookie) cutter. Place on a well-greased baking tray (sheet). Bake at 190°–200°C or 375°–400°F for 15 minutes. Serve hot or cold—either plain, or halved and spread with butter.

Alternatives • Add 1–2 teaspoons finely chopped herbs, eg rosemary, marjoram, sage, nasturtium flowers.
• Add 1–2 teaspoons aromatic seeds, eg caraway, dill, fennel.

BRAN AND OATMEAL BUNS

Makes 24

75 g (1½ cups, 2½ oz) bran
100 g (¾ cup, 3½ oz) wholemeal
(whole-wheat) flour
3 teaspoons baking powder
50 g (⅔ cup, 2 oz) rolled oats
(regular oatmeal)
50 g (2 oz) butter or margarine
6 teaspoons honey or golden syrup
(light treacle)
2 eggs, beaten

Mix bran, wholemeal flour, baking powder and rolled oats in a large bowl. Melt butter in a pan over a gentle heat. Stir in honey. Remove from heat and cool a little. Beat eggs. Stir into warm honey and melted butter. Make a well in dry ingredients. Pour in warm liquid—gradually incorporate all dry ingredients into liquid. At final stages, use hands to ensure an even mixing. Take a small amount of mixture (batter) (2–4 teaspoons). Using hands, shape into a ball. Place on a greased baking tray (sheet). Repeat until all mixture has been used—the mixture is very sticky but workable. Place in a preheated oven at 190°–200°C or 375°–400°F for 12 minutes.

BREAKFAST SCONES (BISCUITS)

Makes 11–12

100 g (¾ cup, 3½ oz) wholemeal
(whole-wheat) flour
50 g (1 cup, 2 oz) bran
4 teaspoons baking powder
2 teaspoons ground cinnamon
¼ teaspoon ground nutmeg
1 apple
3 tablespoons of water
50 g (2 oz) margarine
1½ tablespoons golden syrup (light
treacle) or honey
2 eggs

Mix flour, bran, baking powder, cinnamon and nutmeg in a bowl. Peel and core apple. Cut into thin slices and place in a saucepan with water. Bring to boil, simmer until very soft and remove from heat. Mash well to form a purée. Cut margarine into small pieces and add to apple. Spoon in syrup. Stir well until margarine and syrup have melted and are thoroughly mixed into apple. Set aside until cool. Beat eggs in a separate bowl and stir into apple mixture. Make a well in dry ingredients. Pour in apple mixture—gradually mix wet and dry ingredients. When thoroughly mixed, spoon into well-greased patty tins (cupcake pans) and bake at 200°C or 400°F for 10 minutes. Serve halved and buttered.

CORNMEAL (POLENTA) MUFFINS

Makes 12–14

150 g (1 cup, 5½ oz) cornmeal
(polenta), finely ground
1½ teaspoons baking powder
50 g (½ cup, 2 oz) wholemeal
(whole-wheat) flour
50 g (2 oz) margarine
50 g (¼ cup, 2 oz) granulated sugar
1 egg, beaten
6 tablespoons natural (plain) yoghurt

Mix cornmeal, baking powder and wholemeal flour in a bowl. Rub in margarine with fingertips. Stir in sugar. In a separate bowl, beat egg. Make a well in dry ingredients, pour egg into well and spoon in yoghurt. Gradually blend dry and wet ingredients. Beat a little. Spoon into well-greased patty tins (cupcake pans). Bake at 180°C or 350°F for 15–20 minutes until a little browned.

GOLDEN OATMEAL SCONES (BISCUITS)

Makes 10

150 g (1¼ cups, 5½ oz) wholemeal
(whole-wheat) flour
2 tablespoons oatmeal, finely ground
25 g (1 oz) margarine
1½ teaspoons baking powder
6 tablespoons milk

Mix flour and oatmeal together. Rub in margarine with finger-tips. Stir in baking powder. Warm milk a little. Using a fork, mix into dry ingredients. Drop teaspoons of mixture into greased patty tins (cupcake pans). Bake at 190°C or 375°F for 15 minutes. Cut in half while still hot. Cool and serve buttered.

Note: 1. These scones look rather like rock cakes and are good served hot or cold with a sweet or savoury filling, eg jam, cheese or spread.
2. In place of oatmeal, finely ground porridge oats (rolled oats, regular oatmeal) can be used. I put the oats through the coffee grinder.

Opposite: *Breakfast Scones (top) and Cornmeal (Polenta) Muffins (bottom) are hard to resist when served straight from the oven.*

LUPIN OR PEA FLOUR CHEESE SCONES (BISCUITS)

Makes 10–12
*100 g (¾ cup, 3½ oz) lupin or
pea flour
50 g (½ cup, 2 oz) plain
(all-purpose) flour
50 g (2 oz) margarine
75 g (⅔ cup, 2½ oz) mature
(sharp) cheese, grated
pinch of paprika
3 teaspoons baking powder
1 teaspoon French tarragon, finely
chopped (optional)
2 tablespoons milk*

Mix lupin flour and plain flour in a bowl. Rub in margarine with fingertips. Add cheese, paprika, baking powder and tarragon (if used) to the bowl. Stir to mix thoroughly. Sprinkle over milk. Using a fork, work mixture into a soft dough. Roll out (1–1½ cm (½ in) thick) on a floured board. Cut into rounds with a pastry (cookie) cutter and place on a well-greased baking tray (sheet). Bake at 200°C or 400°F for 15 minutes.

RAISIN SCONES (BISCUITS)

Makes 8
75 g (²⁄₃ cup, 2½ oz) wholemeal (whole-wheat) flour
1½ teaspoons baking powder
25 g (½ cup, 1 oz) bran
50 g (⅓ cup, 2 oz) raisins
1 tablespoon honey or golden syrup (light treacle)
5 tablespoons milk

Mix flour, baking powder and bran in a bowl. Stir in raisins. Gently warm honey and milk. Make a well in dry ingredients. Gradually mix wet and dry ingredients together. Drop spoonfuls of the mixture into well-greased patty tins (cupcake pans). Bake at 190°C or 375°F for 7–10 minutes until lightly browned. Serve hot or cold with butter.

RYE CAKES

Makes 8
100 g (¾ cup, 3½ oz) rye flour
50 g (2 oz) margarine
6 tablespoons milk
1 egg, beaten
2 teaspoons cinnamon, ground
2½ teaspoons baking powder
50 g (½ cup, 2 oz) plain (all-purpose) flour

Place rye flour in a mixing bowl. Make a well in centre. Melt margarine in a saucepan and add milk. Break egg into a separate bowl. Beat well. Mix into margarine and milk. Pour liquid into well, mix wet and dry ingredients together. Beat thoroughly. Thoroughly mix in cinnamon and baking powder and finally plain flour. Spoon into well-greased patty tins (cupcake pans). Bake at 200°C or 400°F for 12–15 minutes. Serve halved, hot or cold, with butter.

Note: 1. Rye flour is low in gluten (*see* notes on pp. 243–4), so wheat flour is added to make a workable and light mixture. I have suggested plain flour, but often use wholemeal (whole-wheat) flour with the bran sieved out—the cakes taste good, but are heavier in texture.
2. In place of butter or in addition to it, I often serve these cakes with fresh natural (plain) yoghurt, cottage cheese or whipped cream.
3. They can also be served as a savoury cake/scone (biscuit) with cheese or herby cottage cheese.

YOGHURT SCONES (BISCUITS)

Makes 15
225 g (1²⁄₃ cups, 8 oz) wholemeal (whole-wheat) flour
3 teaspoons baking powder
50 g (2 oz) margarine
½ egg, lightly beaten
5 tablespoons natural (plain) yoghurt

Mix flour and baking powder in a bowl. Rub in margarine with fingertips. In a separate bowl, beat egg a little and stir in yoghurt. Make a well in dry ingredients. Pour in egg/yoghurt mixture. Gradually blend wet and dry ingredients to make a smooth dough. Roll out (1½ cm/½ in thick) on a floured board. Cut into rounds with a pastry (cookie) cutter. Place on a well-greased baking tray (sheet). Bake at 200°C or 400°F for 15–20 minutes until lightly browned and firm.

Biscuits (Cookies & Crackers)

BRAN BISCUITS (COOKIES)

Makes 20

100 g (¾ cup, 3½ oz) wholemeal
(whole-wheat) flour
50 g (2 oz) margarine
2 tablespoons bran
50 g (⅓ cup, 2 oz) (soft) dark brown
(Barbados) sugar
1½ tablespoons milk

Place flour in a mixing bowl. Rub in margarine with fingertips. Stir in bran and sugar until thoroughly mixed. Add milk, a little at a time, working mixture into a soft dough. Roll out (¼–½ cm/¼ in thick) on a well-floured board—dough will be quite soft and slightly sticky. Cut into rounds or squares. Bake on a greased baking tray (sheet) at 190°C or 375°F for 12–15 minutes until well browned. The biscuits (cookies) should be crisp when cool.

CHEESE STRAWS

Makes 50

100 g (¾ cup, 3½ oz) wholemeal
(whole-wheat) flour
50 g (2 oz) margarine
50 g (½ cup, 2 oz) cheddar cheese,
grated
pinch of cayenne (optional)
1 tablespoon milk

Place flour in a mixing bowl. Rub in margarine with fingertips. Add grated cheese. Season with cayenne (if used). Sprinkle in milk. Using a fork, work into a soft dough. Roll out on a floured board to a thickness of ½ cm (¼ in). Cut into small strips or squares. Bake on a greased baking tray (sheet) at 200°C or 400°F for 12–15 minutes until browned a little. The cheese straws should be crunchy when cool—if they remain soft, replace in a hot oven for several minutes.

Alternative Add 1 teaspoon finely chopped herbs, eg sage, thyme, rosemary.

DIGESTIVE BISCUITS (COOKIES)

Makes 10–12

75 g (⅔ cup, 2½ oz) wholemeal
(whole-wheat) flour
2 tablespoons oatmeal, finely ground
50 g (2 oz) margarine
50 g (⅓ cup, 2 oz) brown ((soft) light
brown) sugar
1-2 teaspoons milk

Mix flour and oatmeal in a bowl. Rub in margarine with fingertips. Stir in sugar. Add milk and work mixture well, first with a fork and then with hands, until a soft dough forms. Roll out on a well-floured board and cut into biscuits (cookies). Place on a greased baking tray (sheet). Bake at 200°C or 400°F for 10 minutes until browned a little.

CHOCOLATE HOOPS

Makes 28–30
100 g (3½ oz) margarine
50 g (¼ cup, 2 oz) raw (demerara, turbinado) sugar
3 tablespoons cocoa powder
1 tablespoon milk
150 g (1¼ cups, 5½ oz) wholemeal (whole-wheat) flour
100 g (3½ oz) (sweet or dark) cooking (sweetened baking) chocolate
1 tablespoon chocolate vermicelli (sprinkles) (optional)

Cream margarine and sugar until smooth. Mix in cocoa. Gradually blend in milk. Finally, stir in flour, a little at a time, to make a soft dough. Take 2–3 teaspoons of dough (about 15 g/½ oz). Roll into a sausage shape approx. 10 cm (4 in) long. Join two ends to make a hoop shape. Repeat until all mixture has been used. Place on a greased baking tray (sheet). Bake at 180°C or 350°F for 15 minutes. Cool on a wire rack.

Melt chocolate in a small pan over a bowl of hot water. Holding biscuits (cookies) with forceps or tweezers, dip each one face down in melted chocolate, sprinkle with vermicelli (if used) and allow to cool and dry on a wire rack.

COFFEE BREAKS

Makes 16
BASE
100 g (3½ oz) margarine
50 g (⅓ cup, 2 oz) brown ((soft) light brown) sugar
1 tablespoon instant coffee*
150 g (1¼ cups, 5½ oz) wholemeal (whole-wheat) flour
a little milk

COFFEE FROSTING
1 tablespoon of top of the milk or thin (single, light) cream
1 tablespoon margarine
½ tablespoon raw (demerara, turbinado) sugar
75 g (½ cup, 3 oz) icing (powdered) sugar
½ teaspoon instant coffee
16 walnut halves

BASE
Cream margarine and sugar. Stir in coffee. Gradually incorporate flour until a dough is formed. Add a teaspoon or two of milk to bind mixture. Press into a shallow baking tin (pan) approx. 18 cm (7 in) square. Bake at 180°C or 350°F for 20 minutes. Cut into squares while still hot and cool on a wire rack—the biscuits (cookies) become crisp on cooling.

COFFEE FROSTING
Gently warm milk and margarine in a pan. When melted, stir in raw sugar, icing sugar and coffee. Mix thoroughly. Increase heat until mixture boils. Beat continuously, allowing mixture to boil gently for several minutes until it thickens and begins to draw away from bottom of pan. Working quickly as frosting hardens readily, spoon a little onto centre of each biscuit. Immediately place a walnut half on top. Leftover frosting can be dropped in teaspoonfuls on a greased baking tray (sheet) to cool, and eaten as sweets (candy).

Note: The biscuits (cookies) can be eaten plain or with frosting on top.
* If coffee granules are used rather than powder, they must be dissolved in the milk first.

Opposite: *Ginger Snaps (bottom right), Chocolate Hoops (bottom left), Coffee Breaks (centre) and Nut Crunchies (top left) — whether for school lunchboxes or suppertime snacks, these treats will appeal to everyone.*

GINGER SNAPS

Makes 22

½ teaspoon baking powder
2½ teaspoons ground ginger
100 g (¾ cup, 3½ oz) wholemeal
(whole-wheat) flour
75 g (⅓ cup, 2½ oz) margarine
75 g (⅓ cup, 2½ oz) raw (demerara,
turbinado) sugar
1 tablespoon golden syrup (light
treacle)

Mix baking powder, ground ginger and flour in a bowl. Melt margarine, sugar and golden syrup in a pan. Add to dry ingredients. Stir well to ensure a thorough mixing. Take 2–3 teaspoons of mixture (batter) and shape into a ball. Place on a well-greased baking tray (sheet) and flatten with a fork until ¼–½ cm (¼ in) thick. Repeat until all mixture has been used. Bake at 200°C or 400°F for 12–15 minutes until browned. The biscuits (cookies) should be crunchy when cool.

NUT CRUNCHES

Makes 16

2 tablespoons oatmeal, finely ground
75 g (⅔ cup, 2½ oz) wholemeal
(whole-wheat) flour
50 g (2 oz) margarine
100 g (½ cup, 3½ oz) raw (demerara,
turbinado) sugar
50 g (½ cup, 2 oz) nuts (eg peanuts
(groundnuts), walnuts), chopped
½–1 tablespoon milk

Mix oatmeal and flour in a bowl. Rub in margarine with fingertips. Stir in sugar and nuts. Add milk and bind mixture together using a fork. Work into a firm dough. Press into a greased shallow tin (pan) approx. 18 cm (7 in) square. Bake at 200°C or 400°F for 17–20 minutes until well browned. Cut into biscuits (cookies) when still warm.

Note: When cold, the biscuits (cookies) should be crunchy—if they remain soft, they may be put back in a hot oven for a few more minutes.

RYE AND CORNMEAL (POLENTA) NIBBLES

Makes 18

25 g (½ cup, 1 oz) bran
3 tablespoons rye flour*
25 g (1 oz) cornmeal (maize meal,
polenta), finely ground
25 g (1 oz) margarine
50 g (½ cup, 2 oz) mature (sharp)
cheddar cheese, grated
2 teaspoons sesame seed, toasted
1 teaspoon sage, finely chopped
1 tablespoon oil

Place bran, rye flour and cornmeal in a bowl. Rub in margarine with fingertips. Add grated cheese, sesame seed and sage. Mix thoroughly. Dribble in the oil. Using a fork, work mixture into a soft dough. Knead a little. Roll out on a floured board. Cut into squares of 3–4 cm (1¼–1½ in) and place on a greased baking tray (sheet). Bake at 190°C or 375°F for about 15 minutes until browned a little. Serve as a pre-dinner nibble, party snack or savoury coffee-time snack.

Note: * Wholemeal (whole-wheat) flour can be used in place of rye flour.

OATMEAL BISCUITS (COOKIES)

Makes 36

125 g (1 cup, 4½ oz) wholemeal
(whole-wheat) flour
200 g (1⅓ cups, 7 oz) oatmeal,
medium or coarsely ground
75 g (⅓ cup, 2½ oz) margarine
3 tablespoons water

Mix flour and oatmeal in a bowl. Rub in margarine with fingertips. Sprinkle in water. Using a fork or hands, work mixture into a dough. Roll out quite thinly (½ cm/¼ in) and cut into squares. Bake on a greased baking tray (sheet) at 180°C or 350°F for 15–18 minutes until very lightly browned.

ORANGE AND DATE TWISTS

Makes 15

100 g (3½ oz) margarine
50 g (¼ cup, 2 oz) raw (demerara,
turbinado) sugar
50 g (⅓ cup, 2 oz) dates, finely
chopped
100 g (¾ cup, 3½ oz) wholemeal
(whole-wheat) flour
2 tablespoons fresh orange juice
100 g (¾ cup, 3½ oz) plain
(all-purpose) flour
3 teaspoons caster (superfine) sugar

Cream margarine and raw sugar. Cut dates into very small pieces. Stir into mixture. Add half of wholemeal flour. Mix thoroughly. Add orange juice. Blend in carefully. Add remaining wholemeal flour and plain flour a little at a time, mixing well between additions, to form a soft dough. Take about 25 g (1 oz) of dough, work a little, and roll into a sausage shape or 'rope' approx. 18 cm (7 in) long. Gently fold in half. Take each end of 'double rope'. Twist in opposite directions. Place on a greased baking tray (sheet). Repeat until all mixture has been used. Bake at 170°C or 325°F for 25–30 minutes. While still hot, sprinkle caster sugar over top. Allow biscuits (cookies) to cool on baking tray.

Alternative Orange and Spice Twists—Substitute 1–2 teaspoons Mixed Cake Spice (see p. 272) for dates.

Note: Other shapes can be formed from the 18 cm (7 in) 'rope', eg coil the 'rope' round and round into a flat round biscuit (cookie); coil the 'rope' round and up rather like a snail-shell shape or loosely knot the 'rope'.

SAVOURY ROLLED OAT BISCUITS (CRACKERS)

Makes 24

75 g (¾ cup, 2½ oz) rolled oats
(regular oatmeal)
100 g (¾ cup, 3½ oz) wholemeal
(whole-wheat) flour
75 g (⅓ cup, 2½ oz) margarine
1 tablespoon water

Mix oats and flour in a bowl. Rub in margarine with fingertips. Add water and work mixture into a fairly dry dough. Roll out (½ cm/¼ in thick) and cut into rounds or squares. Place on a greased baking tray (sheet). Bake at 180°C or 350°F for 18–20 minutes until very lightly browned.

CILLA'S ROLLED OAT BISCUITS (COOKIES)

Makes 30

100 g (3½ oz) margarine

50 g (½ cup, 2 oz) wholemeal (whole-wheat) flour

50 g (¼ cup, 2 oz) raw (demerara, turbinado) sugar

125 g (1⅓ cups, 4½ oz) rolled oats (regular oatmeal)

½ teaspoon baking powder

1 egg, beaten

Gently heat margarine in a pan until melted. Remove from heat and add remaining ingredients. Mix thoroughly. Drop teaspoons of mixture onto a well-greased baking tray (sheet). Bake at 180°C or 350°F for 15–18 minutes until lightly browned.

Alternative Add 4 teaspoons of caraway seeds to biscuit (cookie) mixture (batter) before baking.

Desserts

APPLE TARTS

Makes 10

PASTRY

50 g (2 oz) margarine

100 g (¾ cup, 3½ oz) wholemeal (whole-wheat) flour (from which bran has been sieved)

1½ tablespoons caster (superfine) or icing (powdered) sugar

½–1 tablespoon milk

FILLING

250 g (9 oz) apple purée

75 ml (⅓ cup, 2½ fl oz) thickened (double, whipping) cream

Rub margarine into flour with fingertips. Stir in sugar. Sprinkle over milk. Using a fork, work mixture into a soft dough. Roll out on a well-floured board. Cut into ten rounds 7 cm (2¾ in) in diameter with a pastry (cookie) cutter. Place each round in a well-greased patty tin (cupcake pan). Fill each with a little apple purée. Bake at 200°C or 400°F for 15 minutes. Allow tarts to cool a little, remove from patty tins and place on a wire rack until cold. Whip cream until stiff. Decorate each tart with a little piped cream. Serve.

Alternatives • Add 1 teaspoon finely chopped lemon balm leaves to apple before using.
• Any fruit can be used, eg stewed peaches, plums, blackcurrants. Make sure fruit is not too moist or pastry will be soggy instead of crisp.

Note: Aluminium cake cups can be used in place of patty tins if preferred.

BANANAS IN BRANDY SAUCE

Serves 4

4 bananas

Brandy Sauce (see sauces, p. 227)

100 ml (3½ fl oz) thickened (double, whipping) cream

2 tablespoons walnuts, chopped

Peel bananas and halve lengthwise. Arrange in a shallow serving dish or individual dishes. Spoon over Brandy Sauce. Place in refrigerator for 5–10 minutes to chill a little. Whip cream until stiff. Spoon or pipe over bananas. Sprinkle with walnuts. Serve.

CHEESECAKE

Serves 6–8

BASE

150 g (²/₃ cup, 5½ oz) margarine

75 g (¹/₃ cup, 2½ oz) raw (demerara, turbinado) sugar

225 g (1²/₃ cups, 8 oz) wholemeal (whole-wheat) flour

FILLING

225 g (1 cup, 8 oz) cottage cheese, sieved (strained)

75 ml (¹/₃ cup, 2½ fl oz) natural (plain) yoghurt

50 g (¹/₃ cup, 2 oz) raisins or sultanas (golden raisins)

1 tablespoon honey

1 tablespoon wholemeal (whole-wheat) flour

2 egg yolks

1 tablespoon lemon juice

rind of ½ lemon, grated

90 ml (¹/₃ cup, 3½ fl oz) thickened (double, whipping) cream

3 egg whites

BASE

Cream margarine and sugar in a bowl. Gradually mix in flour. As mixture becomes drier, you may find it easier to use a fork or hands to work in remaining flour. Press evenly to line a springform pan or round cake tin (pan) with a removable base (cheesecake pan), approx. 20 × 6 cm (8 × 2½ in). Set aside while you prepare filling.

FILLING

Sieve cottage cheese into a bowl. Stir in yoghurt, raisins, honey, flour and egg yolks. Stir in lemon juice and lemon rind. Whisk cream until thickened a little. In a separate bowl, whisk egg whites until stiff. First fold cream into filling and then egg white. Carefully spoon filling mixture into base. Bake cheesecake at 150°C or 300°F for 55–60 minutes.

CHOCOLATE MOUSSE

Serves 6

3 eggs, separated

75 g (¹/₃ cup, 2½ oz) caster (superfine) sugar

75 g (2½ oz) (sweet or dark) cooking (sweetened baking) chocolate

3 teaspoons gelatine

4 tablespoons hot water

200 ml (7 fl oz) thickened (double, whipping) cream

3 teaspoons cocoa powder

2 tablespoons nuts, chopped

Separate eggs. Beat sugar and egg yolks until creamy. Set aside. Break cooking chocolate into small pieces. Melt in a bowl over a pan of hot water. Stir melted chocolate into egg and sugar mixture. Set aside in a warm place, but do not allow to become hot. Dissolve gelatine in hot water. Leave to cool a little. Beat cream until thick but not too stiff. In a separate bowl, beat egg whites until they are stiff and form peaks. Take egg and sugar mixture and beat a little more. Thoroughly mix in cocoa. Stir in dissolved gelatine. Beat for 1 minute. Stir in cream. When evenly mixed in, carefully fold in egg white. Spoon into a glass dish or individual dishes. Place in refrigerator to cool and set. Immediately before serving, sprinkle with nuts.

Note: *See* notes under 'Dessert suggestions', p. 295.

CHOCOLATE PUDDING

Serves 2–3

200 ml (7 fl oz) Custard Sauce
(see sauces, p. 226)
2 teaspoons cocoa powder
50 g (2 oz) dark bitter (plain, semisweet) chocolate
1 rounded teaspoon gelatine crystals (powder)
1 tablespoon boiling water

Prepare Custard Sauce. When sauce has thickened but is still hot, stir in cocoa and chocolate, which has been broken into small pieces. Stir well until thoroughly blended.

In a small cup, dissolve gelatine in boiling water. Beat into chocolate sauce. Pour into a glass serving dish or individual bowls. Place in refrigerator to set.

Alternatives
- *Simple Chocolate Pudding*—decorate with whipped cream and 1 or 2 crystallised (sugared) violets *or* borage flowers *or* glacé (candied) cherries.
- *Banana Chocolate Pudding*—slice 2 bananas into a bowl. Add Brandy Sauce (*see* sauces, p. 227). Mix well. Spoon over chocolate pudding when set. Top with whipped cream.
- *Apple Chocolate Pudding*—layer 250 ml (1 cup, 9 fl oz) of sweetened apple purée over pudding when set. Dribble over 1 tablespoon clear honey. Sprinkle with 1 tablespoon chopped nuts.

APPLE TREGEAR

Serves 4

750 g (1¾ lb) (dessert) apples
2 teaspoons lemon balm, finely chopped
2 tablespoons honey or golden syrup (light treacle)
2 tablespoons sesame seed, toasted
150 ml (⅔ cup, 5½ fl oz) thickened (double, whipping) cream
2 tablespoons (soft) dark brown (Barbados) sugar

Peel and core apples. Cut into thin slices. Cook gently with a few tablespoons of water until very soft. Remove from heat, mash a little and stir in lemon balm. Spoon into an ovenproof dish to make quite a thick layer (about 4 cm/1½ in deep). Warm honey until liquid. Add sesame seed. Pour over apple. At the same time, cut apple layer with a knife in a lattice pattern—this allows the honey and sesame to trickle down into apple. Set aside to cool.

Whip cream until thick and stiff. Spoon cream over apple. Using a fork, gently smooth out surface until flat. Sprinkle brown sugar evenly over top. Place under a hot grill (broiler) for 30 seconds to melt sugar. Place in refrigerator to chill.

Note: 1. For this recipe I often use eating apples, eg Granny Smiths. If using cooking apples, which are much more tart in flavour, add a little sugar during cooking.

2. This cold sweet is very light and refreshing and is good to serve after a spicy main course, eg a curry, or as a lunchtime sweet.

Opposite: *A light and tangy dessert, Apple Tregear is a good complement to heavy or spicy main courses.*

BAKED EGG CUSTARD

Serves 6–8

PASTRY

75 g (¹⁄₃ cup, 3 oz) margarine
*150 g (1¼ cups, 5½ oz) plain
(all-purpose) flour*
1 teaspoon ground cinnamon
*1 tablespoon raw (demerara,
turbinado) sugar*
2 tablespoons water

FILLING

500 ml (2 cups, 17½ fl oz) milk
*1½ tablespoons raw (demerara,
turbinado) sugar*
4 eggs
¼ teaspoon ground nutmeg

PASTRY

Rub margarine into flour with fingertips. Add cinnamon and sugar. Mix well. Sprinkle in water and bind together into soft pastry dough. Roll pastry out and line a greased shallow round pie dish (plate) (approx. 20 cm (8 in) in diameter).

FILLING

Pour milk into a saucepan and add sugar. Heat until warmed a *little*, stirring well to dissolve sugar. Remove from heat. Beat or whisk eggs thoroughly into milk. Pour into prepared pastry case (shell). Sprinkle ground nutmeg over top. Place dish in a larger shallow dish or a shallow roasting tin (pan) containing 2–3 cm (1–1¼ in) depth of water. Bake in oven at 130°–140°C or 250°–275°F for 1¾ hours.

Note: I prefer to use plain flour for the pastry as I think it better suits the mild flavour of the egg custard. However, you can use wholemeal (wholewheat) flour with bran sieved out if wished.

COFFEE CREAM

Serves 3

2 tablespoons margarine
*1 tablespoon cornflour
(US cornstarch)*
100 ml (3½ fl oz) milk
1 egg yolk
3 teaspoons instant coffee*
2 tablespoons honey
3 tablespoons natural (plain) yoghurt
*2 level teaspoons gelatine crystals
(powder)*
1 tablespoon boiling water
*100 ml (3½ fl oz) thickened (double,
whipping) cream*

Gently heat margarine until melted and sizzling. To avoid lumps, mix cornflour with a little of milk to make a smooth paste. Add cornflour paste to butter. Stir well. Remove from heat. Carefully blend in remaining milk, avoiding lumps. Return to heat. Cook gently, stirring continuously, until sauce thickens. Beat in egg yolk. Continue heating very gently until sauce thickens further. Remove from heat and cool a little. Stir in coffee, honey and yoghurt. Dissolve gelatine in boiling water, add to sauce and mix thoroughly. Whisk cream until thick and fold into sauce. Spoon into individual dishes. Place in refrigerator to set and cool.

Alternative Vanilla Cream—Substitute ½ teaspoon vanilla essence (extract) for instant coffee.

Note: If using coffee granules, dissolve in a little warmed milk and mix into sauce.

COFFEE MOUSSE

Serves 6

4 tablespoons margarine

2 tablespoons cornflour
(US cornstarch)

200 ml (7 fl oz) milk

2 egg yolks

2 tablespoons granulated sugar

100 ml (3½ fl oz) thickened (double,
whipping) cream

4 teaspoons instant coffee

4 egg whites

2 rounded teaspoons gelatine crystals
(powder)

2 tablespoons boiling water

Heat margarine in a saucepan. To avoid lumps, mix cornflour with a little of milk to make a smooth paste. When butter is sizzling, stir in cornflour paste. Remove from heat and blend in milk. Reheat gently, stirring continuously, until mixture thickens. Add egg yolks. Continue heating gently, stirring until mixture thickens further. Remove from heat. Carefully blend in sugar, cream and coffee—at this stage, sauce is very thick, so take care when blending in cream to avoid lumps and an uneven mixture. Whisk egg whites until they form peaks. Set aside.

Dissolve gelatine in boiling water. Stir into coffee sauce, ensuring mixture is completely even. Fold in egg whites. When thoroughly blended, pour coffee mousse into individual serving dishes. Place in refrigerator to set and cool for several hours.

SUE'S OATMEAL WONDER

Serves 6–8

50 g (2 oz) margarine

50 g (¼ cup, 2 oz) raw (demerara,
turbinado) sugar

1 tablespoon golden syrup (light
treacle)

1 teaspoon bicarbonate of soda
(baking soda)

4 tablespoons boiling water

100 g (¾ cup, 3½ oz) wholemeal
(whole-wheat) flour

150 g (1 cup, 5½ oz) oatmeal,
medium ground

50 g (⅔ cup, 2 oz) coconut,
desiccated (shredded)

50 g (½ cup, 2 oz) walnuts or
almonds, chopped

125 g (¾ cup, 4½ oz) raisins

Gently heat margarine, sugar and golden syrup in a saucepan until melted. Remove from heat. Dissolve bicarbonate of soda in boiling water. Stir into melted margarine mixture. Add flour, oatmeal and coconut and mix thoroughly. Finally, stir in nuts and raisins. Press into a shallow baking tin (pan) (approx. 16 × 20 cm (6½ × 8 in). Bake at 170°C or 325°F for 25 minutes until browned on top. Cut into slices while still warm. Serve with whipped cream.

Note: This can be served plain without the cream as a teatime cake, rather than a dessert.

SWEET OMELETTES *See* recipes under 'Omelettes' on p. 196.

SWEET PANCAKES *See* recipes under 'Pancakes' on pp. 200.

RUM AND DARK BERRY TART

Serves 6

BASE

75 g (1/3 cup, 3 oz) margarine

175 g (1 1/3 cups, 6 oz) wholemeal (whole-wheat) flour

50 g (1/4 cup, 2 oz) caster (superfine) sugar

1 egg yolk

1 1/2 tablespoons water

FILLING

1 tablespoon dark rum

2 tablespoons honey or golden syrup (light treacle)

2 tablespoons water

300 g (10 1/2 oz) blueberries (bilberries) or blackcurrants

375 ml (1 1/2 cups, 13 1/2 fl oz) thick natural (plain) yoghurt

1 tablespoon icing (powdered) sugar

1 egg white

BASE

In a bowl, rub margarine into flour with fingertips. Stir in caster sugar. Add egg yolk and water. Using a fork, work mixture into a dough. Form into a ball, wrap in greaseproof (wax) paper and chill in refrigerator for 30 minutes.

FILLING

Place rum, honey and water in a pan. Heat gently until blended. Add blueberries. Cook very gently, barely simmering, for 1–2 minutes—fruit will soften a little, but should remain whole. Remove from heat. Drain juice from fruit. Set aside fruit, but pour juice back into pan. Simmer very gently until reduced in volume to about 4 tablespoons. Set aside to cool. Place yoghurt in a muslin (cheesecloth) bag or very fine-meshed strainer. Leave for 1 hour to allow excess liquid to drain away.

Remove dough from refrigerator. Working quickly, roll out and line a greased square shallow dish (16 cm (6 1/2 in) square and 2 1/2 cm (1 in) deep)—take care as pastry breaks easily. Place blueberries or blackcurrants in pastry case (shell). Bake at 190°C or 375°F for 20 minutes. Set aside to cool. When yoghurt has drained, remove from muslin bag, place in a bowl and stir in icing sugar. In a separate bowl, whisk egg white until very stiff. Fold into yoghurt mixture. Chill in refrigerator for 20 minutes. When tart is cool, spoon rum and honey syrup over blueberries. Spread yoghurt mixture evenly over tart. Serve.

Alternatives • Prepare fruit and tart base as above, but omit yoghurt mixture. Serve plain or decorate with piped whipped cream.

• Try another fruit if blueberries are unavailable. I often use cape (Chinese lantern, ground cherry) gooseberries with brandy in place of rum—ordinary gooseberries are suitable too, though might need to be sweetened a little more. Halved apricots, peaches or plums can also be used. Use brandy with yellow fruits and rum with dark-red fruits.

• Make individual tarts in patty tins (cupcake pans, tart pans) rather than one large tart.

Opposite: Made here with blueberries, Rum and Dark Berry Tart is suitable for most berry fruits. The tartness of the yoghurt topping perfectly sets off the sweet flavour of the fruit beneath.

PLUMS WITH CINNAMON

Serves 4–6

500 g (1 lb) dark-red plums
4 tablespoons red wine
2 tablespoons brown ((soft) dark brown) sugar
¼ teaspoon ground cinnamon

Halve or quarter plums. Remove and discard stones. Set plums aside. Gently heat red wine, brown sugar and cinnamon until sugar has melted. Add plums and stew very gently for 3–4 minutes or until plums are soft.

Note: If using Victoria plums, which are already sweet, you may wish to reduce the quantity of brown sugar.

RASPBERRY PUDDING

Serves 5–6

1½ tablespoons water
2 teaspoons lemon balm leaves, finely chopped
75 g (⅓ cup, 2½ oz) margarine
75 g (⅓ cup, 2½ oz) granulated sugar
4 tablespoons natural (plain) yoghurt
75 g (⅔ cup, 2½ oz) soya flour (soyflour)
50 g (½ cup, 2 oz) wholemeal (whole-wheat) flour
1 egg
1½ teaspoons baking powder
500 g (1 lb) raspberries

Heat water until almost boiling. Stir in lemon balm. Set aside. Cream margarine and sugar until fluffy. Beat in yoghurt. Gradually add soya flour and wholemeal flour, mixing well between additions. Thoroughly blend in water. Separate egg yolk from white. Add egg yolk and baking powder to pudding mixture. Beat well. Whisk egg white until it is stiff and forms peaks. Fold into pudding mixture.

Place raspberries in a layer on bottom of ovenproof dish (approx. 20 cm (8 in) in diameter). Spoon pudding mixture over top, making a second layer. Bake at 170°C or 325°F for 1 hour.

Note: 1. Loganberries, mulberries, blackberries (brambles), blueberries (bilberries) or similar can be substituted for raspberries.
2. This recipe can be used as a cake recipe if cooked in a cake or loaf tin (pan) without fruit.

HENRI'S RICE PUDDING

Serves 5–6

200 g (1⅓ cups, 7 oz) brown rice
700 ml (2¾ cups, 1¼ UK pints) milk
50 g (⅓ cup, 2 oz) sultanas (golden raisins)
1 tablespoon molasses (dark treacle)

Place rice in pan, add milk and heat. When boiling, stir for 1 minute. Reduce heat. Simmer uncovered for 40 minutes, stirring occasionally (take care during last 10 minutes of cooking that rice doesn't stick to bottom of pan—add extra milk if necessary, 1–1½ tablespoons should be sufficient). Add sultanas and molasses. Stir well. Continue simmering for 2 minutes. Remove from heat. Serve with fresh cream.

Note: This is my version of Henri's rice pudding—Henri always used twice the amount of milk and simmered for twice as long. Often he would add fresh cream during cooking. The result was delicious but very, very rich.

SWEET SOUFFLÉS *See* Vanilla Soufflé (p. 205), Apple and Spice Soufflé (p. 205) and Orange Spice Soufflé (p. 206).

FRUIT CRUMBLE

Serves 3–4

250 g (9 oz) stewed fruit

100 g (¾ cup, 3½ oz) wholemeal
(whole-wheat) flour

50 g (2 oz) margarine

2 teaspoons lemon balm, finely
chopped (optional)

2 tablespoons (soft) dark brown
(Barbados) sugar

Sweeten stewed fruit if necessary. Place in an ovenproof dish. Place flour in a mixing bowl and rub in margarine. Stir in lemon balm and brown sugar. Spoon this mixture over fruit. Bake at 200°C or 400°F for 20 minutes.

PEARS TOPPED WITH CINNAMON CREAM

Serves 4–8

4 firm green pears

2 tablespoons thickened (double,
whipping) cream, whipped

3 tablespoons cottage cheese, sieved

1 tablespoon icing (powdered) sugar

¼ teaspoon ground cinnamon

Brandy Sauce (see sauces, p. 227)

Peel pears, halve lengthwise and scoop out core from each half. Drop into boiling water. Simmer until just tender—8–10 minutes. Drain, cool and arrange in a shallow dish with hollows uppermost. Prepare Brandy Sauce, allow to cool and spoon over pears.

In a bowl, thoroughly mix cottage cheese, icing sugar and cinnamon. Beat mixture a little. Fold in whipped cream. Spoon a little cinnamon cream into hollow of each pear half. Serve.

PEARS WITH CHOCOLATE SAUCE

Serves 4

4 firm green pears

2 tablespoons honey

2 tablespoons water

250 ml (1 cup, 9 fl oz) chocolate
sauce
(see sauces, p. 226)

Peel pears, halve lengthwise and scoop out core from each half. Place in boiling water. Simmer for 8–10 minutes until tender. Drain, allow to cool and arrange in a shallow dish. Heat honey and water gently—allow this syrup to cool. Spoon over pears. Prepare chocolate sauce. Serve hot or cold in a small jug (pitcher).

Alternatives • Arrange pear halves in individual glass dishes, spoon over syrup and then spoon over chocolate sauce. Serve slightly chilled.

• Prepare syrup using: 1 tablespoon rosewater, 1 tablespoon water, 2 tablespoons honey. Proceed as above.

DARK RUM TRIFLE

Serves 4–5

100 g (3½ oz) Chocolate Cake
(see p. 264 for recipe)
2 tablespoons dark rum
250 g (9 oz) red plums, stewed
3 tablespoons arrowroot*
300 ml (1¼ cups, 10½ fl oz) milk
1 teaspoon butter
1½ tablespoons granulated sugar
1½ teaspoons vanilla essence (extract)
100 ml (3½ fl oz) thickened (double,
whipping) cream
2 teaspoons rosewater
1 square chocolate (to decorate)

Crumble cake into bottom of a glass serving dish. Spoon over rum. Place plums on top, making a second layer. In a separate dish, mix arrowroot and a little of milk to a paste. Heat remaining milk in a pan. When almost boiling, stir milk into arrowroot paste, taking care to blend thoroughly. Return sauce to pan. Heat, stirring continuously, until sauce thickens. Remove from heat. Add butter, sugar and vanilla essence. Beat for 1 minute. Set aside until cooled a little. Spoon sauce evenly over plums in serving dish. Set aside until cold.

Pour cream into a separate bowl. Whisk until thick. Carefully blend in rosewater. Spread mixture over arrowroot layer. Chill slightly before serving. Immediately before serving, grate square of chocolate over cream to decorate.

Note: * If arrowroot is unavailable, substitute custard powder or cornflour (US cornstarch). Arrowroot may be available from your chemist/pharmacy if not found in food stores.

SHERRY TRIFLE

Serves 5–6
125 g (4½ oz) plain cake
(see p. 264 for recipe)
4 tablespoons sherry
250 g (9 oz) yellow plums or peaches*
3 tablespoons cornflour
(US cornstarch)
475 ml (2 cups, 16½ fl oz) milk
2½ tablespoons granulated sugar
1 teaspoon margarine
1 cardamom pod (optional)
125 ml (½ cup, 4½ fl oz) thickened
(double, whipping) cream
2 cherries, glacé (candied)

Crumble cake into bottom of a glass serving dish. Spoon over sherry. Cut fruit into small pieces and layer over cake. Set aside. In a small bowl, blend cornflour with a little of milk into a smooth paste. Heat remaining milk until boiling. Pour cornflour paste into hot milk. Stirring continuously, heat sauce until it thickens. Stir in sugar and margarine. Remove from heat. Set aside.

Remove cardamom seeds from pod, crush well and stir into sauce. Allow sauce to cool. Spoon over fruit to make a third layer. Whip cream. Spread over top of cardamom sauce. Decorate with glacé cherries.

Note: * Fresh or lightly stewed fruit can be used.

SOUTH SEAS ISLAND SALAD

Serves 4

2 bananas

2 sweet oranges

2 tablespoons raisins

1 tablespoon dates, chopped

1 tablespoon honey

1 tablespoon lemon juice

400 g (14 oz) ripe pawpaw (papaya)

200 ml (7 fl oz) thick natural (plain) yoghurt

25 g (¼ cup, 1 oz) walnuts, almonds or other nuts, chopped

Slice bananas and cut oranges into small slices. Place in a fruit salad bowl. Stir in raisins and dates. Gently warm honey and lemon juice until well blended. Allow to cool. Stir into fruit. Set aside for ½–1 hour to allow raisins to absorb some of the juices. Skin pawpaw and cut into small pieces. Place in blender (liquidiser). Blend into a smooth purée. Spoon carefully over fruit in bowl, but do not mix the two together. Set bowl in refrigerator for several hours to chill and allow purée to set a little. Immediately before serving, spoon over yoghurt, making a final layer. Sprinkle with nuts and serve.

Note: 1. Ripe pawpaw (papaya) when puréed and allowed to chill will set like custard. If pawpaw is too ripe, it will not set well but can still be used. The resulting fruit salad will be much more liquid, but just as tasty.
2. The yoghurt used must be quite thick—*see* yoghurt-making on pp. 186–7. If desired, yoghurt can be slightly sweetened with a tablespoon or two of icing (powdered) sugar.
3. Apricot purée can be used in place of pawpaw.

CUSTARD PUDDING

Serves 2

Custard Sauce (see sauces, p. 226)

1 rounded teaspoon gelatine crystals (powder)

1 tablespoon boiling water

3 drops vanilla essence (extract)

Prepare sauce according to recipe. Dissolve gelatine in water and stir into sauce. Add vanilla essence. Pour into a serving dish or individual bowls. Allow to set in refrigerator.

Alternatives • *Coffee Custard Pudding*—add 1 tablespoon instant coffee to sauce before adding gelatine.
• *Fruit Custard Pudding*—stir 1 tablespoon jam or 2 tablespoons thick fruit purée into sauce before adding gelatine.

Note: 1. Top with fresh fruit immediately before serving, if wished.
2. Decorate with whipped cream and dribble over 2 tablespoons Easy Fruit Sauce (*see* p. 227).

Dessert Suggestions

Any of the dessert or cake recipes in this section can be served plain, but as alternatives, the following are suggestions. Look for sauce recipes in 'Sauces and Stuffings', pp. 225–7:

Apple Cake (*see* p. 265)—serve with Brandy Sauce or whipped cream.

Chocolate Mousse (*see* p. 283)—serve with Brandy Sauce or Lemon Honey Sauce, with or without fresh fruit.

Chocolate Pudding (*see* p. 284)—serve with Brandy Sauce or Lemon Honey Sauce, with or without fresh fruit.

Coffee Cream (*see* p. 286)—serve with Brandy Sauce or Lemon Honey Sauce, with or without fresh fruit.

Coffee Mousse (*see* p. 287)—serve with Brandy Sauce or Lemon Honey Sauce, with or without fresh fruit.

Coffee and Nut Cake (*see* p. 269)—serve with cream or ice cream.

Custard Pudding (*see* p. 294)—serve with Easy Fruit Sauce.

Fresh fruit, eg bananas, strawberries—in Brandy Sauce or Lemon Honey Sauce.

Ice cream—serve with Chocolate Sauce, or with fresh fruit in Brandy Sauce or Lemon Honey Sauce, or with Brandy Sauce or Lemon Honey Sauce topped with nuts.

Sesame Cakes (*see* p. 270)—serve with whipped cream and Brandy Sauce or Lemon Honey Sauce.

Sweet omelettes (*see* pp. 196–7).

Sweet pancakes (*see* pp. 200–2).

Vanilla Cream—serve with Brandy Sauce or Lemon Honey Sauce, with or without fresh or stewed fruit, or with Easy Fruit Sauce.

beverages

Hot & Cold Beverages

MULLED RED WINE

Serves 8–10
4 oranges
600 ml (2½ cups, 21 fl oz) water
10-12 cloves
¼ teaspoon mace, crumbled
1 stick cinnamon (5 cm/2 in long)
*6 tablespoons raw (demerara,
turbinado) sugar*
1 bottle red wine

Pare thin rind from oranges, leaving behind bitter white pith. Cut away and discard pith. Cut oranges into thin slices. Place in a pan with rind, water, cloves, mace, cinnamon and sugar. Cover pan, bring to boil, simmer gently for 15 minutes. Remove from heat. Allow to stand for a further 15 minutes. Strain juice into a second pan. Add wine, cover and heat until quite hot. Serve.

LIGHT SUMMER PUNCH

Makes 8–10 glasses
360 ml (1½ cups, 13 fl oz) lemonade
juice of 1 orange
1 clove
1 stick cinnamon
½ bottle white wine, chilled
½ bottle rosé wine, chilled
1 medium bottle soda water
4 orange slices, halved

Place lemonade, orange juice, clove and cinnamon in a small pan. Heat until almost boiling. Set aside until cold. Strain through a fine-meshed sieve and pour into a large glass jug (pitcher). Add rosé and white wine, and soda water to taste. Finally, add orange slices.

ROSEMARY-FLAVOURED WINE

1 bottle white wine
2 long sprigs rosemary

Uncork wine, push in washed rosemary sprigs, replace cork and set aside at room temperature for 2 days. After that, place in refrigerator and leave for 1 week. Shake bottle each day during this period to evenly distribute rosemary flavour. You will find the wine faintly and pleasantly rosemary-flavoured.

Note: 1. Besides drinking the wine, you can use it as a skin tonic applied directly by cotton wool or as an additive to bath water. You can also use 125–250 ml (½–1 cup, 4½–9 fl oz) wine as a final rinse after shampooing hair.
2. White, rosé, or red wine can be used and almost any herb or spice that you wish. Some examples are:
• flowering heads of marjoram, sage, thyme, winter savory
• flowers of camomile, rose petals, violets
• leaves of scented pelargoniums (eg rose geraniums), French tarragon
• seeds of cardamom, coriander, fennel, anise, caraway
• cinnamon bark or cloves.

WHITE WINE PUNCH

Serves 6–7

3 medium lemons

2 oranges

400 ml (1⅔ cups, 14 fl oz) water

100 g (½ cup, 3½ oz) granulated
sugar

1 cardamom pod

1 bottle white wine, chilled

1 medium bottle soda water, chilled

12 borage flowers

Pare thin rind from 2 lemons and 1 orange, leaving behind bitter white pith. Squeeze juice from fruit. Place juice, rind, water and sugar in a pan. Remove seeds from cardamom pod. Add to pan. Cover pan, bring to boil, simmer for 1–2 minutes. Remove from heat and set aside until cold. Strain through a fine-meshed sieve. Pour into a punch bowl or similar large bowl. Add wine and soda water. Slice remaining orange and lemon. Add to punch. Finally, sprinkle over borage flowers.

TOMATO JUICE

Makes 2–3 glasses

1 kg (2¼ lb) ripe tomatoes

¼ teaspoon paprika

black pepper

Worcestershire sauce

Cut tomatoes into small pieces. Place in a pan with paprika. Heat gently until boiling. Simmer uncovered, stirring frequently. As you stir, mash and work tomatoes to separate flesh and juice from skin and pips. Once this is done, pass tomatoes through a sieve. Discard contents of sieve. Use strained juice as is or simmer to reduce to preferred thickness. Cool juice and add black pepper and plenty of Worcestershire sauce to taste.

OATMEAL AND ARROWROOT GRUEL

Makes 3 cups

50 g (½ cup, 2 oz) oatmeal, coarsely
ground

600 ml (2½ cups, 21 fl oz) water

2 teaspoons arrowroot*

4 tablespoons water (extra)

8 tablespoons raw (demerara,
turbinado) sugar

Place oatmeal and 600 ml (2½ cups, 21 fl oz) of water in a pan. Cover and bring to boil. Reduce heat. Simmer very gently for 2 minutes. Remove from heat. Allow to stand for a further 5 minutes. Strain through a fine-meshed sieve or muslin (cheesecloth). Replace in pan. Mix arrowroot and extra water in a bowl to a smooth paste. Now heat oatmeal and water. When almost boiling, pour into bowl. Stir thoroughly. Pour back into pan. Heat gently, stirring continuously until it thickens. Stir in sugar. Serve.

Note: 1. This makes a good food/drink for invalids, convalescents or children. 2. * If arrowroot is unavailable, substitute cornflour (US cornstarch). Arrowroot can sometimes be found in chemists or pharmacies if not available in food stores.

DANDELION COFFEE

Dandelion roots can be roasted and ground and used as a coffee substitute. If preferred, they can be mixed with coffee in any proportion that you wish. Besides lacking the stimulant caffeine, dandelion is reputed to have a beneficial effect on many parts of the body, notably the blood and digestive systems, and, in particular, the liver.

Dig up roots in autumn (fall) when foliage is at its lowest and roots are at their fullest with stored food ready for wintering. Wash away soil. Scrub well with a nailbrush. Cut into pieces 1–2 cm (½–1 in) long. Place one layer thick on a flat ovenproof plate or shallow dish. Roast at 150°C or 300°F for 1¼–1½ hours until browned and dry. Allow roots to cool. Pass through a coffee grinder. Prepare dandelion coffee as you would regular coffee, using about 2 tablespoons per 250 ml (2 cups, 17½ fl oz) water, or as preferred. Dandelion coffee can be quite bitter, so drink it weak or medium strength.

Note: 1. Some people suggest using only the long thick roots of the second or third year's growth to improve the palatability of the coffee.
2. One author has suggested steaming cut roots before roasting to enhance flavour.
3. You may need to roast for a longer period if roots are particularly thick or you could try slicing them.
4. Chicory, a close relative of dandelion, can be used as a coffee substitute in the same way as dandelion. Roasted (ground) chicory is widely available from health food stores and some supermarkets. It is a popular drink in the southern states of America, particularly Louisiana. For this reason, it is sometimes known as 'New Orleans' or 'Creole' coffee. It is also widely used in commercially prepared instant coffee.

OATMEAL DRINK

Makes 2 glasses
1 tablespoon oatmeal, coarsely ground
500 ml (2 cups, 17½ fl oz) water
50 g (⅓ cup, 2 oz) raisins
½ teaspoon caraway or anise seeds (aniseed)
1 slice lemon
juice of 1 large sweet orange
25-50 g (⅛-¼ cup, 1-2 oz) raw (demerara, turbinado) sugar
2 orange slices

Place oatmeal in a small shallow pan. Heat gently, stirring continuously, until very lightly browned. Place toasted oatmeal in a pan with water, raisins and caraway (or anise) seed. Cut off and discard all skin and white pith from lemon slice. Add lemon to pan. Heat contents of pan until just boiling. Reduce heat. Simmer gently with pan covered for 5 minutes. Remove from heat, stir in orange juice, and sugar to taste. Strain through a fine-meshed sieve. Serve with orange slices. Serve hot, or chilled with crushed ice.

MALTED MILK

Makes 2 cups

4 teaspoons rolled oats (regular oatmeal)

400 ml (1²/₃ cups, 14 fl oz) milk

1 teaspoon caraway seed

1 teaspoon malt extract

Place rolled oats, milk and caraway seed in a pan. Heat gently. As it warms, add malt extract. Stir until thoroughly mixed. Continue heating. When almost boiling, remove from heat, cover and allow to stand for a few minutes. Strain and serve hot.

Note: 1. This makes a nourishing drink for invalids and children.

2. When chilled, this drink can be used as a base for milkshakes. Add an equal quantity of milk and a little flavouring, eg cocoa powder, and blend for 30 seconds. Cream and/or ice cream may be added for a richer mixture.

3. For extra flavour, bruise caraway seeds before using.

Above: *During long, hot summer days, the delicate and creamy flavours of Peppermint Milk and Strawberry Wine Shake will satisfy your thirst.*

FRUIT CORDIAL

Makes 4 glasses
250 g (9 oz) ripe blackberries
(brambles)
300 ml (1¼ cups, 10½ fl oz) water
pinch of ground cinnamon
1 lemon
100 ml (3½ fl oz) soda water, chilled
100 ml (3½ fl oz) lemonade, chilled

Place blackberries and water in a blender (liquidiser). Blend until smooth. Sieve through a fine-meshed sieve or muslin (cheesecloth). Pour into a pan with cinnamon. Pare thin rind from lemon, leaving behind bitter white pith. Cut away and discard pith, thinly slice lemons. Add with rind to pan. Cover and heat until almost boiling. Set aside until cold. Strain again. Chill. Add soda water and lemonade. Serve.

Note: 1. Any fruit can be used in place of blackberries, eg loganberries, mulberries, raspberries, strawberries, blackcurrants, redcurrants or plums.
2. You may wish to sweeten hot fruit juice before chilling, particularly if you are using a more tart fruit than blackberries.

STRAWBERRY SODA

Makes 2 glasses
200 ml (7 fl oz) strawberry juice*
2 cloves
3 tablespoons port
100 ml (3½ fl oz) soda water, chilled
100 ml (3½ fl oz) lemonade, chilled
10 borage flowers
2 slices of orange

Place strawberry juice and cloves in a pan. Warm gently for several minutes. Set aside until cold. Remove and discard cloves, pour juice into a glass jug (pitcher) and chill thoroughly. Add port, soda, lemonade, orange slices and borage flowers. Serve.

Note: * The strawberry juice must be clear. You can purchase it, or prepare yourself by freezing a quantity of strawberries. On thawing, clear juice separates from flesh. The juice is used as is, or in a recipe as above. The flesh, if blended and simmered with sugar until thick, is used as a strawberry purée for sauces and puddings.

STRAWBERRY WINE SHAKE

Makes 3 glasses
250 g (9 oz) strawberries
200 ml (7 fl oz) rosé wine, chilled
1-2 tablespoons granulated sugar
3 tablespoons (single, light) cream
50 g (2 oz) vanilla ice cream

Place strawberries and rosé wine in a blender (liquidiser). Blend until smooth. Strain mixture through a fine-meshed sieve or muslin (cheesecloth). Rinse blender. Pour sieved liquid into it. Add sugar, cream and ice cream. Blend until thoroughly mixed and frothy on top. Pour into a jug (pitcher). Serve.

Note: This makes an interesting appetiser for a summer brunch or luncheon.

LEMONADE

Makes 4 glasses
juice of 1 lemon
rind of 1 lemon, without pith
100 g (½ cup, 3½ oz) granulated
sugar
650 ml (2⅔ cups, 23 fl oz) water
¼ teaspoon cream of tartar

Place all ingredients in a pan. Cover and heat until boiling. Remove from heat. Allow to stand until cold. Strain and chill. Serve plain or with lemon slices.

Note: If preferred, use only 200 ml (7 fl oz) water and, when cold, add 400–450 ml (14–16 fl oz) soda water.

LEMONADE POWDER

Makes 9–10 glasses
100 g (½ cup, 3½ oz) caster (super-fine) sugar
4 teaspoons lemon juice
3 drops lemon essence (extract)
¼ teaspoon cream of tartar

Place sugar in a bowl. Add lemon juice. Mix thoroughly then spread over a flat plate. Place in a cool oven for several hours or until dry—you may place plate in oven after a cooking session and leave for several hours or overnight. Make sure the oven isn't too hot at first, though.

When thoroughly dry, pound or grind mixture until fine. Stir in lemon essence and cream of tartar. Store in a screw-top jar. Use as required. Use 1–2 teaspoons powder per glass.

SPICED COCOA

Makes 2 mugs
½–1 tablespoon cocoa powder
2 teaspoons granulated sugar
2 mugs milk
4 cardamom seeds (not pods but tiny seeds inside)
1 vanilla pod

Place cocoa and sugar in a jug (pitcher). Add several tablespoons of milk. Mix to a paste. Bruise or slightly crush cardamom seeds. Place in a pan with remaining milk and vanilla pod. Heat very slowly until almost boiling. Pour through a strainer into the jug. Stir cocoa vigorously until thoroughly mixed. Serve.

PEACH ICECREAM MILKSHAKE

Makes 3 glasses
250 ml (1 cup, 9 fl oz) milk, chilled
2 ripe peaches
pinch of ground cinnamon
1 teaspoon port (optional)
75 g (2½ oz) ice cream

Allow ice cream to warm and soften a little. Take 1 peach, skin and stone (pit) it. Chop flesh into tiny pieces. Mix evenly into ice cream. Set to freeze again.

Skin and stone remaining peach. Cut into slices. Place milk, peach slices and cinnamon in a blender (liquidiser). Blend for 30 seconds. Stir in port (if used). Pour into individual glasses. Spoon one-third of ice cream into each glass.

Note: Any other fruit can be used in place of peaches, eg apricots, strawberries, raspberries.

PEPPERMINT MILK

Makes 1 cup
180 ml (¾ cup, 6½ fl oz) milk
1 handful fresh peppermint or spear-mint leaves
pinch of cayenne (optional)

Place milk and mint leaves in a small pan. Cover and heat slowly until almost boiling. Remove from heat. Allow to stand for several minutes. Strain, stir in cayenne if used. Serve.

Note: Peppermint is a herb with digestive and relaxant properties. Cayenne also stimulates digestion.

TOASTED NUT MILKSHAKE

Makes 2 glasses
25 g (¼ cup, 1 oz) almonds, chopped
1½ tablespoons raw (demerara,
turbinado) sugar
250 ml (1 cup, 9 fl oz) milk

In a small pan, gently heat almonds and sugar until browned a little. Pour milk into a blender (liquidiser). Add sugary nuts, scraping pan clean as you do. Blend for 1 minute. Set aside to settle for a minute or two. Pour off milk, leaving behind nuts. Strain milkshake through a fine-meshed sieve or muslin (cheesecloth). Chill and serve.

Note: 1. You can re-blend milkshake after sieving, adding a little vanilla ice cream and/or cream.
2. Float a spoonful of ice cream in milkshake and serve.

BANANA MILKSHAKE

Makes 2 glasses
250 ml (1 cup, 9 fl oz) milk, cold
1 banana
½-1 teaspoon molasses (dark (black)
treacle)
½ teaspoon instant coffee (optional)
2 tablespoons (single, light) cream

Pour milk into a blender (liquidiser). Add banana, molasses and instant coffee (if used). Blend for 30 seconds. Add cream. Blend for a further 15 seconds. Serve.

FLAVOURED EGG MILKSHAKE

Makes 2 glasses
250 ml (1 cup, 9 fl oz) milk
1 egg
2 drops vanilla essence (extract)
½-1 teaspoon cocoa powder
½-1 tablespoon granulated sugar
3 tablespoons thickened (double,
whipping) cream

Pour milk into a blender (liquidiser). Add egg, vanilla, cocoa and sugar. Blend for 30 seconds. Add cream. Blend for a further 15–30 seconds. Serve.

Note: In place of cocoa, use any flavour of your choice, eg strawberry purée, coffee powder or carob powder.

EGG FLIP

Makes 1 large glass
200 ml (7 fl oz) milk
1 egg
dash of Worcestershire sauce
pinch of cayenne
black pepper

Pour milk into a blender (liquidiser). Break in egg. Add remaining ingredients and blend for 30 seconds.

Note: This makes a quick, nourishing breakfast or mid-morning drink.

ICED COFFEE

Makes 2 glasses
4-6 drops vanilla essence (extract)
2 tablespoons granulated sugar
300 ml (1¼ cups, 10½ fl oz)
medium-strength coffee, freshly made
and chilled
100 ml (3½ fl oz) thickened (double,
whipping) cream, chilled
1 teaspoon cocoa powder
pinch of ground cinnamon
1 small square dark bitter (plain,
semisweet) chocolate, grated

Stir vanilla and 1 tablespoon of sugar into coffee. Place in a jug (pitcher). Pour cream into a bowl and add cocoa powder, cinnamon and remaining sugar. Whisk until thoroughly mixed and quite thick. Add cream slowly to jug of coffee and stir gently. Allow to settle for a minute or two. Grate chocolate over top. Serve.

GINGER SYRUP

Makes 8–10 glasses
75 g (2½ oz) fresh ginger
300 ml (1¼ cups, 10½ fl oz) water
250 g (1 cup, 9 oz) raw (demerara,
turbinado) sugar

Grate or very thinly slice ginger. Place in a pan with water and sugar. Cover pan and bring to boil. Remove from heat. Allow to stand until cold. Strain through muslin (cheesecloth) or a fine-meshed sieve. Store in a screw-top jar or bottle.

Use 3–4 tablespoons of syrup per glass. Dilute with hot water or chilled soda water. Add lemon slices for extra flavour if wished.

Note: As a digestive stimulant, take 1–2 tablespoons undiluted when needed.

GINGER CORDIAL

2 lemons
50 g (2 oz) fresh ginger
50 g (2 oz) caraway seeds
100 g (¾ cup, 3½ oz) almonds,
chopped
500 g (3 cups, 1 lb) raisins
1 kg (2¼ lb) granulated sugar
2 litres (8 cups, 3½ UK pints) water,
boiling

Pare thin rind from lemons, leaving behind pith. Squeeze juice from lemons. Grate ginger root. Place lemon juice and rind, ginger, caraway, almonds, raisins and sugar in a bowl. Mix thoroughly. Pack loosely into a stone or glass jar. Pour over boiling water. Cover tightly. Set aside for 2 weeks, stirring thoroughly each day. Strain through a jelly bag. Pour into a clean, dry screw-top jar or bottle. Use as is, or dilute with hot water or chilled soda water.

Note: I found this recipe in a very old cookery book and am afraid I've never tried it. It sounds interesting though, and so have included it for the more adventurous.

LEMON TEA

Makes 2–3 cups
1 lemon
500 ml (2 cups, 17½ fl oz) water
1 teaspoon tea leaves
¼–½ teaspoon caraway seed
2 lemon slices

Pare thin rind from lemon, leaving behind bitter white pith. Cut off and discard all pith. Thinly slice flesh. Place lemon rind, flesh, water and caraway seed in a pan. Cover and bring to boil. Remove from heat. Allow to stand for 5–10 minutes. Strain liquid. Bring to boil again. Place tea leaves in a small teapot. Pour over boiling liquid. Allow to stand for several minutes. Pour and serve with lemon slices. Sweeten with sugar or honey if preferred.

Note: 1. You can prepare a larger quantity of the lemon water and set in refrigerator to be used as desired.
2. You can also chill prepared tea and serve with crushed ice.

MOCK APPLE JUICE

Makes 8–10 glasses
1 small lemon
500 g (1 lb) apple skins and cores
1¼ litres (5 cups, 2¼ UK pints) water
1 small handful lemon balm leaves
4 tablespoons raw (demerara, turbinado) sugar

Pare thin rind from lemon, leaving behind bitter white pith. Cut away and discard pith. Slice lemon. Place lemon slices, rind, apple skins and cores, water, lemon balm and sugar in a large pan. Cover and heat until boiling. Remove from heat. Allow to cool until cold. Strain through a fine-meshed sieve or muslin (cheesecloth). Pour into a jug (pitcher). Chill in refrigerator.

Note: You can make use of apple skins and cores left over from apple piemaking in this recipe. Because of availability, I am forced to use eating (dessert) apples for cooking and this recipe uses those. If using cooking apples, you may prefer to increase quantity of sugar used and/or reduce lemon.

PEAR AND ANGELICA TEA

Makes 2 glasses
2 ripe pears
400 ml (1⅔ cups, 14 fl oz) water
2 small sprigs angelica leaves

Thinly slice pears. Place in a pan with water and angelica. Cover, bring to boil and simmer very gently for 5 minutes. Remove from heat. Allow to stand until cold. Strain and reheat to serve hot, or chill in refrigerator and serve with crushed ice.

Note: 1. You can add a teaspoon or two of a liqueur such as Grand Marnier or Cointreau to each glass.
2. Make a chilled cocktail of ⅓ white wine, ⅔ Pear and Angelica Tea.
3. You can substitute apple or quince for pear in equal quantities.
4. You can substitute any herb of your choice in place of angelica, eg lemon balm, bergamot (bee balm).

SCENTED TEA (PUNCH BASE)

6 scented pelargonium (eg rose
geranium) leaves
500 ml (2 cups, 17½ fl oz) water
3-4 tablespoons powdered glucose or
granulated sugar
3 teaspoons rosewater

Place leaves, water and glucose in a pan. Cover and heat until boiling. Set aside until cold. Strain. Stir in rosewater. Use this tea as a base for a wine or fruit juice punch or background juice in a fruit salad.

Note: As an alternative to pelargonium leaves, you can use any one of the following: cowslips, elderflowers, gorseflowers, primroses, rose petals or buds, violet flowers. A small handful is sufficient.

COOL SUMMER DRINK

Makes 6 glasses
1 litre (4 cups, 1¾ UK pints) water
2 sprigs lemon verbena (each 10 cm
(4 in) long)
50 g (¼ cup, 2 oz) raw (demerara,
turbinado) sugar
juice of 1 lemon

Place water and lemon verbena in a pan. Cover with a tightly fitting lid. Bring to boil. Remove from heat. Allow to stand for 10 minutes. Remove lemon verbena and discard. Add sugar, stir until dissolved, and finally stir in lemon juice. Cover and allow to cool. Pour into a jug (pitcher) and chill in refrigerator.

Note: 1. You can add several slices of lemon and/or borage flowers before serving.
2. Substitute orange juice for lemon juice if preferred.

CUCUMBER AND YOGHURT DRINK

Makes 2 glasses
200 g (7 oz) cucumber, skinned
3 tablespoons water
3 tablespoons natural (plain) yoghurt
2 sprigs salad burnet
75 g (¼ cup, 2½ oz) ice, crushed

Place cucumber and water in a blender (liquidiser). Blend until smooth. Sieve liquid, discarding contents of sieve. Thoroughly beat yoghurt into cucumber juice. Add salad burnet, pour into a jug (pitcher) and chill in refrigerator. Add crushed ice, mix thoroughly and serve.

ORANGE AND FENNEL SEED TEA

Makes 2-3 glasses
2 oranges
600 ml (2½ cups, 21 fl oz) water
½ teaspoon fennel seed
1 cinnamon stick (5 cm/2 in long)
4 orange slices

Pare thin rind from oranges, leaving behind bitter white pith. Halve oranges and squeeze juice. Place juice, rind, water, fennel seed and cinnamon stick in a pan. Cover and bring to boil. Remove from heat. Allow to stand for 5-10 minutes. Strain and serve with orange slices. Sweeten with sugar or honey if preferred. Serve hot, or chilled with crushed ice.

BERGAMOT (BEE BALM) AND ORANGE TEA

Makes 2 glasses
1 orange
1 small handful bergamot (bee balm) leaves
pinch of mace, crumbled
300 ml (1¼ cups, 10½ fl oz) water

Pare thin rind from orange, leaving behind bitter white pith. Cut away and discard pith. Thinly slice orange. Place orange slices, rind, bergamot, mace and water in a pan. Cover and bring to boil. Set aside for 10–15 minutes. Strain and reheat to serve hot, or chill and serve with crushed ice. Offer sugar or honey to sweeten if wished.

Herb Teas

Take a handful of the herb, place in a warmed teapot (three-cup size) and pour over boiling hot water. Allow to stand for 3–5 minutes. Serve. Offer honey or sugar to sweeten if desired, and lemon slices or milk as preferred.

You may use any edible herb you wish. Suggestions are:

- angelica leaves, stems or flowers
- bergamot (bee balm) leaves and/or flowers
- borage leaves and flowers
- camomile flowers
- clover heads
- comfrey leaves
- dill seed
- fennel seed
- ginger—fresh root or dried and ground root
- lavender flowers
- lemon balm leaves
- lemon grass
- lemon verbena leaves
- marjoram leaves or flowering heads
- mint leaves—any of the mint family as preferred
- raspberry, strawberry, mulberry (bramble) or blackberry leaves
- rosemary leaves or flowering heads
- sorrel leaves
- thyme leaves or flowering heads
- violet flowers and leaves
- yarrow (milfoil) leaves or flowering heads.

Herb teas are taken for their flavour and can be consumed for their medicinal properties. Take the time to read up on these if you can (*see* Bibliography for reading suggestions).

Note: Ensure your teapot is not stained with the tannin from regular tea which will spoil the delicate herb flavour.

Opposite: Herbal infusions have been used for many centuries. Soothing and refreshing, Pear and Angelica Tea and Orange and Fennel Seed Tea both have a calming effect and a wonderful aroma.

Flavoured Teas

In many cases, I prefer a herb-flavoured tea rather than the straight herb tea itself. You make a pot of tea in the usual way, perhaps reducing strength if you are a strong tea drinker. To every small pot (three-cup size), add several sprigs of herb or ½–1 teaspoon of seed. Allow to stand and serve with lemon slices or milk as preferred, and honey or sugar to sweeten. You may use any edible herb or seed of your choice, but my favourites are:

- ginger (ground)
- lavender flowers
- rosemary leaves and/or flowers
- thyme leaves or flowering heads
- yarrow leaves of flowering heads.

Fruit Liqueurs

A fruit liqueur is prepared by soaking sweetened fruit in an alcohol such as brandy, port, whisky or gin. Suitable fruits are: apricots, blackberries, currants (red or white), cherries, damsons, elderberries, raspberries, loganberries, mulberries (brambles), peaches, plums or strawberries.

The fruit is washed and dried thoroughly, stoned (pitted) if necessary, and placed in a bowl with half its weight of sugar (raw (demerara, turbinado) or granulated white). When thoroughly mixed, fruit is packed into wide-necked screw-top jars until half full. The jar is filled to the top with alcohol, tightly closed and set aside for 2–3 months. Suggestions are: damson port, strawberry brandy, sloe gin, elderberry gin, orange brandy, cherry whisky.

When using stone fruit such as apricots or peaches, you may crack open stones (pits) of several, roast the kernels and add to fruit. This will add an almond-like flavour to your liqueur. For more detailed recipes and liqueur suggestions, refer to *Amateur Winemaking Recipes* (*see* Bibliography).

PART II
Preserving

Introduction

This section offers the reader a selection of our favourite preserves recipes. I could spend pages discussing the theory, history and methods behind preservation of foods, but this is dealt with far better by David and Rose Mabey in their book *Jams, Pickles and Chutneys*. They have obviously researched the topic thoroughly and I could do no better. Their book and the others given in the Bibliography offer a wealth of recipes beyond those to be found in this section. Enthusiasts please read further, my knowledge here is limited.

Food goes bad either through destruction by its own enzymes or through the growth of microorganisms—bacteria, moulds and fungi. Therefore, to preserve food is to prevent these processes by one of the following methods:

- excluding water, which is a requisite of chemical processes involved in food spoiling, by *drying*
- maintaining a temperature at which none of the chemical processes can occur by *deep-freezing*
- maintaining an environment around food that is stronger than that in which living organisms can grow and multiply, with salt (*salting*), acid or alcohol (*pickling*), or sugar (*jams, jellies, syrups*, etc)
- killing microorganisms present and preventing entry of others through *bottling and canning*.

The original aim of preservation was to enable food that would otherwise be spoiled to be stored until the winter, when food from the land was scarce. But as with all areas of cooking, it developed from a skill into an art so that today we have a vast array of jam, jelly, pickle, chutney, ketchup and sauce recipes from which to choose. Now we perhaps preserve not out of necessity, but out of choice for the tastes of these foods.

As a final note, check a comprehensive gardening manual for methods of fruit and vegetable storage. Keeping these as close as possible to their natural state is best with regard to food value and, of course, saves time and energy. But have fun preserving—don't let it become a boring chore by doing too much.

Bottling

Nowadays, with the availability of domestic deepfreezes, bottling has assumed a lesser importance. However, it is still pleasant and convenient to have several jars of bottled vegetables or fruit. Our favourites are beetroot (beets), tomatoes, peaches and apricots. Despite what some books say, you do *not* have to bottle in brine (for vegetables), or syrup (for fruit): plain water is fine. Direct reference to a book on bottling will give more details, but I will outline the methods I use. (Note that tomatoes are a fruit and therefore are regarded as such in bottling methods.)

Waterbath Method

1. Thoroughly wash and sterilise jars and lids.
2. Prepare vegetable or fruit as desired, eg with corn (maize), with kernels removed from cob; apricots, halved and stoned (pitted); tomatoes, halved or sliced.
3. Fill jars to 3 cm (1¼ in) from top and cover with liquid—water, brine or thin syrup to 1½ cm (½ in) from top. Check for air bubbles and expel any you find.
4. Wipe glass rim around top of jar, replace lid and secure with a screw band.
5. Place jars on a rack in a deep pan so that they do not touch one another. Add water to 3 cm (1¼ in) above jar tops.
6. Cover with a lid, bring to boil and begin timing from this point. At regular intervals, check water level. Maintain it 3 cm (1¼ in) above jar tops by topping up with boiling water as necessary. It is essential to keep water boiling constantly.
7. Remove jars and allow to cool slowly.

8. When completely cold, check for sealing (this depends on the type of seal lids—the packet will explain this) and remove screw band.

9. Store jars in a cool, dark place.

Waterbath Boiling Times

Vegetables	Minutes	Vegetables	Minutes
beans, green (French or runner, string) yellow (wax) etc	120	capsicum (sweet peppers)	60
		carrots	120
		corn (maize)	180
beans, broad (fava)	120	mushrooms	120
beetroot (beets)	120	peas, green	120

Fruit	Minutes	Fruit	Minutes
apples	20	peaches	20
apricots	15	pears	25
berries (except strawberries)	15	plums	20
		rhubarb	10
currants	20	strawberries	15
gooseberries	20	tomatoes	35
guavas	20	tomato purée	35

I have included in the list all fruit and vegetables I feel it is worthwhile to bottle. For further details and times for other foods, please refer to more extensive literature.

Note: All vegetables (not tomatoes) must be boiled in an open pan for at least 10 minutes before tasting or using.

Overflow Method

This method is only for fruit—which includes tomatoes of course.

1. Wash jars and lids well. Dry thoroughly.
2. Prepare fruit as required—halved, sliced, puréed etc—and place in a pan.
3. Add water or syrup to pan. Simmer fruit until well cooked.
4. Just before fruit is ready, place jars in a warm oven to heat thoroughly and immerse lids in almost boiling water.
5. Take one jar, pour fruit mixture in to 3 cm (1¼ in) from top. Now fill right to overflowing with juice only (you may substitute boiling water here), put a lid in place and secure with a screw band. (Before placing lid, gently disturb fruit with a knife to expel any hidden air bubbles.)

   You may need to gently wipe jar rim with a clean cloth or knife to remove fruit bits and pips (seeds) before replacing lid—if these get in the way, a firm seal is prevented.

6. Set jars aside until they are cold. Check for a seal and remove screw bands.
7. Store jars in a cool, dark, dry place.

Note: Jars with an improper seal can be stored in the refrigerator for up to 2 weeks. With these jars, leave screw bands in place to help keep lid on tightly.

Oven Method

This method is for fruit only, including tomatoes. I never found this method in any textbook, but it was commonly used in our area in New Zealand and I found it by far the easiest.

1. Prepare fruit and pack it firmly but not tightly into jars to 3 cm (1¼ in) from top. Set jars in a large shallow dish or oven tray.
2. Pour in water or a thin syrup to cover fruit well.
3. Place tray with jars in a preheated oven at 180°C or 350°F for 1 hour.
4. Just before fruit is ready, immerse lids in almost boiling water.
5. Remove one jar from oven. Top it up to overflowing with boiling water or thin syrup. Place a sealing lid over jar and secure with a screw band.
6. Repeat with remaining jars, removing only one jar at a time from oven.
7. Allow jars to cool. When cold, check for a seal, remove screw bands and store jars in a cool, dark, dry place.

Note: For jars with an improper seal, *see* note under 'Overflow method', p. 313.

BOTTLED BEETROOT (BEETS)

beetroot (beets)
malt vinegar
water

1. Wash and sterilise lids and jars.
2. Prepare vinegar water for beetroot by mixing half water and half malt vinegar. Pour into a stainless steel or enamel pan. Set aside until required.
3. Boil beetroot until tender. Remove from heat, but leave as it is.
4. Place jars in a warm oven to heat thoroughly. Immerse lids in almost boiling water.
5. Heat vinegar water in a covered pan until simmering.
6. Now work as quickly as possible: remove 1 beet, skin it* (discarding skin), slice and place in a hot jar. Repeat, filling jar to 3 cm (1¼ in) from top with sliced beetroot.
7. Pour in vinegar liquid to cover beetroot.
8. Gently disturb slices with a fork to expel any air bubbles.
9. Fill to overflowing with more vinegar water, put a lid in place and secure with a screw band. Set aside to cool slowly.
10. Repeat until all beetroot has been used.

Note: 1. You can use beetroot straight from jar without further cooking.
2. Keep everything as close as possible to boiling point throughout.
3. * To skin beetroot, hold with a fork and rest on a wooden board. Scrape skin away with a blunt knife, and cut away root tip and leaf bases. Slice with a sharp knife. Place immediately in a hot jar. Once practised, you car work up quite a speed. This is important in maintaining high temperature.

Deep-freezing

It is perhaps best here to refer to more extensive literature on deep-freezing or your deepfreeze manual. However, here are a few tips:

- Eggs, I found, were awful after thawing—even the dog refused them!
- Tomatoes may be washed and dried and placed whole into plastic (polythene) bags, sealed and frozen. They are only suitable for soups and stews after thawing, but as a bonus, the skins may be removed with the greatest of ease.
- I store all herbs and spices in the deepfreeze and find they keep their potency much longer.
- Lemon and orange juice store well in the deepfreeze, and are particularly useful for winter coughs and colds.

jams & jellies

I find jam- and jelly-making easy, and not too time-consuming providing I stick to the basic set of rules as follows:

- Don't make too much at a time! For those very busy householders like me, with childcare, goat-milking, hen-feeding, dog-walking etc as daily chores, it is best to make only small quantities of jam at a time. The result is a happier cook and a superior product!
- Prepare a wide variety of jams. This makes the task more interesting and, of course, makes a more exciting larder. If you have 10 kg (22 lb) of blackberries (brambles), try plain blackberry, blackberry and apple, or blackberry and gooseberry jams; or plain blackberry, blackberry and plum, or blackberry and strawberry jellies.
- If you have a good-sized deepfreeze, store fruit until winter. Summer is so filled with gardening chores, picnics and holidays that I try if possible to put off jam- and jelly-making until winter. I enjoy those grey, cold wintry afternoons in my kitchen and cooking seems no chore. A basic preparation of the fruit is required before freezing: wash and dry fruit well and remove stalks and stones (pits), where necessary. Freeze by free-flow method (refer to your deepfreeze manual) and seal in plastic (polythene) bags. The fruit remains loose, making it possible for specific quantities to be removed as required later.

The added advantage gained by storage is that fruits not normally in season together may be combined.

Cost

You must have access to cheap fruit, otherwise jam- and jelly-making become an all too expensive hobby. You can get together with one or several families and buy bulk wholesale and share the fruit amongst yourselves. Or you may grow your own and swap excess produce with friends and neighbours. Also, make full use of 'pick-your-own' days at local fruit-growers. It is a good idea to make use of hedgerow fruit—I was greatly surprised at the variety and abundance of fruit available. You may use rosehips, rowanberries, crab apples, haws, blackberries (brambles), elderberries and mulberries. Also, look out for runaways of the usually cultivated fruits—you may find gooseberries, raspberries, plums and others growing wild, the seeds having been dropped perhaps by birds or passers-by.

The inclusion of hedgerow fruits also makes for a much more interesting larder. Gathering the fruit can turn into a country picnic outing, dog walk or nature lesson for the children. Check with local farmers though before you pick any fruit. In many areas, farmers are spraying out troublesome weeds with toxic chemicals and these areas must be avoided at all costs.

Jam-making
Theory

The theory behind jam-making, briefly, is this: underripe fruit contains a substance called pectin in the walls of the cells. When it is released in the presence of acid, it sets into a jelly rather like gelatine would. Acid is needed to help the setting, but also helps break down the cell walls so that they release their pectin. Sugar is added as a preservative. Bacteria moulds and fungi cannot grow in this 'rich' environment and so jam is prevented from going bad (refer to general notes on preservation at the beginning of this chapter).

A balance of pectin, acid and sugar is essential to a good jam. Fruits low in pectin, and all vegetables when these are used, must have pectin added to them. This can be achieved in several ways:

• Mix fruit of low pectin content with one of high pectin content.
• Add lemon juice prepared from pips (seeds) and skin as described under Pawpaw (Papaya) Jam (p. 323) *or* Strawberry Jam (p. 324)—much of the pectin of lemons is in the pithy white skin and pips.
• Add commercially prepared pectin. The main disadvantage of this is greatly increased cost.

Fruits Low in Pectin	rowanberries	crab apples
cherries	strawberries	damsons
elderberries		gooseberries
haws	*Fruits High in Pectin*	lemons
mulberries	apples	redcurrants
pears	blackcurrants	

Generally, other fruits may be regarded as having a reasonable pectin content, the addition of extra pectin only being necessary where overripe fruit is used.

As fruit ripens, it loses much of its pectin. Slightly underripe fruit contains the largest amounts of pectin and is therefore best when selecting fruit for jams or jellies. Overripe fruit is best used for making fruit purées and sauces.

Jam-making Steps

1. *Choosing the Fruit*—For best quality jam, you should use top quality, slightly underripe fruit. However, we usually pick out the best for bottling or freezing and use second-grade fruit for jam. This is perfectly acceptable, although you may not win any show prizes. If at all overripe, add extra pectin.

2. *Preparation of the Fruit*—Wash and dry fruit well. Prepare according to recipe (apricots must be halved and stoned (pitted), damsons left whole but with skin split). Weigh fruit and then weigh out appropriate quantity of sugar. *Allow 800 g (3¼ cups, 1¾ lb) raw (demerara, turbinado) sugar per 1 kg (2¼ lb) fruit.*

3. *Cooking the Fruit*—Place fruit in a large preserving pan (stainless steel is best, with aluminium next). Add a little water if necessary. Cook over a medium heat, stirring frequently, until fruit is softened and cooked.

4. *Adding the Sugar*—Bring fruit to a good boil. Add sugar a little at a time, always keeping mixture at the boil. Stir almost continuously.

5. *Boiling*—When all sugar has been added, keep mixture boiling as rapidly as possible with pan uncovered to allow evaporation. Stir frequently. Remove any scum that accumulates on surface of jam.

6. ***Testing for a Set***—As jam nears setting point, you will notice a change in the appearance of bubbles on surface—they look thicker, darker and almost gummy. It's difficult to describe, but once you've made jam several times and watched it thicken, you will see what I mean. At this stage, remove from heat. Stir thoroughly. Drop a teaspoon of jam onto a saucer. Place saucer somewhere cool and airy, such as by an open window, and leave for a few minutes. With your forefinger, gently push blob of jam—if it crinkles on the surface as you push through it, jam has reached setting point (this method is referred to as the 'saucer test'). If crinkling is absent or only slight, continue to boil jam for a further few minutes, remove from heat and repeat test. Repeat until you get a positive result. Once you become

more experienced, you will be able to see when jam is about ready and won't have to repeat saucer test too many times before a positive result occurs. Take care that you do not go beyond the setting point or you will end up with gummy unmanageable jam.

Alternatively, you may use a jam thermometer. The jam is boiled until temperature reaches around 105°C or 220°–222°F. Warm thermometer before use and test jam about halfway down—don't let it touch bottom or sides of pan or you will get a false reading.

Although the saucer test sounds messy, it is in fact quick and convenient. I find it much easier than trying to test for temperature through the bubbling mass.

7. *Jarring*—Use wide-necked jars and have them clean, dry and hot to avoid cracking as jam is poured in. Skim any scum from surface of jam, stir once again and ladle into jars. Seal immediately as follows:
   - *With commercially prepared jam pot covers*, place a waxed disc, waxed side down, on jam to cover all of the surface. Push lightly if necessary to exclude air bubbles. Moisten one side of a cellophane disc slightly, place moist side up over pot and secure in place with a rubber (elastic) band.
   - *With wax and a lid*, pour a little molten paraffin wax over surface of jam to seal off from outside. Cover with a clean hot screw lid or a layer of thick greaseproof (wax) paper firmly secured with a rubber (elastic) band.

8. *Storing*—Store jam in a cool, dry place and check periodically for mould growth. If this occurs, do not despair. Scrape off mould. Discard a good thick top layer of jam. Use remaining jam as quickly as possible. If this happens to many jars, improve on hygiene next time, but for now, scrape mould away as described and store remaining jars in deepfreeze.

Note: I always use raw (demerara, turbinado) sugar, but you may use white if you prefer. If you have a jam with large pieces of fruit, allow finished jam to 'rest' for 15–20 minutes before jarring. This will prevent fruit lumps rising to the tops of jars.

APRICOT JAM

1 kg (2¼ lb) apricots, halved and stoned (pitted)
800 g (3¼ cups, 1¾ lb) raw (demerara, turbinado) sugar

A delicious jam, but as with peaches, I prefer to save apricots for desserts. Wash and dry apricots well. Fruit should be cut into chunks and stones (pits) discarded before weighing. Weigh out appropriate proportion of sugar. Add a little water to pan initially to prevent burning. Proceed through stages 3–8 of 'Jam-making steps' (*see* pp. 319–21).

BLACKCURRANT OR REDCURRANT JAM

1 kg (2¼ lb) blackcurrants or redcurrants
800 g (3¼ cups, 1¾ lb) raw (demerara, turbinado) sugar

Top and tail (clean) currants first. Add a little water to pan initially to prevent burning. Proceed through stages 1–8 of 'Jam-making steps' as usual (*see* pp. 319–21).

BLACKBERRY (BRAMBLE) JAM

1 kg (2¼ lb) blackberries (brambles)
800 g (3¼ cups, 1¾ lb) raw
(demerara,
turbinado) sugar

Avoid using overripe fruit—if in doubt, add lemon juice as described under Pawpaw (Papaya) Jam (*see* p. 323). Blackberry and apple make a well-known suitable combination. Add a little water to pan initially to prevent burning. Proceed through stages 1–8 of 'Jam-making steps' (*see* pp. 319–21).

CARROT JAM

500 g (1 lb) carrot, grated
750 ml (3 cups, 26½ fl oz) water
rind of 3 oranges, finely grated
100 ml (3½ fl oz) orange juice
600 g (2½ cups, 21 oz) raw
(demerara, turbinado) sugar
1 tablespoon brandy (optional)
¼ teaspoon ground cinnamon

Place carrot in a pan with water. Cover pan and bring to boil. Reduce heat. Simmer until carrots are very soft (¾–1 hour). Cool carrots a little. Blend (liquidise) until smooth or press through a fine sieve. Pour carrot purée into a preserving pan and stir in orange rind and juice. Bring to boil. Add sugar, a little at a time, stirring frequently and maintaining a boil. When all sugar has been added, boil rapidly until setting point is reached. Stir in brandy (if used) and cinnamon. Jar as usual.

Note: *Lemon rind and juice may be used in place of orange.*

DAMSON JAM

1 kg (2¼ lb) damsons
800 g (3¼ cups, 1¾ lb) raw
(demerara,
turbinado) sugar

Split skins and snip off stalks of damsons before using. Add a little water to pan to avoid burning. As damsons cook, the stones (pits) will separate from flesh. Spoon out as many as you can, then proceed as usual (you may be able to spoon out a few more stones as you go). Continue through stages 4–8 of 'Jam-making steps' as usual (*see* pp. 319–21).

GOOSEBERRY JAM

1 kg (2¼ lb) gooseberries
800 g (3¼ cups, 1¾ lb) raw
(demerara,
turbinado) sugar

Top and tail (clean) gooseberries before use. Add a little water to pan to prevent burning. Proceed through stages 1–8 of 'Jam-making steps' as usual (*see* pp. 319–21).

GUAVA JAM

2½ litres (10 cups, 4½ UK pints)
guava pulp
2 kg (8 cups, 4½ lb) raw (demerara,
turbinado) sugar

To prepare guava pulp, halve guavas. Scoop out flesh and seeds into a large saucepan. Discard skins. Add a little water to pan to prevent burning. Heat guava flesh until boiling. Reduce heat. Boil gently for 5 minutes, stirring well. (This cooking separates flesh from seeds and makes the next stage easier.) Press guava through a sieve to separate seeds from cooked flesh or pulp. Discard seeds. Measure pulp and calculate amount of sugar required according to proportions given. Proceed with jam-making in usual way.

MULBERRY JAM

1 kg (2¼ lb) mulberries
800 g (3¼ cups, 1¾ lb) raw
(demerara,
turbinado) sugar

A delicious jam, but take care that you don't use overripe fruit. If in doubt, add a little lemon juice prepared from pips and skins as described under Strawberry Jam (*see* p. 324). Also, snip off stalks before use. If this is too tedious, resort to mulberry jelly! Proceed through stages 1–8 of 'Jam-making steps' as usual (*see* pp. 319–21).

PAWPAW (PAPAYA) JAM

For each 1 kg (2¼ lb) of prepared
pawpaw (papaya), allow:
1 small lemon
200 ml (7 fl oz) water
800 g (3¼ cups, 1¾ lb) raw
(demerara,
turbinado) sugar

Prepare pawpaw as follows. Halve pawpaw. Scoop out and discard seeds. Thinly pare off skin and discard. Chop flesh into small pieces and weigh. Measure out quantity of sugar required. Set aside. Thinly slice lemon. Place in a pan with water. Bring to boil, cover and simmer for 5 minutes. Strain lemon slices, squeezing as much juice as possible from them. Pour lemony water into a preserving pan. Add pawpaw. Slowly bring to boil, pressing pawpaw with a potato masher to pulp—you may press to a smooth pulp, or allow to remain lumpy if preferred. When boiling, add sugar. Boil briskly until setting point is reached. Jar and seal as usual.

Following page: *Mulberry Jam makes a scrumptious conserve and is a good way of using up fresh mulberries if you have your own tree. Carrot Jam (top) can be made at any time of the year.*

PEACH JAM

1 kg (2¼ lb) peaches, halved and stoned (pitted)
800 g (3¼ cups, 1¾ lb) raw (demerara, turbinado) sugar

A rather heavy jam and not one I make very often, as I prefer to bottle or freeze any fruit for desserts. However, fruit used should be cut into chunks and stones (pits) discarded before weighing. Add a little water initially to prevent burning. Proceed through stages 3–8 of 'Jam-making steps' (*see* pp. 319–21).

PINEAPPLE JAM

1 kg (2¼ lb) pineapple
800 g (3¼ cups, 1¾ lb) raw (demerara, turbinado) sugar

Again, a heavy jam and one I rarely make. Be thorough in paring away all skin and 'eyes' as these will become unpleasant, hard lumps in jam. Cut flesh into tiny pieces. Add a little water initially to prevent burning. Proceed as usual through stages 3–8 of 'Jam-making steps' (*see* pp. 319–21).

PLUM JAM

1 kg (2¼ lb) plums, halved and stoned (pitted)
800 g (3¼ cups, 1¾ lb) raw (demerara, turbinado) sugar

Halve fruit. Remove stones (pits) before weighing. Add a little water to pan to prevent burning. Proceed as usual through stages 3–8 of 'Jam-making steps' (*see* pp. 319–21).

RASPBERRY JAM

1 kg (2¼ lb) raspberries
800 g (3¼ cups, 1¾ lb) raw (demerara, turbinado) sugar

Avoid overripe raspberries or you will not get a good set. Take care with freshness as this fruit goes mouldy quickly. Proceed as usual through stages 1–8 of 'Jam-making steps' (*see* pp. 319–21).

STRAWBERRY JAM

1 large lemon
1 kg (2¼ lb) strawberries
800 g (3¼ cups, 1¾ lb) raw (demerara, turbinado) sugar

Halve lemon, squeeze out juice and set aside (juice is not required). Place pips and lemon halves in a small pan. Add a little water—just enough to cover lemon. Cover and bring to boil. Boil gently for 25 minutes. Remove from heat, squeeze any remaining juice from lemon halves and discard with pips. Pour lemony water into a preserving pan or similar heavy-based pan (not cast-iron). Add strawberries. Bring to boil. When boiling rapidly, add sugar, stirring continuously, until dissolved. Continue boiling rapidly until setting point has been reached. Jar and seal in usual way.

DARK MARMALADE

1½ kg (3¼ lb) oranges
250 g (9 oz) lemons
4 litres (8½ US pints, 7 UK pints)
water
1 kg (4 cups, 2¼ lb) raw (demerara,
turbinado) sugar
2 kg (12 cups, 4½ lb) (soft) dark
brown
(Barbados) sugar

Finely grate peel from half the oranges and half the lemons. Place in a preserving pan. Squeeze juice from all lemons and oranges. Add to pan. Place orange and lemon skins and pips in a muslin (double or triple thickness cheesecloth) bag. Place bag in pan. Cover with water and allow to stand overnight.

The next day, boil contents of pan, uncovered, until liquid volume has reduced by about one-third. Remove muslin bag and squeeze of all its juice. Add juice to pan. Discard contents of bag. Keeping liquid boiling all the time, add sugar 1 kg (2¼ lb) at a time. Continue to boil until setting point is reached. (Test as usual by the saucer method.) Remove from heat. Allow to cool for 5 minutes, stirring occasionally. Pour into hot jars and seal as usual.

GINGERED MARMALADE

1½ kg (3¼ lb) oranges
250 g (9 oz) lemons
4 litres (8½ US pints, 7 UK pints)
1 kg (4 cups, 2¼ lb) raw (demerara,
turbinado) sugar
2 kg (12 cups, 4½ lb) (soft) dark
brown
(Barbados) sugar
1-2 tablespoons ground ginger

Make marmalade according to recipe for Dark Marmalade (above). Immediately before jarring, stir in ground ginger to taste (approx. 1–2 tablespoons). Proceed as usual.

Jelly-making Steps

The same broad principles apply to jelly preparation as described for jam. Therefore, stages 1, 2 and 3 are almost the same for both.

1. *Choosing the Fruit*—For best quality jelly, you should use top quality, slightly underripe fruit. However, as with jam, we usually pick out the best for bottling and freezing, and use second-grade fruit for jelly. If at all overripe, add extra pectin.

2. *Preparation of the Fruit*—Wash and dry fruit well. Prepare according to recipe (apricots must be halved and stoned (pitted), damsons left whole but with skin split).

3. *Cooking the Fruit*—Place fruit in a large preserving pan (stainless steel is best, then aluminium). Add water. Cook over a medium heat, stirring frequently, until softened and cooked.

4. *Straining the Fruit*—At the end of cooking, fruit is cooled and strained of all its juice. So that juice and later jelly do not go cloudy, fruit must be strained through a very fine-meshed material which is made for just that purpose and is called, obviously, a jelly bag. Alternatively, you may strain through several thicknesses of muslin (cheesecloth). Whichever method you use, fruit is poured into bag and the bag is hung up and allowed to drip undisturbed for at least 8 hours. Do not try to speed process by squeezing bag or you will force tiny particles through mesh which will produce cloudiness. If you are preparing a large quantity of one jelly, eg several kilograms of crab apple, split load into four, five or even six lots and strain each separately but simultaneously. I found the easiest way to do this was to hang jelly bags on one or two poles placed across the bath, with one large bowl or pan underneath to catch juice.

The juice is then measured and the appropriate quantity of sugar weighed out. Allow *800 g (3¼ cups, 1¾ lb) raw (demerara, turbinado) or white (granulated) sugar per 1 litre (4 cups, 1¾ UK pints) juice.*

5. *Adding the Sugar*—Pour juice into a preserving pan, bring to boil and gradually add sugar, keeping mixture always on boil.

6. *Boiling*—Now boil rapidly, stirring frequently. Remove any scum that appears on surface.

7. *Testing for a Set*—As jelly nears setting point, you will notice a change in the appearance of bubbles on surface—they look thicker, darker and almost gummy. As with jam, once you've made jelly a few times you will find this easier to spot. At this stage, remove jelly from heat. Stir thoroughly. Drop a teaspoon of jelly onto a saucer. Place saucer somewhere cool and airy, such as by an open window, and leave for a few minutes. With your forefinger, gently push blob of jelly—if it crinkles on surface as you push through it, jelly has reached setting point (this is the 'saucer test'). If crinkling is absent or only slight, continue to boil jelly for a further few minutes, remove from heat and repeat test. Repeat until you get a positive result. Once again, with experience, you will be able to see when jelly is about ready and won't have to repeat the saucer test too many times before a positive result occurs. Take care not to go beyond setting point or you will end up with gummy unmanageable jelly.

Alternatively, you may use a jam thermometer. The jelly is boiled until temperature reaches around 105°C or 220°–222°F. Warm thermometer before use and test jelly about halfway down—don't let it touch bottom or sides of pan or you will get a false reading.

I prefer the saucer test as it is quicker and more convenient.

8. *Jarring*—Use wide-necked jars and have them clean, dry and hot to avoid cracking as jelly is poured in. Skim any scum from surface of jelly, stir once again and ladle into jars. Seal immediately as follows:
- *With commercially prepared jam pot covers*, place a waxed disc, waxed side down, on jelly to cover all of surface. Push lightly if necessary to exclude air bubbles. Moisten one side of a cellophane disc slightly, place moist side up over jar and secure in place with a rubber (elastic) band.

- *With wax and a lid*, pour a little molten paraffin wax over surface of jelly to seal off from outside. Cover with a clean hot screw lid or a layer of thick greaseproof (wax) paper firmly secured with a rubber (elastic) band.

9. *Storing*—Store jelly in a cool, dry place and check periodically for mould growth. If this happens, do not despair. Scrape off mould and discard a good thick top layer of jelly. Use remaining jelly as quickly as possible. If this happens to lots of jars, improve on hygiene next time, but for now, scrape mould away and store remaining jars in deepfreeze.

APPLE JELLY

2 kg (4½ lb) apples
1 litre (4 cups, 1¾ UK pints) water

Cut apples into small pieces (including skin, core, pips etc). Place in pan with water. Cover with a lid and bring to boil. Boil gently until apples are well softened. Strain apples first through a coarse sieve (you may press apples very gently to release a little more juice, but take care not to squeeze too hard or final jelly will be cloudy). Now strain juice through a jelly bag, several layers of muslin (cheesecloth) or a coffee-filter paper.

1 litre (4 cups, 1¾ UK pints) apple juice
800 g (3¼ cups, 1¾ lb) raw (demerara, turbinado) or *white granulated sugar*
2 tablespoons lemon juice

Measure apple juice and weigh sugar in given proportions. Pour apple juice plus lemon juice into a pan, bring to boil and stir in sugar. Continue boiling rapidly until setting point is reached. Jar and seal as usual.

Note: 1. To make use of pulp, press through a fine sieve. The purée produced can be used as a sauce or pie filler.
2. Try a mixture of fruits with apples predominant, eg apple and blackberry (bramble), apple and blackcurrant, apple and gooseberry, apple and elderberry, apple and rosehip, apple and rowanberry.

CRAB APPLE JELLY

2 kg (4½ lb) crab apples
1 litre (4 cups, 1¾ UK pints) water

Choose large, firm, bright-red crab apples. Prepare crab apple juice as for Apple Jelly (above).

1 litre (4 cups, 1¾ UK pints) crab apple juice
800 g (3¼ cups, 1¾ lb) raw (demerara, turbinado) or *white granulated sugar*

Proceed as usual through stages 5–9 of 'Jelly-making steps' (*see* pp. 327–8).

This jelly is delicious in its own right, but can be used as a base to carry other fruits or flavourings, eg crab apple and blackberry (bramble), crab apple and strawberry, crab apple and rowanberry, crab apple and rosehip.

Boil fruits together until soft and pulpy. Strain through a jelly bag and proceed as usual. Crab apple can also be used as a base for herb jelly or spiced jelly.

ELDERBERRY JELLY

2 kg (4½ lb) elderberries
water to cover

Try to pick elderberries that are not too overripe otherwise you will have problems with setting. If in doubt, add extra pectin by any of the methods described on p. 321).

Place elderberries and water in a pan and heat, stirring well. Bring to boil. Simmer until elderberries have cooked and released their juice. Strain through a jelly bag in usual way.

1 litre (4 cups, 1¾ UK pints)
elderberry juice
800 g (3¼ cups, 1¾ lb) raw
(turbinado,
demerara) or *white granulated sugar*

Proceed as usual through steps 5–9 of 'Jelly-making steps' (*see* pp. 327–8).

Note: If adding pectin by making lemony juice, *see* method under Pawpaw (Papaya) Jam (p. 323) or Strawberry Jam (p. 324). Allow 2 lemons per 1 litre of prepared elderberry juice.

HAW JELLY

Jelly is perhaps a misnomer for this conserve. As haws contain very little pectin, even when underripe, it is rarely possible to get a set and vain attempts result in runny jelly or a sticky gum. You can remedy this by the addition of commercially prepared pectin or another fruit, eg apples or crab apples. Both of these, however, alter the fine and delicate flavour of the haws. By general consensus, my family decided to put up with the runny jelly version and to tip their bread or toast accordingly!

Haws certainly make a fine conserve. Haw jelly, with its runny nature, finds a multitude of uses at the table—as a sauce for fruit dishes, desserts, pancakes or sweet omelettes, or in place of honey in any recipe, with a favourable and interesting alteration of flavour.

haws
water to cover

Pick full, fat, soft and red haws. Wash well. Place in a pan and amply cover with water. Boil (covered) until soft and pulpy. Cool and strain through a jelly bag.

1 litre (4 cups, 1¾ UK pints) juice
800 g (3¼ cups, 1¾ lb) raw
(demerara,
turbinado) sugar

Prepare jelly as usual (*see* pp. 326–8). You will not, of course, get a positive saucer test. Continue boiling until cooled drop on your saucer is thick, but not yet gummy.

HERB JELLY

1 handful of herbs, whole or sprigs
per *1 litre (4 cups, 1¾ UK pints) of*
strained juice

Use apple (with or without lemon juice), crab apple, orange or lemon jelly as a base. To every 1 litre (4 cups, 1¾ UK pints) of juice, you need a large handful of herbs—whole leaves or sprigs. Fresh herbs are better than dried.

Prepare jelly in usual way until setting point is reached (*see* p. 327). Bruise herbs, stir into jelly and tightly cover pan. Allow to stand for 5 minutes—keep jelly hot, but do not allow to boil further or you will pass setting point. Stir jelly again. Strain out herbs. Jar and seal as usual. Leave herbs in if you prefer—personally, I like the look of herb jelly with a sprig or two of the relevant herb.

Suitable herbs are: basil, bergamot (bee balm), lemon grass, lemon thyme, lemon verbena, marjoram, mint, peppermint, rose geranium (pelargonium), rosemary, summer savory and thyme.

LEMON JELLY

lemons
water to cover

Cut lemons into pieces (eighths or sixteenths). Place in pan. Cover with water and allow to stand overnight. The next day, heat until boiling. Reduce heat. Allow to simmer gently (covered with a tightly fitting lid) for about 2 hours. Strain through muslin (cheesecloth) or a jelly bag. You may squeeze lemons gently to release more juice.

1 litre (4 cups, 1¾ UK pints) lemon
juice
800 g (3¼ cups, 1¾ lb) raw
(demerara,
turbinado) or *white (granulated)*
sugar

Measure strained juice and weigh sugar, in given proportions. Heat juice until boiling. Stir in sugar. Boil rapidly until setting point is reached. Jar as usual, but it is important to remove all scum before pouring into jars.

Opposite: *Mint Jelly (left) is traditionally served with roast lamb. Crab Apple Jelly (right) makes good use of the sour, apple-like fruit of the tree of the same name — a delectable treat when spread on toast for breakfast.*

ORANGE JELLY

oranges
water to cover

Cut oranges into pieces (eighths or sixteenths). Place in pan. Cover with water and allow to stand overnight. The next day, heat until boiling. Reduce heat. Allow to simmer gently (covered with a tightly fitting lid) for about 2 hours. Strain through muslin (cheesecloth) or a jelly bag. You may squeeze oranges gently to release more juice.

1 litre (4 cups, 1¾ UK pints) orange juice
800 g (3¼ cups, 1¾ lb) raw (demerara, turbinado) or white (granulated) sugar

Measure strained juice and weigh sugar, in given proportions. Heat juice until boiling. Stir in sugar. Boil rapidly until setting point is reached. Jar as usual, but it is important to remove all scum before pouring into jars.

ROSEHIP JELLY

2 kg (4½ lb) rosehips
water to cover

Prepare rosehip juice as given for Elderberry Jelly (*see* p. 329).

1 litre (4 cups, 1¾ UK pints) rosehip juice
800 g (3¼ cups, 1¾ lb) raw (turbinado, demerara) or white granulated sugar
juice of 2 lemons (optional)

Prepare jelly in usual way.

Note: 1. Rosehips are similar to haws so either expect a poor set or mix with another fruit, eg crab apples, in the proportion of 1 part rosehips to 2 parts other fruit.
Prepare fruit juices separately. Combine juices and proceed in usual way.
2. You may prefer to add extra pectin from lemons, as described under Pawpaw (Papaya) Jam (p. 323) or Strawberry Jam (p. 324) to improve 'set'.

ROWANBERRY JELLY

2 kg (4½ lb) rowanberries
water to cover

Prepare rowanberry juice as given for Elderberry Jelly (*see* p. 329).

1 litre (4 cups, 1¾ UK pints) rowanberry juice
800 g (3¼ cups, 1¾ lb) raw (turbinado, demerara) or white granulated sugar
juice of 2 lemons (optional)

Measure juice and weigh sugar in given proportions. Proceed through steps 4–9 of 'Jelly-making steps' (*see* pp. 327–8).

Again, as for haws and rosehips, rowanberry jelly will not set well. For a suitable mix of fruit, try a proportion by weight of 2 parts rowanberries to 1 part crab apple. Prepare juices separately then proceed in usual way.

SPICED JELLY

Use an apple, crab apple, orange or lemon jelly base and add one of the following spicy flavourings (quantities suggested are per 1 litre (4 cups, 1¾ UK pints) of strained juice):

ginger
- use 2–3 teaspoons ground ginger or 1 tablespoon chopped ginger stem. Remove stem before jarring.

cloves
- use ½ teaspoon whole cloves and remove before jarring.

caraway seeds
- use 2–3 teaspoons, which may be left in jelly.

anise seeds (aniseeed)
- use 2–3 teaspoons, which may be left in jelly.

chutneys

& pickles

Chutney may be prepared from almost any fruit. It is essentially spicy and sweet or sour in flavour. It is up to the cook to decide on the final flavour according to the proportions of spices, sugar and vinegar added. Preparation is simple: chop fruit into medium-sized slices or chunks. Add all other ingredients. Boil gently, stirring frequently, with pan uncovered until preferred consistency is reached—thick but not 'solid'. Remember that because of the acidity of chutney, you should use only enamel or stainless steel pans. Jar and seal hot chutney, as described for jams and jellies. Here are a few of my favourite chutney recipes, but do expand on these.

APPLE CHUTNEY

500 g (1 lb) apples
100 g (⅔ cup, 3½ oz) raisins
100 g (⅔ cup, 3½ oz) (soft) dark brown (Barbados) sugar
1 teaspoon ground ginger
100 ml (3½ fl oz) red wine vinegar or malt vinegar
3 tablespoons fresh orange juice
rind of 1 orange, finely grated
½–1 teaspoon mace, crumbled

Peel and core apples. Chop into small pieces. Place in pan with raisins, sugar, ginger, vinegar, orange juice and rind. Wrap mace in a little square of muslin (cheesecloth), secure with white cotton and add to pan. Bring to boil, stirring frequently. Reduce heat. Simmer with pan uncovered until chutney is sufficiently thick (stir occasionally). Remove muslin of mace. Spoon chutney into a hot, dry, clean jar. Seal as usual.

BANANA CHUTNEY

1 kg (2¼ lb) bananas, peeled
1 red chilli (chili pepper) (optional)
500 g (3 cups, 1 lb) (soft) dark brown (Barbados) sugar
500 g (3 cups, 1 lb) raisins
360 ml (1½ cups, 12½ fl oz) red wine vinegar or malt vinegar
6 teaspoons ground ginger

Cut bananas into small pieces. Finely chop chilli (if used). Place all ingredients in a saucepan, heat and bring to boil. Simmer uncovered for 5 minutes. Remove from heat. Jar or bottle as usual.

EGGPLANT (AUBERGINE) CHUTNEY

1 eggplant (aubergine) (400 g/14 oz)
1 onion
2 tablespoons oil
75 ml (⅓ cup, 2½ fl oz) red wine or
malt vinegar
50 g (⅓ cup, 2 oz) raisins
½ teaspoon ground ginger
pinch of allspice
125 g (¾ cup, 4½ oz) (soft) dark
brown (Barbados) sugar

Remove and discard stalk end of eggplant. Cut remainder into cubes of 1–1½ cm (½ in). Do not skin. Set aside. Thinly slice onion. Fry gently in oil, without browning, until tender. Add eggplant and all remaining ingredients. Heat until simmering. Keep tightly covered. Simmer gently until eggplant is very tender, but not yet pulpy. Stir frequently during cooking. Jar and seal as usual.

GREEN TOMATO CHUTNEY

500 g (1 lb) green tomatoes
1 onion
½–1 chilli (chili pepper) (optional)
2 tablespoons oil
1 teaspoon fresh ginger, finely chopped
2 teaspoons golden syrup
(light treacle)
pinch of paprika
black pepper
1 bay (sweet laurel) leaf

Skin tomatoes. Chop into small pieces and place in pan. Thinly slice onion and finely chop chilli (if used). Add onion, chilli and all remaining ingredients to pan. Bring to boil, stirring frequently. Reduce heat. Simmer with the pan uncovered until sufficiently thick (approx. ¾–1 hour). Remove bay leaf. Jar as usual.

RED TOMATO CHUTNEY

1 small onion
1 tablespoon oil
500 g (1 lb) tomatoes
2 cloves garlic
¼ teaspoon of paprika
1 teaspoon chilli (chili pepper),
finely chopped
50 g (¼ cup, 2 oz) raw (demerara,
turbinado) sugar
3 tablespoons cider vinegar
1 teaspoon coriander seed

Thinly slice onion. Fry gently in oil until tender. Meanwhile, skin tomatoes and chop into medium-sized pieces. Finely chop garlic. Add with tomatoes, paprika, chilli, sugar and vinegar to onion. Stir well. With pan uncovered, bring to simmering point. Slightly bruise or crush coriander. Wrap in muslin (cheesecloth) secured with white cotton. Add to pan. Continue to simmer, stirring frequently, until sufficiently thick—approx. 1 hour. Remove and discard coriander. Jar as usual.

TOMATO SAUCE (KETCHUP)

1 medium onion
3 cloves garlic
2 tablespoons oil
750 g (1¾ lb) tomatoes
1 medium green capsicum
(sweet pepper) (optional)
pinch each of ground ginger,
cayenne (optional), allspice
½ teaspoon paprika
100 g (²/₃ cup, 3½ oz) (soft) dark
brown (Barbados) sugar
3 tablespoons dark grape or *malt*
vinegar

Thinly slice onion and garlic. Fry very gently in oil until tender, but do *not* allow to brown.

Chop tomatoes and capsicum (if used) into small pieces. Place tomatoes, capsicum and cooked onion in a blender (liquidiser). Blend until smooth. Pour into a deep pan, add all remaining ingredients and stir thoroughly. Bring to simmering point. Allow to simmer uncovered, stirring frequently, until sufficiently thick. Finally, press through a sieve. Bottle or jar while still hot.

Note: 1. For a good deep-red colour in the sauce, use very ripe red tomatoes. 2. The sauce thickens a little more as it cools so allow for this.

PICKLED RED CABBAGE

1 medium red cabbage,
finely shredded
plain cooking salt, finely ground
spiced vinegar (see Pickled Onions,
p. 340)

Thinly slice cabbage. Place in a large bowl. Sprinkle in plenty of salt, turning cabbage well as you do so. Keep turning and mixing cabbage, adding salt until each piece of cabbage is almost white with salt. Cover with a cloth. Set aside for 24 hours.

Wash cabbage thoroughly in plenty of cold fresh water—it is essential to wash it absolutely free of salt, so take plenty of time and water over this step. Soak in fresh water for 20–25 minutes if necessary. Drain cabbage well in a colander. Dry thoroughly on a cloth. (If bottled wet, it will be soft and soggy.) Prepare vinegar according to instructions under Pickled Onions (*see* p. 340). Pour a little into bottom of a wide-necked jar. Pack a little cabbage into jar. Add a little more vinegar. It is *essential* to exclude all air pockets, which can become sites for microorganism growth. Repeat with alternate additions of cabbage and vinegar, finishing with vinegar. Cover tightly with a plastic lid or several layers of greaseproof (wax) paper. Store for several weeks. Cabbage should be dark red and crisp in texture.

FLAVOURED VINEGAR For herb or spiced vinegar recipes, *see* p. 233.

Opposite: Eggplant (Aubergine) Chutney (left) and Green Tomato Chutney (right) are delicious served with fresh, crusty bread. The beauty of chutneys and pickles is that they can be made when vegetables are in season, and stored for use all year round.

PICKLED EGGS

400 ml (1²/₃ cups, 14 fl oz) red wine vinegar or malt vinegar
2 teaspoons pickling spice
10 eggs, hard-boiled

Heat vinegar and spice in a covered pan until almost boiling. Remove from heat. Allow to stand overnight. Hard-boil eggs, cool quickly, shell and pack loosely in a glass jar. Strain vinegar through fine muslin (cheesecloth). Pour over eggs. Cap tightly and allow to stand for at least 2 weeks before eating.

Note: The longer eggs steep in vinegar, the more pickled their flavour—so eat as preferred.

PICKLED NASTURTIUM SEEDS

100 g (3½ oz) nasturtium seeds
100 ml (3½ fl oz) white wine vinegar
¼–½ teaspoon black peppercorns
¼ teaspoon caraway seeds
1 bay (sweet laurel) leaf

Wash nasturtium seeds. Pick off any pieces of dead flower. Drain well. Dry on a cloth or paper towels (absorbent kitchen paper). Place, 1 seed deep, in a shallow dish or tray. Set in a warm place for 12–24 hours to dry—a warm kitchen, sunny windowsill or even the airing cupboard is suitable.

Meanwhile, pour vinegar into a pan. Add peppercorns, caraway seeds and bay leaf. Cover tightly and heat until almost boiling. Remove from heat. Set aside until nasturtium seeds are ready. Pack seeds into a jar, strain vinegar over seeds and seal tightly. Store in a cool, dark place. Allow to pickle for at least 3 months.

Note: 1. Pickled nasturtium seeds can be used as a substitute for capers. 2. Pick seeds when full grown, green and fat, just after flower has died and fallen away.

PICKLED ONIONS

500 g (1 lb) pickling (very small white onions)
250 g (1 cup, 9 oz) plain salt
150 ml (²/₃ cup, 5½ fl oz) brown malt vinegar
1 teaspoon mixed pickling spices

Peel onions and slice off stalk and root area. Place onions in a bowl. Add salt. Mix well until onions are thoroughly covered with salt. Set aside for 24 hours.

Place onions in a sieve or colander. Wash well under running water to remove every trace of salt. Place onions in a bowl, cover with water and allow to stand for 1–2 minutes. Drain and again rinse well under running water. Drain and dry onions with a cloth or paper towels (absorbent kitchen paper). Pack into a jar. Pour vinegar into a saucepan. Add pickling spices. Bring to boil, remove from heat and allow to cool. Pour vinegar over onions in jar, cover with a tightly fitting lid and allow to pickle for at least 2 months.

PICCALILLI

VEGETABLES

100 g (3½ oz) cauliflower florets
50 g (2 oz) onion
50 g (2 oz) radishes
1 small green capsicum (sweet pepper)
25 g (1 oz) zucchini (courgettes)
50 g (2 oz) cucumber
75 g (⅓ cup, 2½ oz) plain salt

SAUCE

150 ml (⅔ cup, 5½ fl oz) white wine vinegar
2 teaspoons plain (all-purpose) flour
¼–½ teaspoon mustard seed, crushed
½ teaspoon turmeric
½–1 teaspoon ground ginger
2–2½ tablespoons (soft) dark brown (Barbados) sugar

VEGETABLES

Break cauliflower into small florets. Place in a bowl. Thinly slice and chop onion, radishes, capsicum and zucchini. Peel cucumber and cut into tiny pieces. Add all these vegetables to cauliflower. Add salt. Mix thoroughly. Set aside for 12 hours. Wash all traces of salt from vegetables, drain well and immerse in cold clean water. Allow to soak for 30–40 minutes. Drain well. Dry on a cloth or paper towels (absorbent kitchen paper). Set aside.

SAUCE

Blend one-third of vinegar and flour into a paste. Gradually mix in remaining vinegar. Add remaining ingredients. Heat, stirring continuously, until sauce thickens. Allow to simmer, stirring occasionally, for 15–20 minutes. Pack vegetables into a clean jar. Pour sauce over them. Gently turn vegetables with a knife inside jar so that each piece is well coated in sauce. Tightly seal jar.

Note: Almost any combination of vegetables can be used in varying proportions.

SALTED BEANS

Green (French or runner, string), yellow (wax) or purple varieties may be used. Wash and dry beans well. Top and tail them. Cut into pieces or slice as though you were about to cook them. In a wide-necked jar, pack a layer of coarse salt. Pack a layer of beans on top, 2 cm (1 in) thick. Pack a layer of salt, again about 2 cm (1 in) thick, over this. Repeat with layers until jar is full, finishing with a layer of salt. Make sure that beans and salt are packed down as hard as possible in order to exclude all air—microorganisms can survive in air pockets and cause spoilage. Cover jar tightly with a plastic lid or several layers of strong greaseproof (wax) paper. Leave for a day or so. The contents during this time will have shrunk a little, so remove lid and top up with more beans and salt, again finishing with a layer of salt. Cover again tightly. Store in a cool, dark place.

Remove beans as you require them, always re-covering jar tightly to preserve those left behind. Wash beans very well, soak for a minute or two in fresh water, then cook as usual.

Note: Despite thorough washing, the beans always taste a little salty. To reduce this, boil rather than steam.

SAUERKRAUT

I loved sauerkraut when I visited Germany, so I decided to make my own. I found a recipe and followed the instructions to the letter. The result, however, was bland soggy sauerkraut—very disappointing considering the time and effort I had taken. Luckily, however, although much later, my Viennese neighbour put me right. There are three secrets to successful sauerkraut.

• The cabbage must be very, very thinly sliced.
• Not too much salt, as this kills the bacteria needed for proper fermentation.
• Plenty of spices, predominantly caraway seed and black peppercorns.

*2 kg (4½ lb) white (drum head) salad
cabbage (coleslaw type),
finely shredded
60 g (¼ cup, 2 oz) plain cooking salt,
finely ground
2-3 tablespoons caraway seed
¼-½ tablespoon black peppercorns*

Shred cabbage *very* thinly. Place in a large bowl. Sprinkle in salt, turning and mixing cabbage as you do so. Add spices whole (gently bruise in a pestle and mortar for increased flavour if you wish). Continue mixing and turning cabbage until evenly blended. Take a straight-sided container, preferably china, earthenware or glass. Pack cabbage into it. Take this slowly, packing in layers. Press each layer down firmly so that it is tight and all air is excluded, but do not bruise cabbage. Cover with several layers of muslin (cheesecloth), tucking edges down between cabbage and container.

Place a flat china or glass plate—one that fits snugly inside container—over muslin. Press down, then weight heavily. You may use a large rock (well sealed inside a plastic (polythene) bag) or large demijohn or other wide-bottomed container filled with water. Place weighted cabbage in a warm place—around 21°C or 70°F is ideal. The next day, check that cabbage is well immersed in briny liquid of juice and salt. If this is not the case, increase weight and leave for a further 24 hours. If cabbage is still not well immersed (this is essential), add a weak salt solution so that it is. As you proceed through the next steps, ensure that cabbage is always well immersed.

The cabbage ferments, resulting in air bubbles and scum rising to surface. Each day, remove weight and plate. Gently lift off muslin. Rinse all three in warm water, remove any remaining scum from cabbage. Replace muslin, plate and weight. Do this every day until fermentation ceases in 4–5 weeks.

The sauerkraut is now ready to eat, or store as follows: pack firmly into glass jars, covering well with brine solution. Seal with a layer of paraffin wax and cover tightly. Store in a cold place, about 10°C or 50°F. Another method is to pack sauerkraut into preserving jars and carry out the standard bottling technique for vegetables (the waterbath method). *See* pp. 312–3.

SWEET AND SOUR VEGETABLES

VEGETABLES

75 g (2½ oz) carrots

75 g (2½ oz) zucchini (courgettes)

1 medium green capsicum
(sweet pepper)

100 g (½ cup, 3½ oz) cooking salt

SAUCE

1 large tomato, skinned (peeled)

2-3 teaspoons fresh ginger,
finely chopped

2-3 cloves garlic, finely chopped

2 tablespoons golden syrup
(light treacle)

2 tablespoons vinegar

2 tablespoons oil

¼ teaspoon cayenne

Top, tail (clean) and peel carrot. Cut into 'sticks' 2–3 cm (1–1¼ in) long and ½ cm (¼ in) thick and wide. Top and tail zucchini, but do not peel. Cut into similar sticks. Very thinly slice capsicum. Place vegetables in a bowl, evenly mix in salt and set aside for 12 hours.

Wash all traces of salt from vegetables, drain well, immerse in clean cold water and allow to soak for 20–25 minutes. Drain well. Dry on a clean cloth or paper towels (absorbent kitchen paper). Set aside.

SAUCE

Skin (peel) tomato, chop into tiny pieces and place in pan. Add remaining ingredients. Heat until simmering. Stirring frequently, simmer gently for 25–30 minutes. Add vegetables, mix thoroughly and pack into a clean, dry jar. Seal tightly.

Note: 1. I have adapted this recipe from one I found in a very old cookery book. I am not certain exactly how long vegetables will last, so I never prepare more than this quantity and always store it in the refrigerator to be used up fairly quickly.

2. We particularly enjoy this preserve with Chinese-style food or even with a mild curry. Otherwise, serve with cold meat as usual.

sweet &
savoury
PRESERVES

PEANUT BUTTER

500 g (1 lb) peanuts (groundnuts), shelled
5-6 tablespoons peanut (groundnut) oil or other good-quality vegetable oil

Place peanuts in a shallow dish or ovenproof tray one layer thick only. Bake at 170°C or 325°F for 10–15 minutes until lightly browned. Allow to cool. Take a small handful of nuts. Rub between hands to loosen skins from kernels. Repeat until all skins have been loosened. Next blow away skins, leaving behind kernels. This can be done in several ways:

- Toss peanuts gently in a breeze. The skins should blow away, leaving kernels to fall into dish below—a time-consuming process and dependent on a windy day and patience!
- Blow skins away with your breath. Again, time-consuming, but good lung exercise, if laborious.
- Blow skins away with a hair drier—highly technological, but very effective! Take dish to somewhere where mess will not matter greatly. Direct air flow onto peanuts—skins will be gently lifted away leaving kernels in dish.
- Less technological, but also highly effective—use a pair of bellows!

Next grind skinless kernels. This may be done in a mincer or an electric coffee-grinder (I find the latter most effective). Grind to degree of fineness you prefer—smooth or crunchy peanut butter. Place ground peanuts in a bowl. Pour in oil. Using a fork, thoroughly blend ingredients. The final step is seasoning. Add one or more of the following: a little salt, ½ teaspoon caster (superfine) sugar, a pinch of paprika, a pinch of cayenne or a pinch of chilli (chili pepper), finely ground.

LEMON CURD

4 medium lemons (about 600 g/1¼ lb)
125 g (½ cup, 4½ oz) margarine
450 g (1¾ cups, 1 lb) raw (demerara, turbinado) sugar
5 eggs

Finely grate lemon peel and squeeze out juice. Place both in a pan, add margarine and sugar. Heat gently, stirring frequently, until all has melted. Break eggs in a separate bowl. Beat. Add to pan. Continue to heat gently, stirring continuously, until mixture thickens. Pour into hot jars. Seal in usual way.

ORANGE CURD

4 medium oranges (about
600 g/1¼ lb)
125 g (½ cup, 4½ oz) margarine
450 g (1¾ cups, 1 lb) raw (demerara,
turbinado) sugar

Proceed as for Lemon Curd (*see* p. 346), substituting oranges for lemons. If, however, the oranges are very juicy, use juice of only 3½ oranges, otherwise curd will not thicken sufficiently.

CRYSTALLISED (CANDIED) PEEL

4 oranges
2 large lemons
150 g (⅔ cup, 5½ oz) granulated
sugar
150 g (1 cup, 5½ oz) glucose powder

Cut peel from oranges and lemons. Cut into small pieces (½ cm/¼ in cubes). (You may include part of the white pithy skin as you cut, if it is not too thick.) Place peel in a pan. Cover well with water. Cover with a lid and boil gently for 1 hour. Drain peel (reserving juice) and weigh it. You should have around 300 g (10½ oz) of peel. Place in a bowl, sprinkle in sugar and mix well. Cover bowl. Set aside for 24 hours.

The next day, measure reserved juice—you will need 100 ml (3½ fl oz) in total, so add extra water if necessary. Place juice in a pan. Add glucose. Bring to boil, stirring frequently. Allow to simmer for a few minutes. Remove from heat. Add sugary peel. Scrape bowl clean to include all liquid. Stir contents of pan thoroughly. Cover and set aside for 24 hours.

The next day, drain peel of its juice. This may take some time—allow an hour at least. Heat juice. Allow to simmer for several minutes. Remove from heat. Add peel. Stir thoroughly, cover and set aside for 24 hours.

Next day, repeat draining and simmering. The juice should now be very thick and syrupy, and ready for bottling. Repeat one more day if necessary. Otherwise, after adding peel, continue to heat gently until mixture is very hot. Pour into a hot jar. Cap tightly to prevent drying.

ROSEMARY HONEY

1 teaspoon rosemary, finely chopped
250 g (²⁄₃ cup, 9 oz) honey

Add rosemary to honey in a clear glass jar. Tightly cap. Invert jar. Place on a sunny window ledge for a day or two. The rosemary will have passed through honey and now sit floating on 'top'. Turn jar right way up. Again leave for a day or two. Repeat inversion process every few days for 2–3 weeks. The honey will absorb rosemary flavour and be ready for use. Remove rosemary pieces if you prefer. Use honey as a preserve on bread or toast, or in any recipe where rosemary flavour is suitable.

Alternative Any herb can be used in place of rosemary—generally 'sweet' herbs are most suitable, including thyme, marjoram, oregano, basil and lavender.

Winemaking

Winemaking is a vast topic and one I could not adequately cover here. However, I have listed in the Bibliography several very good and inexpensive winemaking books that you may refer to. Over the years, my father has tried most of the recipes and from jolly family visits, I can thoroughly recommend them!

Wherever possible, I make use of hedgerow fruits. Armed with hooked sticks, bags, thick gloves and shoes, we set off to make the fruit collection a country expedition and picnic. You can also make use of garden produce once you have preserved all you need. It's worthwhile checking out the recipes—you can often make use of what would normally be waste. For example, the left-over contents of the teapot may be saved and used for making tea wine. Pea pods can be fermented, too.

I find batches of 5 litres (8¾ UK pints, 5¼ US quarts) suitable (less than this and it becomes too fiddly), and prepare a wide variety. This way the process retains an element of interest and learning, and is not merely yet another chore.

Don't despair with failures though: try blending dubious wines together (but not vinegary ones). The results are often quite impressive. If not, use for 'rough' cooking wine. You will find many recipes in this book which include wine simply because I always have a few bottles of not terribly successful wine around! Vinegary wines may be used as a substitute for vinegar, of course, but do not use them in recipes which require good-quality vinegar. Five litres (8¾ UK pints, 5¼ US quarts) of vinegar can be a rather daunting quantity to cope with alone, so share it with friends. I once flavoured a batch of apple vinegar with small quantities of herbs and spices, poured each into a small bottle, stuck on a pretty label and a fancy bit of ribbon or tape and gave them away as gifts.

So good luck with winemaking and good cheer!

Mincemeat

Our traditional Christmas mincemeat is a little different today from its original predecessor which, as the name suggests, did contain meat. Anyone interested in the history of foods and flavourings should refer to Colin Dence's articles (*see* Bibliography). In brief, he believes that it wasn't until the seventeenth century that the savoury and sweet dish or course were developed as distinct from one another. Before this time, he suggests, food eaten was of a sweet and sour nature with the meat and/or fish, fruit, sugar, spices and flavourings all prepared in the same dish. As the Christian Church, with its religious calendar, had a profound influence on daily meals, a dish might have three different recipes—one for the ordinary day, one for the meatless day and one for the meat and fishless day. With mincemeat, we have a meat recipe and a non-meat recipe. There are, in fact, many variations of mincemeat based on varying the proportions of the ingredients. The ones here are my versions. The English recipe you will note is not entirely fruity due to its suet content. In its meatless fifteenth-century counterpart, the suet may have been replaced by some other ingredient, such as ground almonds—expensive, but used quite frequently in the rich households to which this type of cooking belonged.

ENGLISH MINCEMEAT (FRUITY)

250 g (9 oz) apples
100 g (3½ oz) suet
200 g (1⅓ cups, 7 oz) currants
300 g (2 cups, 10½ oz) raisins
rind of 3 oranges, grated
150 ml (⅔ cup, 5½ fl oz) fresh orange juice
200 g (¾ cup, 7 oz) raw (demerara, turbinado) sugar
2 tablespoons dark rum or *brandy*
¼ teaspoons ground ginger
½ teaspoon ground cinnamon
½ teaspoon ground allspice

Core but do not peel apples. Grate into a bowl. Grate suet into same bowl. Add remaining ingredients. Mix thoroughly. Pack into jars, cover tightly and allow to mature for at least 2 months.

An alternative method, for more immediate use, is to cook mincemeat over a medium heat for 5–10 minutes with the pan tightly covered. Stir frequently during cooking. Use at once or jar and use as required.

AMERICAN MINCEMEAT (MEATY)

1 lamb's kidney (optional)
2 teaspoons butter
50 g (2 oz) suet
250 g (9 oz) apples
100 g (3½ oz) steak mince
(ground beef)
150 g (1 cup, 5½ oz) raisins
100 g (⅔ cup, 3½ oz) currants
2 tablespoons fresh orange juice
rind of 1 orange, grated
½ teaspoon each of cinnamon, ginger,
allspice, all ground
100 g (½ cup, 3½ oz) raw (demerara,
turbinado) sugar
1 tablespoon brandy (optional)

Finely chop kidney (if used). Fry gently in butter until well cooked, but still tender. Place in a large pan. Finely grate suet. Grate or finely chop apple (discard cores, but do not peel). Add suet, apples and all remaining ingredients to pan. Mix thoroughly. Cook over a medium heat, stirring frequently, until mince is well cooked—about 10–15 minutes. Keep pan tightly covered during cooking. Jar while still hot and cover tightly.

Note: Any other meat can be used in place of mince and kidney.

Crystallised (Sugared) Flowers and Leaves

Small edible flowers of sweet violet, heartsease pansy, pansy and borage, and leaves of thyme, salad burnet, mint and pelargonium (eg rose geraniums) may be preserved with sugar for use in decorating cakes and desserts. Pick flowers about mid-morning when still fresh, but dry of dew. Pick with a short flower stalk remaining for easier handling. Holding flower by its stalk, brush evenly with a little beaten egg white (add a very small amount of water to egg white to make it easier to work with if you wish). Sprinkle flower evenly with white caster (superfine) sugar, turning flower so that all surfaces are covered. Both steps must be taken carefully in order to keep petals flat and flower in its open form. It is an exacting but worthwhile job.

As you complete each flower, lay on lightly greased greaseproof (wax) paper on a tray. Set aside to dry for 24–48 hours in a warm, dark place. Leaves are dealt with in the same way. When thoroughly dry, they may be stored for some weeks in a screw-top jar in the dark. If left too long, they will lose their colour.

Note: This is a simplified version of true crystallised (sugared) flowers using gum arabic—see this method in *How to Grow Herbs*, listed in the Bibliography.

PART III
Herb & Spices

Introduction

In this section I hope to cover all the herbs and spices used throughout the book. The range is wide, and in the space available I can offer only a condensed background to each. I have purposely omitted botanical descriptions of plant forms. You *must*, on all occasions, accurately identify any plant before you attempt to use or consume it. Refer to a standard text or a qualified botanist if in any doubt at all. For further reading, refer to the herb books listed in the Bibliography—do read further. The history of herbs is a fascinating combination of fact, myth and belief.

Herb Tisanes

Besides the use of herbs as flavourings in culinary dishes, herbs may be used to prepare refreshing and healthy teas or tisanes. Take a good handful of the fresh herb or 2 rounded teaspoons of the dried herb. Place in a warmed teapot (three–four cup size). Pour in boiling water and allow to infuse for 5 minutes. As an alternative (perhaps a better one in many cases), prepare the tisane in a vacuum flask so that none of the volatile oil is lost. It is this oil which in most cases carries the flavour. Those herbs suitable for tisanes are mentioned in the individual notes that follow. Make sure your teapot is clean inside and not stained with tannin. Otherwise the delicate herb flavour may be spoiled.

Note: Recipes for herb butters can be found on p. 232. Recipes for herb vinegars may be found on p. 233.

A GUIDE TO
herbs &

spices

ALLSPICE • *Pimenta dioica*
Family Myrtaceae

This is the berry of the evergreen pimento tree native to the West Indies and South America, grown in Jamaica in particular. The unripe green berries contain volatile oil in their walls which is lost on ripening. To retain the oil which gives the flavour, berries are picked green, and dried slowly in the sun or in kilns. When fully dry, they are reddish brown and shrivelled, looking rather like black peppercorns. This is why it is sometimes known as Jamaican pepper.

Medicinally, allspice finds value, as do many spices, as a digestive. It stimulates digestive juice flow and is an effective carminative—it is often taken with laxatives to alleviate the griping pains associated with their action. Allspice was included in the British *Pharmacopoeia* until 1914.

Chiefly, allspice is used as a condiment, being somewhat reminiscent of cloves and nutmeg. Add ground allspice to spiced biscuits (cookies), cakes, breads, pastries, spiced or oriental-style dishes, curry powder, pickles, chutneys, mulled wine and fruit punches. Use in moderation as it can prove too bitter and overwhelming.

ANGELICA • *Angelica archangelica*
Family Umbelliferae

Many species of angelica exist, but it is the one above that is of importance medicinally and for flavouring. Originally native to Iceland, Lapland and other northern zones, it has been cultivated for centuries in the temperate zones and in places has established itself as a garden escapee. Although biennial, it may be made to last longer by cutting back the flower heads as they appear. All parts of the plant have value, from the root through to the stems, leaves and seeds.

Medicinally, angelica is used chiefly for pulmonary problems and digestive upsets, but it has been used so widely that some herbalists consider it something of an elixir of life—equivalent to the ginseng of the East.

In history, particularly during the plagues of Europe, angelica was used as a protection against evil and witchcraft. It featured in both Christian and pagan ceremonies. This combined well with its supposed disinfectant properties and so the deanery of St Paul's Cathedral, London, was fumigated daily with angelica root in vinegar (set over hot embers to increase vaporisation).

For flavouring and in cooking, again angelica has been widely used. The powdered root has been used in Norway for making a kind of bread. A distillate of the seeds is used in the preparation of Chartreuse, vermouth and Benedictine. In combination with juniper berries, it is used to flavour gin. The muscatel flavour of Rhine wine is attributed to the secret use of angelica by winemakers. The finely chopped stem and leaves can be used in salads, or, when cooked, eaten as a vegetable. Cooked and sweetened, these can be added to fruit dishes such as rhubarb pie. Angelica is best known, though, as a cake and biscuit (cookie) decoration. Here it is the crystallised (candied) stem that is used. Chopped into small pieces, it can also be added to cake and dessert mixtures (batters). A favourite of ours is as a sweet between-meal nibble or snack—certainly a healthy choice for the children!

Crystallised (candied) angelica, though a little fiddly, is easy to prepare and worth the effort.

1. Take thick stems of second year's growth and cut off leaves where stem forks.
2. Cut stems into lengths of 10–15 cm (4–6 in). Boil gently in water until just tender.
3. Remove stems from water, allow to cool a little. Carefully peel off thin dark-green outer layer.
4. Return stems to boiling water, topping up water level if necessary so that they are well covered. Boil a few minutes longer until they are tender, but not soft and soggy.
5. Drain off water. Weigh stems. Weigh out an equal quantity of white (granulated) sugar.
6. Layer half the sugar on a flat plate or dish. Lay stems on sugar, keeping them slightly apart. Sprinkle over remaining sugar—every part of the stem should be sugar-coated.
7. Cover and allow to stand for 2 days.
8. Place all of the sugary liquid and stems in a pan. Heat gently until just bubbling. Allow to cook until syrup is very thick, but do not let it stick to the bottom. Turn stems frequently during this stage.
9. Drain stems well and lay on greaseproof (wax) paper to dry—this will take several days. Turn stems occasionally to ensure even drying.
10. Dust dry stems with caster (superfine) sugar. Store in a screw-top jar in a dark cupboard.

ANISE (Aniseed) • *Pimpinella anisum*
Family Umbelliferae

Anise is native to the warm countries of the Middle East and was much used in Ancient Egypt, Ancient Greece and by the Romans.

Medicinally, the *seeds* are of value, mostly in treating pulmonary and digestive problems. This is a general characteristic amongst the Umbelliferae family members—cumin, dill, fennel, caraway and angelica are other examples. The characteristic flavour of the seeds is to be found in some alcoholic beverages, such as ouzo and pernod.

Most commonly, the seeds are used to flavour cakes, biscuits (cookies) and pastries, but the leaves, also flavourful, can be used sparingly in salads.

ARROWROOT • *Maranta arundinacea*
Family Marantaceae

Arrowroot is native to tropical West Indies and possibly to tropical America. From there, it has spread to other regions. It has a thick starchy rhizome which is sometimes candied and eaten as a sweet. More commonly, the starch (which includes gums, resins and proteins) is extracted and dried into a powder. This is used as a thickener for sauces and custards. Arrowroot's main value is that it soothes the lining of the digestive tract and is easily digested. It is useful in cookery for invalids or those with digestive upsets and in the diet of young children. In the past, the pulped rhizome has been applied to some poisonous insect bites and to gangrenous sores. Perhaps a more orthodox use was as a base and binding agent in some pills and in barium meals for X-rays.

Note: Arrowroot is often found in chemists/pharmacies rather than food stores.

BASIL (Sweet Basil) • *Ocimum basilicum*
Family Labiatae

Basil is a native of the East and a lover of the sun and warmth. Grown untended, it is an annual, but if the flower heads are pinched off as they appear and the plant is not exposed to cold, it will last longer. There are several basil species and subspecies of *Ocimum basilicum*, all of which vary in leaf form, colour and scent, but have that characteristic blend of spiciness and sweetness. Historically, basil is associated with the Hindu faith and is sacred to Krishna and Vishnu. A basil leaf is placed on the breast of a Hindu at death in the belief that it will guide him or her to Paradise.

Medicinally, the volatile oil that gives basil its pungency is reputed to soothe a disturbed digestion and to calm nervous tension.

In the kitchen, finely chopped basil leaves may be added sparingly to salads, in particular those with a tomato base. Basil leaves may also be included in cooked vegetable, meat, egg, fish or chicken dishes, again particularly those containing plenty of tomatoes and/or garlic.

BAY LEAF (Sweet Laurel) • *Laurus nobilis*
Family Lauraceae

The bay tree has been highly prized for thousands of years and appears in tales of Greek mythology. The Ancient Greeks and Romans prepared wreaths and crowns of bay leaves to honour their heroes of war and their poets, who were highly regarded in those days. Bay was also strewn in houses: it was popular because of its threefold action—insecticidal (fleas and other insects were a common problem in the houses of long ago), antiseptic and aromatic.

In the kitchen, bay leaves are used to flavour stocks, soups, stews, and meat and fish dishes of all kinds. Bay leaf is an important ingredient of the French bouquet garni. Not only is it valued for its flavour, but it is also said to aid digestion, preventing colic and flatulence.

BERGAMOT (Bee Balm, Oswego Tea) • *Monarda didyma* (red bergamot, bee balm) • *Monarda fistulosa* (wild or purple bergamot)
Family Labiatae

The red variety of bergamot is the one most commonly cultivated. It has a striking bright red flower on a tall, erect stem and is full of sweet nectar attractive to bees (and many other insects). Hence one of its common names of bee balm. Wild or purple bergamot has purple flowers and is much less 'showy'.

Bergamot was a plant much used medicinally by the North American Indians living near Lake Oswego, which gave it another of its common names of oswego tea. A Spanish medical botanist, Dr Nicholas Monardez, first reported its use to the 'Old World' in 1577 in a document called *Joyfull newes out of the newe founde world*. Oswego tea became popular with early North American settlers who had limited access to regular tea and, indeed, after the Boston Tea Party protest in 1773, they had no choice but to drink it!

Both these varieties of bergamot contain an aromatic oil very similar to that of the bergamot orange tree. Hence another of its common names of 'bergamot'. The English Earl Grey tea which has become so popular over the last few years is flavoured with bergamot oil from that tree, and not from the herb.

Medicinally, bergamot is said to soothe the digestive system and relieve flatulence. It makes an excellent relaxing herb tea used alone or mixed into a pot of weak regular tea—use both leaves and flowers. Leaves and flower petals may be added sparingly to salads, or used to replace scented pelargonium leaves for making scented finger bowls (*see* p. 374).

BORAGE • *Borago officinalis*
Family Boraginaceae

Borage is an annual plant native to the Mediterranean. It grows in a somewhat straggly form with pretty star-shaped blue flowers. The leaves and stem are covered with numerous tiny prickly hairs which can be off-putting. However, according to the early herbalists, consuming borage lifts the spirits—as Gerard so aptly phrases it: 'Those of our time do use the floures in sallads to exhilarate and make the minde glad.'

The leaves, finely chopped, may be eaten in place of spinach or included in cooked dishes. Make sure they are well cooked though, as the spines can be quite tough. Many writers suggest using the young leaves in salads—the hairiness of them deters me, but you might like to try them. The flowers may be added to salads, cool fruit drinks, wine punches or may be crystallised or sugared and used in cake and dessert decoration.

Note: *See* also notes on garden 'weeds' and flowers on pp. 18–20.

CAMOMILE • *Anthemis nobilis* or *Chamaemelum nobile* (Roman or lawn (perennial) camomile) • *Matricaria chamomilla* or *Matricaria recutita* (German, wild or common camomile)
Family Compositae

Camomile is a herb known of old, taken as a tea for its gentle relaxing properties. In southern Europe particularly, where camomile grows wild and profusely, it is readily available at cafés. There, camomile tea production and consumption remains an industry with a high annual financial turnover. Besides being taken as a relaxing tea, camomile infusion finds many other medicinal applications. It is an anti-inflammatory and tissue healer, and so is applied to wounds, burns, rashes and local skin irritations, as well as being an anti-spasmodic, digestive, anti-allergen and hair tonic (especially blond hair). The flower heads, whole or chopped, may be eaten, perhaps added to a salad to improve palatability.

There are two major types of camomile: the first is Roman camomile—a perennial with a somewhat creeping habit and popular in years past as a lawn plant. Buckingham Palace still has a camomile lawn and Sir Francis Drake is said to have played his historic last game of bowls on a camomile lawn before he set sail to defeat the Spanish Armada. The second type is an annual with a more erect habit—German camomile—and is more often used for consumption. In either case, the flower heads are picked just after opening and infused in boiling water in a covered vessel.

CAPSICUM—Cayenne, Chillies (Chili Peppers), Chilli Powder, Chillipines (Tabasco Peppers), Paprika • *Capsicum* species
Family Solanaceae

The *Capsicum* genus consists of many species and varieties, all indigenous to America where they are used widely by the native Indians, both as flavourings and medicinally. The fruit of the *Capsicum* is always referred to as a pepper since it is characteristically hot and spicy, although some are sweet and mild. The best known of the latter kind is the sweet green or red pepper (bell pepper), eaten as a vegetable and mild enough to be included in salads.

Cayenne	This is a variety of *C. annuum* which includes hot peppers, often sold ground and ready for use. In cooking, it gives a more raw flavour than an equal quantity of chilli (chili pepper). Add a pinch of cayenne to homemade savoury biscuits and crackers, such as cheese straws.
Chillies (Chili Peppers)	These are long red or green peppers which are hot and fiery. They may be finely chopped or ground into a powder. In both cases, pod and seeds are used. Chilli is an ingredient of curry powder and used widely in hot Asian dishes.
Chilli Powder	This may be bought as pure ground chillies (chili peppers) or, more likely, as a blend of chillies and milder herbs and garlic.
Chillipines	These are the tiny orange/red peppers of *C. frutescens*. They are fiery hot. Try adding a little very finely chopped chillipine to stir-fried vegetables.
Paprika	This is the ground pod (minus seeds) of one of the milder *Capsicum* varieties. It is popular in Spanish and Hungarian dishes and is perhaps best known in Hungarian goulash. I am very fond of paprika and use it a lot in savoury dishes and sauces, particularly those including cheese and/or tomatoes.

Medicinally, the *Capsicum* species have been used for centuries. It is mostly hot peppers that are of importance. They are used as a digestive remedy—they stimulate gastric juice flow and can 'disinfect' the upper digestive tract in cases of food poisoning. As a circulatory remedy, they draw the blood to the peripheral vessels, stimulating the circulation and its associated functions.

CARAWAY • *Carum carvi*
Family Umbelliferae

Caraway seeds have been found at the sites of Stone Age dwellings, indicating that they have been in use for around 5000 years. The Egyptians were known to have been fond of caraway and the Bible (Isaiah) makes mention of its cultivation. The Russians and Germans prepare a caraway-flavoured liqueur called kümmel.

The seeds may be used for flavouring or for medicinal purposes. Chiefly, caraway is well known as a digestive—ie it stimulates gastric juice flow—aiding digestion, easing indigestion and especially giving relief from flatulence. It is mild in action and so may be given to children and babies as a gripe water, though dill and fennel seeds are generally preferred for their milder flavour.

In cooking, caraway seeds may be used in sweet and savoury dishes of all kinds. It has gained great popularity throughout Scandinavia and Eastern and Central Europe, where caraway-flavoured cake, biscuits (cookies), black bread and cheese are common fare. There is a tradition that caraway-seed cake is given to farmers to mark the end of the wheat-sowing. Though it is chiefly the seed which is used, the young leaves of the plant may be added to a salad and the roots cooked and eaten as a vegetable.

CARDAMOM • *Elettaria cardamomum*
Family Zingiberaceae

Cardamom is the seed of a reed-like plant native to India. After drying, the seed capsule may be sold green as it is, or may be bleached or half-bleached (to a light brown). Green cardamom is thought most suitable in savoury dishes, and bleached is used in sweet dishes. The seeds are left intact in their capsule until required for immediate use, otherwise much of the spicy aroma is lost. Cardamom may be added to sweet dishes, biscuits (cookies), cakes, pastries, chutneys, pickles, spiced fruit or wine punch, and spicy oriental-type dishes. It is sometimes an ingredient of curry powder. Cardamom is often added to coffee. Besides being a flavouring, cardamom possesses digestive properties and is added to some cosmetic and fragrant preparations. Black cardamoms and Chinese cardamoms may also be purchased. They are not true cardamom, though they belong to the same family, and they differ in flavour.

CATMINT (Catnip or Catnep) • *Nepeta cataria* (erect) • *Nepeta mussinii* (creeping)
Family Labiatae

This is a herb with a mint-like flavour, though somewhat bitter. It is so named because cats adore it and will eat it freely in the garden whereupon they become playful and exuberant. Toy mice stuffed with dried catmint leaves are often sold at fairs and bazaars for cat presents.

Catmint-leaf tea was popular in Europe when imported China tea was beyond the means of the ordinary folk. Medicinally, catmint tea may be used to ease tensions which result in such symptoms as headache, irritability and indigestion. It also is a mild diaphoretic (producing perspiration), and may be taken to ease low-level fevers and to clear the congested feeling associated with head colds and influenza. Finely chopped catmint leaves may be added sparingly to salads.

CHIVES • *Allium schoenoprasum*
Family Liliaceae

As a member of the Allium genus, chives are closely related to garlic, onions and leeks, and so of course have the characteristic onion flavour, though it is mild and easy on the palate. Another member of this genus, *Allium tuberosum*, is similar to chives in form but with a flat leaf. It combines the onion and garlic flavour, hence its name garlic chives. It is also known as Chinese chives.

Finely chopped chive leaves (of either species) may be added to salads or cooked dishes, or sprinkled over as a garnish.

CINNAMON • *Cinnamomum zeylanicum*
Family Lauraceae

The cinnamon tree is an evergreen of the laurel family, which is native to Sri Lanka. The spice we know is the inner bark of the young shoots. The shoots are cut off the tree, and the bark layer is removed. As it dries, the outer thicker layer is peeled off, leaving the inner thin bark which curls into quills as it dries. Smaller quills are packed inside larger ones so that when completely dry, an almost solid cinnamon stick is the result.

Cinnamon was an important spice to ancient civilisations and is mentioned in the Old Testament of the Bible in a context that equates it with gold, silver and myrrh. It was

used chiefly in perfumes and anointing oils. Medicinally, it acts as a digestive, stimulating digestive juice flow.

In cooking, it may be used (powdered) to flavour fruit dishes, desserts, breads, cakes, biscuits (cookies), pastries and savoury foods. It is often an ingredient of curry powder. Whole cinnamon sticks may be used to flavour mulled wine, and wine or fruit punch.

CLOVES • *Syzygium aromaticum*
Family Myrtaceae

Cloves are the dried, undeveloped flower buds of an evergreen tree originally from the Molucca Islands. For economy, the powdered clove stalks have sometimes been used, but the quality is inferior. Clove is a pungent spice reputed to exert a beneficial effect on the digestive system with a soothing and mild antiseptic action. Oil of cloves is added to some pharmaceutical preparations, eg soap, toothpaste, mouthwashes, creams and lotions.

In cooking, it is widely used, though must be added sparingly—add to cakes, breads, biscuits (cookies), pastries, mincemeat, fruit dishes, mulled wine, fruit punches, some meat dishes (eg baked ham studded with cloves) and spicy oriental foods. It is an ingredient of curry powder. An orange or lemon studded with cloves may be hung in the wardrobe or kitchen for fragrance and as a mild insect repellent. A clove orange makes an unusual homemade gift.

COMFREY • *Symphytum officinale*
Family Boraginaceae

Comfrey is a leafy plant native to Europe and Asia, preferring damp conditions. It is of value medicinally because of its allantoin content. This is a chemical which promotes tissue growth, and is particularly of value in damaged tissue such as wounds, muscle and tendon strain, and bone breaks. Besides allantoin, comfrey contains many other chemical constituents, such as the essential oil choline and mucilages, and it finds many medicinal applications. There have been claims in recent years that comfrey may contain harmful substances, but these have not been substantiated and, like anything else, if taken in moderation there is no likelihood of any damaging effect.

Comfrey is of great value as a food since it may contain up to 35% protein and contains vitamin B_{12}. This vitamin is necessary for the maturation of red-blood cells in bone marrow and is rarely found in vegetables. Comfrey is therefore valuable in the diet of strict vegetarians, although it should not be relied upon as the sole source of vitamin B_{12} as it contains only small amounts. Comfrey leaves are rather prickly and so must be cooked. They can be steamed or boiled, and eaten in place of spinach. They can also be included in soups, stews and cooked savoury dishes of all kinds. Young leaves may be coated in batter and deep-fried.

CORIANDER (Chinese Parsley) • *Coriandrum sativum*
Family Umbelliferae

Coriander, sometimes also known as Chinese parsley or cilantro, is an annual plant indigenous to southern Europe, but now more widely spread. It has been cultivated and used by many cultures for centuries and is mentioned in the Ebers papyrus—an Ancient Egyptian medical document dating back as far as the sixteenth century BC.

The leaves have a characteristic odour and are often used in oriental-style cooking or, finely chopped, may be added sparingly to salads. The seeds are sweet and spicy in fragrance— very different from the parent plant. They have been used to flavour some liqueurs, but more commonly they are crushed and used to flavour breads, cakes, biscuits (cookies), pastries and many oriental dishes. Coriander seed is a major ingredient of curry powder.

Medicinally, the seed and the leaf, as is typical of many Umbelliferae members, exert a calming, soothing action on a disturbed digestion.

COSTMARY (Alecost) • *Chrysanthemum balsamita*
Family Compositae

Costmary or alecost is native to western Asia, but owing to its popularity it has been much cultivated and is now naturalised in many parts of Europe and North America. It was highly valued for medicinal purposes, fragrance and flavouring. The Romans can in part take credit for its widespread use, but it really came into its own in Europe in the Middle Ages when aromatics were in great demand. Spain even exported costmary for some time. Early North American colonists took costmary roots with them in their medicine chests and so established the herb there.

Costmary's flavour is a mild combination of mint and lemon, but with a not unpleasant touch of bitterness. Many liken its flavour to tansy. It was once used to flavour ale, hence its other common name of alecost. Young leaves may be finely chopped and added to salads or cooked dishes—meat or vegetarian. My favourite use is with sage and lemon balm, all finely chopped and mixed into bread dough before baking—*see* Mixed Herb Bread on p. 254.

For fragrance, sprigs of costmary can be placed in clothes and linen cupboards and drawers. Dried leaves may be added to potpourris, where they are said to intensify the fragrance of the other herbs.

CUMIN • *Cuminum cyminum*
Family Umbelliferae

Cumin seed is a spice known from the distant past—it was used widely in Ancient Egypt, Greece and Rome, and is mentioned many times in the Bible. It achieved great popularity throughout Europe in the Middle Ages and right up to the seventeenth century, partly due to the fact that it could be cultivated at home when other spices were imported at great cost. (Although native to a subtropical climate, cumin is tolerant of cooler temperatures and may be cultivated successfully in temperate zones.)

In cooking, cumin seed was widely used in savoury dishes and also in breads, biscuits (cookies), cakes and pastries. It is not so commonly found in baking nowadays, being mostly reserved for oriental-style foods. It is an ingredient of curry powder. Cumin's sweet spicy flavour also goes well with eggs and cheese. It is often found in vegetarian dishes.

Medicinally, like many of the Umbelliferae family, it can be used to treat minor digestive upsets.

DILL • *Anethum graveolens*
Family Umbelliferae

Dill is native to the Mediterranean regions and has been known as a flavouring and mild medicine for thousands of years. It is another of the herbs mentioned in the Bible and was also popular in Roman cookery.

The seeds are the part most often used—they are added to biscuits (cookies), breads, cakes, pastries and many savoury dishes and pickles. Dill pickles, cucumbers or gherkins flavoured with dill seed are a North American favourite. The leaves are often added to salads and are especially good with fish and eggs.

Medicinally, dill seed is a good digestive herb with a mild action suitable for babies and young children. Dill-seed water is the base of the well-known gripe water.

FENNEL • *Foeniculum vulgare*
Family Umbelliferae

Fennel is native to Mediterranean regions and has been known and used for at least 2000 years. The Romans were especially fond of fennel.

It is mostly the seeds that are used as they contain the highest proportion of essential oil—this oil gives fennel its characteristic anise-like aroma and its medicinal properties. The seeds may be added to breads, biscuits (cookies), cakes, pastries and savoury dishes of all kinds, in particular fish. Florence or finocchio fennel is a variety with stem bases swollen where they join, so forming a kind of bulb. This may be cooked whole—boiled or steamed and eaten as a hot or cold vegetable dish—or may be finely chopped and eaten as a salad. In both cases, a dressing based on olive oil goes well. Carosella fennel is another variety with thickened stalks which are steamed or boiled and eaten like celery. The leaves of fennel may be added to salads or used to flavour savoury dishes.

Medicinally, fennel-seed tea makes a good eyewash for inflamed or irritated eyes, and is an excellent carminative—it is often included in babies' gripe water. As a slimming device, the seeds, chewed or made into a tea, are said to allay hunger pangs and depress the appetite (they were chewed during the long church sermons of yesteryear to relieve the embarrassment of a rumbling tummy, ready for its Sunday dinner).

FENUGREEK • *Trigonella foenum-graecum*
Family Leguminosae

Fenugreek was a popular herb in Ancient Egypt, Greece and Rome and was used as a cattle food, culinary herb, embalming agent and cloth dye.

The seed, whole or ground, may be used to flavour oriental spicy dishes, in particular curries, and also spicy pickles and chutneys and some kinds of savoury bread. The seeds may also be sprouted and added to salads, or roasted and ground and prepared in place of coffee—though fenugreek does have its own distinctive flavour. In sweet dishes, the seed is used in the Jewish halva or in a Greek dish where it is first boiled until tender, then drained and mixed with honey. Fenugreek leaves and young shoots may be added to salads and savoury dishes of all kinds. Both the leaves and seeds are renowned for their nutrient value and are still popular amongst horse and cattle breeders for giving vitality and a glossy sheen to the coat—presumably it works for humans too!

Fenugreek seed is rich in diosgenin which is much in demand for the production of sex hormones used in the contraceptive pill. Yams now supply most of the industry's needs but fenugreek is a likely alternative as it is easier to cultivate and would find a fourfold use: for diosgenin, seed oil for flavouring, plant remains for cattle fodder and as a soil conditioner (it is a legume and so increases soil nitrogen).

FIVE-SPICE POWDER

This is a condiment used widely in Chinese-style cookery. Its flavour is predominantly of anise, rendered by star anise and fennel, with a hint of clove. Five-spice powder should be used to give a subtle background flavour. In excess, it easily overwhelms the flavour of the other ingredients. Therefore, use only a pinch or two in a dish for three to four people.

The powder may be purchased in any Chinese grocery, delicatessens or some supermarkets. If you prefer, you may prepare your own. Prepare only small quantities at a time (as you will use so little of it). Store in a screw-top jar in a cool, dark place, or preferably in the deepfreeze. The ingredients are as follows:

1 teaspoon Szechuan (Chinese) pepper*

1 teaspoon cinnamon sticks, crumbled

¼–½ teaspoon cloves

2 teaspoons fennel seed

1 teaspoon star anise, crumbled

Pound or grind spices into a fine powder and store as suggested.

Note: * Black peppercorns can be used if Szechuan pepper is not available. Like five-spice powder, Szechuan pepper is commonly found in oriental or specialty stores.

GARLIC • *Allium sativum*
Family Liliaceae

Garlic is native to Asia, but is now cultivated and used widely in most parts of the world. Its value lies in its flavouring and medicinal properties. In Ancient Egypt, a daily dose of garlic was given to the slaves building the pyramids to keep them strong and healthy. It was also a popular herb with the Romans.

Medicinally, garlic has antiseptic properties and is said to be particularly useful against colds, influenza and coughs. Garlic is also a circulatory remedy—it reduces cholesterol levels, regulates the blood pressure and tones the blood-vessel walls.

The garlic bulb is divided into numerous segments and each one is referred to as a clove. A little garlic included in a dish will enhance the overall flavour without itself achieving dominance and is recommended to those on salt-restricted or salt-free diets to give a dish that extra zest which salt-lovers often miss. Garlic may be included in any savoury dish, sauce or dressing in a quantity to suit the consumer. It rarely clashes with the flavour of other herbs. Always use fresh cloves as these contain all of the essential oil necessary to its flavour and medicinal action. Garlic pearls and garlic powder are inferior.

GINGER • *Zingiber officinale*
Family Zingiberaceae

Ginger is native to easten Asia and is mentioned in many early Chinese and Indian manuscripts. It was one of the first spices traded between East and West by Arab merchants. The Greeks and Romans were particularly fond of it.

Ginger grows as an underground rhizome and is harvested when the leaves have died back.

It may be used fresh or dried as follows:

Fresh
- the rhizomes (or 'root' as it is incorrectly named) may be finely chopped or cut into very thin slices and added to any savoury dish. It is often found in Chinese and Indian cookery and also in pickles and chutneys. To store, it may be tightly wrapped in aluminium foil and placed in the refrigerator, where it will last for many weeks, *or*, it may be cut into small pieces, roughly 1½–2 cm (½–1 in) cubes, placed in a jar and covered with sherry. Ginger pieces are removed as required and the sherry, often seen in Chinese recipes, is also used.

Dried
- the rhizomes are thinly scraped, cut into pieces and dried (they should be dried slowly to preserve volatile oil). This will take some time and must be done thoroughly to avoid mould growth during storage which will spoil the flavour. The dried chunks may be stored in a screw-top jar and ground as required—crush first with a rolling pin or large stone, then pass through a standard coffee-grinder. Ground ginger is used widely in sweet biscuits (cookies), cakes, many desserts and is an ingredient of curry powder.

Preserved in Syrup
- the young green rhizome is used here. It is first boiled, then soaked for 2–3 days at a time in several changes of syrup, of increasing concentrations.*

Medicinally, ginger is applied to digestive disturbances. It stimulates gastric juice flow and can calm and soothe in cases of flatulent colic and dyspepsia. It may also be used as a circulatory stimulant.

Note: * This method is very similar to making crystallised Candied Peel (*see* p. 347).

HYSSOP • *Hyssopus officinalis*
Family Labiatae

Hyssop is a herb of ancient use, its name being derived from the Hebrew *esob*, meaning 'holy herb'. It is a herb mentioned several times in the Bible, though historians are in some doubt now over its identity—some believe that the hyssop referred to in the Bible is in fact one of the marjorams. In years past, hyssop was popular as a strewing herb. The succulent branches were strewn over floors so that, when trodden on, they would release a pleasant and refreshing aroma. A strong brew of hyssop tea, like lovage, was used as a body deodorant.

In cookery, hyssop has largely fallen from favour in modern times. However, the leaves may be used to flavour roast meat—I prefer its flavour with beef, though most books seem to regard it as more useful with the meats of a higher fat content, such as pork. It may also be added to stews, casseroles, soups, brawn, sausages and similar meat products, and sparingly added to fruit salads and vegetable salads. Some fruit desserts, notably of cranberries and apricots, may be flavoured with hyssop. Hyssop oil is used as a liqueur flavouring, in particular for Chartreuse, and has a limited use in the cosmetics industry.

LEMON BALM (Balm) • *Melissa officinalis*
Family Labiatae

This plant is native to Mediterranean regions and has been in use for around 2000 years. Principally it had a reputation for being a 'bee herb'—ie bees were very much attracted to it and produced excellent honey from its nectar. It is also believed that lemon balm leaves, rubbed over a hive, guide worker bees quickly back home and prevent the colony from swarming and deserting the hive.

Medicinally, lemon balm is included in that group of herbs believed to be relaxant in action. The volatile oil has a direct effect on the central nervous system inducing calm and relaxation both in the mind and in the viscera. Digestive problems, especially those caused by nervous tension, respond well to lemon balm. In all cases, an infusion or tea of balm leaves is taken.

In cookery, finely chopped leaves may be added to cakes, biscuits (cookies), bread, sauces, salads and any sweet or savoury dishes. A favourite of ours is the addition of the finely chopped leaves to the fruit and the topping of a fruit crumble. A healthy relaxing lemon drink, hot or cold, may be prepared by adding fresh orange or lemon juice to a tea of balm leaves and sweetening with honey.

LOVAGE (Sea Parsley) • *Levisticum officinale*
Family Umbelliferae
Lovage is native to Mediterranean regions, has been in use for thousands of years and was a popular herb with the Greeks and Romans. All parts of the plant may be used—root, stem, leaf and seed—for a variety of purposes: flavouring, medicinal and cosmetic.

Medicinally, the seeds or root may be employed for mild digestive upsets and relief of flatulence. Cosmetically, lovage was used as a deodorant. The leaves may be added to bath or washing water or, for a more direct action, a strong tea of the leaves is applied.

The young stem and leaves may be included in salads, cooked and eaten as a vegetable or used to flavour soups and stews. Lovage is rather like celery in flavour and use. Lovage seed may be added to savoury biscuits (crackers) and bread. Also, the stem may be crystallised (candied) as a substitute for angelica, though it is inferior.

MACE AND NUTMEG • *Myristica fragrans*
Family Myristicaceae
Both mace and nutmeg come from the same tree, which is native to the Molucca Islands, but now much grown throughout the East Indies and other tropical zones. The tree produces a fleshy fruit with a large central kernel. Covering the kernel in net-like strands is mace. Inside the hard shell-like kernel is the nutmeg. Generally, the mace is first removed and it and the kernel are dried separately. When the kernel is fully dried, it is cracked open to release the nutmeg.

Mace • may be purchased whole as 'blades' or ground. It is very similar to nutmeg in flavour, though it is coarser and more bitter. It may be used to flavour savoury, meat, fish, egg and rice dishes, and savoury sauces. Spicy oriental-style dishes may also include mace.

Nutmeg • is spicy and sweet in flavour and is much used in the flavouring of light egg, cheese and milk dishes. It is also used to flavour cakes, biscuits (cookies), pastries, fruit or wine punches, and mulled wine.

Medicinally, nutmeg is used as a digestive and carminative and to relieve nausea. However, excessive or even moderate use can cause hallucination and disorientation.

MARJORAM AND OREGANO • *Origanum majorana* (sweet or knotted marjoram) • *Origanum onites* (pot marjoram) • *Origanum vulgare* (wild marjoram or oregano)
Family Labiatae

Sweet or knotted marjoram is easily identified by its grey-green foliage and round, ball- or knot-like flowers from which its name is derived. The 'sweet' refers to its aroma which does seem to have a degree of sweetness about it. The flower is delicate and light and goes well in salads, with eggs, fish or chicken, or with simple vegetable dishes, such as stuffed zucchini (courgettes). The leaves and flowers may be used. Sweet marjoram is usually referred to as an annual because it cannot stand very cold conditions. In warmer areas, it survives the winter well, though immediately after flowering it must be cut back hard to keep it compact and succulent, so preserving the delicate aroma.

Pot marjoram is more cold-hardy than the sweet variety and so is cultivated in place of the sweet for its truly perennial character. It may be used for flavouring as with sweet marjoram, though its flavour is inferior. There are varieties of pot marjoram grown as ornamentals, many of which have variegated leaves.

Oregano has many varieties, all of which have a stronger, spicier aroma than marjoram. The best I ever found was golden oregano—it had a creeping form with round golden leaves. As it cannot be propagated by seed, cuttings must be obtained. Oregano leaves are used extensively in Italian cookery where a strong, almost heavy, aroma is required to blend with the olive oil, garlic and black pepper so frequently used. I use it a lot with tomato and simple meat dishes.

Medicinally, all the *Origanum* species are used as digestives with mild antiseptic properties. Oregano seems to have achieved the greatest importance medicinally and was also sometimes used as a respiratory agent.

MINT • *Mentha* species
Family Labiatae

The mint genus is a large group with many varieties of each species. A species list is given below with suggestions for culinary uses. All the mints have been popular for thousands of years and are frequently mentioned in early writings. The Ancient Egyptians, Greeks and Romans were all particularly fond of mint and used the various species in cosmetics, medicines and for flavouring. Their fame quickly spread and the mints were introduced and much used throughout Europe very early on. Today we find the mints still very popular and much used commercially. In the cosmetic and pharmaceutical industry they are used in such items as toilet waters, gripe water, toothpaste, creams, lotions and flavouring agents for medicines. Probably the biggest commercial user of mint, notably peppermint, is the confectionery industry—peppermint sweets (candies), chocolates and chocolate creams retaining their eternal popularity. Some liqueurs and cordials are also mint-flavoured, eg crème de menthe.

Peppermint (*Mentha piperita*) • Use finely chopped young leaves in fruit or vegetable salads. A strong tea of peppermint may be used to flavour cakes or fruit punches or may be taken hot or cold as a refreshing beverage.

Spearmint (*Mentha spicata*) • This is the common garden mint. Use as for peppermint, but also to flavour jellies, sauces and vinegars.

Applemint (*Mentha rotundifolia*) • This has a milder flavour than either of the above and is much used in desserts, cakes, jellies, sauces, chutneys, vinegars, fruit punches, vegetable and fruit salads and light savoury dishes, eg baked fish, glazed carrots. Use the young leaves.

Eau-de-cologne or bergamot mint (*Mentha piperita citrata*) • This is mostly of value in cosmetic preparations, but may be added to fruit salads and fruit punches. Use young leaves.

Pennyroyal mint (*Mentha pulegium*) • This has a strong peppermint-like aroma and may be used in place of that herb. Use the tips of the creeping stems.

Watermint (*Mentha aquatica*) • This has a coarser flavour than the others and is used more for medicinal purposes than for flavouring. Use only the leafy tips of the erect stems.

Medicinal uses of the mints are digestive; carminative (of mild action and therefore suitable for babies and young children); antiseptic—used especially for mouth and throat infections; to soothe away headaches, particularly those of nervous origin and to ease nausea.

MUSTARD • *Brassica nigra* (black mustard) • *Sinapsis alba* (white mustard) • *Brassica juncea* (brown mustard)
Family Cruciferae

Mustard has been used as a food condiment for thousands of years. The name is derived from the practice of mixing the ground seed with 'must'—fermented grape juice—giving, of course, 'mustard'. Traditionally, purchased table mustard was a combination of the finely ground seed of both black and white mustards, the proportion of each varying between recipes. As the former is not easy to crop on a large scale, it is nowadays often replaced by brown mustard. Brown mustard is also used in some curry powders and other spice mixtures used in Indian cooking. The flavour of mustard is rendered by essential oils that only develop in the presence of water. When preparing the mustard paste which traditionally accompanies English roast beef, the ground seed is mixed with water and allowed to stand for a time. Other seasonings and vinegar are added later.

The ground seed of any of these species may be added to savoury dishes, especially meat, cheese and fish dishes, sauces, pickles, chutneys and spicy Indian-style foods. The young leaves of white mustard may be added to salads or cooked and eaten in place of spinach.

Medicinally, mustard aids the digestion, particularly of those red meats with which we most associate its use. Mustard seed poultices and baths are often used to relieve the pain of rheumatic and arthritic joints, with some remedial action too.

PARSLEY • *Petroselinum crispum*
Family Umbelliferae

Parsley is a native of central and northern Europe and is perhaps one of the most well-known and used kitchen herbs of the West. It has been used for centuries, as far back at least as the Ancient Greeks and Romans. There are several varieties of parsley, all with slightly different leaf forms. All may be used for culinary and medicinal purposes.

Today, parsley is particularly used as a garnish, and as such, is most often put aside rather than being eaten. This is a sad state of affairs in view of the fact that parsley has excellent nutritive properties. It is rich in iron and mineral elements, and is often prescribed for people suffering from anaemia. The finely chopped leaves may be added to salads, savoury dishes of all kinds, scones (biscuits), breads and savoury biscuits and crackers.

Medicinally, the seeds, root and leaves are used in particular as a diuretic, urinary antiseptic and, as is typical of Umbelliferae members, as a digestive.

PEPPER • *Piper nigrum*
Family Piperaceae

Pepper is a spice of long-standing use and popularity. Throughout the ages, pepper has been one of the most sought-after spices. So much so that in many instances payments for rents, taxes and various levies were paid in peppercorns. It was in the search for the Spice Islands of the Indian Ocean that Vasco da Gama first sailed round the Cape of Good Hope—pepper was a priority item on the list of required spices. It is native to the Malabar coast of India.

The pepper plant is a vine that grows in moist tropical zones, producing clusters of small green berries which turn reddish as they ripen and fall. For *black pepper*, the berries are picked unripe and green, allowed to ferment a little and dried. They shrivel and turn black or brown. For *white pepper*, the berries are picked almost fully ripe, just as they are beginning to turn red. They are soaked in water to soften them, then the dark outer layer is removed. The exposed berry is dried to a creamy-white colour. Both black and white peppercorns contain flavourful alkaloids, such as piperine and piperidine, which stimulate digestive juice flow. Both may be purchased already ground, but for the finest flavour they should be ground immediately before using. 'Mignonette' pepper is a mixture of both black and white pepper in equal proportions.

Medicinally, pepper is employed as a digestive, but also as an antibacterial agent. To this latter purpose, it can be used as a gargle or as a preservative in such foods as sausages and salamis.

ROSEMARY • *Rosmarinus officinalis*
Family Labiatae

Rosemary is, to me, the queen of all the herbs. The history, myth and folklore surrounding this herb are fascinating and I could write for pages! Any condensation of information on rosemary seems an injustice and yet I must do just that. The name 'rosemary' comes from 'ros marinus' meaning 'dew of the sea' and refers to its native position on the hillsides overlooking the Mediterranean Sea. Being a popular herb, however, it is now cultivated almost worldwide. Rosemary is much associated with Christianity. It is said that the beautiful pale-blue flowers were originally white, but when the Virgin Mary hung her cloak on a rosemary bush to dry, they changed their colour to that of her cloak. It is also said that rosemary grows to the height of Christ in 33 years—the age at which he was crucified. Thereafter, it will grow only in breadth and thickness. Such are the legends surrounding this wonderful herb.

Rosemary is rich in a strong volatile oil and is much used for culinary, cosmetic and medicinal purposes. In the kitchen, rosemary is said to aid fat digestion, so the leaves are added to the richer dishes, especially those of lamb or pork which, having a high fat content, may be difficult to digest. Finely chopped rosemary leaves may be added to soups, sauces, savoury dishes of all kinds, breads, biscuits (cookies), crackers, cakes, scones (biscuits), jellies and some sweet dishes. It is an ingredient of the French bouquet garni. A sprig of rosemary added to the hot coals of a barbecue will mildly flavour the meat and is supposed to repel flies and mosquitoes.

Medicinally, rosemary has antiseptic and insecticidal properties. It can be used on wounds or as a general skin cleanser and tonic, and as a hair conditioner.

SAGE • *Salvia officinalis*
Family Labiatae
Sage is one of the trio of best-known country herbs still in use today, the others being thyme and parsley. One of its commonest uses is in sage and onion stuffing, used primarily to stuff poultry and which may be purchased commercially. Sage was widely used in years past in flavouring and for medicines, and gained the reputation as something of a cure-all for a great variety of ailments. 'How can a man die who has sage in his garden?' says a well-known Arab proverb. Sage ale and sage tea were popular brews in all country kitchens. The latter was so sought after by the Chinese that they traded their highest quality tea with Holland in exchange for sage. One of the oldest of the British cheeses is one called Derby sage or, more commonly now, 'sage Derby'. It is rather like blue-vein cheese, though the veins are of ground sage and the cheese itself is milder in flavour and creamier in texture.

Sage leaves may be used to flavour cheese or egg dishes, salads, savoury dishes and sauces of all kinds; as well as meat dishes, especially those of the fattier meats, such as pork and lamb. Herb-flavoured sausages, of the kind small family butcheries still produce today, often contain sage among the assortment of flavouring herbs. Sage-flavoured apple jelly and sage vinegar are other popular uses.

Before the days of commercially prepared toothpaste, sage was much used as a tooth cleanser and whitener. It was ground with sea salt, dried and powdered. Bees love the nectar of sage flowers and anyone preparing a bee garden must include sage. The resultant honey, besides having the finest of flavours, is said to be particularly nutritious.

SALAD BURNET (Garden Burnet) • *Sanguisorba minor (Poterium sanguisorba)*
Family Rosaceae
See 'Garden weeds and flowers', pp. 18–20.

SAVORY • *Satureja hortensis* (summer savory) • *Satureja montana* (winter savory)
Family Labiatae
The savories are amongst the oldest of the herbs known and used in Europe for medicines and flavouring.

Summer savory is an annual, is mild in flavour and suitable for use in egg, cheese, bean, meat or vegetable dishes, sauces, dips, herb vinegars and jellies.

Winter savory is a perennial with a strong spicy flavour which the Romans were particularly fond of and which was popular before imported spices from the East became readily available. It can be used in dishes requiring a stronger, coarser flavour—stews, casseroles, roast meat and poultry, sausages and offal dishes. It may also be used in vegetable, egg or cheese dishes.

The savories should be included in bee gardens as bees love its nectar. Potpourris may also contain savory.

SCENTED PELARGONIUMS (Geraniums) • *Pelargonium* species
Family Geraniaceae

Pelargonium species are natives of southern Africa, and as members of the Geraniaceae family, are often referred to as 'geraniums'. There are very many *Pelargonium* species, each with its own distinctive aroma. Examples are lemon, rose, nutmeg, peppermint, almond, coconut and apple. The species of greatest economic importance is *P. graveolens*, the rose-scented pelargonium or rose geranium, because the extracted oil may be used as a substitute for the more expensive rose oil much in demand throughout the cosmetics industry. Pelargonium oil in its own right is used in cosmetics, particularly in perfumes for men—deodorants, aftershaves and the like.

For culinary flavouring, a strong tea of the leaves may be used as the liquid component in jellies, sauces, custards, cakes and desserts. Scented cream for desserts may be prepared by infusing pelargonium leaves in the liquid cream over a very low heat for 30 minutes. The cream container must be tightly covered. For delicately scented finger bowls, prepare a strong tea of the leaves, pour into pretty china or glass bowls and in each float a young pelargonium leaf. For garnishing, use fresh young leaves or, for a more exotic touch, prepare sugared leaves (*see* method under 'Sugared flowers and leaves', p. 350).

SESAME • *Sesamum indicum*
Family Pedaliaceae
Sesame is native to tropical zones and was cropped in Egypt as far back as 1800 BC. It was also an important crop in Africa, America, India and China. It is the seed of the plant which is of importance. Sesame seed has a high proportion of protein and is rich in polyunsaturated oils. Extracted sesame oil is excellent for cooking and as a salad oil. It is often recommended for those on a low-cholesterol diet.

The seeds develop a strong nutty flavour after toasting. To do this, gently heat a shallow layer of seeds in a covered pan until they turn golden brown. Shake the pan periodically to move the seeds around and ensure an even toasting. The seeds will begin to pop open as they toast, hence the need for the lid. Add toasted sesame seeds to savoury dishes, especially egg- and cheese-based ones, sweet dishes of all kinds, vegetable salads, fruit salads, breads, biscuits (cookies), sweet and savoury crackers, pastries and cakes. Sesame seed is often sprinkled over bread (or cakes) immediately before baking for flavour and decoration. Sesame seed crushed into an oily paste (rather like peanut butter) and flavoured with lemon juice and garlic is called 'tahini', and is a popular Middle Eastern dish.

SORREL • *Oxalis acetosella* (wood sorrel) • *Rumex acetosa* (garden (broad leaf) sorrel) • *Rumex acetosella* (sheep sorrel) • *Rumex scutatus* (French (buckler leaf) sorrel)
Family Polyganaceae
See 'Garden weeds and flowers', pp. 18–20.

TANSY • *Tanacetum vulgare* (common tansy)
Family Compositae
Tansy is best known as a perennial border shrub. It has clusters of bright yellow button-like flowers which are excellent for drying. Used in dried flower arrangements, the bright yellow colour fades only very slowly. The flowers and leaves have a bitter aromatic taste not popular these days. It is also not popular, it seems, with insects, and was therefore much used as an insect repellent in the days before mothballs and commercially prepared insect sprays. Traditionally, it was also used as a roundworm treatment.

Tansy cakes, puddings and pancakes were popular in the eighteenth century and tansy was as essential to Easter fare in England then as Christmas turkey is to a traditional Christmas dinner today. Tansy leaves and flowers can be made into a weak herb tea or added *sparingly* to salads, cooled fruit purées, cakes or puddings.

Note: Tansy can be poisonous in *large* doses and is best avoided by pregnant women.

TARRAGON, FRENCH • *Artemisia dracunculus*
Family Compositae

French tarragon is a native of southern Europe and is a widely used culinary herb, though it is perhaps most associated with French cuisine. There are two species of tarragon—French (*Artemisia dracunculus*) and Russian (*A. dracunculoides*). The French has the finer, sweeter flavour of the two and is the one favoured for culinary purposes. It can only be propagated through root-cuttings and should be renewed every few years to maintain vigour and flavour. Because it dies down for the winter even in mild climates, it must be dried or frozen if continued use is desired. This must be done with extreme care as the flavourful volatile oil is easily lost.

Tarragon is best known for its use as a poultry flavouring, in particular with chicken. Use the leaves whole or finely chopped. It can, however, also be used to flavour soups, stews, roast or grilled (broiled) meats, fish dishes, egg and/or cheese dishes, salads, salad dressings, mayonnaise, sauces and some pickles. Tarragon vinegar and tarragon butter are also popular.

THYME • *Thymus vulgaris* (garden thyme)
Family Labiatae

The name thyme is thought to be derived from either the Greek word *thymon*, meaning to fumigate, or *thumus*, meaning courage. Whichever is the case, the Greeks certainly valued the medicinal and flavouring properties of this herb. Thyme was introduced into Britain and Europe by the Romans. Its popularity has continued right through the ages, so that even today it is one of the most well-known and used of the kitchen herbs. Bees are also especially fond of thyme nectar, the resultant honey being highly valued.

Medicinally, herbalists use thyme as a digestive, expectorant and powerful antiseptic. The antiseptic action comes from a component of the volatile oil called thymol. It has been shown to be 20 times more powerful than phenol which is a standard laboratory antiseptic. Thymol is still much used in the pharmaceutical industry in products such as mouthwash, toothpaste, tooth powder and soap. In cosmetics, it may be included in scented water and some perfumes.

In the kitchen, thyme finds a multitude of uses—in soups (it is an ingredient of bouquet garni), stews, casseroles, on roasting meat and poultry, in fish, egg or cheese dishes, in stuffings, sausages, sauces, biscuits (cookies) (sweet or savoury), cakes, breads, pastries, fruit punch or vegetable dishes. Thyme tea may also be used as an antiseptic cleanser for all working surfaces, implements and furniture.

Besides this species, there is also the wild species from which garden thyme has probably been cultivated. It is often, therefore, called mother-of-thyme—*Thymus serpyllum*. Other varieties are scented: lemon (*T.* x *citriodorus*), caraway (*T. herba-barona*) and orange (*T. vulgaris* var. *fragrantissimus*). Those grown as ornamentals are: woolly thyme (*T. pseudolanuginosus*), silver thyme (*T. vulgaris* 'Argenteus') and golden thyme (*T. vulgaris* 'Aureus').

TURMERIC • *Curcuma domestica* • *Curcuma longa*
Family Zingiberaceae

Turmeric is a native of South-East Asia and has been in use for well over 2000 years. It is a close relative of ginger. Like ginger, the part used is the thick fleshy underground stem or rhizome. When the leaves die down, the rhizome is dug up and scrubbed well. It may be used fresh or, more commonly, dried and powdered. To make turmeric powder, the rhizome is broken into pieces, boiled in water for about an hour and dried thoroughly—this will take several days at least. It is then ground to a fine powder. For a finer flavour, the skin may be removed before grinding. Commercially, this is done by machine (the books refer to it as 'polishing'). I found it impossible to do by hand and so resorted to scraping before drying. This inevitably leads to loss of some volatile oil and flavour. To reduce this to a minimum, drying must be done quickly, though at a fairly low temperature and in the dark.

Turmeric powder is used to flavour and colour curries, spicy oriental dishes, rice, sauces, pickles and some chutneys. Commercially, it is used to colour such food products as cheese, margarine, butter, liqueurs, cordials and mustard. The fresh whole rhizome may be finely chopped and added to dishes as one would use ginger, eg curries and stir-fried vegetables.

In the past, turmeric was much used as a dye, often substituting for saffron which is more difficult to cultivate in quantity. The aromatic oil, curcuma oil, is extracted and used in some perfumes and cosmetics.

VANILLA • *Vanilla planifolia*
Family Orchidaceae

Vanilla is native to Mexico and Central America and was used widely by the Aztecs for flavouring their favourite chocolate drinks.

The vanilla plant is a climbing orchid with long seed pods. These are collected before ripening and are made to ferment. The processing takes several months and results in the deposition of vanillin crystals on the outside of the pod—it is this vanillin which gives the flavour. Good-quality vanilla pods are long, dark brown and flexible, with a strong aroma. Vanilla essence (extract) is made by steeping the crushed pods in alcohol to extract the vanillin. Artificial vanilla essence is made either from eugenol, an extract of cloves, or even by the processing of sucrose, waste-paper pulp or coal tar. None of the artificial flavourings has the subtlety of flavour of the real thing.

For flavouring, pods may be soaked for 10–15 minutes in the warmed liquid of the recipe, eg water, milk or wine, that is to be added to the dish. The pod then may be dried and restored for future use. Always store pods in a screw-top jar in a cool, dark place. Vanilla sugar is prepared by placing a pod in a jar of sugar. The sugar must be stirred occasionally to ensure an even flavouring. Allow the pod to remain until the degree of flavour required is reached. Add vanilla sugar to your coffee or chocolate drinks, or to cakes, biscuits (cookies) and sweet pastries. When using vanilla essence, use only a few drops as it is quite strong.

Vanilla is used widely in commercially prepared food products, eg ice cream, chocolate, soft drinks and some liqueurs. It is also sometimes used in the preparation of perfumes and even tobacco.

VIOLETS • *Viola odorata*
Family Violaceae

The well-known deep violet colour and sweet scent of violets are much used in the cosmetics and perfumery industries, in pharmaceutics and in the confectionery industry.

For home use, young leaves and flowers can be added to fruit or vegetable salads, used to flavour wines, cordials and jellies, or sugared or crystallised (candied) (*see* p. 350), and used as a garnish for cakes, biscuits (cookies) and desserts. The dried flowers and leaves are often included in potpourris and in articles like scented bags and sleep pillows. Violet syrup is an excellent cough remedy and expectorant. It is prepared by infusing flowers and leaves in a strong honey and water mixture. The heartsease or wild pansy (*Viola tricolor*) is a close relative and can be used in place of violets or in addition to them in any of these suggestions.

YARROW (Milfoil) • *Achillea millefolium*
Family Compositae

The name *Achillea* was given in the belief that it was this herb that Achilles used to staunch the bleeding on the wounds of his soldiers in the Trojan wars. Indeed, in herbal medicine today, yarrow is applied to wounds and is taken internally for its beneficial effect on the circulatory system. It also improves digestion and is cooling to fevers.

Yarrow leaves can be added to meat or vegetable dishes and to salads. As it is a bitter herb, choose only the young leaves and add sparingly. To improve palatability when used in salads, include sweet ingredients, eg apples, bananas or sultanas (golden raisins), or use a sweet salad dressing, perhaps one based on fresh orange juice. Alternatively, add a few leaves to the teapot when preparing regular tea. An infusion of yarrow leaves in water can be used as a hair and scalp tonic—apply it as a conditioner after shampooing.

APPENDIX:
Planning a Menu

Here I hope to offer the reader a quick aid to planning menus. If planning a picnic or a formal main course, reference to the relevant list will give all the suitable dishes in this book. I particularly wanted to include this in my book in sympathy to others like myself who have spent hours poring over cookery books sorting out recipes.

When planning the whole menu, use a good measure of commonsense. You would not want a cheesy hors d'oeuvre and a cheesy main course or vegetable side dish with cheese. Similarly, if the main course is rich, choose a relatively simple and light dessert. Otherwise, make your own choices with the meal-planning. Use the following list as a guide only. They cover my preferences, but may not be yours.

Note: You will have to check through recipes as you choose them and adjust quantities to suit your use. For example, a dish serving four people as a main course would serve eight or more as an hors d'oeuvre.

Breakfast

See hot vegetable recipes
Buckwheat Brunch (p. 27)
Savory Rolls (p. 38)
Savory Kumara Flat Cake (p. 34)

See beef recipes
Rissoles (Meat Cakes, Hamburgers) (p. 104)
Beef Sausages (or Burgers) (p. 112)

See pork recipes
Pork Sausages (or Burgers) (p. 125)
Scrapple (p. 126)

See lamb recipes
Brains with Mushrooms (p. 138)
Haggis (p. 138)
Kidneys à la Crème (p. 139)

See fish recipes
Stuffed Trout (p. 172)
Trout Baked with Yoghurt (p. 172)
Tuna Fish Kedgeree (p. 175)
Whitebait Fried with Sage (p. 175)

See egg recipes
Egg Rolls (p. 190)
English Egg Bread (p. 192)
Omelettes, savoury (pp. 194–6)

Omelette with Rainy Day Filler (p. 196)
Omelettes, sweet (pp. 196–7)
Pancakes (pp. 197–202)
Buckwheat Pikelets (Drop Scones, Pancakes) (p. 202)

See cheese and egg recipes
Welsh Rarebit (p. 215)

See bread recipes
Bread (pp. 250–61)

See scone (biscuit) recipes
Scones (biscuits) (p. 272)

Light Supper or Lunch Dishes

I have made my selection here based on several criteria. Most importantly, the dish in question had to be simple and light on the digestion. Also, it had to be either quick and easy to prepare and cook, eg an omelette, or be the kind of dish that could be prepared beforehand and eaten cold, eg a savoury flan or pasties. I have in mind a simple lunch for a busy family or a late evening supper, perhaps after returning from the cinema.

For a more formal lunch or supper menu, refer to 'Main courses' (*see* pp. 380–1). Pick out a few of the less elaborate dishes.

See hot vegetable recipes
Grilled (Broiled) Cheesy Vegetables
   (p. 26)
Buckwheat Brunch (p. 27)
Eggplant (Aubergine) Ruffle (p. 32)
Savory Rolls (p. 38)
Stuffed Tomatoes 1, cold (p. 47)
Stuffed Tomatoes 2, cold (p. 48)
Tarragon Lunch (p. 54)
Stuffed Zucchini (Courgettes)
   (p. 54)
Apia Fruit Zucchini (Courgettes)
   (p. 51)
Bean and Corn Pie (p. 25)
Cabbage and Coriander Pie (p. 28)
Carrot Tart (p. 30)
Cheese, Carrot and Caraway Pasties
   (p. 30)
Savoury Kumara Flat Cake (p. 34)
Cheesy Leek and Bacon Pie (p. 35)
Mushroom Quiche (p. 36)
Tomato and Basil Pie (p. 46)
Zucchini (Courgette) Quiche (p. 52)
Zucchini (Courgette) Pie (p. 52)
Tasty Turnip Dish (p. 49)
Turnip Bed (p. 50)

See bean recipes
Beansprout Pasties (p. 68)
Spiced Dhal (Dal) (p. 66)
Green Hummus (p. 65)

Lentil Patties (p. 66)
Tomato Beans (p. 69)
Hot Tomato Beans (p. 69)

See beef recipes
Lettuce Leaf Rolls, cold (p. 100)
Rissoles (Beef Cakes, Hamburgers),
   cold (p. 104)
Cornish Pasties (p. 109)
Tongue, cold (p. 111)
Beef Sausages (or Burgers) (p. 112)

See pork recipes
Bacon Joint with Mustard and
   Tarragon Sauce (p. 115)
Liver Pâté 1 (p. 124)
Pork Sausages (or Burgers) (p. 125)
Scrapple (p. 126)

See poultry and game recipes
Cold Chicken in Tarragon Sauce
   (p. 141)
Chicken in Mayonnaise (p. 144)
Chicken Salad (p. 144)
Liver Pâté 2 (p. 149)
Turkey and Lovage Pie (p. 152)
Deep-fried Rabbit with Sour Sauce
   (p. 152)
Rabbit and Noodles (p. 153)
Fried Rabbit with Sweet Sesame
   Sauce (p. 154)

See fish recipes
Friday Pie (p. 166)
Rosemary Fish Triangles (p. 168)
Fish Pâté (p. 167)
Prawns (Shrimp) and Asparagus
   with Fennel Sauce (p. 174)
Tuna Fish Kedgeree (p. 175)
Whitebait Fried with Sage (p. 175)
Fish with Caraway and Rice
   (p. 171)

See egg recipes
Egg Rolls (p. 190)
English Egg Bread (p. 192)
Saturday Eggs (p. 191)
Omelettes (pp. 194–7)
Pancakes (pp. 197–202)

See cheese recipes
Savoury Apple Pasties (p. 208)
Mary's Macaroni Cheese (p. 208)
Malcolm's Macaroni Cheese (p. 209)
Pizza 1 (p. 210)
Pizza 2 (p. 212)

See cheese and egg recipes
Cheese and Potato Cakes (p. 213)
Cheese Fondue or Dip (p. 214)
Welsh Rarebit (p. 215)
Cheese and Egg Pie (p. 215)

Hors d'Oeuvres

See hot vegetable recipes
Bean and Corn Pie (p. 25)
Grilled (Broiled) Cheesy Vegetables
   (p. 26)
Buckwheat Brunch (p. 27)
Stir-fried Cabbage with Eggs (p. 27)
Stuffed Cabbage (p. 28)

Stir-fried Choko (Chayote, Mirliton)
   with Herbs (p. 32)
Eggplant (Aubergine) Ruffle (p. 32)
Sardine-stuffed Eggplant
   (Aubergine) (p. 33)
Stuffed Eggplant (Aubergine)
   (p. 33)

Eggplant (Aubergine) Bake (p. 34)
Spiced Kumara and Spinach (p. 35)
Mushrooms in Red Wine (p. 38)
Silverbeet (Swiss Chard), Chicken
   and Noodles (p. 44)
Stuffed Silverbeet (Swiss Chard)
   Leaves (p. 45)

Vegetarian Stuffed Capsicum (Sweet
    Peppers) (p. 42)
Potato-stuffed Capsicum (Sweet
    Peppers) (p. 41)
Baked Potato Layers (p. 41)
Savoury Pumpkin (Winter Squash)
    (p. 44)
Tomato Hors d'Oeuvre (p. 47)
Stuffed Tomatoes 1 (p. 47)
Stuffed Tomatoes 2 (p. 48)
Vegetable Variety (p. 50)
Vegetarian Moussaka (p. 48)
Oatmeal-stuffed Zucchini
    (Courgettes) (p. 51)
Tarragon Lunch (p. 54)
Stuffed Zucchini (Courgettes)
    (p. 54)
Apia Fruit Zucchini (Courgettes)
    (p. 51)
Cabbage and Coriander Pie (p. 28)
Carrot Tart (p. 30)
Cheesy Leek and Bacon Pie (p. 35)
Mushroom Quiche (p. 36)
Tomato and Basil Pie (p. 46)
Zucchini (Courgette) Quiche (p. 52)
Zucchini (Courgette) Pie (p. 52)

See salads
Avocado Salad (p. 56)
Avocado in Tarragon Dressing (p. 56)
Stuffed Avocado (p. 55)
Cheesy Avocado (p. 55)
Avocado Boats (p. 55)
Spicy Avocado (p. 56)

See bean recipes
Bean Dish (p. 68)

Spiced Dhal (Dal) (p. 66)
Green Hummus (p. 65)
Lentil Patties (p. 66)
Tomato Beans (p. 69)
Hot Tomato Beans (p. 69)

See beef recipes
Sweet and Sour Beef in Egg Rolls
    (p. 95)
Dark Mince (Ground Beef) (p. 99)
Lettuce Leaf Rolls (p. 100)
Peppery Liver (p. 111)
Oxtail Stew (p. 110)
Tongue (p. 111)

See pork recipes
Bacon Joint with Mustard and
    Tarragon Sauce (p. 115)
Pork Fried Rice (p. 121)
Pacific Pork (p. 122)
Liver Pâté 1 (p. 124)
Scrapple (p. 126)

See lamb recipes
Brains with Mushrooms (p. 138)
Haggis (p. 138)
Stuffed Hearts (p. 139)
Kidneys à la Crème (p. 139)

See poultry recipes
Chicken in Mayonnaise (p. 144)
Chicken Salad (p. 144)
Salisbury Chicken (p. 145)
Liver Pâté 2 (p. 149)
Turkey and Lovage Pie (p. 152)

See fish recipes
Friday Pie (p. 166)

Rosemary Fish Triangles (p. 168)
Southbridge Fish (p. 167)
Fish Pâté (p. 167)
Fish with Basil (p. 169)
Prawns (Shrimp) and Asparagus
    with Fennel Sauce (p. 174)
Deep-fried Fish with Sour Sauce
    (p. 170)
Stuffed Trout (p. 172)
Stuffed Trout with Apricot Filling
    (p. 172)
Trout Baked with Yoghurt (p. 172)
Alafua Fish (p. 174)
Tuna Fish Kedgeree (p. 175)
Whitebait Fried with Sage (p. 175)

See egg recipes
Curried Stuffed Eggs (p. 190)
Egg Rolls (p. 190)
Eggs with Orange Sauce (p. 190)
Saturday Eggs (p. 191)
Suppertime Eggs (p. 191)
Sweet and Sour Eggs (p. 192)
Omelettes (pp. 194–7)
Pancakes (pp. 197–202)
Soufflés (pp. 204–6)

See cheese recipes
Pizza 1 (p. 210)
Pizza 2 (p. 212)

See cheese and egg recipes
Cheese and Onion Pudding (p. 213)
Cheese and Potato Cakes (p. 213)
Cheese Fondue or Dip (p. 214)
Cheese and Egg Pie (p. 215)

Main Courses

See hot vegetable recipes
Sardine-stuffed Eggplant
    (Aubergine) (p. 33)
Stuffed Eggplant (Aubergine) (p. 33)
Stuffed Marrow (Summer or Yellow
    Squash) (p. 39)
Silverbeet (Swiss Chard), Chicken
    and Noodles (p. 44)
Stuffed Silverbeet (Swiss Chard)
    Leaves (p. 45)
Tasty Turnip Dish (p. 49)

See bean recipes
Bible Pork with Lima (Butter)
    Beans (p. 116)
Mexican Stew (p. 136)

See beef recipes
Boiled Brisket (p. 94)
Winter Stew (p. 96)
Sweet and Sour Beef in Egg Rolls
    (p. 95)
Sweet Pepper Curry (p. 95)
Coriander Beef (p. 98)
Barbecued Porterhouse Steak
    (p. 98)
Tomato Steak and Dill (p. 97)
Kebabs (p. 96)
Ginger Beef (p. 98)
Steak Divine (p. 100)
Steak with Pepper Sauce (p. 100)
Dark Mince (Ground Beef) (p. 99)
Lasagne (p. 99)

Meatballs (in a sauce) (p. 103)
Moussaka (p. 102)
Pawpaw (Papaya) Mince (p. 103)
Rissoles (Beef Cakes, Hamburgers)
    (with a sauce) (p. 104)
Spaghetti Bolognese (p. 104)
Tai Tapu Beef (p. 105)
Beef and Potato Casserole (p. 106)
Silverside with Onion Sauce (p. 108)
Roast Sirloin (Standing Rib) with
    Marjoram (p. 107)
Beef and Rice (p. 108)
Beef Olives (p. 109)
Roast Rib with Mushrooms (p. 106)
Peppery Liver (p. 111)
Oxtail Stew (p. 110)

See pork recipes
Bacon Joint with Mustard and
    Tarragon Sauce (p. 115)
Spaghetti Pork (p. 115)
Fruit Pork Chops (p. 118)
Pork Chops with Hyssop (p. 118)
Pork Chops and Dill Seed (p. 118)
Sweet and Sour Pork (p. 117)
Pork with Watercress (p. 120)
Lemon Pork Curry (p. 116)
Pork and Wine (p. 116)
Loin of Pork with Sesame (p. 117)
Spicy Pork Meatballs (p. 123)
Mustard Pork (p. 117)
Orange Pork Roast (p. 120)
Roast Pork Dish (p. 121)
Pork Fried Rice (p. 121)
Pacific Pork (p. 122)
Spare Ribs with Plums (p. 122)
Liver and Bacon Casserole (p. 124)

See lamb recipes
Stuffed Breast (Flap) of Lamb
    (p. 130)
Spicy Lamb Chops (p. 128)
Barbecued Lamb Chops (p. 128)
Lamb with Bean Sprouts (p. 130)
Rolled Fillet of Lamb with Apricot
    Stuffing (p. 129)
Roast Knuckle of Lamb with
    Apricots (p. 127)
Lamb Curry (p. 132)
Middle Neck with Yoghurt (p. 132)

Mexican Stew (p. 136)
Lamb Parcels (p. 134)
Lancashire Lamb (p. 133)
Roast Shoulder of Lamb (p. 136)
Haggis (p. 138)
Stuffed Hearts (p. 139)

See mutton recipes
Mutton with Mustard (p. 137)
Thursday's Mutton (p. 137)

See goat recipes
Goat Chops with Cucumber and
    Potato Sauce (p. 140)
Mountain Goat Curry (p. 130)

See poultry and game recipes
Barbecued Chicken in Marinade
    (p. 141)
Basic Chicken Stew (p. 140)
Chicken Curry (p. 142)
Fruity Chicken Curry (p. 142)
Cold Chicken in Tarragon Sauce
    (p. 141)
Chicken Pot (p. 141)
Whole Chicken with Orange
    (p. 146)
Chicken with Ginger (p. 144)
Chicken with Noodles (p. 145)
Apia Duck (p. 148)
Duck with Orange Sauce (p. 146)
Young Mallard with Lemon and
    Sherry Sauce (p. 149)
Guinea Fowl Baked in Yoghurt (p. 150)

Guinea Fowl for Reuben (p. 151)
Roast Turkey (p. 151)
Deep-fried Rabbit with Sour Sauce
    (p. 152)
Rabbit and Leek Casserole (p. 153)
Rabbit and Noodles (p. 153)
Rabbit Braised in Hot Chilli Sauce
    (p. 152)
Roast Rabbit with Apple and Lemon
    Sauce (p. 155)
Fried Rabbit with Sweet Sesame
    Sauce (p. 154)

See fish recipes
Fish with Basil (p. 169)
Sweet and Sour Fish (p. 171)
Pineapple Fish (p. 168)
Polynesian Fish (p. 170)
Deep-fried Fish with Sour Sauce
    (p. 170)
Stuffed Trout (p. 172)
Stuffed Trout with Apricot Filling
    (p. 172)
Trout Baked with Yoghurt
    (p. 172)
Alafua Fish (p. 174)
Fish with Caraway and Rice
    (p. 171)

See egg recipes
Egg Rolls (p. 190)
Rosemary Noodles and Eggs
    (p. 191)
Soufflés (pp. 204–6)

Vegetarian Main Courses

See hot vegetable recipes
Stuffed Cabbage (p. 28)
Eggplant (Aubergine) Bake (p. 34)
Eggplant (Aubergine) Ruffle (p. 32)
Vegetarian Stuffed Capsicum (Sweet
    Peppers) (p. 42)
Stuffed Pumpkin (Winter Squash)
    (p. 43)
Stuffed Tomatoes 2 (p. 48)
Vegetable Variety (p. 50)
Vegetable Moussaka (p. 48)
Tarragon Lunch (p. 54)
Bean and Corn Pie (p. 25)
Cabbage and Coriander Pie (p. 28)
Carrot Tart (p. 30)
Mushroom Quiche (p. 36)
Tomato and Basil Pie (p. 46)

Zucchini (Courgette) Quiche (p. 52)
Zucchini (Courgette) Pie (p. 52)
Cheese, Carrot and Caraway Pasties
    (p. 30)

See bean recipes
Beans in Peanut (Groundnut) Sauce
    (p. 65)
Bean Dish (p. 68)
Spiced Dhal (Dal) (p. 66)
Green Hummus (p. 65)
Tomato Beans (p. 69)
Hot Tomato Beans (p. 69)

See egg recipes
Egg Rolls (p. 190)
Rosemary Noodles and Eggs (p. 191)

Saturday Eggs (p. 191)
Suppertime Eggs (p. 191)
Sweet and Sour Eggs (p. 192)
Omelettes (pp. 194–7)
Pancakes (pp. 197–202)
Soufflés (pp. 204–6)

See cheese recipes
Savoury Apple Pasties (p. 208)
Mary's Macaroni Cheese (p. 209)
Malcolm's Macaroni Cheese (p. 209)
Pizza 1 (p. 210)
Pizza 2 (p. 212)

See cheese and egg recipes
Cheese and Onion Pudding (p. 213)
Cheese Fondue or Dip (p. 214)
Cheese and Egg Pie (p. 215)

Main Course Side Dishes

See hot vegetable recipes
Sage Beans (p. 26)
Stir-fried Cabbage with Eggs (p. 27)
Stuffed Cabbage (p. 28)
Baked Red Cabbage (p. 29)
Cabbage with Cheese (p. 27)
Rosemary Carrots (p. 31)
Cauliflower with Mushroom Cream
    Sauce (p. 31)
Spicy Cauliflower Cheese (p. 31)
Cauliflower with Turmeric Sauce
    (p. 32)
Stir-fried Choko (Chayote, Mirliton)
    with Herbs (p. 32)
Eggplant (Aubergine) Ruffle (p. 32)
Grilled Cheesy Chokos (Chayotes,
    Mirlitons) (p. 33)
Chokos (Chayotes, Mirlitons) with
    Oriental Sauce (p. 33)
Spiced Kumara and Spinach (p. 35)
Parsnip and Carrot Purée (p. 40)
Parsnip Nest (p. 40)
Leeks and Potatoes (p. 36)
Leeks in Peanut (Groundnut) Sauce
    (p. 36)
Mushrooms in Red Wine (p. 38)
Indian Okra (Lady's Fingers,
    Gumbo) 1 (p. 38)
Indian Okra (Lady's Fingers,
    Gumbo) 2 (p. 39)
Herbed Stuffed Onions (p. 40)
Peas with French Sorrel (p. 39)

Baked Potatoes (p. 42)
Baked Potato Layers (p. 43)
Savoury Potato and Marrow
    (Summer or Yellow Squash)
    (p. 43)
Oven-cooked Potatoes (p. 43)
Savoury Pumpkin (Winter Squash)
    (p. 44)
Peppery Rice (p. 44)
Turmeric Rice (p. 142)
Creamy French Sorrel (p. 46)
Oriental Sprouts (p. 46)
Tomato Hors d'Oeuvre (p. 47)
Stuffed Tomatoes 2 (p. 48)
Oatmeal-stuffed Zucchini
    (Courgettes) (p. 51)
Stewed Zucchini (Courgettes)
    (p. 51)
Zucchini (Courgettes) with
    Rosemary Sauce (p. 53)

See salads
Avocado Salad (p. 56)
Avocado in Tarragon Dressing
    (p. 56)
Stuffed Avocado (p. 55)
Cheesy Avocado (p. 55)
Avocado Boats (p. 55)
Spicy Avocado (p. 56)
Beetroot (Beets) with Lemon Sauce
    (p. 57)
Red Cabbage Salad (p. 57)

Mixed Green Salad (p. 57)
Cauliflower Salad (p. 58)
Easter Salad (p. 58)
Cucumber and Dill Salad (p. 59)
Egg Salad (p. 60)
Fennel (Finocchio) Salad (p. 59)
Mixed Herb Salad (p. 60)
Herbs and Lettuce Salad (p. 61)
Spicy Leeks (p. 61)
Autumn Salad (p. 60)
Macaroni Salad (p. 61)
Val's Mushrooms (p. 62)
Pineapple Salad (p. 63)
Pineapple and Pawpaw (Papaya)
    Salad (p. 63)
Potato Salad (p. 62)
Brown Rice Salad (p. 62)
Fruit Rice Salad (p. 64)
Savoury Rice (p. 64)
Basil Tomatoes (p. 64)
Spicy Tomatoes (p. 64)
Watercress Salad (p. 65)

See bean recipes
Beans in Peanut (Groundnut) Sauce
    (p. 65)

See poultry recipes
Turmeric Rice (p. 142)

See egg recipes
Yorkshire Pudding (p. 204)

Picnic

See hot vegetable recipes
Bean and Corn Pie (p. 25)
Cabbage and Coriander Pie (p. 28)
Carrot Tart (p. 30)
Cheese, Carrot and Caraway Pasties
    (p. 30)
Cheesy Leek and Bacon Pie (p. 35)
Mushroom Quiche (p. 36)
Savory Rolls (p. 38)
Tomato and Basil Pie (p. 46)
Zucchini (Courgette) Quiche (p. 52)
Zucchini (Courgette) Pie (p. 52)

See salads
Stuffed Celery Sticks (p. 58)

See bean recipes
Beansprout Pasties (p. 67)
Lentil Patties (p. 66)

See beef recipes
Lettuce Leaf Rolls (p. 100)
Cornish Pasties (p. 109)
Tongue (p. 111)
Beef Sausages (or Burgers) (p. 112)

See pork recipes
Liver Pâté 1 (p. 124)
Pork Sausages (or Burgers) (p. 125)
Scrapple, cold (p. 126)

See poultry recipes
Liver Pâté 2 (p. 149)
Turkey and Lovage Pie (p. 152)

See fish recipes
Friday Pie (p. 166)
Rosemary Fish Triangles (p. 168)

See egg recipes
Curried Stuffed Eggs (p. 190)

See cheese recipes
Savoury Apple Pasties (p. 208)
Pizza 1 (p. 210)
Pizza 2 (p. 212)

See cheese and egg recipes
Cheese and Potato Cakes (p. 213)
Cheese and Egg Pie (p. 215)

See bread recipes
Breads (pp. 250–61)

See cake recipes
Cakes (pp. 264–72)

See scone (biscuit) recipes
Scones (biscuits) (pp. 272–6)

Bibliography

Food and Cookery Books

Ashbrook, F. G., *Butchering, Processing and Preservation of Meat*, Van Nostrand Reinhold Co., New York, 1955.

Claiborne, C. and Lee, V., *The Chinese Cookbook*, Sphere Books, London, 1974.

David, E., *French Provincial Cooking*, Penguin, Harmondsworth (revised edition), 1969.

Dence, C., 'Herbs and spices through the ages', *The Herbal Review*, a quarterly publication of the Herb Society, London, vol. 3, nos 1, 2, 3, 4; vol. 4, no. 2; 1978–79.

Desrosier, N. W. (ed), *Elements of Food Technology*, AVI, Westport, 1977.

Escoffier, G. A., *A Guide to Modern Cookery*, Heinemann, London, 1957.

Janick, Schery, Woods and Ruttan, *Plant Science—An Introduction to World Crops*, Freeman, San Francisco (second edition), 1974.

Jordon, J., *Wings of Life*, Crossing Press, New York, 1976.

Mabey, D. and R., *Jams, Pickles and Chutneys*, Penguin, Harmondsworth, 1976.

Mabey, R., *Food for Free*, Collins, London, 1972.

Mackenzie, D., *Goat Husbandry*, Faber and Faber, London, 1970.

Reader's Digest (ed), *The Cookery Year*, Reader's Digest Association, London, 1981.

Schery, R. W., *Plants for Man*, Allen & Unwin, London, 1954.

Storch, J. and Teague, W. D., *Flour for Man's Bread: A History of Milling*, University of Minnesota Press, Minneapolis, 1952.

Thomas, A., *The Vegetarian Epicure*, Penguin, Harmondsworth, 1973.

Turner, E. (ed), *The Colour Book of Indian Cooking*, Octopus Books, London, 1978.

United States Department of Agriculture, *Handbook of Nutritional Contents of Foods*, Dover Publications, New York, 1975.

Westland, P., *A Taste of the Country*, Penguin, Harmondsworth, 1976.

Wood, B., *Let's Preserve It*, Granada Publishing, London 1972.

Herbs and Plants

Day, I. and Carmichael, I., *A Guide to Spices*, The Herb Society, London, 1978.

Eagle, R., *Herbs, Useful Plants*, British Broadcasting Corporation, London, 1981.

Fitter, R. and Fitter, A., *The Wild Flowers of Britain and Northern Europe*, Collins, London (third edition), 1978.

Grieve, M., *A Modern Herbal*, Peregrine Books, Harmondsworth, 1976.

Hall, D., *The Book of Herbs*, Pan Books, London, 1976.

Levy de Baïracli, J., *The Illustrated Herbal Handbook*, Faber and Faber, London, 1974.

Loewenfeld, C. and Back, P., *The Complete Book of Herbs and Spices*, Reed, Wellington, 1974.

Loewenfeld, C. and Back, P., *Herbs for Health and Cookery*, Pan Books, London, 1965.

Philbrick, H. and Gregg, R. B., *Companion Plants*, Watkins, Dulverton, 1967.

Stewart, M. (ed), *The Encyclopaedia of Herbs and Herbalism*, Orbis, London, 1979.

Sunset Books (ed), *How to Grow Herbs*, Lane Books, Menlo Park, 1972.

Thomson, W. A. R. (ed), *Healing Plants: A Modern Herbal*, Macmillan, London, 1980.

Winemaking

Acton, B. and Duncan, P., *Making Wines Like Those You Buy*, The Amateur Winemaker Publications, Andover, 1981.

Berry, C. J. J., *One Hundred and Thirty New Winemaking Recipes*, The Amateur Winemaker Publications, Andover (second edition), 1974.

Berry, C. J. J. (ed), *Amateur Winemaker Recipes*, The Amateur Winemaker Publications, Andover, 1973.

Miscellaneous

Blackie, M. J., *Successful Smallfarming*, Methuen Publications (NZ) Ltd, New Zealand, 1981.

Evans, R. E., *Rations for Livestock*, Bulletin No. 48, HM-SO (15th Edition), London, 1960.

Index

(Numbers in *italics* refer to illustrations)